High School Students Unite!

High School Students Unite!
Teen Activism, Education Reform, and
FBI Surveillance in Postwar America

••

AARON G. FOUNTAIN JR.

The University of North Carolina Press Chapel Hill

© 2025 The University of North Carolina Press
All rights reserved
Set in Charis by Westchester Publishing Services
Manufactured in the United States of America

Library of Congress Cataloging-in-Publication Data
Names: Fountain, Aaron Gregory, Jr, author.
Title: High school students unite! : teen activism, education reform, and FBI surveillance in postwar America / Aaron G. Fountain Jr.
Other titles: Teen activism, education reform, and FBI surveillance in postwar America
Description: Chapel Hill : The University of North Carolina Press, 2025. | Includes bibliographical references and index.
Identifiers: LCCN 2025022645 | ISBN 9781469691817 (cloth ; alk. paper) | ISBN 9781469691824 (pbk. ; alk. paper) | ISBN 9781469686431 (epub) | ISBN 9781469691831 (pdf)
Subjects: LCSH: United States. Federal Bureau of Investigation—History—20th century. | High school students—Political activity—United States—20th century. | Teenagers—Political activity—United States—20th century. | Student movements—United States—20th century. | High school students—Civil rights—United States—20th century. | Vietnam War, 1961-1975—Protest movements—United States. | BISAC: SOCIAL SCIENCE / Ethnic Studies / American / General | SOCIAL SCIENCE / Activism & Social Justice
Classification: LCC LB3610 .F68 2025 | DDC 303.48/408350973—dc23/eng/20250617
LC record available at https://lccn.loc.gov/2025022645

Cover art: *Top: Students Holding Signs. Bottom: Student Rights Demonstration.* Both from the *Militant* Photographic collection, Box 2, Folder 12, Hoover Institution Library & Archives.

For product safety concerns under the European Union's General Product Safety Regulation (EU GPSR), please contact gpsr@mare-nostrum.co.uk or write to the University of North Carolina Press and Mare Nostrum Group B.V., Mauritskade 21D, 1091 GC Amsterdam, The Netherlands.

To

the various former youth activists who passed away before the publication of this book. And to my niece, Raven.

Youth of America v. President Johnson 68
Eintou poem by J. A. Dennis

The world
Sacrifices
Its greatest potential
When famished minds feast on half truths
Youthful tears cries for change
Where's the knowledge,
Johnson?
Johnson,
Where's the knowledge?
Youthful tears cries for change
When famished minds feast on half truths
Its greatest potential
Sacrifices
The world.

Contents

List of Illustrations, ix

Acknowledgments, xi

Abbreviations, xv

Prologue, 1
The Making of a High School Student Activist

Introduction, 9

Part I
Politics

1. From Civil Rights to Student Rights, 25
   San Francisco's High School Free Speech Movement

2. The Backbone and Organizers, 47
   Building a High School Antiwar Movement

3. The Rise of Independent Student Organizations, 71
   The New York High School Student Union

4. Vietnam and Student Rights, 96
   The Antiwar and High School Movements Unite

5. The Voice of the Movement, 114
   The High School Underground Press

Part II
Race

6. Blowouts, Sit-Ins, and Walkouts, 141
   High School Student Uprisings

7. Student Rights as Civil Rights, 164
   Philadelphia's Student Bill of Rights Campaign

8   Violence and Reform, 185
    Cleveland's Collinwood High School Race Riots

    Part III
    Surveillance

9   Troublemakers, 215
    School Administrators and the FBI

10 To Save the Children, 242
    Parents and the FBI

    Epilogue, 259
    High School Student Activists in Adulthood and Memory

    Appendix 1. List of Independent High School Student Organizations, 271

    Appendix 2. List of High School Underground Newspapers in the United States, 285

    Notes, 309

    Bibliography, 347

    Index, 365

Illustrations

Steve Wasserman, 2

"High School Students Unite!" illustration, 11

The *Activist Opinion*, 35

High school antiwar protesters, 49

Flyer for the 1967 SMC conference, 59

New York High School Free Press, 85

Demonstration in front of Martin Van Buren High School, 89

Students holding signs, 97

Grant Cooper, 117

Police at Woodward High School, 142

Student rights demonstration, 166

Collinwood High School Riot, 195

Acknowledgments

This project began in 2012 when I was an undergraduate and a Ronald E. McNair Scholar at Winthrop University in Rock Hill, South Carolina. Neither I, my advisor Andy Doyle, nor McNair Director Cheryl Fortner could have foreseen what this project would eventually become. Over the course of thirteen years, many people have contributed to its development, and I am deeply grateful. I especially appreciate the various historians whose colloquiums and seminars helped shape my thinking.

Special thanks go to Cara Caddoo, Ellen Wu, Amrita Myers, Peter Guardino, and Alex Lichtenstein for their support during critical moments. Circumstances beyond my control nearly derailed this project. During the pandemic, when I was an unemployed PhD candidate, Cara Caddoo provided me with a job, while others rallied to assemble emergency funds that helped me make it through the Fall semester of 2020. I am also deeply grateful for the opportunity to work at the *Journal of American History*, where I gained insight into the scholarly process. I had the pleasure of engaging in meaningful conversations with the staff, including Benjamin Irvin, Stephen Andrews, Anne Gray Fischer, Tina Irvine, Hannah Alms, Liam Kingsley, Amy Ransford, and others. Reading scholars' rough drafts and witnessing the extensive revisions even the most esteemed academics undergo was an eye-opening experience.

My graduate school peers were instrumental in helping me develop this work. Matthew Gordon, Jake Hagstrom, Sam Bass, Stephen Buono, Andy Aguilera, Bobby Wells, Kathleen Doll, Matthew Johnson, Daniel Story, Ruth Almy, Samson Ndanyi, Amanda Waterhouse, Amanda Lanzillo, Sydney-Paige Patterson, Gloria Lopez, Stephanie Huezo, Natalie Levin, Miguel A. Cruz-Diaz, Gloria Colom, Hannah Craddock, Denisa Jashari, and Jeffrey Cisneros were just a few of the many peers I met at Indiana University. I am especially grateful to Jazma Sutton for our thoughtful conversations as coworkers at the *Journal of American History* and as fellow graduate students who spent countless hours in the Neal-Marshall Black Cultural Center. Her belief in making academic work accessible to general audiences, out of genuine care for the subjects, deeply influenced my writing style. Charlene

Fletcher-Brown provided sisterly guidance and encouragement throughout my graduate studies, while Carl Suddler offered advice and support, especially after my father's untimely passing. Alexis Smith and I shared countless Facebook messages about graduate school and life, and I will always remember her help with interview preparation for my first public history job in Cleveland, Ohio.

This book was completed while I worked full-time jobs. I am deeply grateful for the encouragement and support of Kathleen Crowther, Margaret Lann, Anne Donte, Stephanie Phelps, Jamie Miles, Tom Jorgensen, and many others at the Cleveland Restoration Society in Ohio. To the Smithsonian's National Museum of African American History and Culture in Washington, DC, I extend heartfelt thanks to my former coworkers on the web team for their praise and support. The curatorial team taught me how to make my writing accessible to a museum audience.

Outside of work, I regularly shared portions of this project with the Writer's Center in Bethesda, Maryland, and the DC Writers' Salon. Presenting my work to nonacademic audiences was invaluable for refining its narrative flow. After I confidently shared what I thought was a clever introduction, one writer remarked, "This reads like a dissertation." It was simple but incredibly helpful advice.

I am especially appreciative of the individuals who agreed to be interviewed and who provided documents from their private collections. No project is completed alone, and while I cannot name everyone, I must give special thanks to Steve Wasserman, one of the first people I interviewed for my second summer research project. He came highly recommended by everyone I spoke to at the time, and we have stayed in touch for twelve years. I am also deeply grateful to Susan Bailey, who sent me heartwarming messages almost daily. Her knowledge of Black history in Philadelphia rivals that of any historian.

Paula Garb, who sadly passed away in August 2024 while working on her memoir, gave me unforgettable advice. After reading a peer-reviewed article I had written, she reminded me that while teenage activists were precocious, "we were still kids." Her words echoed a sentiment expressed by Delaney Tarr, one of the Parkland activists I saw speak in Chicago in 2018, who said, "We're still awkward teenagers," in response to media portrayals of their intellectual sophistication. Inspired by their insights, I made it a priority to highlight the humanity of the individuals I write about.

Throughout the course of this research, I have often been asked whether I was an activist in high school. The short answer is no. Due to five years living with a parent struggling with drug addiction and experiencing two abandonments within the span of three months, I attended eight different high schools in three states (a story that could fill a memoir). However, during this research, I often saw aspects of myself in my interviewees. Like some of them, I developed a strong interest in politics in high school and became frustrated when my peers did not share the same passion.

Although my father passed away after my first year of graduate school, I will always be grateful for his strictness, his understanding of the value of education despite being a high school dropout, and his commitment to prioritizing my sister and me in every decision he made. As I've gotten older, I've come to understand how challenging it must have been for him to be unable to work full-time due to a violent mugging that left him on disability at just twenty-four years old. Yet, he worked tirelessly to give my sister and me a semblance of a normal childhood.

He moved us to our birthplace, Bethlehem, Pennsylvania, because he did not want to raise us in Jamaica, Queens, New York. Living in a predominantly Puerto Rican neighborhood exposed me to more diversity than he had encountered as a child. Until I was eleven, we lived in safe neighborhoods, attended good schools, and occasionally took family trips. My father certainly wasn't perfect, but I am certain that I would not have reached my current position in life without his parenting.

Abbreviations

ACLU	American Civil Liberties Union
ASD	Active Students for Democracy
BSU	Black Student Union
CHIPS	Cooperative High School Independent Press Syndicate
CRU	Community Relations Unit
FBI	Federal Bureau of Investigation
FOIA	Freedom of Information Act
HIPS	High School Independent Press Service
HSPA	High School Principals Association
HSSAW	High School Students Against the War
HSSU	High School Student Union
LNS	Liberation News Service
MID	Military Intelligence Detachment
MSU	Minnesota Student Union
PFT	Philadelphia Federation of Teachers
RSU	Radical Student Union
SDS	Students for a Democratic Society
SIC	Student Information Center
SMC	Student Mobilization Committee
SOEAL	Students' Organized Education and Action League
SSOC	Southern Student Organizing Committee
UC	University of California
UFT	United Federation of Teachers
USG	Union of Student Government
USM	United Student Movement

VBSAM	Van Buren Students Against Militarism
VDC	Vietnam Day Committee
YRP	Youth for Radical Progress
YSA	Young Socialist Alliance

High School Students Unite!

Prologue
The Making of a High School Student Activist

Geography is fate. That is the lesson Steve Wasserman recalled when reminiscing about his childhood. This lesson, however, extends beyond his personal narrative and echoes the arcs of his grandfather and father. Solomon Wasserman was born in Chełm, Poland, in 1897. In 1922, he bid farewell to his homeland and immigrated to New York City. There, he forged a new life, secured employment as a sewing machine operator, and later became an organizer for the International Ladies' Garment Workers' Union. He soon immersed himself in the world of Jewish progressives by contributing short stories, nonfiction essays, and columns to Yiddish-language newspapers, most notably the left-wing publication known as the *Morgen Freiheit*.[1]

In 1930, Solomon and his wife Rebecca welcomed the birth of their son Abraham, nicknamed Al. Born in the Bronx, Al's family lived in workers' cooperative housing called the Coops. He grew up in a Yiddish-speaking household and learned English on the playgrounds of the public school he attended. Following his high school graduation, he matriculated into the Cooper Union for the Advancement of Science and Art, pursuing a degree in civil engineering. Love followed his scholarly pursuits, as he joined in matrimony with his high school sweetheart, Ann Dragoon. Their romance blossomed during their time as counselors at Camp Kinderland, a summer retreat established in 1923 by Jewish union activists in upstate New York. The camp aimed to provide working-class families with an escape from city life while instilling the values of secular Jewish culture, including a commitment to social justice. Together, they traveled westward to Portland, Oregon, where Al got a job with the Oregon Highway Department to help build a road connecting Mount Hood to Portland. The two then began a family of five, bringing Steve into the world in 1952, followed by his sister Rena in 1955, and Sherry in 1957. After a stint in Sacramento, the family settled in Madras, Oregon, a small town located in the heartland of the state.[2]

If Wasserman had remained in the modest confines of Madras, his upbringing would have likely shaped him into a provincial lad, perhaps even an ostracized liberal. Yet, destiny took an unexpected turn for young

Steve Wasserman, Berkeley High School student body president, in the fall of 1969. He is holding in one hand a gavel, in the other Chairman Mao's Little Red Book, and boasting a cigar with a "Nixon's the One" campaign button stuck on the end. Courtesy of Berkeley High School Library.

Wasserman in August 1963. Driven by a desire for cultural diversity, his father Al accepted a transfer with the Bechtel Corporation and moved to the San Francisco Bay Area. The timing was propitious. While temporarily lodged in a motel as his parents searched for a permanent home, Wasserman read his way through *The Adventures of Sherlock Holmes*. Fortuitously, one station broadcasted the gathering at the National Mall in Washington, DC, the March on Washington. He watched the civil rights demonstrators demand jobs, equality, and human dignity. Yet, Wasserman's political education did not conclude with the awe-inspiring scenes from the nation's capital.[3]

His parents espoused progressive political leanings, a characteristic that influenced his maturing mind. Al made a career change and pursued the field of law. He became involved in the National Lawyers Guild, a progressive association of legal professionals, and eventually assumed the role of president of the Berkeley-Albany chapter of the American Civil Liberties Union. Moreover, he was a longtime subscriber to the intellectual periodical *I. F. Stone's Weekly*, as well as *The Minority of One*, edited by

M. S. Arnoni, a Holocaust survivor and a stalwart of left-wing ideals. Within the pages of the latter publication, Wasserman read Eric Norden's seminal three-part exposé on Vietnam, an exotic and unknown land at the time to most Americans. Norden's piercing words peeled back the curtain on the United States' secret military involvement embodied in a growing group of advisers. "It proved to be quite a prophetic article," Wasserman recalls.[4]

Wasserman's early maturation in matters of governance, his parents' embrace of progressive ideals, and the relocation of his family to Berkeley laid the groundwork for his involvement in left-wing causes. Wasserman soon found himself swept into a whirlwind of events. The saga commenced with the Free Speech Movement, an uprising that engulfed the University of California (UC) in the autumn of 1964. The ensuing years bore witness to an embryonic antiwar sentiment, manifested through the teach-ins and demonstrations organized by Berkeley's Vietnam Day Committee (VDC) in 1965. Concurrently, the nascent Black Panther Party took root in the neighboring city of Oakland in October 1966. The summer of 1967 heralded the emergence of an increasingly noticeable counterculture, as San Francisco became a vibrant epicenter of alternative lifestyles and societal experimentation. In November 1968, the student strike for Black studies at San Francisco State College confronted a brutal response from law enforcement. And in May 1969, the eruption of protests over UC's suppression of People's Park triggered a month-long occupation of Berkeley by a combination of local police forces and National Guard units, ordered by then-Governor Ronald Reagan.[5]

Although these developments involved mostly college-age adults, Wasserman was no mere spectator. Once the Free Speech Movement at UC began, he often participated in protests at Lower Sproul Plaza, a social area on the campus. Even as a junior high school student, he joined his father in attending much of the thirty-six-hour Vietnam teach-in that gripped UC's campus in May 1965. There, they saw and heard speakers that ranged from Norman Mailer, I. F. Stone, Paul Krassner, Mario Savio, Senator Ernest Gruening, and philosopher Bertrand Russell, who all talked about the Vietnam War. Wasserman also participated alongside university students in numerous antiwar demonstrations. Having attended multiple VDC meetings, he sought to educate his peers about the US government's growing involvement in Indochina and created the Vietnam Analysis Committee (VAC) in the fall of 1965, which received the approval of Garfield Junior High School officials. However, the approval was not without its tribulations. Before the

VAC could strategize, Wasserman and his comrades faced disciplinary action, suspended from school for wearing black armbands with peace symbols to protest the war. Eventually, in January 1966, the VAC mounted its own antiwar rally, where the local press reported on the several hundred students who participated. At the gathering, Wasserman and his peers passed out copies of the 1954 Geneva Accords, an agreement that had aimed to temporarily partition Vietnam along the seventeenth parallel, with the promise of a unifying election in 1956. Alas, the specter of a communist victory cast a dark shadow over these aspirations, as US authorities, gripped by fear, moved to prevent the election from taking place.[6]

As antiwar activists planned the October 1967 Stop the Draft Week, some students at Berkeley High decided to organize their classmates to participate in the demonstrations by walking out of school. Wasserman joined them. His peers held meetings in basements, where they strategized actions. The students then spread awareness by creating and distributing flyers and leaflets around the school. Principal Emery Curtice learned of these activities after an unidentified source informed him about the impending walkout. Curtice then advised teachers to mark participants absent.[7] On the first day of the demonstrations in Oakland, more than 100 Berkeley High students walked out of their fifth-period classes, marched to UC's campus, and made their way to Oakland. Some demonstrated for one or several days, while others stayed for the whole week. The demonstration eventually turned into a police riot where Wasserman was tear-gassed for the first time. On the third day, twenty-two Berkeley High students were among the ninety-one protesters arrested. Police apprehended them for a few hours and later released them into their parents' custody.[8]

In the week following the April 4, 1968, killing of Martin Luther King Jr., Wasserman joined his friend Ronald Stevenson, the founder and chairman of the Black Student Union (BSU) at Berkeley High School, and organized a strike of 2,000 fellow students, demanding the establishment of a Black studies and history department. However, within this united front, a difference emerged between him and Stevenson. Their divergence of opinion centered on a central question: Should the program be elective or mandatory? Stevenson advocated for a voluntary approach, granting students the choice to participate, while Wasserman harbored apprehensions about this path, fearing that white students might readily opt out of enrolling if granted such freedom. Wasserman believed that the program's voluntary nature would likely only attract Black students. To him, this presented a dilemma, for he firmly felt that white students, too, must acquire knowledge of Black history. "After all," he explains, "how could you consider yourself truly educated if, you say, you only knew about Abraham Lincoln and not Frederick Douglass. Or if you only knew about John Brown, but did not know about Nat Turner." Such historical figures "might seem obvious today," he states. "I assure you in 1968, they weren't as obvious."[9]

Solidarity became Wasserman's and his friends' rallying cry as they stood arm in arm with the protesters of People's Park. The presence of martial law outraged residents who felt that the police and armed forces were out of control and behaving with disproportionate brutality. Patrolmen deemed any gathering of more than three individuals as unlawful and stopped and frisked residents. Reports circulated of individuals being handled roughly or subjected to physical violence, while others fell victim to theft of their personal belongings. In an act of defiance, Wasserman and several scores of his compatriots undertook a weeklong sleep-in at their school. They declared their safety was in jeopardy as long as armed soldiers and patrolmen guarded the streets. Excluding weekends, they vowed to continue until both the police and the National Guard stood down.[10]

Emboldened by the activism of their Black peers and the National Guard's occupation of Berkeley, in the fall of 1969, Wasserman and his friends formed the Berkeley High School Student Union (HSSU) with a vision to champion educational and societal reform. Its members had experience in antiwar and women's liberation activities. Students Leni Schwendinger and her friend Jenny Stone recorded antiwar protests and dispatched footage to Vietnam. Equipped with cameras, both hitchhiked to Central California and clandestinely entered an active military base to interview servicemen. Together, the group spent the summer of 1969 reading Herbert Marcuse's *Repressive Tolerance*, C. Wright Mills's *The Power Elite*, and an array of other scholars, which helped inform the ideological foundations of the group. Using the typesetting machines at the Black Panther Party's national headquarters in Berkeley, the HSSU published an underground newspaper called *Pack Rat*, in which it covered antiwar activities, racial discrimination, women's liberation, student rights, and other contemporary topics. When the HSSU tried to distribute the paper on campus, school officials suspended its members. The city's local daily newspaper, *Berkeley Daily Gazette*, reprinted the cover of the publication on the front page with the headline, "Pack Rat . . . Radical paper on HS [High School] Level." However, the school officials' action was ephemeral, as the school board later overturned the suspensions. This decision was largely attributed to the persuasive arguments put forth by the parents of

Wasserman and his fellow students, who advocated for their rights to freedom of the press. The discussion extended well into the early hours of the following morning and ended in a compromise.[11]

Wasserman once again found himself an active participant in major events of the times. In September 1969, the Chicago Seven faced federal charges that included conspiracy and crossing state lines to incite riots during the 1968 Democratic National Convention. To support the defendants, while in his last semester as a high school senior in November 1969, Wasserman traveled to Chicago. He knew three of them personally. He met Jerry Rubin while organizing Garfield Junior High's first antiwar protest. Activist Tom Hayden had "taken an interest in my rabble-rousing protests at Berkeley High School during People's Park." And he met Black Panther Party member Bobby Seale through his close friendship with schoolmates who had joined the group. He arrived at the apartment of Leonard Weinglass, one of the defense attorneys, which served as a "crash pad and general meeting place for the far-flung tribe of supporters and radical nomads." Upon his arrival, he remembered the place enveloped in a "cloud of pot smoke," accompanied by the "dulcet sounds" of the Beatles' "Here Comes the Sun" playing on a turntable. Around midnight, Illinois Black Panther Party chairman Fred Hampton entered the building. "You could feel the barometric pressure in the room fall with Hampton's entrance," he wrote. One month later, Chicago police killed Hampton in his sleep, after he had been drugged and betrayed by a Federal Bureau of Investigation (FBI) informant.[12]

At Berkeley High, Wasserman ran for student body president against Richard Beibel, co-founder of the Supporters of American Ideals, a conservative, pro-war youth group. "The contest was viewed by many as a clash between the ultra-left and the far-right," summarized student Merritt Cliffton in the 1970 Berkeley High yearbook. But neither candidate "represented the farthest-out extremes of his position." According to Cliffton, Wasserman's tenure was marked by shortcomings due to his off-campus activities. He tried to make the Board of Control (BOC) meetings more open to the student body, but the HSSU's activities split the BOC between "Steve's radical faction and those who supported a more traditional view of high school life." The dysfunction of the BOC led some students to demand a recall to replace Wasserman. These factions were motivated by the Vietnam Moratorium Day and the student suspensions over *Pack Rat*. Cliffton concluded that few of Wasserman's plans gained traction "because they were more dream than substance. . . . Good intentions alone could not overcome the problems of Berkeley High School."[13]

As the boundaries of the HSSU's activism expanded beyond the confines of Berkeley, the group captured the attention of the FBI in June 1970. FBI Director J. Edgar Hoover stumbled upon an article in the Liberation News Service, which detailed that the Berkeley HSSU "has called a nation-wide conference of high school radicals." Prompted by this discovery, he urged the San Francisco office to "promptly submit information" on the group and establish contact with the Chicago office, the designated host city for the conference.[14] The National High School Conference represented the HSSU's most ambitious endeavor, aiming to organize fellow high school student activists from across the nation. It intended to follow the event with two regional gatherings in September, accompanied by a fall offensive. Activists acknowledged the significant rise in high school student activism, primarily concentrated at the local level. However, they believed that the time had come to broaden their scope and operate on a national scale. By doing so, activists maintained they could "attack the roots of the educational system, such as state education codes," and eventually begin to "directly affect this whole oppressive system."[15]

Despite its ambitious plans, the reality of the situation became apparent during the conference. One participant from Indianapolis reported that only around forty individuals attended the event, hailing from "such exotic places as New York, California, and Texas." "Although many of the ideas discussed showed a high level of consciousness," recalled the attendee, "the idea of a group of 40 people mobilizing a national high school strike in September appeared to me to be unfeasible." Most high school students, they continued, "aren't even organized on a local level."[16] None of the FBI's informants were aware of the conference until agents contacted them in July, a month after the event had taken place. Furthermore, the investigation into the HSSU was ephemeral, lasting a mere four months, as most of its members had graduated from high school that spring.[17]

After graduating from high school a semester early, Wasserman traveled to Cuba in February 1970 to cut sugarcane and demonstrate his solidarity with the Cuban people. Like many leftists, he admired the revolutionary Che Guevara and Cuba's resistance to US imperialism. Domestically, his activism captured the attention of two journalists, who interviewed him for their upcoming book on student activists, *The High School Revolutionaries*. The resulting material appeared in *Look* magazine, which republished his interview.[18]

Wasserman's commitment to progressive causes extended far beyond his high school years. He graduated from UC Berkeley with a degree in criminology in 1974. Following in the footsteps of his grandfather, he ventured into the realm of publishing. He worked for Francis Ford Coppola's *City Magazine of San Francisco* and the *Los Angeles Times* as the deputy editor of the Sunday Opinion section and op-ed page, and later, as editor of its Sunday book review. In Los Angeles, he founded the Los Angeles Institute for the Humanities at the University of Southern California and later served as the principal architect of the *Los Angeles Times* Festival of Books. He migrated to New York to work in high editorial positions for *New Republic* Books; Farrar, Straus and Giroux; Random House; and Yale University Press. Along this journey, he found himself routinely in the orbits of literary luminaries, forging deep bonds with authors like Christopher Hitchens, whose writings he was the first to publish in the United States. Later in life, he returned to the Bay Area to work as publisher of Heyday, one of California's most distinguished independent, non-profit presses.[19]

Juxtaposed with the average American high school student, who had more interest in prom, popular culture, and pep rallies than politics, Wasserman's experiences as an activist appear extraordinary. But he was one of hundreds of thousands, perhaps millions, of teenagers politicized by local and national developments. Many, like him, came from liberal households. Others did not. Nonetheless, they all fought for civil rights, an end to the war, student rights, and curriculum reform; created underground newspapers and independent student organizations; organized demonstrations; and forged national networks. They achieved some victories, experienced setbacks, and many were monitored by local and federal law enforcement. Geography shaped their experiences. And this book tells their story.

Introduction

High School is closer to the American experience than anything else I can think of. We have all been there [and while] there, we saw nearly every sign of justice and injustice, kindness and meanness, intelligence and stupidity, which we are all likely to encounter later in life.
—Kurt Vonnegut Jr., *Our Time Is Now: Notes from the High School Underground*

The average person immediately defaults to college campuses when they think about student activism. This book focuses on a different setting. It tells the story of a political development originating in secondary schools across the nation, which contemporaries referred to as the high school movement. This activism, I contend, constituted a teenage-led education reform campaign, with adolescents' actions and ideas forming a significant ideological pillar in the history of school reform. Furthermore, the expansion of constitutional rights for minors coincided with surveillance operations and the modernization of school security. Through a series of character-driven, curated stories arranged chronologically and thematically, this book aims to illuminate how high school students in the 1960s and 1970s spearheaded their own social movement, which deserves recognition alongside other prominent grassroots developments of the era. Given that nearly thirty thousand public and private secondary schools existed in the United States during this period, I largely follow independent student organizations, publications, and notable events.[1] You can certainly study student activism at individual schools or within specific neighborhoods, but this book seeks to uncover the broader citywide, regional, national, and international networks that teenagers established. It explores how these networks enabled them to remain informed about each other's actions. Even the government surveillance that followed these activists recognized the significance of these connections.

One notable example of these networks comes from the title of this book. The slogan originated from an illustration that showcased a cartoon of two male figures—one white, one Black—with clenched fists, standing in solidarity. Beneath the drawing, in bold letters, the message read, "High School Students Unite!" This image first appeared in 1968 in the pages of the New York City-based High School Independent Press Service, known as HIPS, a print syndicate that disseminated "weekly packets of news and illustrations of high school uprisings, busts, dress codes, discipline, and politics" to subscribers nationwide.[2] For at least seven years, its "Unite!" illustration appeared plastered on flyers and leaflets and was reproduced in underground newspapers from Lawrence, Kansas, to Vancouver, British Columbia.[3] Even without the accompanying image, the slogan became one of the most ubiquitous phrases used in the high school movement when students sought to organize politically.

For years, historians and education scholars have worked diligently to recognize high school students' contributions to some of the most significant social movements of the 1960s and 1970s. These young activists stood on the frontlines of the civil rights, Black Power, and Chicano movements. They pushed for racial integration, community control, Black and Chicano studies, and the removal of police from campuses.[4] Others participated in progressive movements revolving around the environment, women's liberation, antiwar protests, and even sparked debates about long hair and school violence.[5] From Boston to Los Angeles, their actions showed that high school student activism was a nationwide phenomenon.

Yet, our understanding of this era does not reflect how many contemporaries experienced this movement. Although much of high school student activism was neighborhood and campus-based, teenagers routinely formed independent organizations and underground newspapers that traversed their city and metropolitan area. Furthermore, they used preexisting networks and established new ones to connect with like-minded peers across the country and, to a small extent, abroad. Many of the characters that appear in this book grew up hundreds and even thousands of miles away from one another yet had some form of contact with each other while in high school. Through underground newspapers, regional and national conferences, written correspondences, public demonstrations, and word-of-mouth, they raised awareness of a national student movement and helped alleviate the feeling of isolation. Academia, government officials, and American popular culture caught wind of these developments as well. For a brief period, the topic of high school student activism appeared as the subject of focus in congressional testimonies, theses and dissertations, books, magazines, and even several episodes in the Emmy award-winning primetime show *Room 222*.[6]

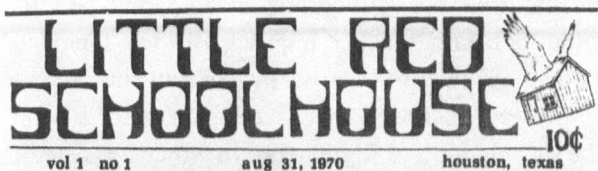

The "High School Students Unite!" illustration reprinted on the cover of an underground newspaper in Houston, Texas, in August 1970. Courtesy of Harrell Graham.

But as time progressed, this history has faded from popular memory. Only a handful of historic student uprisings received any recognition on their fiftieth anniversary.[7] The rest have been forgotten. As of August 2025, according to the Historical Marker Database, which is crowdsourced by thousands of hobbyists and has over 200,000 active markers in the United States, there were only four reported markers that dealt with historic high school student activism.[8] During my various research trips across the country, I found that many archivists, librarians, public historians, and even lifelong residents were unaware of past protests, organizations, and underground newspapers in their communities. "I do not know if there was

Introduction 11

any 'student activism' at that time that your correspondent would be interested in," wrote an alumnus of a San Francisco high school when I inquired about its campus newspaper back in 2015.[9] The passage of time has failed to erode this presumption. In 2022, I served as the lead historian for a public history project called the Cleveland Civil Rights Trail in which I assisted in installing historical markers, creating a website, and conducting oral histories. But when I read the list of potential sites gathered through community surveys, there were no high school protests listed as suggestions.[10] While leading the project, I once delivered a lecture on the civil rights movement in Cleveland and briefly mentioned the city's largest student uprising at John Hay High School—a controversy that spanned five months from 1968 to 1969. To my surprise, only one person in the audience was familiar with the event. It turned out she had been a participant.

There are several reasons why this amnesia has occurred. First, by the early 1970s, the national media started paying less attention to high school protests, and the subject became more of a local story. Even at its height, national coverage was short-lived. Second, firsthand accounts of the 1960s made passing references to high school students or no mention at all. Furthermore, some of the earliest accounts of this era stopped in 1968, 1969, or 1970, just when high school student activism peaked.[11] Third, the ad hoc nature of organizing left behind spotty archival records. Teenage activists often lacked office space, and it was common for them to congregate at private residences. High schools themselves rarely maintain archives, and many do not even have the entire collection of their campus newspapers. Given that many of the students' political activities were unauthorized, school officials discarded printed materials far more often than they preserved them. Last, as education scholar Jon Hale noted, there continues to be a tendency reinforced through media outlets, conferences, and public commemorations to characterize student activism as being "synonymous with *college* student activism."[12]

High School Students Unite! seeks to restore the high school movement to its rightful place in history. By doing so, it makes several key observations regarding teenagers' roles within the histories of education, rights, childhood, youth, and policing.

First, during the 1960s and 1970s, teenagers emerged as significant social actors and thought leaders in debates on school reform. Traditionally, and even today, the voices of high schoolers are notably absent in discussions about education.[13] Yet, youth activism forced school officials to contend with students' ideas about what schools should be and how they could better promote equality. Although teenagers' demands for change were often met with resistance or inaction, they left short- and long-term imprints on the American education system. Some school districts appointed students as nonvoting members on school boards, liberalized dress codes, increased minority representation among faculty, revamped curricula, established open campuses, and enacted bills of rights specifically tailored for high school students. Through public demonstrations, meetings with school administrators, and writings, these activists expressed their grievances and provided alternative ideas about education. When they went to the courts, young people reshaped constitutional law. Rather than being mere recipients of an expanded definition of citizenship, students actively fought for rights.

Second, student rights did not just emerge through court rulings; they were also shaped by school boards and individual schools through negotiations and public pressure. While the Supreme Court's decision in *Tinker v. Des Moines* established a legal foundation for student rights, this broader movement extended beyond the courtroom. The case itself, sparked in 1965 by junior high and high school students in Des Moines, Iowa, involved students wearing black armbands to protest the Vietnam War. After the youth were suspended, they sued the school, leading to the landmark ruling that protected students' free speech rights.[14] Student rights cover myriad concerns that have only received growing attention since the 1960s, including due process, symbolic expression, dress codes, pregnancy, and disabilities. Educators, then and now, have viewed the concept as detrimental to the education system.[15] Reflecting on schools during the 1960s, a high school principal in Indianapolis alleged that *Tinker* "wrecked all of the discipline in high schools."[16] But the on-the-ground reality was more nuanced. In various communities, students organized campaigns, drafted bills of rights, and renegotiated school policies pertaining to dress codes, due process, and disciplinary measures. Their success did not come easily. Many administrators resisted or narrowly interpreted *Tinker*. Attorney Ira Glasser, who served as the executive director of the New York Civil Liberties Union, routinely encountered these tactics at the time. In one case in upstate New York, a school principal had suspended a student for wearing a green armband that referenced environmentalism. "And I cited and explained the *Tinker* case, and the principal actually said to me that case was different," Glasser recalls. "I asked why, and he said, 'Well, those are black armbands.'"[17]

Third, and a point that requires some elaboration, the overwhelming left-wing-oriented high school student radicalism constituted a significant ideological pillar in the history of school reform. Historians know much about students' *actions* during this period, but they know little about their *ideas*. High school student radicalism mainly consisted of two concepts. The first was the belief that high school students constituted an oppressed group akin to racial minorities, women, and poor people. As administrators sought to restrict political activities during school hours, a growing number of students found themselves questioning their entitlement to constitutional rights and viewing educational institutions as inherently oppressive. Puzzled by the paradox of studying the Constitution and American democracy while simultaneously being denied the very rights granted within those documents, they grappled with a fundamental question. How could students be expected to grasp the principles of democracy when their schools seemingly disregarded those very principles? A student from Queens, New York, expressed bafflement after facing scrutiny for wanting to either sit or leave the classroom during the Pledge of Allegiance as a form of political protest. "How can a school which requires every student to take American history, which stresses the Constitution, which contains the First Amendment, deny First Amendment rights to students?" she asked. "Aren't students citizens?"[18] They sought to remedy this contradiction and routinely pushed for school reform to make education more "relevant."

The second concept of high school student radicalism dealt with young activists arguing that high schools stood as *pivotal* institutions that needed to be reformed *before* any larger meaningful societal change could occur. "The schools of a society are a part of, and the reflection of, that society," exclaimed sixteen-year-old Aimee Sands in a *New York Times* letter to the editor in 1969. "In order to change our sick and corrupt society, we must begin by changing our sick and corrupt school system."[19] From the students' perspective, high schools reflected and reinforced the racial, gender, and socioeconomic disparities that were pervasive across the nation. As compulsory institutions, they saw in school reform the potential for students to enact changes that would forge a more egalitarian society.[20] Within this context, they put forth an argument: school officials should grant them the opportunity to exercise their constitutional rights within school to nurture their development as engaged citizens in adulthood. They proposed various remedies, which school administrators often resisted. It reinforced activists' conviction that high schools perpetuate a culture of mass conformity and uphold the status quo. Regardless of the personal sentiments harbored by students toward administrators, it was undeniable that without their cooperation, young activists would have struggled to achieve many of their goals.

Lastly, student activism and school violence led to the modernization of school security. Although conventional wisdom deems school police a necessity in modern times, some school officials once saw the proposal as inconceivable. In response to "lawlessness" in public schools in Brooklyn, New York, in 1957, Superintendent of Schools William Jansen opposed a grand jury recommendation to station uniformed city policemen in every public school in the city. "To me," he began, "the proposal to have an armed policeman regularly stationed in every school is unthinkable."[21] Circumstances changed in the next decade. Between the mid-1960s and the early 1970s, high schools became sites of disturbances. School officials, politicians, and local newspapers often failed to identify the root causes of these issues and amalgamated them into a vague definition of "high school unrest." Seeking to maintain order and security, school boards, under the sway of concerned parents, teachers, media reporters, and administrators, implemented a range of measures: stationing armed and unarmed police officers and security guards within public schools, mandating identification cards, fortifying campus grounds, and installing surveillance cameras. In many circumstances, students contested the placement of police and security guards on campus. Through public protests or debating the idea with school officials, students argued for alternative solutions to achieve a more accommodating environment.[22] However, it is crucial to note that white violence in schools led some Black students and their parents to demand police protection.[23] While some scholars have highlighted students' calls for the "wholesale abolition of student suspensions and school police," critiques of campus security varied given the local circumstances. At some schools, students protested the presence of police. But in racially tense environments, such a call was risky.[24]

More importantly, school officials' growing reliance on using law enforcement to handle disciplinary matters *included* privately contacting and collaborating with the FBI and police intelligence units. Scholars have correctly noted that a "complex interplay" of government officials, parents, student organizers, teachers, and administrators shaped and contested school policing and student discipline. But security apparatuses were diverse in scope, employed gradually, and far more invasive than what scholars have uncovered.[25]

There is a well-documented history of federal, state, and local law enforcement agencies targeting political groups and individuals across the United States. White leftists, as well as American Indian, Chicano, Puerto Rican, and Black activists, were frequently subjected to heavy surveillance, repression, and sometimes violence, often outside the bounds of the law.[26] Government agencies in Australia, Canada, England, and New Zealand also spied on leftist movements, including secondary school students.[27] In this context, it is not surprising that American teenage activists were also under scrutiny. But there are some differences. Records show that while adult activists faced severe tactics—like attempts to incite violence or create internal divisions—teenagers were primarily monitored. By 1968, however, the FBI escalated its approach, conducting counterintelligence operations to stifle youth activism in high schools.[28] What stands out is the role school officials, parents, and fellow teenagers played in these investigations. They willingly acted as informants for the FBI, police, and military intelligence, with pupils reporting on their classmates. Parents often reached out to the FBI to report on their own children's political activities.

Most investigations rested on the belief that outside agitators had orchestrated student protests. School administrators, parents, elected officials, police, and others often portrayed teenagers as docile and apolitical, who only engaged in politics because of outside influences. However, the reality was more nuanced. Students usually lacked the infrastructure to operate effectively. John Eklund, a former youth activist in Milwaukee, Wisconsin, recalls, "We didn't have the resources to organize, publish newspapers, or work media." Antiwar groups in Milwaukee targeted him and his peers, but as Eklund remembers, "there was really nothing nefarious about this and if anything, we welcomed being taken seriously by these adults."[29] Students sought *assistance* from older activists.[30] They usually needed to be part of or collaborate with a political organization to organize and access its office space, mailing list, mimeograph machine, and other equipment. As one antiwar organizer in Chicago recollected, "I worked with them, but I wasn't organizing by myself; it was the high schoolers who were doing the organizing." If they "wanted leaflets and they wanted them left under the bushes outside a neighbor's house because of their parents, then I would organize that."[31] The students themselves had to handle writing, distributing, and organizing because they needed to be relatable to their peers. Adult radicals did indeed target teenagers unsolicited, but many were often rebuffed by disinterest, hostility, or school officials who called the police to apprehend them when they appeared on campus.

The high school movement produced a plethora of student-produced artifacts, but sadly, many of these records have been lost over time.[32] As stated previously, teenagers seldom created archives and artifacts they saved vanished with the passage of time, having been misplaced, destroyed, lent to friends, or lost with the passing of those who held them. Former youth activist Keith Hefner donated the largest archival collection of high school underground newspapers to Temple University in Philadelphia. "But I retained like [the] fifty best and the correspondence," he tells me. Unfortunately, a basement flood destroyed them after he gave them to a student publishing an underground newspaper before he relocated to New York.[33] While school newspapers and yearbooks can offer glimpses into student life, they had strict administrative oversight and served as the gatekeepers of memory. Former youth activist Estelle Schneider highlighted this issue during an interview with the Columbia Center for Oral History Research. She pulled out her 1969 yearbook from James Monroe High School in Queens, New York, and stated the yearbook committee had omitted any references to the social unrest that took place that year. Instead, it printed nursery rhymes.[34]

These long-standing issues do not directly apply to this book, but challenges remain. Two types of collections have played a pivotal role in uncovering long-lost student-generated materials: private archives and FBI files. I have been fortunate enough to gain access to the private collections of various former activists and school officials who allowed me to interview them and examine records in their possession. In instances when physical visits were unfeasible, they shared copies of the documents via email or traditional mail. Altogether, I have collected over one thousand pages of documents. An exceptional encounter occurred when Robert French, a former principal at a junior high school in Palo Alto, California, welcomed me to his home and granted me entry to over six hundred pages of documents that he had recently donated to a local archive. He rescued these records when they were on the brink of destruction during an office cleanup at Palo Alto High School in the 1970s. In his garage sat boxes consisting of underground newspapers, leaflets, flyers, letters, memos, and an array of materials documenting the student protest that engulfed the district. Private archives, however, do have challenges. Some former activists, despite initial assurances, failed to invite me to their homes. Others cut off communication without providing any explanation. In numerous cases, these individuals had no idea what exactly they possessed, thus leaving my inquiries shrouded in mystery. Still, the records various former activists have graciously shared with me have been more than helpful.

FBI files have provided valuable insights that historians have often underappreciated due to their inaccuracies in reporting. Since 2014, I have filed over 1,800 Freedom of Information Act (FOIA) requests. Through this process, I uncovered surveillance and counterintelligence operations targeting at least 370 high school groups, underground newspapers, public demonstrations, and incidents of school violence between 1961 and 1976. These files range in length from just two pages to over seven hundred. This arduous effort began in August 2014. I had long suspected the possibility of FBI surveillance after reading an interview in which several Palo Alto students boasted about being monitored. However, my initial FOIA requests were unsuccessful, as I was unfamiliar with the process. Thankfully, I remembered political scientist Stephen Smith telling me he would be shocked "if the FBI did not spy on high school students." I kept that in mind. When I started graduate school, I decided to write a seminar paper on the New York High School Student Union. I contacted a former member who shared digital scans of memorabilia. Among the images, I found two pages of the group's FBI file. My jaw dropped. Eureka, I thought, what I had long suspected had been confirmed. A professor provided me with a FOIA template, and I immediately submitted a request concerning the group. But I was too late. The FBI had destroyed all the documents in three separate instances: 1979, 2010, and just four months before my request in April 2014. Although devastated, I was not deterred. Recognizing the risk of losing this history, I began compiling a list of every student organization I encountered during my research. Positive matches quickly accumulated, with connections from Minneapolis, El Paso, Providence, Rhode Island, and beyond. Over the next ten years, I continued this effort and diversified the search to include underground newspapers, high schools that experienced social unrest, and individual students. My pursuit was so indefatigable that during my first visit to the National Archives in College Park, Maryland, a staff member recognized my name and asked, "Are you the guy who's been submitting all those requests on high school students?"

The motive to retrieve these records was not solely rooted in a desire to safeguard this history; rather, it stemmed from a broader observation. Undoubtedly, these files contain unverified accusations, misspelled names, and incorrect associations. However, the individuals who aided these investigations inadvertently turned FBI agents into unintentional archivists.[35] Parents, school officials, police officers, private citizens, and fellow students confiscated records from activists who distributed them on school campuses, street corners, and during meetings, or simply discarded them as litter. Within these files, I have reconstructed an archive of long-lost student-generated artifacts. They include underground newspapers, pamphlets, flyers, leaflets, meeting minutes, and other records. Much of this book could not have been written without these files. Alongside these materials are also numerous records and personal correspondence that were not produced for public consumption. Police records, school districts' intercommunication files, and letters from parents abound in these collections. In writing and phone calls to the FBI, parents relayed their deep concerns about not only their children's political activities, but also the alleged threat radical materials posed to youth in the community at large. Nonwhite adults are notably absent as informants for the most part. Black and Latino parents, given the troubled relationships both communities had with the police, were highly unlikely to work clandestinely with law enforcement to spy on their own children.

However, my efforts reveal an unfortunate truth: the complete extent of FBI surveillance on teenagers will forever remain unknown. Among the over three hundred cases I have confirmed, more than one hundred have been reported as lost or destroyed, either partially or entirely discarded. The number of false negatives is also unknowable. Occasionally, documents that the FBI initially reported as nonexistent emerged years later or after I saw the index number in another case file. Moreover, police departments and state government agencies deliberately discarded their records to avoid public embarrassment.[36] This fact signifies not only the absence of law enforcement documents but also the disappearance of numerous student-produced materials.

Some readers may wonder why it has taken so long to uncover FBI surveillance operations on high school students. Have historians been too hyper-focused on college campuses? Have we paid too much attention to major cities, national organizations, and prominent individuals? These assessments have validity. But to put it simply, most high school political activities were short-lived. Teenage activists often struggled to keep their operations afloat for more than one school year. Many individual activists found themselves as members of multiple organizations and contributors to various underground publications. Only a handful of groups received media coverage beyond their local communities. Given these circumstances, much of high school student activism has flown under historians' radar. Few would presume that a short-lived, campus-based underground newspaper in Lincoln, Nebraska, would have an FBI file, but it did.[37] Government surveillance was not restricted to major urban centers. It also occurred in suburbs and small towns.

To preserve the many forgotten names of the high school movement, *High School Students Unite!* features appendices that list numerous independent student organizations and underground newspapers that existed during the 1960s and 1970s. Teenage activists created myriad short-lived political groups. The membership of these organizations spanned from individual schools to entire metropolitan areas and formed to address various issues. Underground newspapers were far more numerous than these groups. Most of them vanished after a single issue; therefore, it remains impossible to determine the exact number that ever came into existence. Yet, I recorded the names of over one thousand publications as I sifted through archives, scrolled through microfilm, scanned digitized newspapers, and even flipped through school newspapers in a storage closet at a high school in Indianapolis.[38] Given the aforementioned limitations, the two lists are not meant to be comprehensive. But what they reveal is that high school student activism occurred in locations typically unassociated with radical politics.

To tell an intimate account of the high school movement, *High School Students Unite!* follows various characters. I have conducted over seventy oral history interviews over the course of a decade. It is crucial to note that despite being politically precocious, these young activists were still teenagers who experienced the joys and challenges of adolescence. All the feelings of happiness, pleasure, romance, loneliness, pain, and jealousy existed in their lives. Some were the brightest students at their schools, while others struggled academically. Many had cherished childhood memories, and others shared traumatic experiences like the premature death of a parent. Yet, most wanted to tell their stories. When I initially reached out to these former youth activists, I often sensed a surge of excitement that someone, anyone, was interested in documenting their movement. "Wow!" exclaimed one interviewee who responded to my letter. "It's not only a blast from the past, but also a bit shocking that anyone would be interested."[39] On several occasions, I reconnected friends who lost touch with each other fifty years ago and received messages of gratitude. As these young activists transitioned into adulthood, many of them continued their involvement in political activities, and their experiences in youth activism shaped their careers. They ventured into fields such as the arts, politics, labor relations, and various other endeavors. A surprising number of them became academics.

I found most interviewees through simple trial and error by mailing letters and sending emails. Some hard-to-locate persons came through recommendations. Others were serendipitous. In one notable instance, David Jacobs, a Stanford University archival specialist, handed me his business card as he was intrigued by my interest in high school radicalism records. Instantly, I recognized his name. I confirmed that he was indeed the same individual mentioned in an FBI file I possessed concerning the Radical Student Union in Palo Alto, California. We then agreed to do an interview. Of course, some potential interviewees declined my invitation for various reasons undisclosed to me. Unfortunately, there have been dozens of instances where I sought to contact former activists, only to discover that they had passed away a few months or a year prior to my request. The most regrettable episode occurred when I postponed an interview with former youth activist Neal Hoyman. In 1968, he founded a student group called the Charlotte Student Union in Charlotte, North Carolina. Parents and school administrators accused it of having outside influence and contacted the FBI to investigate its members. He eagerly wanted to share his story, but when I attempted to reconnect, his sister Michele informed me that he had passed away a year before.[40]

Most urgently, there is a need to preserve their stories. Former high school student activists are aging. Their memories are also fading. Hefner saw the memory lapse of his former peers when he attended his fortieth high school reunion. "Because I was an activist, some of my strongest memories were of protests, some of which turned into small riots and then school assemblies to talk about the issues. A very big deal at the time," he recalls. "But not a single person I talked with remembered them!" A reporter who was interviewing him for the event was reluctant to report his recollection because "she couldn't corroborate them with anyone else!" Hefner later provided the reporter with news clippings from the high school and a profile piece of him in *The New York Times* as evidence.[41] His experience was not an anomaly. When I began doing research on high school students in the anti-Vietnam War movement, an alum who oversaw San Francisco's Mission High School records told me confidently, "Nothing happened." With this book, I seek to correct this collective gap in our historical knowledge for scholars and non-scholars alike.

Part I **Politics**

∙∙

We find, however, that fundamental rights of the constitution are not found in the schools. The right to petition and to assemble are not only discouraged, but often denied.

—General Purpose of the [Minnesota] Student Union, 1969

1   From Civil Rights to Student Rights
San Francisco's High School Free Speech Movement

This story begins in 1965, but high school student activism certainly precedes this year. There is a rich history of teenagers politically organizing during the 1930s. Most notably, Black Southern youth initiated numerous campaigns against segregated schools and facilities throughout the 1950s and 1960s.[1] However, if we mark the beginning of the high school movement as the moment when students began advocating for their rights as *students*, then debates regarding free speech were among the earliest major controversies. Civil rights activism was the first flashpoint. In October 1964, fifteen-year-old Canzetta Burnside testified in court after she and dozens of other students had been suspended for wearing "freedom buttons" in their segregated high school in Philadelphia, Mississippi. A similar incident occurred in Sharkey County, Mississippi, in January 1965 when over 100 students wore Student Nonviolent Coordinating Committee (SNCC) buttons in defiance of the principal's order to remove them. The burgeoning antiwar movement became another flashpoint of contention from 1965 to 1966. School officials suspended students in Des Moines, Iowa; Euclid, Ohio; Nyack, New Jersey; Berkeley, California; and Chicago, Illinois, for wearing armbands to protest the war in Vietnam.[2]

Amid these controversies, high school students in San Francisco launched a long-forgotten, citywide campaign for free speech rights. But rather than wearing insignias, the center of controversy dealt with an underground newspaper. Coinciding with a campus uprising at UC Berkeley, one newspaper dismissed the endeavor as a "junior Free Speech Movement."[3] But this effort was organic. It lacked theatricality and a charismatic figurehead like Mario Savio and featured no massive protests or indelible political speeches delivered by young activists. Instead, it was a battle of ideas. These young activists espoused distinct perspectives on their predicament as minors and engaged in debates that hinged upon historical and contemporary notions of childhood, citizenship, the arbitrary demarcation between childhood and adulthood, and the paradox of teaching students about democracy while simultaneously curtailing their constitutional rights in school. They belonged to a citywide group called the Students' Organized Education and Action League, commonly known by its acronym SOEAL (pronounced "soul"). Comprising primarily white students from middle- and upper-middle-class households, many of whom hailed from families with direct and indirect ties to the Communist Party or who supported the civil rights movement, the group was held together by a common bond. "I realized later, what really held them together is they were all red-diaper babies," recalled former SOEAL member Peter Shapiro. "I mean, without exception."[4] In April, San Francisco's Superintendent Harold Spears ordered a district-wide ban against the group's publication. However, with the superintendent's ban in effect, the group pivoted swiftly, rallying around the issue of free speech. Ultimately, the students failed in their endeavor to lift the ban. Nevertheless, many of the ideas these young activists expressed would reverberate throughout the high school movement.

The Origins of SOEAL

During his formative years, Jesse Tepper found himself captivated by the civil rights movement. Born in New York City in the late 1940s, he moved to California with his family when he was an infant. "I got a sister who is a year younger [than me] who was born out here. I got brothers who are twins to each other. . . . None of them consider me a native although I've been here for sixty-plus years," he recalls jokingly. "My folks thought it would be good for us to live in a suburb when I was ten." Weighing options, the family moved to the Marin County suburb of Terra Linda. It was a peculiar place for young Tepper. "I remember age nine to ten walking around asking, where's the library? Where's the movie theater? Where's the shopping center? Totally a fish out of water," he remembers. However, the matrimony was short-lived as his parents divorced before his high school years, leaving his mother to relocate to San Francisco to raise him and his three siblings. Together, they navigated the challenges of a single-parent household. Filling the void left by his father's absence, Tepper took on adult responsibilities at an early age. He ensured his siblings were fed, escorted them to school, and tended to his mother's needs, whether it was fetching her morning coffee or getting her cigarettes before she went to work.[5]

Remarkably, the weight of domestic obligations failed to completely obscure Tepper's attention to political developments in the city. He became acquainted with the civil rights movement through his mother's involvement in a short-lived local organization. Through her connections,

Tepper crossed paths with Nathaniel Burbridge, the chairman of the local National Association for the Advancement of Colored People (NAACP), who would forever have Tepper's admiration. "He was one of my heroes," he recalls. Burbridge had led several successful civil rights demonstrations against Auto Row and the Sheraton-Palace Hotel. As an adolescent, Tepper yearned to contribute to Burbridge's cause, but Burbridge politely declined. He was wary of inviting undue scrutiny and accusations of manipulating minors that often dogged civil rights proponents. At the age of fourteen, Tepper enrolled in the private, elite institution Lick-Wilmerding High School as a "charity kid. Smart kids, but without connections." He remembers his peers' immense wealth. "One of my classmates' grandfather owned the Empire State Building," he recalls. Others came from notable hereditary lineages. One of them arrived at school every day in a Corvette. Although he had the academic prowess to study alongside his more privileged peers, he found himself drawn to political activism. The gravitational pull of that world lured him into a circle of like-minded peers from other high schools in the city. On picket lines and through formal introductions, he met fellow teenagers whose upbringings were both similar to and more radical than his own.[6]

One of those students he met was Betsy Brown, whose childhood reflected the influence the Communist Party had on the members of SOEAL. Born on January 2, 1951, in San Francisco, Brown grew up in a family of "Jewish Communist atheists." Her father, Archie Brown, was born in Sioux City, Iowa, on December 16, 1911, to Russian Jewish immigrants. After the family farm hit financial troubles in 1924, he, his father, and older brothers moved to California in search of work and settled in Oakland. Archie developed antiracist attitudes through a series of incidents. When his brother Carl attempted to get him elected as president of the Science Club, a teacher advised that an underclassman could not be president, but his brother felt it dealt with Archie's ethnicity. In another episode, when Archie worked as a newsboy, police apprehended him. During the interrogation, the officer called him "negative terms as far as being a 'Jew.'" In one incident that left a sense of shame, Archie joined in with boys who taunted a Black girl by calling her a "nigger." Coincidentally, Archie and the girl were neighbors and had played with each other. When the girl returned home and told her family what had happened, her brother cornered Archie and punched him "so hard that he wound up on the floor." Thereafter, the relationship with the family shattered. Archie carried "great shame" and decided to oppose racism wherever it existed.[7]

He also became a Communist. In 1928, the *San Francisco Call* and *Post Enquirer* merged and laid off half of the newsboys. Viewing such a move as unjust, considering that he delivered the mail, he assisted in the newsboy strike. Originally, the group sought assistance from the American Federation of Labor, but the organizers rejected them because they only wanted skilled workers. They did, however, find support from the Trade Union Education League, which consisted of union radicals. Having seen the backing that the Communist Party had given to the workers' movements, Archie soon joined the Young Communist League.[8]

For Archie to identify as an open Communist carried great risks. Anticommunist politics in California laid the groundwork for future conflicts that reverberated through the corridors of public education. The coexistence of communists and fervently patriotic groups forged a volatile atmosphere. Among these factions, the conservative Better America Federation emerged, committed to eradicating what it deemed "radical" literature from schools. Simultaneously, police departments homed in on labor activists and those affiliated with leftist causes. Exploiting the fears stoked by the Red Scare, business leaders deployed tactics to quell unionization efforts among farmworkers. Nevertheless, the Communist Party thrived in the 1930s, bolstered by its involvement in maritime and agricultural disputes. As the Cold War crystallized as an all-encompassing reality, the state of California and its officials took decisive action. State officials wielded their authority to banish school textbooks from classrooms. They imposed employment bans on those with communist leanings and enforced loyalty oaths upon churches, charities, and veterans. In this calculated onslaught, public schools emerged as the next target. In 1941, the state forged its own Committee on Un-American Activities, whose mandate encompassed scrutinizing the activities of communists on university campuses and in public schools alike. A decade later, in 1951, the state passed a measure affording the dismissal of schoolteachers accused of indoctrinating their pupils with communist ideas. Consequently, state employees, educators, and scholars who transgressed these stringent measures found themselves terminated. To some, these efforts were commendable. Among their champions stood the Senate Interim Committee on Education, which expressed its "deep gratification" upon witnessing the removal of teachers who invoked their Fifth Amendment rights.[9]

As a young adult, Archie faced multiple arrests by the Oakland police for participating in Communist parades and violating an anti-speaking ordinance. He worked as a longshoreman and collaborated with veterans of the Spanish Civil War within the Abraham Lincoln Brigade. In 1947, his name appeared on a list compiled by the American Coalition of Patriotic Societies, submitted as testimony before the House Committee on Un-American Activities. His political activities prompted his wife to relocate Betsy and her three daughters to live with their grandmother in Southern California while Archie went into hiding during the McCarthy era. He resurfaced when he ran for a position on the city's board of supervisors and successfully had his name included on the ballot. In 1965, he achieved a significant victory when a Supreme Court decision affirmed the rights of Communists to hold union positions.[10]

Brown's journey to political activism was modeled not only by her father but also driven by the example set by her mother, Esther, who worked as a legal secretary. Like Archie, Esther was the daughter of Russian Jewish immigrants who left Russia for New York because of their political activities. She also belonged to the Communist Party but refrained from being as public as Archie. Esther traveled to Mississippi for the Freedom Summer campaign and went to New Orleans to work as a legal secretary for a law firm. She brought Betsy to antiwar marches, civil rights demonstrations, and union picket lines. The family also hosted dinners where they engaged in various insightful conversations.[11]

The civil rights movement and Communist Party shaped Tepper and Brown and much of the ideological basis of SOEAL, but the group still needed members to have practical experience, especially in the realm of publishing. That is where co-founder Jonathan Bennett entered the picture. Bennett found his political grounding within the civil rights movement. Born in New York, Bennett's family relocated to Arizona when he was almost six years old. However, during his junior high school years, his parents moved again, this time settling in San Francisco. Like Tepper, Bennett also matriculated into Lick-Wilmerding High. Dinner table conversations shaped his worldview. Racism, sexism, world peace, and other topics that resonated with leftist political circles took center stage in these dialogues. Bennett's first foray into political engagement materialized through his involvement with the Committee for Non-Violent Action, a pacifist collective committed to thwarting aboveground nuclear testing. Subsequently, he found himself drawn into the Bay Area civil rights movement and actively participated in a group known as the Student Congress of Racial Equality (SCORE). There, he honed his skills in crafting newsletters and developing his leadership abilities. However, an inherent imbalance manifested within SCORE, as white students predominantly occupied the leadership positions.

Consequently, seasoned civil rights activists kindly requested that the leadership step aside and cede their positions to Black students, affording them the opportunity to develop their own leadership acumen. As a result, Bennett chose to disassociate himself from the group, yet he retained the skills he had acquired.[12]

SOEAL had numerous other members who shared characteristics similar to those of Tepper, Brown, and Bennett. Peter Shapiro's father, older sister, and cousin were politically active. Unlike his peers, Shapiro was not a red diaper baby. His cousin notably was a prominent figure in SLATE at UC Berkeley and a key organizer of the 1960s protests against the House Un-American Activities at City Hall. Shapiro himself became active after the civil rights demonstrations in Birmingham, Alabama. Bennett invited him to meetings with SCORE, but later "SCORE didn't seem to be going anywhere," he said, "especially its youth group. They broke away and started this thing." Among SOEAL's ranks, some were his close friends, while others were more casual acquaintances.[13] Carol Pittman, a biracial girl, was raised in a "family of communist journalists." Her father, John Pittman, founded a Black-run newsletter called *San Francisco Spokesman* (later renamed *The Spokesman*). Its endorsement of the San Francisco General Strike in 1934 led to conservative vigilantes damaging its office building. John moved to New York after the incident and met his future wife, Margrit Adler, a German immigrant who never finished school under Nazi-era policies. In 1938, she fled to the United States, where her brother resided, and joined other antifascist emigres from Germany, as she herself once secretly belonged to an antifascist organization, and worked on the bilingual newspaper, the *German American*. Carol spent three years in the Soviet Union before returning to the United States. She lived just a few blocks away from Brown and often visited her home.[14] Mark Citret's parents became close friends with Al and Mini Bock, two prominent local Communists who lived a few doors down from the family. Through conversations between the Bocks and his parents, Citret developed left-wing perspectives on various political issues. The protests at UC captivated him to such an extent that he lost a friend who saw him as becoming increasingly obnoxious. He eventually joined SOEAL after Shapiro introduced him to the group.[15]

SOEAL had two other members who, like Citret, were influenced by members of the Communist Party. After returning from World War II, Elisabeth Semel's father became involved in the Veterans of Foreign Wars, a progressive alternative to the American Legion. He and Elisabeth's mother became friends with couples who, together, established the Sunset Nursery School,

San Francisco's first cooperative nursery school. During the war, her mother was a reporter for the *San Francisco Chronicle*, but after the war, women at the paper lost their positions to men. She did public relations work, was active in the local civil rights movement, became executive director of the San Francisco Conference on Religion, Race, and Social Concerns, and later of the San Francisco Jewish Community Relations Council.[16] Semel met Kate Northcott in junior high school, and they bonded over their shared love for the Beatles. Northcott's parents met while attending college in Texas before the outbreak of World War II. After moving to San Francisco, both of them became involved with members of the Communist Party and other individuals they encountered through their work. For instance, the family lived next door to the Bocks, who helped them find the home. Northcott's mother actively advocated for causes such as the Fair Housing Initiative and fought against the construction of a freeway that would cut through the city.[17]

Semel attended Lowell High School and became friends with a girl who would provide SOEAL with an international connection. Paula Garb had a family background intertwined with the Russian Revolution. As a nine-year-old Jew, Garb's father found himself caught in the conflict. The February Revolution of 1917 marked the downfall of the imperial government, followed by the October Revolution, which ushered the Bolsheviks into power in that same year. In this context, the Red Army, composed of Bolshevik forces, clashed with the White Army, a coalition of factions opposing the Bolsheviks. Tragically, thousands of Jews perished in antisemitic pogroms during the war. Amid this chaos, Garb's father lived in a small Russian town where he suffered the devastating loss of most of his family at the hands of anti-Bolshevik forces. However, he and two siblings, hiding under the house, miraculously survived and were assisted by Bolshevik organizations until 1922. The Garb orphans immigrated to the United States to reconnect with their grandparents. From that point on, he maintained an enduring admiration for the Bolsheviks. Garb adopted her father's worldview, later identifying as a "red-diaper baby." Growing up during the McCarthy era, she concealed her family's political leanings.[18]

Even during a period of anticommunist politics, Garb wanted to immerse herself in local and global affairs. That moment came when she stumbled upon a flyer tacked onto a library bulletin board. It advertised a lecture at San Jose State University talking about the war in Vietnam in the context of Graham Greene's book *The Quiet American*. In 1963, Vietnam held little resonance within the American consciousness. However, she knew her father appreciated the book's author, so she decided to attend the event.

There she received another flyer about an antiwar demonstration in San Francisco, scheduled for the next day. With tears brimming, she implored her father for permission to attend the march. Initially, he declined, but ultimately reversed course. As a veteran of World War II, he understood some conflicts were necessary, while others were not. The avoidable conflicts, to him, only inflicted upon innocent civilians the torments he had endured as a child. "I got my way, and that changed my entire life," Garb said.[19]

The experience in San Francisco motivated Garb to move closer to the action. Residing in Santa Clara, a forty-mile expanse separated her from the city. She desired a new milieu. In her view, her classmates at Santa Clara High School were folks who were "shallow," not interested in politics, and she felt stuck in a "swamp." Over the summer, she successfully coaxed her parents into arranging her transfer to Lowell High in San Francisco, where they discovered an elderly woman seeking a roommate. Her family eventually relocated to San Francisco during her senior year. There, Garb met Semel, Northcott, and other like-minded peers.[20]

The members of the group held a genuine fondness for each other. When Citret first met Garb, he admitted, "I was a little intimidated by her because she was much more sophisticated than the rest of us high school kids." There was "something kind of alluring about her. . . . When you're in high school, and you know there are just some girls who are not interested in high school boys, and they end up dating college seniors. That's sort of what Paula was like." But Garb had her own insecurities about her looks and intellect. She felt a tinge of jealousy toward Semel's ability to consistently achieve straight A's and excel in tests. "Lis was in my classes, and she was so bright . . . it really pissed me off," she states. "She got straight A's on tests [and] didn't miss one question, ever. She was very high energy." These personal attitudes were typical adolescent anxieties, but they failed to hinder their collaborative work. The academic backgrounds of the members varied. While young activists were usually the brightest pupils in their schools, the composition of SOEAL included both high achievers and individuals who struggled or put in minimal effort to get by academically. Citret notably repeated a grade. He recalls his poor editing skills, jokingly stating, "I don't know how I was editing copies, but I was doing that. . . . I'm sure there were a lot of grammatical and syntactical errors because they had editors like me." Tepper, on the other hand, never held a strong interest in school and admitted to graduating in the bottom 13 percent of his class. In contrast, Garb, Semel, and Northcott thrived in their studies. Yet, they all possessed an interest in political affairs.[21]

The *Activist Opinion*

The *Activist Opinion* made its official debut in February 1965. The first issue alerted readers that SOEAL published the newsletter and promised fresh content every three weeks. From the beginning, the group aligned itself with the civil rights movement, both in the South and locally in San Francisco, and soon after with the nascent antiwar movement. It envisioned the paper as an "attempt to inform the San Francisco Bay Area youth about liberal and progressive activities and organizations in this area." It noted that although many "new political youth groups" have emerged, there had been a "strange lack of an effective progressive political organization for high school and junior high school students." SOEAL opened itself to "all young people 12 years and older" who agreed with the preamble and statement of purpose, which declared "We believe that as young people, it is our duty to bring about peaceful coexistence, complete disarmament, freedom for all people, and self-determination and freedom from oppression for all the nations of the world." The publication encouraged contributions from youth and wanted readers to know what was on their fellow peers' minds.[22]

SOEAL members strategized ways to distribute the paper and received mixed reactions from consumers. The group sometimes printed the paper in temporary chairman Frank McMurray's father's office or at the office of the W. E. B. Du Bois Club. They reached their audience wherever they could. Tepper took to selling the newsletter on his commute home, proclaiming, "I'd be waiting for the bus and on the bus, I'd say, 'Get your *Activist Opinion*, $0.05.'" Pittman distributed copies at her school, Woodrow Wilson High. Citret passed out copies at Lick-Wilmerding since district policies did not apply to his school. However, distributors did not always get the reaction they wanted. At Lowell High, a jock hurled a rock at Garb's head while she and some friends distributed copies of the newsletter. Citret's paternal grandmother "offered to buy all the issues and burn them." Her husband would yell in response, "'You can't afford to buy all those issues. They're worth far more than a nickel a piece." Citret's grandmother was a former educator for sixty years. "It wasn't that she objected to them ideologically[,] . . . it was the fact that the school board banned it . . . and to her, the school board was God. What they said was the gospel."[23]

The *Activist Opinion* covered a range of topics from a left-wing perspective, which largely reflected the radical upbringing of the writers. Citret credited an article he wrote arguing that the 1965 Watts riots in Los

Angeles were an "insurrection in response to decades of institutional abuse" to dinner table conversations with the Bocks.[24] On the Vietnam War, the writers viewed American imperialism and civil rights struggles as deeply intertwined. When police in Selma, Alabama, brutalized civil rights demonstrators in March 1965, SOEAL published an editorial arguing that political officials had a willingness to "send millions of dollars and thousands of men to fight in Vietnam," but were "unwilling to send any kind of force into Alabama where US citizens are fighting for their rights."[25] Furthermore, the writers' knowledge of the history and complexity of the conflict highlighted an admirable trait of rigor. In an article titled "Continued Madness in Vietnam," the group condemned a public statement made by Defense Secretary Robert McNamara as spurious after he claimed the South Vietnamese death toll demonstrated the people's willingness to defend their country. "If that last incredible statement proves anything," the group wrote, "it demonstrates how desperate our government is to sell the American people on the War in Viet Nam." Countering President Johnson's desire for "'unconditional negotiations' with North Viet Nam," it noted that the "Viet Cong is made up primarily if not entirely of South Vietnamese" and received its weapons by capturing them from South Vietnam's government troops. Therefore, it was "difficult to see the sense of appealing to the Hanoi government if a cease fire is really desired." Speculating about the possibilities of where the conflict could shift, the group concluded, "One thing is still clear—the United States is not combating aggression in South Vietnam. If anything, it is engaging in it."[26]

Unbeknownst to SOEAL, the FBI and the San Francisco Police Department's Intelligence Unit had been secretly monitoring the group. Beginning in late March, Special Agent in Charge Curtis Lynum received three copies of the second issue of the *Activist Opinion* from various sources. On March 25, an anonymous individual, presumably the mother of a Lowell High School student, mailed him copies of the newsletter along with an antiwar leaflet and expressed her eagerness to aid the investigation. Lynum obliged the request.[27] Meanwhile, Special Agent Melvin Blatch happened upon a copy of the newspaper through his own son, a student at George Washington High.[28]

As fate would have it, on April 1, Lynum received a tip-off from San Francisco police officer Cecil M. Pharris. Pharris handed over not only the newsletter but also a flyer promoting a party organized by SOEAL. To add to the intrigue, Pharris included a copy of a letter he received from his informant, who disclosed that the newsletter had been discovered at Aptos Junior High School. The revelation prompted school administrators to sum-

Vol. 1 no. 5   june 7 - june 28   price 5 cents

"For here we are not afraid to follow truth wherever it may lead-- nor to tolerate any error so long as reason is left free to combat it."
—Thomas Jefferson

EDITORIAL: THE DOMINICAN REPUBLIC

The era of gunboat diplomacy has arisen, Phoenix-like, from its ashes in all its regalia, complete with a "peace-keeping force" of 30,000 United States Marines. The position of the United States in the politics of the Western Hemisphere has finally been made crystal clear for all well-wishing liberals who really think that the Organization of American States, The Alliance for Progress, and the United Nations have some political significance. The U.S. supports democratic constitutionalist governments apparently only when they will pledge total allegiance to the United States.

When one looks behind all the administration's planted stories one discovers one basic admission that no member of the government is willing to make, but which is the entire basis for our invasion of the Dominican Republic. That is that in a fluid situation, where no government is in control, powers sympathetic to the United States cannot possibly win without our direct
(Con't. on pg. 2)

******   *   ******   *   ******

STUDENTS PICKET DR. SPEARS FOR RIGHTS

In the last two weeks 50 to 100 students have, on four occasions, picketed the offices of Dr. Spears, Superintendent of Schools, to demand that all student organizations be allowed to hand out or sell literature in the public schools. These demonstrations, organized by the student group which publishes the Activist Opinion, were called only after 7 weeks of unsuccessful appeals to the Board of Education and Dr. Spears to change the present rules which deny individual students and student organizations their normal constitutional rights of freedom of speech and freedom of the Press.

-History-

This conflict between students and administrators stated on April 5 of this year when Dr. Spears announced that the Activist Opinion, two editions of which had been sold inside San Francisco schools by that date, could no longer be sold on school grounds.
(Con't. on pg. 7)

* * *

ANNOUNCEMENTS   -IN THIS ISSUE-

The fifth issue of the *Activist Opinion.* Courtesy of Kate Northcott.

mon a student to their office. This pupil, in turn, confessed to receiving the publication from Tepper, who allowed him to pocket two cents for every copy sold. Troubled by the ever-deepening reach of the organization, the informant confided in Pharris, remarking, "Cecil[,] they seem to be getting further down the age ladder more and more. Next, we will have the elementary grades picketing."[29] Given the available evidence, it is unlikely that school officials had any involvement in or knowledge about this investigation. However, the mere existence of the publication on campuses instilled suspicion among certain residents of the city. Interestingly, the police had one member already under surveillance. After the school district banned the publication, Brown went to the police station to retrieve a permit for a planned march. Little did she anticipate the encounter that awaited her. Pulling forth a file bearing her name, the officer posed a query that left her momentarily astounded, "Are you Elizabeth Brown?" She confirmed, and he followed with, "Are you Archie Brown's daughter?" Confirming the familial connection, Brown then asked for the permit, received it, and left. She admits not being experienced enough to know what the officer implied with his question.[30]

One article, which later became controversial for the group, focused on racial segregation in the city's public schools. Many of SOEAL's founders had been engaged with local civil rights efforts and recognized, as Tepper put it, "Northern segregation being different from Southern segregation." The Bay Area's reputation for liberalism and social tolerance often masked a history of racial violence, leading school officials to view discrimination as a distant problem and dismiss accusations of racism. White residents condemned blatant racial terrorism in the South more often than they acknowledged structural discrimination within their own communities. Yet, SOEAL knew the reality.[31] A student gathered data from the NAACP and reported on overcrowding and "shamefully deteriorated school buildings" in predominantly Black schools in the city.[32] SOEAL also reported that students from the predominantly white Hunter's Point Naval Reservation were bused across town to attend the lily-white Winfield Scott School, effectively separating themselves from the neighboring majority Black communities.[33]

SOEAL reported on a problem local civil rights activists have long sought to highlight. Following the Supreme Court's 1954 ruling in *Brown v. Board of Education* mandating desegregation in public schools, Black leaders in San Francisco organized meetings with school administrators and board members to urge the city to integrate its own voluntarily. But these sessions repeatedly ended without any tangible commitments. A significant issue was the absence of an official census on the district's racial demographics. This lack of information allowed school officials to dodge accusations of de jure segregation and demand proof from their critics. Recognizing this gap in quantitative data, *Sun-Reporter* publisher Carlton B. Goodlett initiated a "Study Our Schools" campaign in 1959, beginning with a well-attended conference. This event birthed the Study Our Schools committee, which proposed that parents finance an evaluative study of the school system, investigate complaints of discrimination in teacher hiring, and employ an independent authority to lead the inquiry. Additionally, the committee aimed to support mayoral candidates who could appoint a school board member to represent the Black community.[34]

Despite mounting pressure, district administrators maintained that discrimination in public schools did not exist. Superintendent Spears even testified before the US Commission on Civil Rights, asserting that San Francisco's school assignment policies were colorblind. Even with a pending lawsuit against the district, Spears declared, "I don't think we'd be vulnerable at all, not on any counts." He added, "We build the schools where they're needed, where the children live. There are bound to be some that are all-Negro or all-White, or largely so."[35] Ironically, his remarks hinted at the existence of segregated schools within the district, yet he portrayed them as incidental rather than the product of deliberate policy. The school district eventually agreed to conduct its own racial census of its schools and released the information in August 1965. It revealed what community activists had long alleged. Racial imbalance was widespread, especially in the elementary schools. Out of ninety-five elementary schools, seventeen had an enrollment of greater than 90 percent white, twenty-four were at least 57 percent Black, and nine were over 90 percent Black, while fourteen schools had Asian populations that were over 30 percent. Whites, Blacks, and Asians made up 57, 28, and 15 percent of the elementary student population, respectively.[36] But for SOEAL, highlighting this issue and others set it on a collision course with the school district.

The Fight to Repeal the Ban

Before the group could publish the third issue of the *Activist Opinion*, Superintendent Spears banned its distribution from the city's public schools on April 5, 1965. School administrators took issue with articles in the publication that criticized FBI Director Hoover, the House Un-American Activities Committee, and school segregation. The newspaper also included advertisements for showings of Russian-made films at the American-Russian Institute, an organization labeled as communist by California state officials. "There could be no disagreement relative to a factual finding that this publication constitutes propaganda," stated Irving Breyer, the school board's legal counsel. Breyer had previously supported school officials' ban on the sale and distribution of left-wing publications on school grounds.[37]

Yet rather than quelling the fervor of its publishers, this act of suppression stoked their defiance. Undeterred, SOEAL taunted the ban in the third issue of the paper, displaying the front page with a proclamation: "All Students Beware: This Newspaper Is Banned."[38] The group used this issue to focus on school administrators and the fight for free speech. The editors recounted that the principal of Lincoln High School had informed McMurray that he could no longer sell copies of the newsletter on campus. The official then posted a notice on the daily bulletin, stating that unauthorized literature could not be distributed at the school. When the superintendent extended the ban citywide, McMurray and managing editor Bennett approached Breyer to inquire about lifting the ban. With knowledge of the law, particularly because McMurray's father was an attorney, they challenged Breyer's assertion that the law used by Spears prohibited the school board from allowing the distribution of literature not under the school's control. McMurray and Bennett referenced section 8454 of the State Education Code. Attorneys had informed them that it granted the school board the authority to permit such distribution. They argued that the schools had, in fact, banned a publication that was not under their control.[39] In another editorial, the students contended that Superintendent Spears's rationale for banning the newspaper was "nothing but a poor cover-up for suppressing a newspaper which gives the students a point of view different than that found in our textbooks." They accused school administrators of stifling independent thought and violating students' rights to a free press and the right to hear all sides of every issue.[40]

The ban came amid several incidents regarding free speech and symbolic expression in high schools throughout the Bay Area. At Lowell High, administrators initially banned California state assemblyman John Burton from speaking about the war when students requested his presence, but the administration and the students compromised by agreeing to invite a figure who would speak from an opposing position.[41] Lowell High faced another controversy when the school's dean of girls instructed senior Mary Stack to remove three nude sketches from an art display in the hallway, citing their unsuitability for minors. Stack initiated a petition, which revealed that most students had no objections to the drawings. In response, school administrators threatened to suspend her, but ultimately withheld the suspension, and the controversy eventually subsided.[42] Claiming that the school tarnished its image of academic excellence, the students wrote, "If the intent is to create carbon copy students, then the administration should admit this, and that free expression does not exist."[43] Simultaneously, the principal of Lincoln High, swayed by his own convictions, firmly rejected McMurray's request to extend an invitation to a speaker who espoused the abolition of the House Un-American Activities Committee.[44] This episode unraveled just as both Berkeley High and Tamalpais High Schools grappled with their own struggles, as students attempted to invite left-wing speakers onto campus in response to the presence of conservative speakers.[45]

In the face of these perplexing acts of repression aimed at curtailing free speech, the students penned an editorial that raised a fundamental question: Does the First Amendment apply to high schools?

> It is time the high schools made a searching examination of their policy toward the student press. For what purpose do the schools support newspapers: Is it to indoctrinate its students into right-thinking avenues? Is only the controversial pap of the Walt Disney school of journalism allowed; or is it to instill in its students the belief that perhaps freedom of the press is not merely a slogan, but a basic right which must be defended at every turn? If it is the former, then we expose student newspapers for the farce they often are, merely official organs for the administration's policies. If it is the latter, we applaud the sentiment, but wish the administration would keep its well-trained, Victorian, non-controversial nose where it belongs, and allow the students the freedom they are told about in Civics. END CENSORSHIP OF THE STUDENT PRESS![46]

SOEAL turned its words into action as several members attended the next school board meeting on April 27. Addressing the board first, McMurray proclaimed SOEAL had no affiliation with other organizations and consisted entirely of junior and senior high school students. "My organization feels that, as citizens of the United States," he began, "they have a right, under the First Amendment, to publish a newspaper and sell it to fellow students." He believed the purpose of education was to "teach students how to think and how to make choices." But this mission, in a democracy, could not succeed "by presenting the students with only one small part of the spectrum of ideas and opinions." A true "democratic method of education" presented every side and permitted students to make up their own minds. The lack of free speech rights, he believed, would have profound consequences. "An educational system which leaves the student unfamiliar with different points of view is not going to produce thoughtful voters," he claimed. "How can we, as students, be expected to acquire a real understanding and appreciate [sic] of democracy when we learn from our civics classes?" Furthering this argument, he quoted a social studies textbook that explained the importance of the First Amendment, and then he claimed the same officials who made them read the textbook had abridged their freedom of speech. McMurray did not expect the school board to endorse students' opinions, but his group wanted "it [to] recognize our right of freedom of the press and our readers' right to freedom of intellectual investigation."[47] For McMurray, the high schools were inherently contradictory because they instructed students about democracy but forbade its existence during school hours. A fulfilling education, McMurray believed, allowed students to actively practice their rights.

Written expressions of support also found their way to the forefront. Tepper presented a statement from one of his teachers, C. Franklin Kelley, another person Tepper greatly admired. Kelley immigrated to the United States after escaping the Nazis, identified as a conscientious objector, and held several doctoral degrees. In class, he introduced students to the writings of Alexis de Tocqueville and historical documents like the Magna Carta, all to develop their critical thinking skills. Tepper felt nervous before speaking, but he "remembered a couple of tricks like looking in a mirror and be familiar with what you're talking about." While acknowledging the limits of private school instructors in shaping public school policies, Tepper read Kelley's letter, in which he offered to "endorse [students'] genuine interest in thinking and publicly expressing their lively and serious concern for certain human and civil rights."[48]

A few sympathetic adults sat among the audience. Dan Jackson of the San Francisco Federation of Teachers acknowledged that public schools were "charged with preparing students to assume rights and responsibilities of citizenship in society." In this regard, he contended that students possessed an inherent right to hear dissenting viewpoints. He explained that teachers should have been "rather encouraging and stimulating to find youngsters with the interest and concern of public questions to seek to propagate their ideas, however unpopular or ill-conceived they might be." The classroom, he continued, remained inextricably linked to "the confrontation with the issues of our times." Commissioner Edward Kemmitt asked whether the Federation backed the *Activist Opinion*. Jackson responded that the board needed to establish ground rules. "To a teacher, academic freedom is just as much a tool of the trade as a hammer is to a carpenter, and any invasion of that academic freedom is taking the tools of our trade from us," he asserted. Commissioner James E. Stratten interjected, asserting his belief that the Federation supported the publication. Stratten then offered an analogy. "I would also say that the carpenter using the hammer as a tool uses it for constructive ideas and constructive things," he began. "When the carpenter starts breaking people's windows with the hammer, he's no longer a carpenter, he's a destructive individual and his hammer is taken away from him." The audience erupted in applause. Stratten then expressed his admiration for the written work produced by the young authors and commended Jackson for his enthusiasm for the students.[49]

The board persisted in its interrogation of Jackson regarding the controversial publication. Stratten publicly disapproved of the insults and "untrue statements . . . perpetrated by teachers, inspired by teachers" and carried out by youngsters. Commissioner Ernest Lilienthal, seeking further clarification, asked Jackson whether the publication had a faculty supervisor and exactly how much academic freedom existed. Jackson responded by claiming that academic freedom should not be limited to teachers' mere presence. To him, it also "include[d] the right of a student to advocate his idea before other students. . . . I don't see how you can set students aside as a different classification of citizens from the rest of citizens," he explained. Commissioner Joseph A. Moore Jr., drawing from the pages of George Orwell's dystopian novel *1984*, posed a hypothetical scenario for consideration. "Suppose this publication . . . kept issuing issues, and their premise was that 2 plus 2 was 5," he began. "Would it be your thought that we should continue to permit that to be published and let the children make up their minds?" Jackson responded with no, but Moore pressed on, "Where would you draw the line?"[50]

The clash of perspectives raged on, unabated, as the adults engaged in an exchange with students. Amid this heated atmosphere, one adult voice emerged, resolutely denouncing the publication and resurrecting age-old narratives that questioned the cognitive capacity and emotional maturity of minors to handle the full spectrum of academic freedom. Leon Market, representing the West of Twin Peaks Council, commenced his statement by underscoring the vital role of minors in this contentious affair. He posited, "If we don't consider that one of the prime keystones, then what is to prevent someone from coming into the schools with a paper extolling the use of marijuana or LSD?" He commended the board's decision to ban the paper, asserting that without such a measure, they would "ultimately . . . have chaos in the high schools."[51] On the other side of the divide, a student seized the moment to address the ban on the publication and shed light on the absence of Black history courses. Balboa High student Kit Wilson approached the board with an impromptu speech. She admitted that all students needed some experience in school and often read adult newspapers and opinions.

"They state their opinions. They tell the news. Why can't we?" she asked. As a Black student, she noted that the school board had done a poor job integrating Black history into the curriculum.[52]

The subsequent proceedings of the meeting fell on the premise of the artificial line between childhood and adulthood and the autonomy of the publication itself. At the heart of the debate lay the question of when precisely a student reached maturity. Following inputs from a few students and adults in attendance, Commissioner Kemmitt stated that mature people could make their own opinions but followed up with, "At what age is the so-called student mature?" He expressed his belief that an individual attained maturity when they could receive information, digest it, and make independent decisions devoid of coercion. Stratten followed up and directed his attention to McMurray and inquired about the article on school segregation in San Francisco. When McMurray acknowledged that Shapiro had obtained sources from the NAACP, Stratten contended that there were individuals within the community who would exploit students as conduits for propagandistic endeavors. Nonetheless, before the meeting adjourned, Superintendent Spears concluded that the publication "was not conducive to the educational interests of the school."[53]

The exchange of words between students and administrators illuminated the disagreements in defining childhood and the evolving role of education. In the wake of World War II, the surge in the number of Americans enrolling in high schools mirrored the rising demand for a well-educated population in white-collar and technical professions. Parents increasingly grappled with concerns regarding whether their children would receive the knowledge and skills needed to thrive in an increasingly competitive society.[54] During the late 1960s, psychologists such as Jerome Bruner and Jerrold Zacharias championed constructivism, which posited that children were active participants and learn best with engagement. These ideas stood in direct competition with the influential scholar James B. Conant's advocacy for tracking, a system that segregated students into paths leading to college or basic skills and vocational training courses.[55] Meanwhile, the members of SOEAL, deeply influenced by the civil rights movement, believed that a comprehensive education went beyond the classroom and included covering controversial topics. To them, the creation and circulation of an underground newspaper that discussed political and local affairs not only enriched their educational experience but also provided a platform for practicing active citizenship. However, administrators held steadfast paternalistic attitudes, which hardened as students began challenging school policies. Coupled with the prevailing climate of anticommunism, these administrators perceived the students as mere pawns manipulated by outsiders.

The school board meetings also highlighted evolving conceptions of youth. Influenced by diverse factors such as public policies, economics, geography, and culture, the understanding of what it means to be a child, particularly a teenager, is inherently bound to a specific historical context. By the mid-1960s, American social scientists began acknowledging that teenagers' accelerated social maturation and increased dependence resulted from the nation's newfound affluence and compulsory education. California Institute of Technology President Lee DuBridge stated, "There is no question that today's teen-ager coming to one of the major colleges is better educated and more seriously motivated than ever before." The statistics spoke volumes. In 1900, a mere 13 percent of American children between the ages of fourteen and seventeen were engaged in formal schooling. By 1940, this figure skyrocketed to 73 percent, and by the mid-1960s, it stood at around 95 percent. This transformation fundamentally changed the lives of American teenagers. Social scientists keenly observed that this rapid educational expansion and the dwindling guidance of parents compelled teenagers to mature at an accelerated pace. Schools, cafeterias, drugstores, and the freedom of the open road filled the void once occupied by familial structures. These assessments, however, predominantly reflected the experiences of white middle- and upper-middle-class youth, often neglecting the nuanced realities faced by their nonwhite and less affluent counterparts.[56] Amid the board meetings, certain sympathetic adults recognized these societal transformations. On the other hand, others still viewed teenagers as too immature to engage in sophisticated conversations.

The fourth issue of the *Activist Opinion* appeared shortly after the board meeting, with SOEAL standing firm in its position. On the front cover, the publication featured a quote by Benjamin Franklin: "When men differ in opinion, both sides ought equally to have the advantage of being heard by the public." The students recounted the events of the meeting and acknowledged that despite the conservative attitudes of the board members, they were responsive to public pressure.[57] The publishers welcomed criticism from fellow students, and one critical respondent agreed with Superintendent Spears that the publication interfered with schoolwork. The writer explained that he and his friends had chosen to read the newspaper during several classes, thus validating Spears's decision to ban it.[58]

Although SOEAL initially appeared defeated after the board refused to lift the ban, the group decided to attend the subsequent meeting on May 11 to discuss the issue further with board members. Shapiro and Garb joined McMurray and Tepper, and all four had portrait photographs taken by the *San Francisco Chronicle*.[59] McMurray reiterated the points made in the previous meeting and challenged Superintendent Spears's assertion that the publication interfered with the educational process. He began by stating, "The student is best served by being allowed access to all kinds of ideas, facts, and opinions." His comments were brief. Tepper, following his lead, proceeded to read three letters, including one from his teachers and another from the lawyers' guild. Although all three expressed disagreements with certain content in the *Activist Opinion*, they all identified freedom of speech as the fundamental issue. One board member displayed signs of fatigue due to the lack of novelty in the debate. Some adults in attendance spoke in favor of either lifting or upholding the ban. A gentleman named Reubin Bennett asked whether the school board was as "concerned with the mental health of our students as it is with the physical health." John F. Wormuth, a Lincoln High student and representative of the Committee for America, asserted, "I feel that the organizations which attempt to start a free-speech movement in the schools, as such, are giving youth in its entirety a bad name." "They are not defending democracy," Wormuth continued, "for they are using democracy . . . as something for their mere appendage." At the meeting's conclusion, the board members held firm in their stance on the ban, reiterating that the publication was irresponsible and that freedom of speech and the press were rights that entailed responsibility and privilege. Kemmitt underscored this sentiment, stating, "Anyone who takes advantage of this privilege in an irresponsible manner violates my rights in the future to use this privilege."[60]

A few weeks later, SOEAL organized a picket line outside the school board's office. Around thirty to forty students marched, their voices resonating with civil rights hymns such as "We Shall Overcome" and "America the Beautiful." One student displayed a sign bearing the words, "You have opinions, why are you afraid of ours?" The protesters pledged to persist in their picketing until Spears relented. Local journalists, however, remained unsympathetic. A reporter from the *San Francisco Chronicle* depicted the participants as "well-scrubbed and neatly dressed, tend[ing] to blur the image of any oppressed minority."[61]

The *Chronicle*'s investigation uncovered a historical precedent of a free speech controversy in the city nearly half a century earlier. Alvin J. Greenberg recounted his expulsion from Lowell High School in 1916 due to his involvement in an unauthorized publication known as the *Scholastic Rebel*. The board of education had refused Harold B. Matson, the editor of the paper, permission to attend Lowell High until he ceased its publication. The *Scholastic Rebel* held controversial positions on issues such as military training in schools and militarism. Similar to present-day high school radicals who linked their predicament to broader political causes, Greenberg reflected on how he connected his battle with the school board to the American Revolution, Sun Yat-sen's crusade in China, and the struggle for home rule in Ireland.[62] The historic context did not persuade the district. At a subsequent school board meeting, it unanimously upheld Spears's ban, with Spears reiterating that while students had the freedom to express themselves outside of school, such liberties were not permitted within the school's confines.[63]

At least one school adopted a more liberal approach regarding the *Activist Opinion,* even with the ban intact. Initially, Lowell High barred the circulation of a petition seeking the repeal of the ban on the *Activist Opinion* within its premises. However, Principal J. A. Perino reversed course. Prior to this development, two students had submitted a petition to the California State Board of Education, urging the lifting of the district-wide ban and advocating for "free written and spoken expression of thought by all students." While their success extended only to their own school, Perino granted students the freedom to voice their opinions in the school newspaper while pledging to scrutinize and curtail any inflammatory or libelous material.[64]

SOEAL's high school free speech campaign ultimately failed, but the group continued operations through the next school year. Notably, Paula Garb traveled to Helsinki, Finland, in June 1965, where she attended the World Congress for Peace, National Independence, and General Disarmament as a representative of SOEAL. Various peace groups representing nearly 100 countries attended the conference. Garb reported that the delegates of South Vietnam presented a moving experience and later expressed solidarity with the Dominican Republic, which had recently been invaded by American forces. Additionally, she attended a workshop on Vietnam, which was the "most important and well-attended." Garb wrote how impressed she was by the mutual respect delegates showed one another. "Americans were able to cry with the Vietnamese. The people of Israel were able to discuss their conflict with the Arabs."[65] While in attendance, she received an invitation to travel to Moscow by train. She thought, "I'm going because I've never been there, and that was my father's homeland. He said all these great things about the Bolsheviks and the lies of the capitalists made about the Soviet Union." There, she met a Russian tour guide who became her future husband.[66]

By 1966, SOEAL began to gradually decline. The group shifted its focus to the Vietnam War and organized a demonstration involving fifty people in front of the Fillmore Auditorium.[67] Many of the core members had graduated from high school. Others became less active within the organization. Semel and Northcott, motivated by a desire to protest the elitism at Lowell High, transferred to their neighborhood school, the majority Black Polytechnic High School. They found solace and a sense of belonging there, where the glaring inequalities became readily apparent. Semel completed high school at sixteen in 1967, while Northcott finished later that same year after taking summer courses. Citret, on the other hand, retreated to his interest in photography.[68]

SOEAL failed in its effort to repeal the ban, but it represented a burgeoning trend among adolescents, both in the city and throughout the nation. Influenced by the civil rights movement and increasingly engaged in antiwar activism, its members imbibed protest tactics and absorbed arguments about citizenship. Remarkably, even those members who may have been lackluster in their academic pursuits displayed an astounding level of sophistication in their writings and exchanges with school board members. Gradually, the students in SOEAL came to perceive the "student" as a politicized identity, one that crystallized through the lens of repression.

The controversies surrounding free speech marked a pivotal shift in high school student activism. Previously, battles for educational reform had centered on school integration. Although racial disparities remained unresolved in certain school districts and issues of racial imbalance persisted, students collectively rallied around the cause of free speech, seeing it as inextricably linked to civil rights and antiwar struggles. Their open defiance of the postwar era's prevailing anticommunist sentiments and traditional notions of childhood signaled a paradigm shift in the mindset of politically engaged teenagers. During the Cold War, children had been thrust to the forefront, deemed in need of protection against communist subversion. Students now challenged the in loco parentis doctrine, asserting their maturity and autonomy in arriving at their own convictions. SOEAL eventually disbanded in 1966, but teenage activists in San Francisco continued to organize politically. The antiwar movement served as a vessel to forge connections beyond their local communities and make the burgeoning high school movement national. Through these networks, students who lived hundreds and thousands of miles apart became increasingly aware of each other's struggles.

2 The Backbone and Organizers

Building a High School Antiwar Movement

In 1967, the average American high school student harboring doubts about the Vietnam War was isolated. If they tried to converse with their peers about the conflict, they likely would have been met with blank stares or outright hostility. After all, most teenagers, like most citizens, supported the war. Even if their parents had skepticism of President Johnson's rhetoric, they tended to keep their reservations to themselves. To discuss the topic in school was ill-advised. News of massive protests in coastal cities and college towns seemed like far-off lands to many students across the country. Sixteen-year-old Maurice Isserman felt this sense of seclusion in his small town in eastern Connecticut, where antiwar protests were virtually nonexistent. Isserman's school imposed strict appearance codes. Boys had to keep their hair short, and girls were required to wear skirts with hemlines below the knee. "More importantly," he recalled, "nobody in my high school or community was vocally opposed to the Vietnam War—except, it seemed, me." But everything changed for him on April 15, 1967, when he attended his first antiwar protest in New York City, organized by the Spring Mobilization to End the War in Vietnam. "When I reached the Sheep Meadow," he remembered, "suddenly I found I was lonely no longer."[1]

The crowd was predominantly young and white, but Isserman also saw people of different races and ages, and groups such as veterans and trade unionists. With an estimated 400,000 people in attendance, he likely missed the high school contingent present that day. They were not mentioned in his recollection. Had he mingled with them, he would have found peers who shared his antiwar stance and had experienced repression for their actions. He probably would have been shocked to discover that through one of the protest's sponsors, these young activists were gearing up to publish a national newsletter and spearhead a high school-centric antiwar effort. Teenagers in urban areas were among the first to mobilize against the war, but these developments eventually reached youth who lived in areas like Isserman. He was not alone.[2]

The anti-Vietnam War movement helped build a national high school movement, but this success was not guaranteed. Initially, teenagers opposed to the war organized small, collective actions or met one another through local peace groups. Encountering like-minded individuals at meetings and demonstrations led them to establish their own organizations, frequently adopting names such as "High School Students Against the War" or "High School Students for Peace." The preexistence of these groups was crucial for adults to recruit students into larger organizations. They also recognized the need for independence and respect. "If high school students are to be organized against the Vietnam War," wrote one writer in a paper for the National Coordinating Committee in 1966, "the students must be free to develop their own leadership, their own perspective, and their own strategy based on the given conditions of the community in which they exist." Youngsters would "have no respect for an organizer that attempts to impose a fixed ideology on them . . . or that attempts to recruit teen-agers as lackeys for an adult operation."[3]

Various peace groups aimed to mobilize teenagers, but the Student Mobilization Committee (SMC) achieved the most success from its inception in 1966 until its dissolution in 1973. As a national organization, the SMC created networks among high school students nationwide. It sponsored regional and national conferences and published a newsletter, the *Student Mobilizer*. As the organization grew, its offices received a steady stream of letters from teenagers eager to establish chapters, seek resources, and voice their political grievances. Many came from unlikely areas where antiwar activism felt as foreign as a penguin in the desert. In September 1968, a girl from Charleston, West Virginia, using the pseudonym Jorma Williams, wrote a letter to an SMC staff member and informed them, "I'm in a junior high that is very anti-anti-draft, if that makes sense." She claimed to be the only person who wore peace buttons at her school and routinely received criticism for her actions. But she managed to find like-minded high school students around the city and asked the office for materials to form a chapter.[4] The SMC responded to numerous letters from teenagers like Williams. It provided organizational strategies, published works, and reduced the sense of isolation.

Most Americans, then and now, think of the antiwar movement as just a series of major demonstrations occurring one after another, like a slideshow. However, like all social movements, it included a variety of tactics, evolving ideologies, internal disputes, and other complexities. High school

Students holding up a banner that reads "We Are the Majority. Bring all the G.I.s Home now! High School SMC." The *Militant* Photographic Collection, box 2, Folder 12, Hoover Institution Library & Archives.

students were vital participants. They persevered amid persistent challenges such as isolation, parental authority, censorship, transient leadership, and entrenched ideas of childhood innocence. For the entirety of the antiwar movement, teenagers organized conferences, distributed leaflets in schools and cities, recruited peers in public spaces, held street rallies, worked in offices after school, and sustained the movement's momentum. Adult organizers greatly admired their dedication and hailed them as the "backbone and organizers of the SMC."[5]

High school antiwar activism spread nationwide, but two communities—San Francisco and Detroit—exemplify the themes of small, collective actions, citywide organizing, and building networks. In San Francisco, high school students established the city's first youth-oriented antiwar group, which the SMC later absorbed. Meanwhile, in Detroit, teenage antiwar activists formed a high school chapter of the SMC and built regional and national networks.

The Backbone and Organizers 49

San Francisco's High School Students Against the War

Raised in a politically active household in San Francisco, Katharine Harer's beliefs formed early. After a period of isolation at a remote boarding school, she returned to the city, bringing with her a sharpened sense of purpose that led her to found San Francisco's first high school antiwar group. She was born in Oakland, raised in San Francisco, and grew up in a white working-class household. Her father worked as a longshoreman at the docks and served as a rank-and-file leader of the International Longshoremen and Warehousemen's Union, while her mother, who was also active in the office workers' union, performed several office jobs, taking on work as a bookkeeper and a clerk, among other professions. Both of Harer's parents identified as socialists and participated in the antiwar, civil rights, abortion rights, and Fair Play for Cuba Committee. The latter group championed the Cuban Revolution as a "socialist alternative to Soviet-style communism." As a child, Harer participated in civil rights picket lines and later recalled them as enjoyable and educational since they had taught her to fight for just causes. She also received a political education by sneaking out of her room at night to eavesdrop on strategy sessions her parents held with other socialists.[6]

When her parents sent her to John Woolman School, a Quaker school in Nevada City, nearly 150 miles away from San Francisco, she took a pause on activism. She had taken the opportunity because her older siblings had had rough experiences at her neighborhood school, Balboa High. Furthermore, she believed Woolman would allow her to explore her interest in writing. But her time there was one of constant delight and frustration. "Everybody's worldview there was about peace. It wasn't antiwar, it was peace," she recalls. "In those days, those of us who were more socialist, radical, didn't use the word 'peace.' We'd say, 'don't call it the peace movement, call it the antiwar, we're trying to do something, we're trying to end the war.'" Woolman had a socialist club, but it had only three members. Although the school facilitated conversations about peace, justice, and kindness, Harer realized "you're up in the woods. There's nowhere to do anything." Craving to be part of the action in the Bay Area, she and a friend sneaked away from the school and hitchhiked to Berkeley to participate in antiwar demonstrations.[7]

The taste of being in such a dynamic atmosphere, such as the Vietnam Day teach-ins at UC, was exhilarating. It only increased her longing to return to activism. After two years at Woolman, she convinced her parents to bring her back to San Francisco. She felt conflicted by the decision. "As much as I liked it because it was so beautiful and I could write poetry and be in a class with seven people and study history, literature, and science, I felt I was missing what was going on in the world." She was "very frustrated by not being able to contribute to the antiwar movement." In San Francisco, she attended Polytechnic High School to explore her interest in studying drama. Poly High sat in the Haight-Ashbury district, drawing in mostly Black students, as well as a significant number of working-class whites and Asians. She loved the school, the teachers, and the diversity. Its proximity to urban amenities provided joy. She could visit head shops in Haight-Ashbury and wander over to Golden Gate Park, where she and other kids rolled down Hippy Hill. At Poly High, she met students who came from families who were active in the labor movement. Concurrently, she grew close to a group of friends who had become involved in the counterculture but considered themselves apolitical.[8]

Harer's family's connections with socialists and communists exposed her to a political network and made it easier for her to meet some familiar faces in the Young Socialist Alliance (YSA), the youth group of the Socialist Workers Party, of which her parents were members. She knew several YSAers personally as they had come to parties and meetings at her home. A YSA member asked whether she wanted to start a high school antiwar group. Though Harer had little experience in political organizing, YSA members mentored her and allowed the group to hold meetings in their office. To recruit students for the group, Harer reached out to her close circle of friends at Poly High, and others reached out to students at Lincoln High. They were a small group of young people, mostly white and middle class, but nearly all were quite politically conscious since their parents were currently or had formerly engaged in radical politics.[9]

The High School Students Against the War (HSSAW) originated as a discussion group. It later became affiliated with the United Committee, a coalition of various antiwar organizations from across the Bay Area, which allowed the group to use its headquarters. However, in terms of organizing its peers, the HSSAW faced a daunting task. Most high school students in San Francisco were apathetic about the war in Vietnam in 1966. Harer argued in a newsletter that the apathy probably stemmed from "basic ignorance" of facts. They received, she continued, "fabricated lies on all sides," but these deceptions could be vanquished with truths. The group planned to work within schools and suggested that students could use official school organizations like human rights clubs to raise awareness. HSSAW wanted the war to become part of a regular dialogue and felt that the lowering of the draft age posed a real threat to high school students. Despite the challenges, the group remained quite optimistic. "The whole field of high school antiwar work is really exciting," Harer claimed in her newsletter article, "mainly because it is a new one with a great deal of possibility for success." She promised that if the war continued, "There will be high school students working alongside the rest of the antiwar movement to see that these ends are met."[10]

According to one of the organizers, a few individuals created the group and received assistance from the VDC chapter at San Francisco State College. Drawing on a longer history of the Left organizing among teenage peace activists, the VDC declared that one of its main goals for the summer was to help "high school students who oppose the war to get organized" by providing moral support and distributing leaflets. However, the group acknowledged that the students themselves "quickly got going on their own." HSSAW members leafleted two summer schools to organize a discussion group and collected almost a dozen names for the August 6 antiwar demonstration. Harer's parents often assisted in organizing these events. For her group, they wanted "to make some kind of impression and get more high school kids to follow us, or to at least get people to know what high school students against the war was, and that we should have a really big presence at these demonstrations." The event itself brought out about 3,000 people who marched up Market Street. As with most contemporary reporting on the antiwar movement, the press devoted little attention to the march and dismissed demonstrators as "long hair waving" protesters. Reporters did not acknowledge the high school presence at the march. But their attendance helped them recruit more teenagers to the cause. The students had marched with fifteen people in the event, holding a banner that read "High School Students Against the War." More than twenty high schoolers who saw the sign approached the group shortly after the demonstration to join the organization. By the end of August 1966, the group consisted of students from eight different public and private high schools across the city.[11]

Peace groups had long aimed to organize high school students, continuing a tradition of the American Left recruiting secondary school students. In the 1930s student movement, the American Student Union, the largest student organization of that period, linked urban teenagers with labor and civil rights organizations and peace demonstrations. The group notably established high school chapters and appointed a high school chair to build a student movement within secondary schools, which were more intolerant, repressive, and paternalistic than colleges. This tradition persisted into the early 1960s when the Student Peace Union organized conferences to educate high school students about its stance on nuclear weapons. In November 1961, for example, the group distributed over 1,000 leaflets at several high schools in Rochester, New York.[12]

Even though the average senior was close to draft age, most young people supported the war. They published pro-war statements in news columns. The home environment and parental patriotism shaped their views. Teachers taught the domino theory, which theorized that if one nation fell to a Communist takeover, the surrounding nations would eventually succumb to its expansion. Students who lived in the countryside would rarely have any discussion about the war that questioned its purpose. The poet W. D. Ehrhart recalled that teachers in his rural Pennsylvania high school were influenced by a conservative milieu that discouraged critical conversations about the war. The lack of challenging dialogue led him to enlist in the Marines, only to be emotionally scarred by the conflict for life. Such indifference occurred at San Francisco's Lowell High, when an editor in the school newspaper responded to criticism about the lack of coverage on contemporary issues by claiming most students "aren't interested." Yet, young activists still sought to organize their peers and raise awareness of antiwar sentiment among their population.[13]

The HSSAW epitomized a broader trend of teenagers forming community-based antiwar groups aimed at engaging their peers. These groups varied in structure, some being ad hoc while others were more formal. Just a month after President Johnson committed ground troops in April 1965, a small group of youth in Baltimore, Maryland, calling themselves the Baltimore High School Students for Peace, picketed and distributed leaflets for two hours in front of the United States Post Office to demand an end to the war. One participant remarked to a reporter that they "wanted to make people aware of dissenting opinion. . . . People are taking the war too complacently."[14] Other students formed official organizations. In June 1966, over a dozen students in Pittsburgh, Pennsylvania, created the Pittsburgh High School Students for Peace in Vietnam and gradually expanded its membership through independent and collaborative actions. Its initial activities were minimal, but the group maintained that "there is great potential in this area."[15] Some of these groups emerged from adult-led organizations. In Providence, Rhode Island, sixteen-year-old Anne Finger began attending meetings sponsored by the Rhode Island Committee for Peace in Vietnam. "Most of the members are college-age or older. I was the youngest, but they always let me participate without taking special notice of my age," she relayed to a journalist. After participating in rallies and demonstrations both within and outside Providence, she and a friend eventually formed the Rhode Island High School Students for Peace in 1968.[16]

During the fall of 1966, the HSSAW became more organized and extended its reach beyond San Francisco. Activists scheduled weekly classes on Vietnam and worked to raise funds for the November 5–8 mobilization against the war. They also aimed to convince high school officials to stock school libraries with more information on Vietnam, civil rights, peace action, and conscientious objection. There is no evidence that school officials acted on these demands. But HSSAW members were resolute in their mission to make information about the war accessible to their peers. Organizing efforts extended across the bay as well. In Oakland, students, primarily from Oakland Technical High School, formed a group called Students Against the War, which published its own newsletter, *DOVE*.[17] This group worked in tandem with HSSAW and collaborated with the United Committee.[18]

The emergence of the SMC would transform localized high school organizing into a national movement. A reported 257 students from college and high school campuses in the United States, Canada, and the US territory of Puerto Rico attended the founding conference in Chicago from December 28 to 30, 1966. The SMC formed with the intent of marshaling campus opposition. However, it emerged amid competing ideas within the antiwar movement about whether to appeal to the broadest audience possible or base itself primarily on students and demand an immediate withdrawal of troops. It was in a "state of disarray" upon its first publication of *Mobilizer*, which it created to organize students against the war. The gathering held workshops and drafted proposals for the spring. The organization proposed that April 8–15 be designated as Vietnam Week, culminating in transporting students to New York and San Francisco as part of the Spring Mobilization scheduled for April 15. It proposed that Vietnam Week focus on bringing home the troops, opposing the draft, and ending "campus complicity with the war effort."[19] Impressively, the group would eventually grow to become one of the largest, longest-lived peace organizations in the country. Furthermore, as the organization established itself, it would play a significant role in doing outreach work to high school students who would expand its focus beyond ending the war.

Practicality can undermine ambition. High school antiwar activism, at the time, was strictly local. Prior to SMC's formation, small collective actions characterized much of teenagers' activities. Yet this local organizing paved the way for teenagers to eventually join the SMC and, in the process, establish networks with like-minded peers well beyond their community. By 1967, the SMC developed crucial contacts on the East Coast, in the Midwest, and out West.

The HSSAW became absorbed into the national antiwar movement following the establishment of the SMC. On February 16, 1967, the SMC reported that several high school students from Los Angeles had attended a two-day conference in San Francisco earlier that month. At this event, the attendees learned about existing high school groups in the Bay Area and were encouraged to form a citywide group in Los Angeles. The students began organizing. They used radio phone-in shows, underground newspapers, leaflets, and word of mouth to connect with other students who opposed the war. By March 5, a report noted that students from fifty high school campuses participated in the founding meeting of the West Coast High School Students Against the War. Among the speakers was Susi Montauk, a student at Oakland High School and a Bay Area organizer for HSSAW. The West Coast HSSAW aimed to raise funds to travel to San Francisco to support the upcoming April 15 demonstration and began collaborating with the Spring Mobilization Committee and the SMC to schedule classes on the war.[20] A similar organizing effort took place in New York City. In February 1967, activist Maxine Orris founded the High School SMC, drawing sixty-four students from twenty-seven high schools to the inaugural event. Attendees agreed to organize local groups and activities, build antiwar movements within each school, and coordinate these activities during Vietnam Week. The group also planned its own march on April 8.[21]

In the spring of 1967, the HSSAW intensified its political activities and became an integral part of the broader antiwar movement. Internal reports from the SMC indicated that high school students were becoming increasingly involved in the movement, with actions spreading from San Jose to Los Angeles.[22] San Francisco's SMC outreach coordinator, Kipp Dawson, reached out to Harer, hoping she could lend her organizing expertise to other SMC chapters, particularly one in Boston, to assist with summer projects.[23]

Dawson emerged as a significant figure in the high school antiwar movement, despite having graduated from high school in 1962. Born in Los Angeles during World War II to a Jewish mother and father who were social justice activists, Dawson became involved in progressive politics from an early age. Her mother, a labor activist, was a member of the International Longshoremen and Warehousemen's Union and was a rank-and-filer in the

Communist Party of the United States of America. Attending union meetings with her mother, Dawson absorbed the powerful dynamics of unionism. She also vividly recalls FBI agents visiting their home to intimidate her mother and their neighbors.[24]

Dawson grew up in a housing project for World War II shipyard workers, which evolved into a postwar racially and ethnically diverse community, providing a sanctuary from the outside world's intolerance. Her mother's remarriage introduced her to a mixed-race family dynamic, as Dawson gained two stepsiblings and, in 1957, a biological sibling when her mother and Black stepfather had a child together. Her stepfather, born to a migrating family from Louisiana and working as a longshoreman, stayed away from politics but supported his wife's activism. Race was a constant presence in Dawson's life. In at least one incident, the police had stopped them, suspecting a Black man had kidnapped a white family. Walking around town, Dawson observed the stark differences in how strangers treated her Black siblings compared to her and her lighter-skinned brother. She even remembers a time when police apprehended one of her brothers, mistaking him for a robbery suspect. Having witnessed police brutality against civil rights demonstrators on television and reading *Jet* magazine, to which her family subscribed, Dawson's civil rights awareness increased.[25]

Dawson's unique upbringing groomed her to recognize the conservative culture at Berkeley High, where racially segregated fraternities and sororities dominated student life, even determining where people sat during lunch. Undeterred, Dawson and a close-knit group of friends formed a civil rights organization initially called the Anti-Anti Club, later renamed Students for Equality, during the 1959–1960 school year. The founders, including Brenda Malveaux and Tracy Sims, came from politically active households and were inspired by civil rights activists in the South.[26] The group convened weekly at various locations on campus, attracting anywhere from five to forty participants. It organized educational programs, invited speakers to campus, held discussion forums, recruited fellow students to join members on picket lines, and went together to hear Malcolm X when he spoke near the UC campus in 1961. As the civil rights movement gained momentum in the area, Dawson stepped back from her leadership role, graduating a semester early in January 1962 at sixteen. She continued her education at San Francisco State College, where she remained active in the civil rights movement and served as a high school and college student coordinator with the SMC in the antiwar movement.[27]

Dawson helped organize the April 15, 1967, demonstration that took place in both New York and San Francisco. In New York City, up to 400,000 protesters marched from Central Park to the United Nations, led by Dr. Martin Luther King Jr. In San Francisco, over 50,000 people filled Kezar Stadium, a gathering that the *San Francisco Examiner* dubbed "the largest West Coast protest yet against the war in Vietnam." Protesters endured intermittent rain as they marched and sat through the event. A significant portion of the participants consisted of 7,000 trade unionists, but students made up the largest section. Unlike New York, no draft card burning demonstrations took place in San Francisco. Serving as executive director of the demonstration, Dawson greeted speakers and arranged the stage. She and other antiwar activists saw the antiwar movement's growing fervor, "but none of us, on either coast, had any idea how huge the turnout would be that day." Dawson sat between Dr. King's wife Coretta Scott King and singer Judy Collins. Addressing the crowd from the stage at the center of the stadium, she spoke into a microphone and declared, "We are here to demonstrate our belief that the soldiers have the right to protest the war in Vietnam. . . . We are joining with the soldiers in their demand—that they be brought home now." The crowd "responded with a mighty roar that I can still hear."[28]

The April 15 demonstration showed activists that the antiwar movement was on the upswing. For high school students, it marked the beginning of a burgeoning movement that would go beyond actions in local communities. A rock-and-roll band riding a truck featured a banner that read "West Coast High School Students Against the War."[29] The opportunity for HSSAW to become part of a nationwide high school antiwar movement disappeared just as soon as it emerged. When Harer graduated from high school in 1967 and prepared to matriculate at San Francisco State College, the group she had founded dispersed. Its last major action occurred when it encouraged peers to come out for mass mobilization on April 15. Calling the war illegal and unconstitutional, the group warned, "After graduating, most high school students will be drafted to die on foreign battlefields in a cause that is not theirs."[30] Nonetheless, the HSSAW had only a few dedicated members. The group never had a large membership, nor did school officials publicly comment about it because most of its activities occurred off campus.[31]

Although small in membership, the HSSAW represented the most effective efforts of high school students in San Francisco to rally around the Vietnam War across the city after the demise of SOEAL. It connected the city with other teenagers across the state and the country. The group did not push much for school reform, but it adopted an early notion that high school students were a distinct subset within the antiwar movement. By 1967, teenagers increasingly became organized not just on a citywide level, but on a national scale.

Building a National High School Antiwar Movement

Prior to the April 15 demonstration, the SMC had scheduled a national student antiwar conference for May 13 to 14 in Chicago. Its previous division with other antiwar groups ceased, notably with *Bring the Troops Home Now Newsletter* dissolving itself and turning over its mailing list to the SMC. Several members from other groups joined the organization. The May conference originally sought to map out a summer project of antiwar activity. Dawson had moved to New York immediately after the April 15 demonstration to work for the SMC's national office. In early May, Dawson circulated a position paper to the staff in which she declared that April 15 showed "local organizing and large protests are the two sides of a successful antiwar movement: They are interlinked and dependent upon each other." She then proposed October 21, in "hopefully Washington," for a "massive action that would culminate the summer and early fall activity." The date fell on a Saturday for technical reasons, allowing the largest number of participants, and long enough into the semester to allow for campus organizing.[32]

The SMC Chicago conference marked a significant shift in its high school outreach efforts. Prior to the event, it noted the SMC "has been able for the first time to organize significant numbers of high school students in protest action against the war."[33] Held at the University of Chicago's campus in May 1967, about 600 people attended, including twenty-four high school students. Several debates occurred over opposing 2-S draft deferments, viewed as discriminatory against nonstudent youth, and whether to change SMC's statement of aims to include "promoting" draft resistance rather than supporting individual rights to noncooperation with the military system. Differences abounded, but no power struggle for control over the organization occurred. Before the event, the SMC anticipated "the largest participation yet from high school students." It hoped those in attendance who were disorganized could learn from high school antiwar activists on both the West and East coasts, who it hoped would be present. "It seems that the West Coast and New York City are the leading areas of high school anti-

A CALL TO A NATIONAL STUDENT ANTI-WAR CONFERENCE

The Student Mobilization Committee is a broad coalition of student groups which organized Vietnam Week, April 8-15, and coordinated student participation in the giant April 15 demonstrations against the war. To evaluate the results of this mobilization and to plan future projects for the summer, we are calling for a national conference in Chicago on May 13 and 14. There will be a nominal registration fee.

600 New York High School Students demonstrate on April 8 to kick off Vietnam Week →

MAY 13 and 14 in CHICAGO

For more information about the Student Mobilization Committee, about the conference, or about housing, please fill out the following and send to:

STUDENT MOBILIZATION COMMITTEE

NEW YORK (national office)
Student Mobilization Committee
29 Park Row
New York, N.Y. 10038
Phone: (212) 233-4535

CHICAGO Office
Student Mobilization Committee
3101 W. Warren
Chicago, Illinois 60612
Phone: (312) 638-2725
If no answer, 226-5107 or 525-5722

☐ Please send me more information about the Student Mobilization Committee

☐ I plan to attend the May 13-14 conference and (☐ need) (☐ do not need) housing.

☐ Enclosed is my . . . . . . contribution to help the Student Mobilization Committee

Name
Address
City
State   Zip
School or Organization

A flyer sponsoring the 1967 SMC conference in Chicago includes a photograph of high school demonstrators in New York City. Courtesy of Howard Swerdloff.

war activity in the country," read a correspondence letter. Conference planners sought to have attendees leave with "as many ideas as possible on how to build the anti-war movement on high school and college campuses." Notably, the event concluded with the formation of a national high school antiwar organization.[34]

The National High School SMC, headquartered in New York City, emerged out of the Chicago conference. SMC recognized that, unlike college students, "high school students are isolated and disorganized nationally." But they "represent a vast manpower resource which cannot be ignored by anyone interested in building a mass movement." The organization recognized the distinct differences between high school and their collegiate counterparts, with "parental authority problems" and less political freedom cited as the two main reasons. It believed most adolescents would respond more favorably to each other than to college students. These factors made it "evident that high school students must organize themselves." Continuing, the group claimed, "The high school student's organization must be neither an exact model of nor subservient to the Student Mobilization, and this position must be kept clear." To keep them connected, it created a national communication link between groups on both coasts through a contact list and newsletter.[35] Maxine Orris, a member of the New York High School SMC, echoed this sentiment. She believed the formation of a National High School SMC would allow students to create their own independent programs on a national scale.[36] For the summer and fall, the group planned to organize regional committees and conferences, among other projects.[37]

The May conference in Chicago set the stage for another mass mobilization in Washington, DC, but more importantly, the various high school students who attended the gathering would use the momentum to organize their peers back in their communities. The SMC published a list of contacts it made at the Chicago conference to allow "closer correspondence between High School Mobilization groups" than the forthcoming newsletter. It asked members to inform the New York High School SMC about their organizing efforts. Given the proximity, most new contacts came from Illinois and nearby states, which included Ohio, Michigan, and Wisconsin. Other areas, such as Massachusetts, Georgia, Minnesota, San Francisco, and Los Angeles, had one individual contact.[38] Although adult SMC organizers had long credited California and New York students for being the most organized, youth in Detroit assisted in building a high school antiwar movement not only in their city but throughout much of the upper Midwest.

Detroit High School Student Mobilization Committee

Gordon Fox's doubts about the Vietnam War surfaced as soon as President Johnson committed ground troops. After attending a demonstration in Washington, DC, in 1966, he returned to Detroit and organized a local antiwar group for his peers. His commitment only grew, and he would eventually help build a national network of high school antiwar activists.[39]

Born in 1952 in Detroit, Fox grew up in a majority Jewish neighborhood in the city's northwest, the son of an attorney and a psychologist. His interest in political affairs began in childhood after a newspaper article about political unrest in Cuba caught his eye, leading to an unforgettable, insightful conversation with his father. Together with his parents, he participated in ban-the-bomb demonstrations, influenced by their background as former members of the Communist Party and their connections with pacifists. By March 1965, as US troops landed in Vietnam, Fox had become active in the antiwar movement.[40]

He had no trouble diving into activism early on in Detroit. The city had vibrant antiwar groups, which included the Detroit Committee to End the War in Vietnam (DCEWV), which emerged in February 1965 following the bombing campaign of North Vietnam. This group organized numerous local demonstrations and events across the city and sponsored teach-ins, debates, speakers, and films. One notable effort was its support for a group of Cass Technical High School students who, in December 1965, faced exclusion from school for wearing black armbands to protest the war.[41]

Fox soon grew disillusioned with how the *Detroit Free Press* covered the local antiwar movement. In December 1966, he attended a day-long, antidraft seminar at Central Methodist Church, sponsored by a committee of clergymen opposed to the war. He listened attentively and even asked a question during the event. Reflecting on the seminar, Fox wavered between conscientious objection and noncooperation, themes heavily discussed at the conference. However, when he read the news article on the gathering, he felt irritated by the inaccuracies. He wrote a letter to the editor criticizing the reporter for grossly underestimating the crowd size and accused television stations of mischaracterizing the conference as a forum for young men to learn how to avoid military service. "No such thing happened at the conference," he wrote. "This is worse than just reducing the size of the crowd; this is making up news."[42]

Like many high school antiwar activists, Fox's initial involvement in the movement did not come through the SMC. Instead, he attended an event in Washington, DC, called the Voters' Peace Pledge March, sponsored by the National Committee for a Sane Nuclear Policy. Women for Peace organized bus rides from Detroit. There, he met people who mentioned an electoral campaign, and he then ventured into electoral politics, supporting a candidate who ran against a pro-war incumbent. Although the candidate lost, Fox wanted to keep being active and organizing students. Thus, he helped form a small local group called Young Students for World Peace, which later became the Detroit High School Students for Peace. But he needed help. He called the DCEWV, where its members suggested he attend a meeting, which led to his involvement with the group. From there, he connected with like-minded peers. This interest propelled him to attend the SMC's national conference in May 1967. After carpooling to Chicago with friends from Detroit, he and they decided afterward to form a high school-based chapter of the SMC.[43]

Over the course of the summer of 1967, the SMC eroded the persistent feeling of isolation among student activists. The season presented a prime opportunity for organizing. Orris announced plans for a national publication called the *High School Student Mobilizer* and laid out four summer projects: organizing in summer schools, sending caravans to camps and resorts, holding forums, and counseling students on the draft in East Harlem. Chicago and San Francisco reported active participation in the High School SMC.[44] Nationwide, the SMC observed antiwar activities spreading locally, "much of it in new places." By August 1967, the SMC had established active high school antiwar committees in Los Angeles, Minneapolis, Detroit, Milwaukee, Boston, New York, Palo Alto, California, and Tucson, Arizona.[45]

The Detroit High School SMC began publishing the *High School Mobilizer*, a youth edition of the *Student Mobilizer*. This publication provided the organization with a platform to connect their movement with the actions of high school SMCs nationwide. In the first issue, the editors acknowledged that "for years high school students have played an active role in the anti-Vietnam war movement" but lacked their own organization. Historically, teenagers had worked within established antiwar committees both on and off campus. The 1967 Chicago conference challenged "the old role of high school students. . . . and a new national organization, the National High School Student Mobilization Committee, was established." Three of the youth involved in forming this group were from Detroit. The Detroit chapter formed thereafter to raise awareness about the "unjust, illegal, and racist" war. "And not only this—Americans, and especially high school students, have the right and responsibility to make their opposition to the war manifest," it wrote. "That high school students who will soon be fighting on the front lines have the right to insist that the government cannot speak for them . . . [and] have the power to help bring the 'dirty war in Vietnam' to an end."[46]

The publication served as more than a mouthpiece for the group; it also became a brochure for upcoming events and a source of information on high school antiwar activities throughout North America. Georgina Bermann of the Greater Boston High School SMC contributed a short letter detailing her community's actions. "Tonight, we will leaflet at the Boston War Memorial Auditorium. How do you like that for a place to leaflet?" she wrote. The newsletter also spotlighted the antiwar activities of high school students in Montreal, Quebec, highlighting their involvement in street rallies, films, tapes, speakers, meetings, leafleting, and marches. The final page featured a cut-out section for readers to express interest or make a monetary contribution, along with their contact information.[47]

In its quest to build a national high school antiwar movement, the Detroit High School SMC, along with other chapters, hosted regional conferences. These gatherings were essential in connecting geographically isolated students within a space of shared interests. In the late summer of 1967, regional high school conferences occurred nationwide. In August, activists in Cambridge, Massachusetts, held the Regional-National High School Antiwar Conference, attracting students from New England, New York, and even Detroit. Simultaneous conferences took place in Kansas City, Phoenix, Arizona, and Richmond, Virginia. The Massachusetts conference featured speakers and saw ideological divisions emerge. Some participants wanted high schoolers to organize around the war and the draft, while others sought to focus on issues like dress regulations, subpar cafeteria food, and related concerns. Ultimately, the conference passed three resolutions: support for the upcoming October 21 demonstration, a strike against the Levi & Strauss Company, and the creation of a national high school antiwar conference in Chicago over the Thanksgiving holiday.[48]

In Detroit, Fox and another peer organized a Midwest conference for high school students.[49] In a write-up, the Detroit High School SMC captured the essence of this endeavor, acknowledging that "organizing high school students against the war is a concept which has aroused the enthusiasm of older sections of the peace movement for some time," but "it is a task that has been made difficult by a generational gap." This dynamic shifted in the summer of 1967, as "dedicated high school anti-war activists" formed the Detroit High School SMC and recruited interested students through leafletting high schools and holding rallies. The organizers discovered a persistent problem: "many high school students are not aware of the existing anti-war organization in Detroit—that there really was no vehicle through which high school age opponents of the dirty war could express their views and plan activities specifically geared to high school students." This recognition underscored the "urgent need" to organize, promoting a call for a high school conference scheduled for September 8–10, 1967. The event sought to address the unique challenges faced by students, who not only grappled with "being directly affected by the war (the draft in particular), but also the problems in organizing other high school students against the war."[50]

The conference featured speakers like Jim Zeleski, an Air Force veteran who had served in Vietnam, and Sue Claus, a high school student from Canada. Attendees, journeying from as far as Minneapolis and Toronto, were educated on high school activities in diverse locales.[51] Despite lower-than-expected attendance, the post-conference write-up noted that the students resolved to support an October demonstration in Washington, DC, exchanging ideas on high school organizing, the draft, and free speech issues. They committed to mobilizing both city and suburban students as soon as the teacher strike concluded. "Numerous circumstances" affected attendance, but the conference yielded "concrete resolutions." Among them was a strong endorsement for the upcoming antiwar demonstration in Washington, DC, with a call to engage all high schools in the march under their own banners. They also passed a resolution backing GIs exercising their free speech rights on army bases and advocating for education on the draft and "all forms of resistance to it." Workshops on high school organizing, the draft, and free speech issues illuminated the intersection of student rights and antiwar activism. Claus, representing the Students Against the War in Vietnam in Toronto, detailed the "various activities going on in the nationwide Canadian organization, including a teach-in campaign to get the anti-war speakers in every school." Other attendees, like Bill Scheer from Minneapolis, shared their stories and gathered information to bring back to their communities.[52]

The meeting extended into the weekend, featuring a general assembly where attendees listened to a Vietnam veteran from Chicago, antiwar poetry recited by Professor David Herreshoff, and various other speakers. Attendance dwindled, but the organizers managed to collect enough funds to cover expenses. On Sunday, the conference included film screenings and a plenary session. Following the event, the Detroit High School SMC committed to mobilizing students across the city and its suburbs once the teacher strike concluded. They planned to bring in antiwar speakers from the DCEWV and establish their own committees within high schools. The group also declared its intent to attend the national high school antiwar conference in Chicago over the Thanksgiving holidays, vowing to be in Washington, DC, in full force." It proclaimed, "High school organizing is really moving!"[53]

As the SMC and other antiwar groups geared up for the upcoming mass mobilization in Washington, DC, Mobe activists at the May conference in DC agreed to hold a multi-tactical protest in the nation's capital on October 21. Given the unexpectedly high turnout at the April 15 demonstration, they anticipated over a million marchers. Amid internal disputes, former VDC leader Jerry Rubin proposed that the action should target the Pentagon. Rubin, who viewed the Pentagon's five-sided structure as "a symbol of evil," believed that protesters would "drive the evil spirits away." The Mobe consented to hold the protest there against activists Fred Halstead's annoyance that Rubin did not know the Pentagon was in Virginia. On August 28, they held a press conference in New York to announce that on October 21–22, Americans would "shut down the Pentagon." This saber-rattling by some leaders unsettled moderate members, who harbored reservations about the protest in the weeks leading up to the demonstration.[54]

The approaching March on the Pentagon catalyzed a surge of correspondence from high school students to the SMC offices in the fall of 1967. In anticipation of this major event, students nationwide sought guidance and resources to organize their peers. This influx of letters usually arrived before significant antiwar demonstrations. Weeks ahead of the October 1967 march, a high school senior from San Mateo, California, wrote to the San Francisco regional office, urgently requesting brochures to "wake up the other kids befor [sic] the 21st!"[55] Similarly, students from Fairfield, Connecticut, who formed the Fairfield Students Against the War, sought logistical assistance. "We have no idea on how to get our people down to Washington, how to raise money to do so, etc.," the letter read.[56] A student from Hockessin, Delaware, reached out for information, posters, and buttons, expressing, "I intend to be there, and I hope that with your help I will be able to bring some people with me" to Washington, DC. Dawson responded with details of the plans for the upcoming event.[57]

Another reason for the spike in high school students' interest likely stemmed from the Johnson administration's policy of military escalation in Vietnam, which led to the deployment of more than 400,000 US troops, a massive bombing campaign, and high casualty rates on both sides. To meet the increased demand for troops, President Johnson placed nineteen-year-olds at the top of the draft list on June 30, 1967. Before the enactment of this official change, a paper written by Oberlin College student Tim Rowton circulated at the SMC conference in Chicago in May 1967. He interviewed about fifty high school students in three schools in Lorain, Ohio, and noticed that after Johnson's proposed preferential drafting of nineteen-year-olds, "the war has become one of their main concerns." The students expressed "strong opinions on the war, something very unusual a few years ago." Consequently, for a president deeply concerned about the growing unpopularity of the war, Johnson made a decision that infused more energy into the antiwar movement. Government officials in Washington, DC, witnessed the first and largest confrontational demonstration in October 1967 as protesters exhibited their loss of faith in nonviolence. When officials noticed that the number of protesters ranged anywhere between 50,000 and 150,000, they ordered 25,000 troops to guard the White House and the Pentagon.[58]

On October 21, over 100,000 people converged at the Lincoln Memorial. Youth dominated the crowd, but it also included lawyers, accountants, teachers, housewives, and seasoned political organizers. Attendees listened to various speeches. Pediatrician Dr. Benjamin Spock declared, "We do not consider the Vietnamese north or south the enemy. . . . They have only defended their country against the unjust onslaught of the United States. . . . The enemy, we believe in all sincerity, is Lyndon Johnson." The crowd then moved toward the Arlington Memorial Bridge with government helicopters buzzing overhead. It began to fracture, with several hundred demonstrators veering off into the Virginia woods toward the Pentagon. MPs and US marshals soon encircled these splinter groups. Protesters, undeterred, tested the Pentagon's defenses. One person placed flowers in rifle barrels, a symbolic gesture of peace against the machinery of war. High-ranking military officials watched from the rooftops. Inside the building, government officials peered from their windows to observe the spectacle. As midnight approached, the government began to clear the plaza. While most of the crowd had dispersed, a determined few thousand remained, engaging with troops, burning draft cards, spray-painting slogans on the Pentagon walls, and starting campfires on the mall. Government officials responded swiftly and forcefully. In a dense V-shaped formation, forces moved slowly but relentlessly into the demonstrators. Some protesters were met with the brutal force of marshals' boots and rifle butts, and clouds of tear gas or mace filled the air. The aftermath saw 683 arrests, fifty-one jail terms up to thirty-five days, fines totaling $8,000, numerous injuries, but remarkably, no deaths. In the wake of the demonstration, Halstead reflected, "the movement as a whole began to embrace the idea [of reaching out to GIs] with some enthusiasm." The protest had not only sparked a strategic shift but also garnered extensive press coverage.[59]

Fox, alongside countless high school students from across the nation, took part in the March on the Pentagon in Washington, DC. The *Detroit Free Press* noted that Detroit teenagers were among the crowd. One student from Cass Tech helped hold up a sign for the Detroit High School Students for Peace. Another student recounted their parents' fear, saying, "We heard all the talk about troops and possible violence. But I promised my parents I would not take part in any civil disobedience." Fox, however, felt frustrated once again with the local press's coverage of the demonstration. "Why does the *Free Press* insist on giving the impression that the march was quite small?" he asked. He refuted the allegation that marchers threw tear gas. "I saw the soldiers throwing the grenades, and I choked on the tear gas. The Army had masks; we had nothing to protect ourselves with. Why would we try to gas ourselves?" he asked again. His critiques were valid. Throughout the antiwar movement, the press often emphasized violent and radical behavior, undercounted crowd sizes, and ignored the political arguments of protesters. Coverage of demonstrations overshadowed the tedious, unglamorous work of organizing. Fox also bristled at the press's portrayal of antiwar marchers as "groovies, the far-outs, the hippies and the Free Men." "Perhaps," he suggested, reporter "Saul Friedman needs his eyes checked, although he seemed to notice the girls in miniskirts."[60]

During the Thanksgiving holiday in 1967, the National High School Conference convened in Chicago, drawing 120 students from November 24 to 26 at the University of Chicago High School. The idea for a conference emerged during SMC's May 1967 conference. Fox and other high school antiwar activists decided to arrange phone calls to find one another in DC during the March on the Pentagon. "We thought it would be a great idea to have a national high school antiwar conference," Fox recalls. The teenage demonstrators met in a designated spot during the event and discussed the idea of organizing a future event. At the Chicago conference, Bill Scheer of the Twin Cities High School SMC reported that participants from twenty cities, including Toronto, ranging in age from thirteen to seventeen, were in attendance. The conference opened with an address by antiwar activist Rennie Davis, who spoke about the suffering he witnessed in Vietnam. Attendees participated in workshops covering civil liberties, national action, local organizing, nonviolence and noncooperation, human rights, the draft, student rights, education reform, and Vietnam. Toward the end, they debated the structure of the High School SMC, coalescing around a commitment to end the war and enhance coordination among local groups. Fox recalls the event as largely unsuccessful in terms of turnout and its failure to create a national high school SMC, but he thoroughly enjoyed meeting like-minded peers from different locations. "It was pretty cool," he remembers. "It was wonderful to meet people who were just like you and your friends. At least one of them continues to be a good friend today." He stayed in touch with Chicago high school activist Geoff Mirelowitz, and the two "spent a fair amount of time on the phone" discussing their experiences, clashes with administrators, and typical adolescent interests.[61]

The Detroit High School SMC, along with other chapters, played a crucial role in building a national high school antiwar movement with extensive networks. While SMC activists saw high school students as untapped workforce, their success hinged on the fact that teenagers were already organized or involved in local peace groups. However, the SMC's exclusive focus on opposing the war and building contacts led adult organizers to overlook the unique challenges faced by their younger members. Consequently, many high school SMC chapters found themselves drawn into First Amendment rights struggles.

The High School Antiwar Movement and Student Rights

On November 27, 1967, three panelists joined a student moderator on WBAI Radio Broadcast in New York City to discuss the high school movement against the war. Steven Share of Martin Van Buren High School facilitated the conversation, opening with a series of probing questions: "How effectively organized are the students? What are the rights of students, teachers, and the schools? Is the high school movement student-led? For the benefit of the [New York] Daily News, is there any communist influence? How much pressure is there from the Board of Education?" Leonard Boa, a teacher at John Bowne High School in Flushing, Queens, began by recalling his recent trip to Washington, DC, for the March on the Pentagon. "I was most impressed by the youthfulness of the demonstrators," he reflected. "Not only were there college youth, but high school youth as well. And I thought to myself, there must be a growing movement in the high schools of New York City and throughout the country to protest this most horrible, egregious, and unjust war." Upon returning home, Boa discovered that about 100 students had decided to form a peace club at John Bowne High. The students met informally at a member's home on an irregular basis because the principal refused to recognize the club, despite the fact that it met the requirements of having at least twelve members and a faculty adviser, which Boa himself chaired. At the moment, the students were drafting a petition with nearly 500 signatures, intending to present it to the principal in January.[62]

The nearly hour-long conversation underscored not only the burgeoning antiwar sentiment in the city's high schools but also the persistent challenges of repression, hostility from administrators and fellow students, and the murky definition of student rights. Wendy Fisher, a student at The Bronx High School of Science, had spearheaded a nascent antiwar group with over 100 active members. Laura Heming, chair of the New York High School SMC, began her group in February 1967, initially organizing around the April 15 demonstration and later expanding to address the war, the draft, and student rights. Ira Glasser, Associate Director of the New York Civil Liberties Union, provided much of the legal analysis on student rights. He noted that his office had received more complaints about dress codes, distribution of leaflets, and other issues concerning student rights than any other matter. "Without having done an extensive study on that subject, that certainly is my impression. They come in at the rate of two or three a day," he told the panelists. Although the panelists all shared stories of rights violations, nobody had a clear definition of what student rights entailed.[63]

Share turned to Glasser for clarification, particularly as he himself had encountered trouble with school administrators regarding leaflets and had sought the American Civil Liberties Union (ACLU) help. Glasser explained that the question was broad since it is a fuzzy area still in need of clear determination. However, the ACLU believed students had the same First Amendment rights as adults, provided these rights did not interfere with the daily educational process. Glasser observed that disruptions were rarely the case. Anyone, he argued, could distribute a leaflet on the sidewalk if it did not cause a disruption, and he believed students learned more from such practical engagement than from textbooks. Glasser also pointed out that teachers had no issue with the existence of pro-war organizations, noting that principals often responded with repression. This visceral reaction concerned the ACLU because it represented "a greatly contradictory policy to be teaching the principles of American democracy in the classroom and to be flagrantly violating them by the structure of the school." This contradiction led him to a crucial realization:

I often wonder how students are supposed to believe anything they read in [James] Madison and [Thomas] Jefferson about the Bill of Rights when the facts of their school are that freedom of association with regard to the forming of clubs is prohibited. That freedom of the press does not exist, that distributing leaflets is frowned upon, to say the least, and threatened with suspension. And that the whole all the things protected by the Bill of Rights that children are taught should be revered, are in fact repressed on the grounds that students are not people; therefore, do not have the rights of people. I think what this teaches students is that authority and discipline and conformity and obedience are the values that the society prizes most.[64]

Though the conversation among the panelists occurred just two years into the antiwar movement, the issues they raised would echo throughout the high school movement. The SMC would eventually come to place high school student rights at the core of its outreach. However, in certain bastions of activism, some members grew disillusioned with their treatment within the organization and began to forge their own path in the fight for constitutional rights. Adult-led antiwar organizations' singular focus on ending the war often left high school members feeling sidelined. Some youth remained with the SMC, but others came to see the war and the repression from school administrators as intertwined. In response, some teenage activists formed their own independent organizations focused on student rights and school reform. These groups sprouted nationwide, with the largest and most influential one emerging in New York City in the fall of 1968.

3 The Rise of Independent Student Organizations
The New York High School Student Union

On April 28, 1969, writer Fred Ferretti's article on teenage activists appeared in *New York Magazine*. The account offered a glimpse into the high school movement in New York City through the lens of an organization called the New York High School Student Union. This group had begun planning a citywide boycott in May to compel the district to heed its ten demands. Members Laurie Sandow and Charlotte Brown, a white girl and a Black girl, respectively, shared their insights with Ferretti. Sandow explained that the origins of the Union emerged from a schism in the National SMC during the spring of 1968. The rift occurred between the Trotskyites and Independents on how the antiwar movement should proceed. The former group wanted to focus exclusively on the war, while the latter group desired to address issues beyond the conflict, "to find out what was creating the war, to go past the meetings and the office work, the ideological games." The divisiveness eventually divided the SMC and summarily convinced the members of the High School chapter that they had grown irrelevant. Sandow recalled that the philosophy of the Independents became the nucleus for the Union. Referencing its view, Sandow concluded, "When you look beyond, you naturally come to the schools." Over the summer, the members used Students for a Democratic Society's (SDS) 114th Street brownstone fraternity, housed off the Columbia campus, where they held workshops and study-ins. On September 21, 1968, they officially formed the Union at a founding conference.[1]

Ferretti might have found the structure of the organization peculiar, labeling it as an "amorphous organization." It had no officers, titles, or leaders. But it did include a representative committee, office staff, and locals in most of the city's schools. These locals had complete autonomy and were not required to follow any direction, despite some provided by the Representative Committee. "People participate on any level they want," said Brown, "on any level they can give." Sandow followed, "High school students realize that when you have a leader, you look to that leader. . . . We don't want to have to depend on one person, so we have no leaders."

Although leaderless, it had more structure than when it first began, where meetings included vague dialogues and shouting matches. "And what yelling! And the male chauvinism! Wow! It's all there. And the personality conflict!" Brown mentioned. But a stronger sense of internal development emerged from the initial chaos. The Union published a newsletter called the *New York High School Free Press*, put together by a volunteer staff and funded through ads, newsstand and subscription sales, and donations. One member claimed the paper had a circulation anywhere from 10,000 to 40,000. The teacher strike in the fall gave the Union strength. It provided students with a significant amount of allotted time to organize.[2]

Adult-run organizations viewed high school students as allies but often marginalized or completely ignored the unique issues they faced. For much of the high school movement, teenage activists worked within preexisting organizations or as youth divisions bearing the group's name. By 1968, however, teenagers began forming their own independent groups to address concerns unique to high school students. They often called themselves unions, alliances, coalitions, committees, or fronts, and used names such as "concerned students." While such groups had existed since the beginning of the high school movement, many were single-issue-focused, lacked any organizational structure, and had few active members. By the late 1960s, multifaceted organizations proliferated and continued emerging well into the 1970s. Black Student Unions emerged as the most ubiquitous groups, but many later became official school organizations. Completely independent ones drafted constitutions, a statement of purpose, and, unlike the New York HSSU, members usually held official titles. These groups frequently incorporated the name of the school, city, county, metro area, or state they represented, bearing names such as Seneca (High School) Student Rights Committee in Louisville, Kentucky, Portland High School Rights Coalition in Oregon, Montgomery County Student Alliance in Maryland, Greater Rochester High School Student Union in New York, and the Minnesota Student Union in the Twin Cities.[3] Regardless of the name, these groups signified that students sought to advocate for themselves as a special interest group akin to teacher unions and parent-teacher associations. Through these organizations, students published and distributed printed materials and organized direct actions. Their formation made it easier for journalists to recognize the existence of the high school movement, as they sometimes received lengthy write-ups in newspapers and education journals.

Among the various groups that emerged in the late 1960s, the New York HSSU is arguably the most significant. At its peak, the Union consisted of a citywide coordinating council and locals in 108 public and private schools, making it one of the largest—if not the largest—high school student organizations in the country. Its underground newspaper covered a wide range of topics, focusing primarily on student rights, race, Vietnam, and, in later years, women's and gay liberation.[4] While a full recounting of its activities would require an entire book unto itself, a glimpse into its origins, structure, operations, and the media attention it solicited offers a snapshot of how local concerns shaped the goals and campaigns of these independent student organizations.

The Origins of the Union

"I had been in the Boy Scouts from the time I was eleven years old," Bruce Trigg said, reflecting on his involvement with the New York HSSU. "The Boy Scouts are very patriotic, but in those days, it was sort of an idealistic patriotism." All the men he encountered in the Scouts served in World War II, and coming from a Jewish household, the war had "a very special resonance." But growing up in New York City, he found himself surrounded by more liberal-minded students whose political views and lifestyles would challenge his deeply held values. Over the course of his high school years, this idealistic Boy Scout, who believed in the inherent righteousness of his country, would find himself clubbed and punched in the face by police at the 1968 Democratic National Convention in Chicago.[5]

He was born in 1951 in the Flatbush neighborhood of Brooklyn, New York. His grandparents on his father's side had immigrated from Bialystok, Poland, to New York City in 1904. Bruce's grandfather worked as a cigar roller and developed tuberculosis, prompting him to move to Denver, Colorado, where sanitariums were located. There, his son Maurie—Bruce's father—was born. Maurie would go on to college but dropped out after his first year to assist the family. In the late 1920s, the family returned to New York, where Maurie's uncle owned a furniture business in Brooklyn. Bruce's mother, Bernice, was born in Brownsville, Brooklyn, and raised mainly by her grandparents, who were "quite poor." Her father had immigrated from Germany but died prematurely. Bernice worked in a garment factory in midtown Manhattan when Bruce was a child and later labored as a teletype operator for one of the large garment corporate offices. Maurie, on the other hand, was a credit manager for the millinery business, but it went defunct by the 1950s, so he worked as a traveling salesman for much of Bruce's childhood. When he was just six months of age, his parents relocated to Bayside, Queens, to a predominantly working-class Jewish community where they stayed with his grandmother in a four-room garden apartment. Maurie and Bernice were both of Jewish heritage, but neither was religious. Neither of them possessed a college degree. Like any family with aspirations for their children, they had high expectations for Bruce. "I have an older brother, who has had developmental and emotional problems much of his life," he stated. "So, there was a lot of pressure on me to be the successful son, to go to college, and to become a doctor. Which, ironically, is exactly what I've done."[6]

Unlike many of his future peers, Trigg's parents were not politically active, nor did he encounter radical politics. He remained active in the Boy Scouts upon entering high school and spent his summer break at the camp in New York City. The Boy Scouts in American culture "are a familiar part of the furniture," as a "well-worn fixture of the household that seemingly has always been there." Founded in 1910, its membership grew from virtually nothing to 361,000 boys and 32,000 scoutmasters by 1919. Stretching back to the 1870s, organizing activities sought to improve and build middle-class boys' characters.[7]

He absorbed the culture of the Scouts, but he found himself in an unfamiliar environment when he entered Martin Van Buren High School. The school was a world away from his working-class upbringing. There, he encountered students from affluent families, working-class kids of German, Irish, and Italian heritage, and Black students bused in from Jamaica, Queens. He noticed many of these students were tracked into either college preparatory paths or general courses. In gym class, conversations often revolved around post-high school plans. "If you weren't going to college," he remembered, "Vietnam was clearly in your immediate future." The various students he encountered at Van Buren High, whom he initially met in junior high, held liberal perspectives and opposed the Vietnam War. He initially resisted these views and remained steadfast in his belief that America was on the right side of history. However, the influence of classmates who wore their hair long, smoked marijuana, and vocally opposed the war gradually began to erode his convictions.[8]

Over time, Trigg became more receptive to left-wing politics, especially after meeting fellow student Josh Kiok. Kiok was born to a mother who worked as a public school teacher in New York City. His father died suddenly when he was two years old; thus, he inherited his left-wing politics from his mother. Kiok enrolled in Van Buren High in 1966 and joined a small group of about two dozen students called the Van Buren Students Against Militarism (VBSAM). The VBSAM advocated for the abolition of military assemblies where students "were forced to listen to the spiels of military recruiters." It showed North Vietnamese propaganda films at a local Unitarian Church and campaigned vigorously to change the school's dress codes. Its activism extended to supporting the civil rights movement by raising donations for the Southern Christian Leadership Conference's Poor People's Campaign in 1968. Although the group met off campus, it maintained an official presence at the school by forming a front organization called the "'Asian Affairs Club,' which due to school rules, had to have a teacher for a faculty adviser." It enlisted a liberal faculty member for this role, but the group eventually let the club "wither away" due to its ineffectiveness within the constraints of school administration.[9] The group frequently encountered hostility on campus. Someone routinely tore down stickers antiwar students posted on campus. However, one inventive member devised a clever plan. "He was a creative kid," said Trigg in response to an activist he knew. "There was some sort of crystal that he could mix up in a chemistry lab, and he put them under the stickers." When a kid pulled the sticker off, it exploded. The *New York Daily News* even reported on the incident at Van Buren High with the headline, "Peace-Sticker Booby Trap Hurts Boy."[10]

Trigg could not escape the antiwar activities at his school. The VBSAM organized student participation in various demonstrations, including the March on the Pentagon. Trigg attended this event, his first one, with his assistant scoutmaster, who was a student at Queens College. "I picked a heck of a protest to be my first demonstration," he recalled. "It was overwhelming and mind-boggling." This experience deepened Trigg's involvement in activism with "kids who were sort of the more intellectual, the more rebellious spirits, the more artsy types." His first girlfriend was an outspoken leader in the antiwar movement. In one instance, she mentioned to him Marxist revolutionary Che Guevara, who had recently been murdered in October 1967. Trigg asked, "Lucia, he's a communist, isn't he?" "You bet he is!" she replied. Trigg's evolution as a self-identified radical had not blossomed yet. Supporting a communist was unthinkable to him. He tried to draw a clear line of demarcation between his ingrained patriotism and growing opposition to the Vietnam War.[11]

On April 26, 1968, the VBSAM joined the National Student Strike Against the War. Spurred by wavering public attitudes toward the conflict, SMC organizers planned the next major demonstration for April 26–27, called the International Student Strike Day. The event would take place on Friday and Saturday to encourage activities on high school and college campuses. While

The Rise of Independent Student Organizations   75

the moment seemed ripe when planned, the timing for the event could not have been more unfavorable when it occurred. Public appetite for mass demonstrations waned that month. City neighborhoods still lay in ruins because of the urban uprisings that had occurred shortly after Martin Luther King Jr.'s assassination on April 4. Municipalities had pulled vast numbers of public resources to combat agitated protesters and fires set to vehicles and buildings. Images of crowds marching in the streets became ubiquitous. Nonetheless, the New York City Board of Education reported that city schools had about 100,000 absences. The VBSAM joined the action. Members plastered stickers advertising the strike around the school. Some hawks ripped them off. Once again, one person placed some stickers "up over a wad of presumably homemade contact explosive just a few days before the strike." On the day of the demonstration, the VBSAM formed a picket line in front of the school. Pro-war proponents counter-picketed. Some threw eggs, and one member was assaulted.[12]

The growing and vibrant antiwar movement led Trigg to start attending SMC meetings in Manhattan. The group split when he attended its meeting for the first time. "For many people, it would've been the ultimate turnoff: you go to your first big national meeting, and people are just like that, screaming at each other," he recalled. "But I was just absolutely fascinated by it. It was so interesting, and I wanted to know: who on earth is Trotsky? Because . . . that wasn't my family's interest at all. In fact, I was always very envious of my friends—many of the leaders in the antiwar movement I now know were red diaper babies." His intellectual curiosity grew. He started volunteering for the Fifth Avenue Peace Parade Committee and encountered teenagers from other city schools.[13] Many high school students went to the Committee's office on Seventeenth Street in Manhattan after school. The group "provided us with facilities to publish our little antiwar newspapers," one former Union member recalled. "You would meet students from all over the city there—from Bronx Science, from Seward Park, Brooklyn Tech, you name it." Trigg enjoyed his time at the office. The adult organizers respected their younger members. "I knew nothing," he said, "and there I was sitting at these important meetings, and people respected my opinions and encouraged us to participate. So, it was . . . quite a learning experience."[14]

The students Trigg encountered would eventually go on to form the Union. Just like their counterparts across the nation, they met through newly established and preexisting antiwar organizations. Many had experience in "localized, in-school antiwar groups and as volunteers" with the High School SMC. Youth such as Dana Driskell, Reginald Lucas, and David

Fenton had organized their peers at the Bronx High School of Science as members of the Bronx Science Committee for Political Action. Laurie Sandow and Charlotte Brown attended the High School of Music and Art in Manhattan and were leaders of the Music and Art Students Against the War in Vietnam. At John Bowne High School in Queens, Union cofounders Howard Swerdloff and Paul Shneyer participated in the John Bowne Students for Peace and contributed to the school's underground newspaper, *John Bowne Was a Pacifist*.[15] Jamaica High School student Jeffrey Schwartz grew up with liberal parents but admitted he "wasn't very politically conscious" during his early teenage years and initially supported the Vietnam War. However, the summer of 1968 proved to be a turning point. While on a family vacation at Letchworth State Park in western New York, he met a young woman and listened to radio coverage of the Democratic National Convention. Reflecting on the experience, he said, "I couldn't exactly tell you why, but I just identified with the demonstrators."[16] These students came from mostly white and Black upper-middle-, middle-, and working-class households. Furthermore, many of the members had far more radical upbringings than Trigg. Some of their parents once belonged to the Communist Party and had educated them about political issues. Andrew Jackson High School student Elk Gene's parents, both of whom were former members of the Communist Party, had encouraged him to participate in contemporary political struggles.[17] James Monroe High School student Estelle Schneider grew up with working-class Jewish parents. Her mother was a former member of the Communist Party, and her father once belonged to the Young Communist League. They both taught her about the international proletariat, the rights of working people, humanism, and tolerance for others.[18]

Other members had their political grounding in the civil rights movement. Robert Newton had two politically active parents. His father served in the Abraham Lincoln Brigade during the Spanish Civil War, and his mother brought him to the March on Washington in 1963. She had earned a doctorate at the University of Chicago and sent him and his sister to "Freedom School" at a local church during the New York School Boycott on February 3, 1964, where 450,000 students boycotted school to protest school segregation. Maxine Orris's parents were both involved in leftist organizing at a young age. When she was eleven, Orris had become an active member of the Student Nonviolent Coordinating Committee and established a high school chapter upon matriculating into Elisabeth Irwin High School in Manhattan. She notably joined SMC and helped in preparing for Vietnam Week. Adult leaders gave her the responsibility of putting together a high school SMC to garner teenage support for the upcoming demonstration. Afterward, she established the New York High School SMC, mimeographed antiwar fliers, and distributed them throughout the city.[19]

Others, like Trigg, had apolitical upbringings. Howard Swerdloff was born in 1951 to a father who worked as a commercial artist and a mother who stayed at home. The family was "typical lower-middle class," having moved several times throughout Queens. As a World War II veteran, his father purchased, through the GI Bill, a home situated in an ethnic Italian neighborhood that gradually became diverse. Reflecting on his past in a piece he wrote as a self-identified political radical, Swerdloff confessed, "I used to be the biggest patriot in the country. I cheered wildly when John Glenn went up and marched proudly in my Boy Scout uniform on Memorial Day. This country was the greatest in the world." Swerdloff had plenty of opportunities to get into trouble. He often hung around juvenile delinquents. But as desegregation occurred and the Vietnam War escalated, he began to identify with marginalized groups. Like other members of the Union, he spent considerable time in Manhattan, engaging with the Fifth Avenue Peace Parade Committee and eventually the High School SMC. At these gatherings, he encountered peers with radical upbringings and heard political arguments that were "much more sophisticated than what some of them had been exposed to in the past. This was a training ground for people like me who had no real political upbringing." Swerdloff attended various political demonstrations: Vietnam Week, the March on the Pentagon, picketing Secretary of State Dean Rusk when he visited the Hilton, and even the rally at the Democratic National Convention in Chicago.[20]

Trigg's new social circle was different from anything he had experienced, but he did not yet identify as a radical. His worldview shifted in the summer of 1968. He served as a scoutmaster in Long Island for the first month in June. In August, a trip to Chicago changed his perspective on the country dramatically. Vice President Hubert Humphrey entered the presidential race and pledged to continue the war despite widespread opposition to the conflict. Senator Robert Kennedy won the California Democratic primary in June, an event which many antiwar liberals celebrated. An assassin's bullet ended any hope his base had for his nomination. The Democratic Party's position on the war would be decided at the convention in August. The Mobe, which had organized the March on the Pentagon, planned to hold demonstrations outside the convention. In preparation for the event, Chicago's Mayor Richard Daley sealed off the site with barbed wire and refused to grant permits to protesters, purposefully stalling other requests. Additionally, he placed 12,000 police officers on twelve-hour shifts, mobilized more than 5,000 National Guardsmen and provided them with riot training, and called in 6,000 US Army troops equipped with flamethrowers, bayonets, bazookas, and machine guns mounted on Jeeps. Small, disruptive protests occurred throughout the weekend of August 24. Police broke up an encampment at Lincoln Park with tear gas and nightsticks. Inside the convention hall, another disorder occurred. Although 80 percent of registered Democrats voted overwhelmingly for antiwar candidates, the party's leadership tried to repress it. A group of antiwar delegates proposed a plan to the platform committee that called for a de-escalation in Vietnam akin to what Senators Eugene McCarthy and Kennedy had proposed. But the committee endorsed a pro-war plan. On August 29, both senators had received the vast majority of the primary votes cast. But convention delegates handpicked by the party machine leaders nominated Humphrey for president.[21]

The crowd outside erupted. Someone lowered the American flag, and the police moved in and bloodied numerous protesters. Disillusioned by the police response, antiwar liberals who originally tried to moderate protests earlier, believing it would ruin McCarthy's chances, joined in with the radicals. Some hurled rocks at the police. Soldiers chased protesters through the streets of downtown Chicago and sprayed them with tear gas. The protesters dispersed, circled in, and regrouped throughout the chaos.[22] Trigg was in the crowd. He not only witnessed the police attack unarmed protesters, but he was also clubbed and punched in the face. Swerdloff, reflecting on the incident two months later, labeled the event as "Czechago"—a portmanteau of Czechoslovakia and Chicago—drawing a parallel between Soviet troops and tanks seeking to crush a liberal Czech movement and the police crackdown in Chicago. Trigg avoided arrest, but upon leaving the city, he began developing a sense that opposition to the war in Vietnam was part of a global movement. He even began calling police "pigs," a term he had previously detested. "I came back from Chicago a committed revolutionary and was [one] already when we had our first meeting of the High School Student Union," he remembered. "I was a hardened veteran of the battle of Chicago." Swerdloff noted that the group's experience in Chicago helped them gain "some celebrity." They returned to New York as "big shots—we had made the world notice us."[23]

The Birth of the Union and Its Structure

The Union formed amid a teacher strike in New York City that began in May 1968. This conflict ignited in the Ocean Hill-Brownsville district of Brooklyn, a predominantly Black neighborhood where an experimental school district had formed. After the community board transferred some white educators out of the district, teachers went on strike. The strike carved a deep chasm between Black and white New Yorkers. Schools across the city closed from May until mid-November. Over one million students lost nearly two months of school time.[24]

Union members now had additional time to continue networking, organizing, and advocating for various political and social causes. After a series of meetings in the summer of 1968, a group of about 200 students from twenty-five high schools in New York City convened for the last time on September 21 at the New York Society of Ethical Culture in Manhattan. They had assembled a "founding conference" to establish what would become the New York HSSU. This organization would represent all high school students in the city and oppose the war in Vietnam, call for Black liberation, fight for student rights and school reforms, and raise a radical consciousness among the city's youth. During the previous school year, school officials had repressed students' political activities on campuses. These actions led some students to believe that schools perpetuated the status quo and failed to encourage students to question and challenge societal norms. Trigg articulated this belief succinctly: "We started to reach this analysis of the schools as this totalitarian institution that was closely allied with the war machine and with all the class and race divisions and inequalities in society." Gradually, he continued, "it emerged a sense that schools were these key institutions for turning out soldiers and functionaries. What went on [in] the schools were essentially a microcosm of the society that we were increasingly in opposition to." Through the new organization, students could coordinate collective actions and gain a greater voice in school operations.[25]

From the outset, the New York HSSU sought to create a non-authoritative group and give members as much autonomy as possible. In a proposal on the design of the organization, the students decided to establish a steering committee that met weekly and would handle finances, mailing, public relations, leaflets, and call emergency meetings. A representative committee would meet biweekly and receive two votes from each local, along with two representatives to vote on union-wide policy decisions. The task of establishing local groups in as many city schools as possible made it necessary to bequeath autonomy to the locals. Students at various schools wanted to address their own issues; having a citywide group that dictated policies to all the locals might have created internal frictions. The students also proposed that the New York HSSU would hold a general meeting every two months.[26] Anyone could join, which allowed the group to "ultimately become racially, ethnically, and socioeconomically diverse with students from traditional high schools as well as the city's more prestigious, college-preparatory school facilities." This structure allowed the group to coordinate collective actions more efficiently since representatives had a presence in various high schools in the city.[27]

With the group officially established in September 1968, the New York HSSU expressed jubilant optimism for the upcoming school year. "This is the first time high school students have had an organization that combines local high school organization with a citywide coordinating body to win our rights," a pamphlet read. "We're sick of having no say in the institutions that run our lives. We're sick of having our basic rights to look the way we want, to leaflet, petition, and speak our mind denied because we're under 21 (not that people over 21 have these rights either)."[28] The students characterized the group as an antiwar, antiracist, and student rights organization. Believing that high school students constituted an oppressed group, the Union made a provocative statement:

> The main thing that's taught [to] us in school is how to be good niggers, obey the rules, dress in our uniforms, play the game, and no, don't be uppity! Oh, we're trained for participating in "the democratic process"—we have our student government—they can legislate about basketball games and other such meaningful topics. Don't mention the curriculum—they'll tell us what to learn. Oh, we can express our complaints in the school newspaper—but the principal says what gets printed and don't embarrass the school's reputation. Not only are we forced to attend school in the first place, we have to carry ID cards at all times, walk on the right side of the hall, and if the teacher doesn't want us to, we can't even take a PISS!
>
> Many of us are finding out that the only way to be free and to be treated like human beings is to stand up and fight for our rights. Last January, in many city H.S.'s, when chicks were sick of freezing their assess off because they had to wear skirts, they said HELL NO, had a pants strike, and now chicks can wear pants in NYC public high schools. When the principal of Brandeis refused to let the kids

there hear Rap Brown speak, they walked out of school and heard Rap out there. The kids at Food & Maritime still were on strike when schools closed in June, demanding simple reforms like student government. And of course, last April 26, 200,000 of us declared our disgust at going to school for 12 years so we can kill Vietnamese.

THIS FALL we're prepared to demand a change, because now we have an organization that will make the Bd of Ed shiver (private schools too). It's called the N.Y. High School Student Union and we are you.[29]

The Union likely drew inspiration from literature professor Jerry Farber's 1967 article, "The Student as Nigger," which used provocative language to highlight the powerlessness of college students. Farber argued that students were akin to "niggers" because they were "politically disenfranchised" and expected to "know their place." While the article's use of a racial slur was deeply problematic, it became one of the most reprinted pieces in the high school underground press.[30] With the Union now established, students were positioned to challenge school policies and persuade administrators to grant them greater political rights as minors.

New York High School Free Press

The strike gave the New York HSSU a vital opportunity to establish an underground newspaper, which was a ubiquitous endeavor among student activists nationwide in the mid-1960s. Across the country, underground newspapers emerged as New Leftists began crafting radical newsletters to disseminate new ideas and "inspire political tumult." Publishers welcomed rank-and-file participation in every aspect of production, opening their pages to anyone eager to voice left-wing perspectives and fostering a sense of community among political radicals and bohemians. Readers could find these papers almost anywhere—head shops, offbeat bookstores, and street vendors in hip neighborhoods, or at public gatherings such as "'poetry readings, political meetings, art gallery openings, light-shows and other freakouts—anywhere [there was] a captive audience.'" The rise of photo-offset printing technology made producing these newspapers both affordable and accessible. With a typist, a pair of scissors, and a jar of rubber cement to paste copy onto backing sheets, one could produce several thousand copies of an eight- or sixteen-page tabloid for just a few hundred dollars. A cheaper, albeit lower-quality, option was to use a power mimeograph machine, which was easier to operate and cost a few hundred dollars.[31]

By 1966, underground newspapers started to interconnect through loose networks such as the Underground Press Syndicate (UPS) and Liberation News Service (LNS). These became the primary communication channels for New Leftists. The LNS, launched in 1967, offered a radical alternative to the Associated Press. UPS facilitated a free exchange of articles, news stories, and reviews among the underground press. LNS, on the other hand, aimed to "centralize newsgathering and dissemination in the underground media." It regularly distributed packets of articles, editorials, photos, and political cartoons to hundreds of college and community newspapers, which could freely print as much material as they wanted. Over time, LNS reached millions, mailing weekly packets to nearly 300 subscribers by 1969.[32]

In New York City, teenage activists pioneered one of the first high school press syndicates. By 1969, education writer Diane Divoky estimated that about 500 such publications had appeared over the past couple of years. Some lasted a year or more, while others folded after a single issue.[33] Most were campus-based, though a few were citywide. However, there was no network to connect these publications or track what fellow high school students were doing in their communities. For a brief period in 1968, the High School Independent Press Service (HIPS) in New York City filled this gap, serving as a national syndicate for the high school movement. Operating out of the LNS office at 160 Claremont Avenue in Manhattan, HIPS modeled itself after the organization. The LNS announced in a brief write-up that "a new press service especially for the growing network of high school underground papers has been established in New York City." Like LNS, HIPS sent weekly news packets to several hundred high school publications, receiving about sixty papers, and boasting 400 subscribers, who were charged a nominal and often uncollected fee of $4 a month. "HIPS is very much in the revolutionary bag," one staff member told a freelance writer. "I suppose we're just as bad as the [*New York*] *Times* in being biased. But underground papers are more interesting to read than the *Times*. They don't start with the usual 'who, where, when, what, why.' HIPS gets people to think. Gets them radicalized before they get into college. If that happens, chances are a fourth of them will never get to college."[34]

Sixteen-year-old Tom Lindsay founded the organization. A skilled writer and cartoonist, he created HIPS's iconic "High School Students Unite!" poster. In an interview with two book authors, he relayed to them that he was the son of a preacher. "I went to church; I was a nice kid. But it's a drag being a nice kid," he said. After rejecting a social script, he "started rebelling in a lot of ways." He stopped attending church, began smoking cigarettes, started going to parties, "started making it with girls, stopped getting good grades, skipped school on nice days . . . and just started fucking around." He began hanging out with other teenagers like him. Like many members of the Union, which he joined, he went to the March on the Pentagon and witnessed people get teargassed. Prior to working on HIPS, he, along with a friend, created an underground paper titled *The Searcher* in Wellesley, Massachusetts. He abhorred the dress code. "No cocksucker is going to tell me to get my hair cut unless I also have the power to tell him to grow his hair long," he asserted. He later moved to New York and enrolled in Brandeis High School. After moving to New York, he began working on HIPS for several months and helped distribute it.[35]

But HIPS quickly ceased operations, hampered by its inability to turn a profit and limited staff to sustain its operations. As the New York HSSU took shape, the workers of HIPS began to address the communication gap between high school activists and adult organizations. "Those people [SDS] don't understand the problems of kids in New York City," wrote the staff writers. "We gotta work our own problems out and HIPS takes too much of our time." By the fall of 1968, HIPS's staff redirected their energies toward the *New York High School Free Press*, the official publication of the New York HSSU.[36]

The *New York High School Free Press* ran as a monthly sixteen-page tabloid where students discussed both local and national events, aired opinions about their schools and society, and chronicled the political activities of high school students across the country. The students received office space from the *New York Free Press* and the *New York Review of Sex* on West 72nd Street off Broadway. Jack Banning, the publisher of the *Free Press*, offered the students a small desk, a file cabinet drawer, and an IBM computerized typesetter. Reflecting on his decision, Banning confessed to a freelance writer, "Sometimes I regret that decision. They're kids. They're noisy. They love big meetings and endless discussions, but they are relevant and they are sharp." When Swerdloff requested permission to use the office equipment on weekends and at night, Banning acquiesced "because I felt it was necessary." "The high schools were about to blow up," he continued. "The Establishment was trying to stop them from even distributing their leaflets near schools. I thought it would be better to let them blow off a little steam." The staff members taught them how to use the IBM typesetter in one day, which, according to Banning, normally took two weeks. A woman who sold ads for the publication also sold them for the students. Ads from major record companies such as Columbia Records, as well as subscriptions and donations, funded the newspaper.[37]

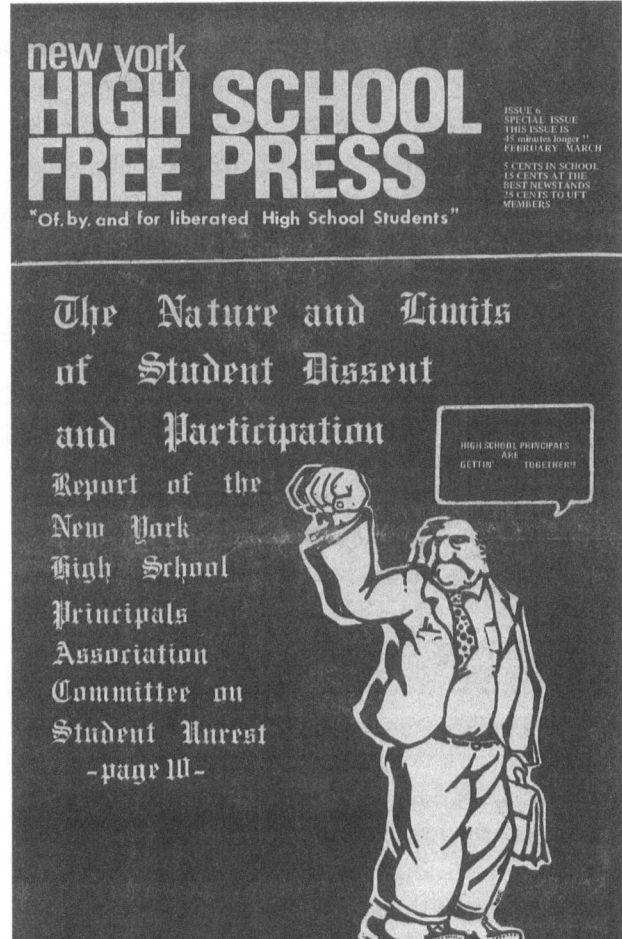

Cover of the *New York High School Free Press*. In possession of author. Used with permission by Howard Swerdloff.

Freelance writer Nicholas Pileggi captured a snapshot of the *High School Free Press* office on a typical day. At first glance, the environment appeared chaotic and comedic. The staff indulged in a variety of snacks—"fried clams, popcorn, ice cream, barbequed chicken, potato chips, oranges, apples, Fritos, halvah, candy bars, processed cheese, packaged cake, and peanuts"—all wrapped up in greasy paper bags spread out over the desk, the seats of chairs, and on the two-foot-high stacks of the *Free Press* and *Screw*. Amid the clutter, Pileggi saw Swerdloff erupt with excitement. "Dynamite!" he yelled, as he snatched a letter from the drawer and waved it above his head. "We've got a distributor at Cardoza [a Queens high school]." Mark Rose, a fifteen-year-old from Bronx Science and the makeup editor, joined the fray, shouting, "A letter from Paramount Pictures!" All eyes turned to Rose as he read aloud: "Because of the controversial nature of this movie, we would appreciate you sending one Black and one white reviewer to this preview and perhaps running the articles simultaneously." Reginald Lucas, another fifteen-year-old Bronx Science junior, suggested Rose, who is white, would attend as the Black reporter, and Lucas, who is Black, would go as the white one. Rose, caught up in the jest, quipped, "Man, I'm grooving. Yeah! I'm a brother. Man, I got soul." These were, after all, typical teenagers—laughing, joking, and indulging in poor dietary choices—yet, they were politically astute beyond their years. "Everyone just writes what he feels," Swerdloff explained. "And it comes out true."[38]

At its peak, the *New York High School Free Press* had a circulation of around 40,000 copies every three weeks and lasted for roughly two years. Union members delivered copies to the city's junior and senior high schools throughout the city.[39] The paper incorporated HIPS's style of reporting by chronicling the political activities of high school students nationwide in a section titled "High School Students are Gettin' Together." It linked readers to the broader high school movement. The *High School Free Press* even had an official student photographer who traveled throughout the city to document demonstrations.[40] To manage the distribution of tens of thousands of copies, the students established contacts with peers at other schools and enlisted adult allies. Given their age and the legal restriction on driving, they coordinated with SDS members for logistic support. Those organizers often tried to sway them toward their ideology, but the students remained unimpressed. "We would always tell them, 'We don't need your help, we were doing fine without you,'" recalled former Union member Jamie Friar. The group viewed outsiders as potential distractions from their primary focus on school issues.[41]

Although these youth claimed to be enlightened, sexism remained a persistent issue in the Union, which was also a problem in the high school movement overall. Even in periods when people called for change, they still "cling to traditional patterns, habits, roles, and customs."[42] In Palo Alto, California, a male member of the United Student Movement openly criticized the group for its male chauvinism. He observed that men dominated political decisions and leadership roles, often displaying arrogance and self-righteousness. Self-reflectively, he admitted to valuing passivity in female members, a trait he would never tolerate in a male peer and argued that embracing women's liberation could strengthen their fight against capitalism.[43] Girls, meanwhile, tackled their own issues independently. Similarly, the authors of *Red Tide*, a Los Angeles-based underground student paper, highlighted sexism in rock culture, school textbooks, and the education system.[44] In Baltimore, female students at Towson High School distributed a leaflet questioning gender roles, asking, "Why do we take typing? So we can be secretaries when we leave school and do nothing but be pretty, please the boss, and type boring letters other people have written."[45] If anything, these young activists adopted the language of the high school movement to argue that society and schools were inherently oppressive to girls. In the Union, white males typically dominated leadership positions and discussions. Members Schneider and Katherine Mulvihill recalled the sexist attitudes within the group, noting that male members often made unpleasant comments about women and rarely took female members seriously. Schneider and Mulvihill occasionally discussed the sexist nature of their male counterparts among themselves. Over the course of time, the *High School Free Press* covered women's liberation.[46]

The Union Confronts the Teacher Strike

The Union formed primarily as a student rights organization, but its initial activities centered around the ongoing teacher strike. Leaders and members of the United Federation of Teachers (UFT) framed the strike as a labor dispute, but many students saw it through the lens of race. The students chose to align themselves with local activists in the Black community, who were advocating for community control of schools in their neighborhoods. During a general meeting, one New York HSSU member declared, "We are against the teacher strike. The strike, which in itself, is racist and is a show against the centralization of black control of the black community."[47] As teachers picketed the schools, New York HSSU members crossed the picket lines and attempted to reopen them. Trigg remembered that liberally minded teachers "who had liked us because we were antiwar activists," began "calling us fascists for trying to cross a picket line." The shop and gym teachers, who were more conservative, called them communists. "I remember being taken aback at being called a communist and a fascist on the same day," he recalled.[48]

Once the students crossed the picket lines, they reopened the schools and held classes taught by volunteer teachers. These makeshift classes, however, were short-lived as police officers or school janitors would soon discover them and force everyone to leave.[49] By supporting Black community control activists and defying the picket lines, the Union presented itself as a student organization unafraid to challenge the status quo. Its actions served as a powerful conduit to channel the attitudes of some of the city's youth toward the teachers' strike. For the remainder of the strike, the group organized a sit-in at UFT headquarters and continued to hold "liberation schools" within the buildings. Additionally, two Union members visited the Ocean Hill-Brownsville school district, toured its grounds, and interviewed its controversial administrator, Rhody McCoy. This visit directly contradicted the UFT's claims of "chaos and anarchy in the halls."[50]

The strike concluded shortly after the *High School Free Press* published its interview with McCoy, dashing any hopes for community control. UFT members were scheduled to return to work on Tuesday, November 19. Teenage activists were dismayed by their exclusion, and that of the larger Black community, from strike-related negotiations. The UFT and the Central Board of Education reached an agreement to "make up time," ensuring that UFT members would earn "retroactive income for the thirty-six days lost during the strike," and to provide students with lost teaching time. In a move that would trigger severe backlash, this agreement extended the school day by forty-five minutes and added nine extra days to the academic calendar. In response to this agreement, the New York HSSU, along with the High School Coalition and the Afro-American Student Association, organized a citywide strike. Just weeks after schools reopened, students across the city boycotted classes to express their discontent with the extended school days and the cancellation of holidays. On November 29, the school district reported that 35 percent of students participated in the boycott. In the immediate aftermath, the *High School Free Press* printed an article titled, "Fuck Your 45 Minutes." An anonymous writer declared that the strike "scared the Board of Education, the UFT, the whole racist bureaucracy into dealing with us." Stressing the significance of students uniting, the writer stated, "Now that we got our shit together, we can win."[51] At some schools, official student organizations co-sponsored the event. In Queens, the Martin Van Buren High School Student Union Local and the G.O. Executive Committee called for a strike. Both groups argued that "the extra five minutes tacked on to each period has no educational value, and will serve only to pad the teachers' pockets."[52]

Demonstrations occurred elsewhere around the city. Some students picketed and protested outside their schools. But thousands went to a student demonstration at the United Nations Plaza in Manhattan at 1:00 p.m. on November 27. The Citywide Student Strike Committee, which included

The start of a demonstration to protest the lengthening of the school day in front of Martin Van Buren High School on November 27, 1968. The boy holding the sign was in one of the frats, showing how the Union was able to unite a diverse array of students. Courtesy of Josh Kiok.

leaders from the Union, the Brooklyn-based African American Student Association, and other groups, organized the "African American Friday" boycott that drew a "teenaged crowd ranging in size anywhere from at least fifteen hundred to possibly as many as four thousand." Those among the crowd held signs that expressed their displeasure with the agreement. Similar events occurred in the days and weeks that followed. Students throughout the city skipped their classes and picketed schools. A few incidents devolved into violence, injury, and police intervention.[53]

Police nabbed Trigg and Kiok at Van Buren High's demonstration after a teacher conversed with a police officer and pointed directly to them as the leaders. The officer hauled them into the rear of a paddy wagon and darted off to chase other students. Inside the van, another officer told them to go home, so they avoided arrest. Trigg then broke the news to his parents. "I remember telling my parents that I had nothing to do with the big strike that occurred, basically a riot at the school," he recalled. But the real bombshell came in the mail—a suspension letter from school. He remembered his "parents just flipping out. Their son, the [future] doctor, how could you get expelled?"[54] Kiok received a similar letter on November 27, addressed to his

The Rise of Independent Student Organizations 89

mother, Helen. "I regret that it has been necessary to suspend your son Josh Kiok," Principal Maurice Bleifeld wrote. He summoned her for a meeting on December 4 at 3:00 p.m. to discuss her boy's potential return to school, provided he stayed home during school hours in the meantime.[55] Trigg's parents refused to reenroll him unless he renounced his political activities. But he refused. "So, I spent a few weeks going to protests around the city and finally got a letter from the New York Civil Liberties Union . . . telling the principal that my suspension was illegal," he recalled. Principal Bleifeld called Trigg's parents and struck a deal: Bruce would graduate early in January, as he had enough credits. "And they'd be rid of me, and I'd be rid of them. So that was actually the end of my high school career at Martin Van Buren," he said. He then moved out of his parents' home, which "had become unbearable from all the tension," and moved with his first girlfriend to the Lower East Side. He remained active with the Union while working for the Fifth Avenue Peace Parade Committee.[56]

The strike, despite its mixed outcomes, managed to achieve notable successes. By its conclusion, school officials reassessed certain agreements from the initial negotiations. In December, the UFT moved to renegotiate the extended school hours and the elimination of school holidays. This renegotiation led to the Board of Education's January announcement that schools would indeed close for Easter Week. The Board maintained the longer school day and mandated adherence to the new schedule from January 30 to April 22.[57] While the district did not meet all the students' demands, the strike's impact was undeniable. School officials likely would not have reconsidered the plan without the student mobilization. Although most students did not join the protest, the substantial percentage that did forced school officials to seek a resolution to restore order within the schools. Newton delivered a statement on News Anchor Roger Grimsby's 11:00 p.m. Eyewitness News Report in December 1968, which encapsulated the students' desire to have their voices heard:

> Our press statement put out by the high school student union: The growing demonstrations and acts of violence seen by the city in the past week were made necessary by the immoral agreement signed by the UFT and the Board of Education. The New York High School Student Union and the Citywide Student Strike Committee consider this agreement unfair and detrimental to the success of the New York City educational system. Such demonstrations will continue to be held until the city realizes there are more important

figures involved in UFT. In the past all decisions have been made by a few bureaucrats. High school students were expected to obey like robots. Therefore, as of now, we are taking a strong stand on this issue. In the future, the Board of Education will have to deal with the students as they deal with the teachers in times of crisis.[58]

The week of student unrest culminated in a delegation of twelve student leaders from the Union, the African American Student Association, and the Citywide Student Strike Committee meeting with Milton A. Galamison, the Vice President of the Board of Education. On December 9 and 11, the group addressed their concerns regarding the UFT strike resolution and the disciplinary actions following the demonstrations. The students called for the elimination of the forty-five-minute school day extension, amnesty for all participants in the protests, and the return of the "stolen holidays." Galamison assured them he was "in favor of no reprisal for the whole thing."[59]

In response to the student mobilization, administrators took a more punitive stance. To quell further unrest, they suspended and expelled students for their political activities and, as Trigg experienced, forced them to graduate a semester early. Anticipating this backlash, the New York HSSU established the High School Legal Defense Committee to protect students' rights.[60] By January 1969, many original leaders had graduated due to administrative pressure. In December 1968, school officials expelled Swerdloff for his activism. His family sought help from the ACLU, which negotiated a deal: Swerdloff would receive his diploma as long as he never returned to school. He graduated from John Bowne High School in January 1969, six months ahead of schedule. Most principals, believing a few students caused the unrest, saw this strategy as a way to restore order in their schools.[61]

In January 1969, the High School Principals Association (HSPA) of the City of New York released a report expressing its concerns about student unrest in high schools. The report framed the uprisings as a reincarnation of the turmoil that had beset college campuses. Believing that the Board of Education, the mayor, and the Superintendent of Schools had failed to address "clear and present dangers," the HSPA called for protection against what it described as a small group of agitators. Principals were resolute in their pursuit of tranquility, but acknowledged that students had legitimate concerns about the "very real defects and inadequacies in our education system." However, the HSPA offered no new compromises to address students' demands, citing the limitations imposed by their roles: "the principal is not an absolutely free agent operating in a vacuum. His duties, responsibilities, and accountabilities are clearly spelled out for him."[62] Although the HSPA had laid out principals' legal obligations, the unfulfilled demands left the students unsatisfied. The HSPA's inability to accommodate students' desires only increased tensions between students and administrators.

Media Attention and Criticism

While the UFT strike consumed much of the Union's energy, the organization and its underground newspaper tackled a broad range of topics that nurtured a radical political consciousness among New York City high school students. By 1969, Union members had achieved a level of celebrity. Factors such as geography, race, and the group's sheer size captivated and, in some cases, terrified many observers. Freelance writer Diane Divoky highlighted the group in a cover story for the *Saturday Review* in February 1969, and *The New York Times*'s Pileggi humorously titled his March 1969 article "Revolutionaries Who Have to be Home by 7:30." The piece featured a moment where a member suddenly realized he needed to be home by a specific time.[63] Documentary filmmaker Stephen Sbarge followed the group around during the teacher strike and some later activities. He then produced the 1970 film *Ira, You'll Get into Trouble,* distributed by Newsreel, a radical film distribution and production group.[64] Swerdloff remembers Sbarge driving them around in a Land Rover. He took them to Times Square, where they watched Clint Eastwood westerns at midnight.[65]

School administrators, on the other hand, had suspicions about the organization. They insisted that outside agitators were manipulating the students. Public officials regularly claimed that independent student organizations had adult leadership because their activities mirrored those of more seasoned activists. Dr. Bernard E. Donovan, the Superintendent of Schools, believed that adults were the true organizers. When asked about the New York HSSU in March 1969, he responded, "There is too much printed material and general similarity for me to believe it is not being led by adults."[66] Yet, members of the group stood defiant against this allegation. "Outside agitators?" Union member Charlotte Brown asked in a *New York Magazine* article in April 1969. "The agitators are the students. Our principals and teachers don't seem to want to acknowledge that we can think."[67] Brown reversed the argument to criticize administrators, stating, "They should be proud of us. To say we're being led certainly doesn't speak well for the school system. They're pointing out their own failure."[68]

Nonetheless, the claim that outside agitators were pulling the strings persisted. *High School Free Press* distributors routinely encountered repression. In Sbarge's documentary, one girl recounted to a group: "Two hours later, after I get done selling them, the dean comes in and he said, 'All right, come down with me,' and I said ok. 'Take your papers too.' So, I come down with him. He turns to page three where they have a big headline 'Fuck your 45 minutes.' 'Now listen, do you think this is nice? What are you trying to do to these poor kids? We have a responsibility here to educate, not corrupt.' He's giving me this whole story. It turns out in the end they confiscated the papers."[69] Secretively, the FBI monitored the group likely on similar suspicion of outside influences. On November 21, 1968, the FBI placed the Union under an internal security investigation, which lasted nearly nine months.[70]

One incident of suppression reached the US District Court in March 1969. Schwartz claimed Jamaica High Principal Louis Schuker had punished him for distributing the *High School Free Press* near campus grounds. In January, Schuker suspended Schwartz for his refusal to surrender copies of the newspaper and his encouragement of a peer to do the same. Schwartz argued that he was never formally charged with violating a school regulation, nor given a proper hearing, and that his punishment was unconstitutional. However, the court ruled against Schwartz, stating that informal conferences had been held and determining that his suspension was based on defiant behavior rather than an infringement of his free speech rights.[71]

The Spring Offensive

In the spring of 1969, the New York HSSU embarked on another ambitious citywide initiative. By then, students across New York City had come to recognize their collective power. The Union called for a "Spring Offensive," a term borrowed from antiwar mobilizations, to demand school reforms and challenge the bureaucratic constraints imposed on students. Planned for April 21 to May 19, the group aligned the event with past antiwar demonstrations held every spring since 1965. One argument in favor of this demonstration dealt with the Union's claim that 12,000 students had been suspended in the previous school year. In response to this issue as well as others, the group drew up ten demands: it called for no suspensions, no police in schools, no identification cards, and no military recruiters in schools. It also called for open admission to college, a job, and decent housing for dropouts and students who decided not to attend college, Black and Latino studies departments, community control of the schools, student power, and an end to "general and commercial diplomas." Realizing that these demands would not come easily, the Union called on students to protest the schools between its proposed dates.[72]

As the Spring Offensive approached, students across the city were already organizing and submitting their own demands to reform their schools. These demands included having more inclusive and representative faculty, improving school facilities, abolishing nonacademic general courses, and removing military recruiters and police officers, who had been stationed in high schools following the Ocean Hill-Brownsville Teachers' Strike. Throughout the proposed offensive, students staged sit-ins, walkouts, and student-faculty conferences. *The New York Times* reported about eighty instances of student disturbances at thirty-eight city schools between April 16 and May 9.[73] On April 20, some Black and Puerto Rican high school students presented fifteen "non-negotiable" demands to the Board of Education, designating the next day as "D-Day" if their demands were not met. The Board's lack of response led to demonstrations and violence at numerous schools over the following weeks. Most protests occurred in April, coinciding with uprisings on college campuses throughout the city. Some schools saw students occupying cafeterias and auditoriums, even setting fires in basements. Other schools closed the following day after protests that caused severe property damage.[74]

The Union continued its activities into the next school year, but many of its founding members had finished school. In response to the spring unrest, school officials expelled many student activists, while others received diplomas despite missing over a month of school. Some students received suspensions, while others dropped out altogether.[75] Newton, absent for most of the spring, returned in the fall only to drop out a few weeks later. Mulvihill left school after the teachers' strike to become more involved with political organizations.[76]

Having graduated from high school in January, Trigg, Swerdloff, and other Union members received an invitation from activist Linda Morse to Berkeley, California, in the summer of 1969. High school student activists in the region had organized the Bay Area High School Liberation Conference. Many radical groups attended the meeting, including the Black Panthers, Brown Berets, Red Guard, and La Raza, as well as the film production company Newsreel and community radio station KPFA. This conference marked the beginning of a loose coalition of preexisting and new student rights groups, which coalesced into the Bay Area High School Student Union. Debates between Maoist and anarchist thinkers shaped the structure of the organization. Trigg spoke about the formation and evolution of the New York HSSU. He explained that it grew out of the antiwar movement, where students realized "we had the basis for a strong union after the success of the high school anti-war strike." He detailed the teacher strike, its racial dynamics, and the vitriol they faced, being labeled "everything from fascists to communists to nigger-lovers." He also discussed the strike against the extended school day, their collaborations with other student groups, and the demands they were currently proposing to the school board. Organizers had doubts about achieving anything substantial, yet the Bay Area High School Student Union took shape. Trigg's speech provided a political education for Bay Area youth, who had little connection with New York City students outside of antiwar activism.[77]

The New York HSSU emerged alongside many independent student organizations in the late 1960s and early 1970s. The reasons for their formation varied, but nearly all fought for school reform and represented students as a collective body of shared interests. They represented a shift in thought in the high school movement as students increasingly saw themselves as a political constituency with issues as important as those of PTAs, teacher unions, and other special interest groups. Many of these groups are worthy of their own exclusive study, given how impactful they were in negotiating with school officials and engaging with local media. Local circumstances, however, shaped the issues they addressed and how effectively they could organize. If the teacher strike had not happened, the Union would have likely taken longer to mobilize students citywide. But because of the incident, much of its attention centered on the fallout.

Internal rifts in the antiwar movement and the indifference of adult-led organizations to teenagers' unique plights led to the idea of the New York HSSU and possibly other independent student organizations. However, by 1969, the SMC began to recognize these issues and started to prioritize student rights as a major component of its efforts to end the war. Its embrace of the issue led to a surge in interest among young people across the country and further built the high school movement.

4 Vietnam and Student Rights
The Antiwar and High School Movements Unite

On April 22, 1969, Joanna Misnik of the New York SMC sent a letter, along with clippings and reprints, to the New York Civil Liberties Union "so that you get an idea of what the Student Mobilization Committee's involvement in high school rights is." The letter also conveyed a recent realization among SMC members:

> Our primary purpose, of course, is to organize campus and high school students to oppose the Vietnam war and to engage in actions and educational projects against it. With the recent upsurge of high school participation in the antiwar movement, especially evident on the April 5th to 6th demonstrations, high school students play more and more of a role in our organization. As they have begun to be involved, we have discovered more or less empirically that the fight for their RIGHT to express their political views goes hand in hand with organizing them against the war. That is, the repressive character of the high school set-up is in a limited way analogous on a civil liberties basis to what antiwar GIs face in the army—the myth that neither are protected by the Constitution as regards free speech and expression, that somehow they are exempted. This myth must be challenged on a civil liberties basis to win the right to organize the high school antiwar sentiment.
>
> The next issue of the *Student Mobilizer*, our national publication, will officially launch this orientation for us—defending the right of high school students to oppose the war and express this opposition as a free speech right.[1]

Since the inception of the antiwar movement, teenage activists have continually grappled with issues surrounding First Amendment rights and the parameters of nondisruptive protests. Many faced disciplinary actions for protesting the war on campus. Yet, adult-led groups like the SMC often overlooked the issue. The formation of the New York HSSU brought the issue of disenchantment to adult organizers' attention. However, a significant shift occurred in 1969. The Supreme Court's ruling in *Tinker* provided antiwar

A member of the High School SMC holds a sign demanding "Full Rights for High School Students." Another student holding a sign demands an end to the war. The *Militant* Photographic Collection, box 2, Folder 12, Hoover Institution Library & Archives.

organizers with the legal language needed to defend students' rights to protest the war. With this newfound judicial support, the SMC began to foreground student rights struggles in high schools, eventually incorporating this issue as a major tenet of its broader campaign to end the war. To understand this evolution in thought, we must delve into several stories that captured the attention of SMC organizers, each involving high school members who faced disciplinary actions for their activism.

Paula Smith and the Chicago High School Students Against the War

One of the first student rights incidents that came to the SMC's attention occurred in Chicago in March 1969, involving a Catholic school student named Paula Smith. Raised in a conservative, middle-class household—her father owned trailer parks in Indiana while her mother was a homemaker—Smith had no known radicals in her family or among her early friends. Entering high school, she had little inclination toward political activism. However, her perspective changed as the family frequently traveled across North America. "You hear various things, but as they say, there's nothing like seeing it for yourself," she recalled. During these trips, Smith saw the stark poverty experienced by Mexican Americans and the entrenched racial segregation in the South. "I remember the Southwest," she began. "Mexican-American kids used to come up to you with no clothes on trying to sell you beans for ten cents. That's how they live." When she encountered racially segregated bathrooms, she relayed, "These are things that are impressed upon you, and you realize whether you are middle class, working class, or what, that there is something wrong." Smith did not initially see herself as particularly political, but she felt a deep urge to address these injustices. "I didn't know what to do until I got my hands on some antiwar literature," she said. These documents, from the Chicago High School Students Against the War, galvanized her into action. As a freshman, she joined the group, attended meetings and demonstrations, and became part of the broader antiwar movement.[2]

Organizing against the war among Chicago high school students launched following the SMC's Chicago conference in May 1967. Eighth-grader Geoff Mirelowitz, along with a friend, attended the event and subsequently became active in the SMC. They soon connected with other high school students around Chicago and its suburbs, and together they initiated efforts to form their own organization. This small collective of twenty to thirty youths undertook their first major action by initiating a march against the war on August 6, 1967, to mark the anniversary of the atomic bombing in Hiroshima. Mirelowitz did much of the organizing for the demonstration and contacted Roosevelt University professor and well-known activist Staughton Lynd, who agreed to speak at the event. Lynd had traveled to North Vietnam on a fact-finding mission with Tom Hayden and others. When high school students began mobilizing en masse, Mirelowitz and his peers formally established the Chicago HSSAW in 1968. It became the main organizer of high school antiwar activity in Chicago with contacts in dozens of schools.[3] Additionally, the group quickly came under scrutiny from the *Chicago Tribune* and the Chicago Police Department's Red Squad. A November 8 article alleged that a Trotskyite communist organization had begun recruiting local high school students "under the guise of a student peace group." Police officials soon took notice. On November 11, an officer from the police intelligence division wrote on a leaflet advertising a citywide SMC meeting, "I would like more information about High School Students Against the War." The group remained under Red Squad surveillance well into April 1969.[4]

Chicago SMC staff member Kitty Cone played a vital role in supporting HSSAW's work. That included helping to prepare HSSAW leaflets, posters, and buttons, and facilitating logistics for distributing materials—even coordinating covert drop-offs for students wary of their parents' reactions. "If they wanted leaflets and they wanted them left under the bushes outside a neighbor's house because of their parents, then I would organize that," she remembered. Cone had muscular dystrophy, which weakened her physically and forced her to use a wheelchair. Yet, Mirelowitz, who met her when he was either thirteen or fourteen, remembered that he never thought of her as "handicapped," but rather as "the hardest working person I had ever encountered; totally dedicated to the movement and equally dedicated to encouraging every young person she met to shoulder as much responsibility for leading the movement as they were willing to take." Her medical condition did not appear to "keep her from doing anything she felt had to be done. If there was ever a 'tireless organizer,'" Mirelowitz recalled, "Kitty Cone was that person." She was "the person most responsible for working with the large number of high school students who were flooding into the movement against the war."[5]

Cone taught Mirelowitz and many others the basics of political organizing. She ensured the group attached a coupon to the bottom of every leaflet it distributed so readers who wanted to volunteer could send their name, phone number, and home address. In a small office, much of the work the group did consisted of calling and talking to every potential volunteer. "Those coupons paid off," Mirelowitz remembered. "We had two or three phone lines in that very small space, and Kitty and I spent countless hours together calling those names, getting to know the young people on the other end of the phone, and involving them in the movement." Cone also led by example. That translated into the teens realizing that any successful meetings, large demonstrations, or rallies depended on the "'little things.'" She instilled in them to value what they accomplished together. Through it all, the Chicago HSSAW became a success, and "the motor force behind that effort was Kitty Cone."[6]

The zeal and dedication of the Chicago HSSAW earned it praise from the YSA, who hailed the group as "one of the healthiest high school anti-war coalitions in the nation."[7] The YSA acknowledged that since the anti-Vietnam War movement began, "high school students ha[d] been in the forefront of almost every major anti-war action," often acting "completely on their own, or with minimal assistance from college-orientated groups." "From Boston to Berkeley," it continued, "high school students have made up a huge percentage of nearly every major anti-Vietnam demonstration in the past four years."[8] The SMC also deemed the Chicago HSSAW a success. By the summer of 1969, the group had organized two high school rallies and played a leading role in three antiwar demonstrations. It had established contacts in over 130 schools, with plans for further expansion. This network allowed students to build confidence, gain organizing experience in their own schools—whether antiwar sentiment existed or not—and most importantly, erode feelings of isolation. Mirelowitz became a key contact for students sending inquiries to the SMC. In January 1969, a fellow member asked him to write an article on the Chicago HSSAW's activities for the next issue of the *Student Mobilizer*, noting that "the *Mobilizer* needs regular articles on high school activities—in the past that has been one of the weaknesses of the paper."[9]

The police riot at the 1968 Democratic National Convention further catalyzed Smith's politicization. "I went to look on as a neutral observer, with the nice attitude that everything's going to be fine: I'm just going to have a good time like everybody else," she recalled. Armed with a camera, she ended up with "my head beat in" and was arrested. She joined the crowd clashing with police. Though she claimed police killed her friend, no official reports confirmed this. Following this event, Smith embraced anti-police sentiments and identified as a socialist, convinced that the government did not operate in the best interests of most Americans. She believed the US government served its own interests and advocated for its replacement with a more suitable alternative. Eventually, she joined the YSA, which supported socialist democracies, revolutions worldwide, Black liberation, and antiwar sentiments.[10]

Smith's radicalization must have seemed odd to her peers at the Academy of Our Lady, where no radical activities took place. Located in Chicago's South Side, the all-girls school was comprised mostly of middle-class white students from conservative households. Nevertheless, Smith managed to form a group of students who opposed the war or questioned its merits, calling themselves the Concerned Students Against the War Within the Catholic High School. They held classroom debates and meetings at her home, which raised suspicions from their peers and adult leaders. Girls became hostile toward them. School officials questioned members, accusing

Smith of smoking marijuana and labeling her a militant. Catholic schools were far more restrictive than public schools. Although many high schools had dress codes, Catholic institutions mandated uniforms and prohibited any showing of knees "because that's a sin." Political organizing in other area Catholic schools was "very hush-hush." Smith lamented, "You see very few examples of open political activity. . . . I hate to say it, but very few Catholic girls will become active on their own."[11]

Smith's activism ultimately led school officials to expel her from school on February 19, 1969. The administration refused to provide a formal explanation, though officials later told reporters that Smith was "defiant, militant, and revolutionary." Sister Martinus insisted Smith's expulsion had nothing to do with her political views, citing instead "impudence, disrespect, absenteeism, and vandalism." Principal Sister Mary Lenore added, "I don't care about her political views. She has caused us trouble for the last year and a half. She has erratic behavior and has become very insolent. After a year and a half, she needs a change in environment, and we could no longer help her." But Smith contended that school officials expelled her for allegedly inciting a riot between Black and white students.[12]

In response, the Chicago HSSAW issued a call to action, distributing a leaflet titled "An Attack on Free Speech at Academy of Our Lady." The leaflet outlined the incident and urged readers to contact Sister Lenore. It described the expulsion as the "latest effort of the school administration to suppress the political ideas of some of their students." The leaflet detailed how Smith had been prohibited from distributing literature on campus after handing out a leaflet printed by the Chicago HSSAW. Consequently, she had faced increasing harassment from officials. Despite her campus-based, antiwar group holding meetings at her home, the Chicago HSSAW noted that the following week, Sister Lenore called the students into her office and warned them not to continue their activities because "their education was at stake." They would, she cautioned, be "'picked out one by one.'" Having been summoned to the school's main office twice "for such vague charges," Smith arrived at the office, and officials told her she was suspended from school. She received no written note, explanation, or a date when or if she could return. The Chicago HSSAW labeled Sister Lenore's action as a "serious infringement of the basic rights of political freedom as guaranteed in the First Amendment." It then encouraged readers to write or call Sister Lenore and send copies of their letters to the HSSAW office.[13]

In solidarity, about forty concerned students, parents, and clergymen organized a demonstration on March 8 at the Chancellery office of the

Chicago Archdiocese. The demonstrators demanded Smith's reinstatement and an end to the suppression of free speech and the distribution of literature within parochial schools. Representatives from the city's antiwar scene, universities, religious institutions, the ACLU, and Chicago HSSAW attended the gathering. Teenage picketers, calling themselves the Committee to Defend the Rights of High School Students, came from the Academy and several Catholic high schools in Chicago's northern suburbs to protest in front of the Catholic school board. They invited Sister Lenore to defend her actions, but she declined. Chicago's Catholic schools appeared more hostile to activism than public institutions. In Fall 1968, for example, officials at Trinity High School in suburban Oak Park forcibly "graduated" Laura Miller after her name appeared in the *Tribune*'s article about the Chicago HSSAW.[14]

Not all members of the Chicago HSSAW were pleased by the focus on Smith's plight. Jay Schaffner, who attended Niles High School, remembers: "The age groups that the Panthers were talking to were the same age as Paula. To make Paula the cause célèbre when you're getting Panthers who are getting shot down . . . and Paula is being expelled from a Catholic school. There was somewhat of a disconnect. So, to build a student rights movement around her case, as unjust as it was, it sort of fell flat." He sympathized with her, but as someone who, along with his peers at Niles High, collected food for the Panthers and the Young Lords, he felt the YSA was out of touch. "I don't think it was on the same level as the nationwide campaigns [as to] what was happening to the Panthers. I think what the YSA was trying to do was transpose it as one vs the other," he states.[15]

Ultimately, the Chicago HSSAW fell short of getting Smith readmitted into the Catholic school. But other controversies ensured that the issues of student rights and antiwar activism among high school students remained intertwined.

East Cleveland's Button Lawsuit

Other student rights struggles coincided with Paula Smith's expulsion as school administrators ignored the *Tinker* ruling. One case in East Cleveland, Ohio, demonstrated that even judges interpreted the ruling differently, given the circumstances.

On March 11, 1969, Shaw High School Principal Donald L. Drebus found himself at odds with junior Thomas Guzick Jr. Drebus had suspended him for refusing to remove an antiwar button that advertised an upcoming demonstration in Chicago on April 5, sponsored by the SMC. Guzick defended his actions to a local reporter, calling it "a silent protest." His defiance challenged Shaw High's forty-year-old rule prohibiting buttons, emblems, or insignia unrelated to school activities. Administrators, already wary of racial tensions in a school that had shifted from predominantly white to 70 percent Black by 1969, feared that the button could spark unrest. Shaw High had a history of racial violence, and officials wanted to avoid any more flare-ups. Guzick was not having it. "The school said if I wore my button," he began, "everybody else would wear theirs and we would have a racial disturbance. It seems the school feels we are nothing but a bunch of animals."[16]

Yet, the District Court cited the *Blackwell v. Issaquena Board of Education* case in upholding the prohibition of all buttons in the high school. The case stemmed from an incident in Mississippi in 1964 when school administrators suspended Black students for wearing and distributing "freedom" buttons after forbidding the buttons. In 1965, the Supreme Court ruled that students engaging in symbolic protest should be "quietly deferential to school officials on terms that those authorities specified." Essentially, only polite protest would be tolerated. In *Guzick*'s case, the district judge argued that buttons and insignia "are taken to represent, define and depict the actual division of the students in various groups." "The buttons tend to polarize the students into separate, distinct, and unfriendly groups," the judge wrote. The court felt that if the policy did not remain intact, "some students will attempt to wear provocative or inciting buttons and other emblems," which would "exacerbate an already tense situation." The Circuit Court elaborated on the lower court's decisions, stating, "In our view, the potentiality and the immenseness of the admitted rebelliousness in the Shaw students support the wisdom of the no-symbol rule." Previous rulings that struck down claims for free expression offered substantial evidence that the students would or did cause disruptions. But the lower courts in *Guzick* ruled on predictions about buttons that had never been allowed in the school in the first place. The *Cleveland State Law Review* pointed out that *Tinker* and *Guzick* were inconsistent since students could express themselves politically in a racially homogenous school but not in a racially tense one.[17]

In the fourth issue of the *Student Mobilizer Wallposter*, published in May 1969, the SMC reported on the *Guzick* case alongside other controversies. The issue opened with a declaration: "High school students have been waging a militant struggle around the country to ensure their rights to organize their fellow students." The Chicago HSSAW featured prominently, as it sought to distribute leaflets in high schools to galvanize support for an

April 5th action. Another story occurred in Maplewood, New Jersey, where administrators suspended forty students at Columbia High School for handing out leaflets outside school grounds that promoted the same April 5 demonstration in New York. The SMC noted that the school district's explanations failed to "answer the test questions set up by the U.S. Supreme Court *Tinker* decision."[18] Further north, in Binghamton, New York, about fifty students at Central High School signed an open letter requesting permission from their principal to organize against the war on campus. They proposed distributing leaflets, wearing armbands, and introducing classes on Black history and Marxism. The principal, however, accused them of "fomenting trouble and distributing pornography" and demanded their presence at a meeting with their parents and local probation officers. He even circulated a xeroxed copy of an "obscene leaflet," accusing the students of distributing it, though they had never seen the document. The principal refused to engage with their demands. After enduring harassment from police and other students, the group sought legal assistance, framing their battle as one of free speech for high school students.[19]

Well-publicized stories from Chicago, East Cleveland, and elsewhere put the issue of high school student rights on SMC's radar. These trends compelled it to address a concern among its core constituents. High school students' participation had been "steadily rising," but the group recognized the need to modify its approach.[20] On October 10, 1969, the national steering committee held a meeting where it decided "we should give our high school work a national focus." It established two high school project directors for the West Coast and the national office based in New York City. It also decided that November 20 would be the day "for focusing on high school rights around the country." It proposed teach-ins and assemblies with speakers from the ACLU or a strike in more active areas. To establish stronger forms of communication, it mailed out a questionnaire to learn about the activities or plans in certain areas. It stated its goals to put together a pamphlet to learn what had occurred in the previous year and what was happening currently.[21] This shift in focus coincided with the efforts of student activists in New York City. In December 1969, student representatives of the Black Student Union, New York HSSU, YSA, and the High School SMC held a conference to discuss ways to "win the rights of full citizenship" in their proposed Bill of Rights to the school board.[22] The SMC likely adopted this document as a model for its own High School Bill of Rights, making student rights a central tenet of its broader anti-war efforts. This move significantly boosted the group's popularity among high school students until the antiwar movement's demise.[23]

SMC's High School Bill of Rights

The SMC's National Student Antiwar Conference occurred in Cleveland, Ohio, from February 14 to 15, 1970. As usual, these attendees came by bus and plane, as well as by carpooling or hitchhiking. Hosted at Case Western Reserve University, the SMC had organized the conference to strategize antiwar actions for the coming spring. Its major issues appeared on banners plastered across the walls of Adelbert Gym. Slogans like "BRING ALL THE GI'S HOME, NOW!"; "FULL RIGHTS FOR HIGH SCHOOL STUDENTS! FREE SPEECH FOR GI'S! WAR MACHINE, OFF CAMPUS! SELF DETERMINATION"; and "SMC to END the WAR in VIETNAM" captured the urgency and breadth of its demands. Organizers held workshops and panels on various topics, such as Black liberation, GI and high school organizing, and the international antiwar movement. According to the SMC, over 3,500 antiwar activists showed up, making it, in the words of Halstead, "the largest working conference in the history of the antiwar movement." He added, "A major indication that the campuses were going to be far from quiet that semester on the war issue." However, the conference was far from harmonious. Ideological rifts surfaced over whether the organization should expand into a multi-issue entity capable of succeeding SDS or remain singularly focused on the war. Tensions peaked a day before the conference at a preliminary workshop when high school students staged a walkout. One youth stood up and declared, "I don't want to sit through all the bull again, like this afternoon." The college crowd, he implied, had monopolized the convention and marginalized high school voices.[24]

Atlanta, Georgia, native Jeff Berchenko was one of nearly 500 high school students from across the United States who attended the conference. He found himself surrounded by fellow teenage activists eager to exchange ideas and learn from each other's struggles. Some arrived from cities with vibrant youth movements. Others, like Berchenko, came from areas where organizing was in its infancy.[25] Berchenko led Atlanta's High School SMC, also known as the High School Mobe. He regularly contributed to Atlanta's leading underground newspaper, *Great Speckled Bird*, where he did not mince words about the city's underwhelming antiwar scene. "The Anti-War Movement continues to exist in Atlanta. Barely," he wrote. After listing the usual explanations—lack of Southern progressiveness and insular antiwar groups—he nailed the core issue. "Everyone agrees on one major reason: Atlanta has lacked a successful high school anti-war group," he argued. "Of the different groups in Atlanta, the high school students are a great untapped source of anti-war sentiment."[26]

He then proceeded to act on this shortcoming. In the following weeks, he organized a high school conference at Emory University in late January by advertising it in the *Great Speckled Bird*. The event drew seventy-five students from seventeen high schools, all eager to create an independent, citywide high school organization to tackle issues like the war, women's liberation, and racism. While some participants advocated for a public stance against racism, others desired a singular focus on the war. The former faction prevailed, with attendees acknowledging the inseparability of opposing the oppression of the Vietnamese people and confronting the repression faced by Black Americans. Attendees also shared tales of repression experienced personally or incidents that they witnessed at their school. In response, they decided to demand the freedom to leaflet on school grounds, form political organizations, send invitations for speakers into classrooms, and liberalize dress codes for girls. In one of the group's first actions, it showed up at a school board meeting to voice its concerns about administrators harassing antiwar students.[27]

Berchenko reported from Cleveland on the high school caucus, which grappled with the "special difficulties of high school organizing." The attendees identified the transient nature of student bodies, censorship of free speech, and pervasive feelings of isolation as major obstacles in building a robust high school antiwar movement. Students felt isolated and hamstrung by a lack of freedom of speech in cities with lackluster antiwar activism. Mirelowitz and others led the high school workshop. The group considered a motion to split the high school SMC from the national organization, but attendees shot it down. After intense debates over parliamentary procedures, the group reached a consensus to distribute newsletters to SMC chapters. This initiative aimed to help fledgling groups learn from more established movements. Additionally, the caucus successfully passed the High School Bill of Rights.[28]

Prepared by activists before the gathering in Cleveland, the High School Bill of Rights represented the culmination of antiwar activism and, in turn, students' experiences with repression from school officials. For years, administrators had thwarted students' attempts to distribute leaflets on campuses, receive official recognition for student organizations, and invite antiwar speakers to balance out the visits of military recruiters. Furthermore, the reality of parental authority, notions about childhood innocence, paternalistic attitudes among school officials, and hostile campus environments made adult leaders realize that high school students had to overcome unique barriers. The group spent a month debating what the document should include and exclude, as it labeled the first draft inadequate. "The problem of repression in high schools is deeper than temporary political issues," one staff member wrote. "We are forced to acknowledge the fact that often students are deprived of their civil liberties because of deep-rooted beliefs and attitudes that simply will not be changed by a sheet of demands." After various edits and critiques, staff members decided that the document should provide an outline of rights and serve as a source of strength to students.[29]

The document outlined six fundamental rights for high school students: freedom of political activities, speech, and the press; due process; free elections; an end to the "war machine"; and the right to determine curriculum and evaluate teachers. Addressing the "No War Machine" clause, the document asserted that students had the right to "be free from the presence of any influence of federal agencies not directly involved in the educational process." It also included the termination of all military programs like ROTC and military recruitment, as well as the prohibition of police intervention in school disputes. The committee that approved the document concurred that students were entitled to exercise all rights enumerated in the United States Constitution, the Bill of Rights, and all subsequent amendments, as well as those established by the United States Supreme Court.[30] The SMC heralded its adoption as the dawn of a new era, labeling it as an "integral part of the fight against the war," and quoting a United Nations charter: "An attack on one is an attack on all." Organizers believed the document laid "the basis for broadening the antiwar movement." The New York regional office underscored its significance, noting that it showed "those who are angered by the manipulation and authoritarian treatment of high school students that the organized antiwar movement is a powerful ally in their struggle and that the two movements must be linked."[31] According to SMC, the antiwar and high school movements had officially united.

The High School Bill of Rights had no legal weight, but it resonated deeply with students who viewed it as more than a symbolic gesture. The *Great Speckled Bird* reprinted the document, and Berchenko's group, High School Mobe, planned to make it "our major piece of high school SMC literature."[32] In March, his group presented its demands at another board meeting. The *Atlanta Journal* mistakenly reported the list of demands as patterned "after a 'Bill of Rights' drafted by a coalition of New York students." The group sought the right to distribute leaflets on school grounds without administrative permission, to belong to any political or social organizations, even those "which champion unpopular causes," and to be free from military recruiters and any "military programs like ROTC." No reports emerged on the board's response, but it likely mirrored the inaction seen across the country when students presented their demands.[33]

The High School Bill of Rights proliferated like wildfire. It appeared in underground newspapers nationwide, becoming a rallying cry for students from Salem, Oregon, to locations where the SMC had barely made a dent. New chapters emerged in Seattle, Portland, and Austin, Texas.[34] Its popularity caught the attention of school administrators, who quickly moved to crack down on its presence on campuses. In March 1970, about twenty-five students, mostly girls at a junior high school in North Bethesda, Maryland, picketed the school following the suspension of a ninth grader who had tried to distribute the document along with buttons. Tensions escalated into fistfights and shoving as more "conventionally dressed youngsters" arrived and began "taunting the picketers." Police arrived and restored order.[35] In Orlando, Florida, in September 1970, school officials suspended six students after fifty protesters and over 100 onlookers held an impromptu meeting on the front lawn of Winter Park High School, where they distributed the Bill of Rights document.[36]

Unlike past correspondences, which typically involved teenagers writing to SMC offices before upcoming antiwar demonstrations, the group now received letters from students eager to form new chapters. One student from Virginia wrote to the SMC office, explaining how she became interested in the organization after a friend showed her a copy of the High School Bill of Rights. "Not even one statement in the bill is recognized by my local high school," she wrote. Even as a senior, she felt "this is the time to finally take some action" and asked for more copies and information on forming a chapter.[37] The SMC remained committed to student rights struggles. Throughout 1970 and 1971, office staff diligently collected newspaper clippings documenting junior high and high school students organizing campaigns for their own bills of rights.[38]

Government Surveillance and Parental Objection

SMC's rejuvenated outreach to high school students did not go unnoticed by the FBI. The Bureau had long monitored SMC's high school chapters.

These included groups in Detroit, Kansas City (Missouri), Los Angeles, Minneapolis, New York, San Francisco, and even Milwaukee despite the absence of an official group there.[39] With the adoption of the High School Bill of Rights, the FBI's efforts to undermine the organization intensified. In March 1970, just a month after the national conference, the Cleveland field office sought Hoover's authorization to initiate counterintelligence operations against SMC's "vigorous efforts to organize high school students." The FBI managed to persuade a former member, disillusioned with SMC, to pen a letter to a local newspaper accusing the organization of "perverting the idealism and anti-war sentiments of high school students and using them for the propagation of the YSA philosophy." By July, the FBI's efforts escalated. It identified a source and his associates who had shown a "keen interest in the activities of radical student groups who were then beginning to infiltrate the high schools." Hoover approved the distribution of various publications circulating in New Left circles, including alternative publications with content "containing items relating to the high school scene." The office dispatched the materials to the source before the new school year began, believing "factual information concerning the subversive ramifications of the SMC" could preemptively curb high school agitation. In August, the FBI instructed the source to "alert high school administrative personnel to the potentially disruptive tactics of the SMC and to the control of this group by the YSA."[40] Whether these tactics worked remains unclear. But it is plausible that the opposition from parents played a more significant role in curtailing SMC's activities than the FBI's covert tactics.

Just a month after the FBI launched its first counterintelligence operation in the Cleveland area, in April 1970, the SMC chapter in Cleveland Heights found itself under intense scrutiny. Cleveland Heights, bordering the east of Cleveland and adjacent to Case Western Reserve University, was a majority-white community in 1970. It housed a mix of middle- and upper-middle-class Catholic, Protestant, and Jewish residents, with a growing number of Black families moving into the area. In April 1970, three mothers from the Cleveland Heights Unit of the Western Reserve Women's Republican Club submitted a letter to school board members, administrators, and "some interested public officials in our area." They expressed concern about the existence of SMC chapters at Cleveland Heights High and Roxboro Junior High Schools. Officials had approved both chapters earlier in the year. At a recent PTA meeting at the junior high, parents voiced their concerns to the principal about why the SMC had been allowed to form as an extracurricular activity. He explained that the group received a charter because two faculty members agreed to serve as sponsors and that it fell within the school board's guidelines on "Rights and Responsibilities of Students." Additionally, he emphasized that the SMC aimed to protest the war and study ways to implement a withdrawal. The parents were unconvinced. In their letter, they argued that the "objective of the National SMC are more extensive than those limited objectives presented" to school officials. They provided him with several issues of *US News and World Report* that described SMC's philosophy as "Trotskyite School of Communism." "We object to the presence of the SMC in any school in our system not only because of its political philosophy, which we believe to be subversive," they claimed. "But also, because qualified observers . . . have stated unequivocally that narcotics frequently move hand-in-hand with such 'New Left' organizations." They alleged that rumors of drug use at Roxboro had circulated and feared that the "liaison of SMC groups in our schools" with nearby universities could "provide additional sources of narcotics to our students."[41]

In response to the school board's booklet, the group published its own "Parents' Bill of Rights and Responsibilities." Since parents are "legally, morally, and financially responsible for the actions and activities of minor children," the document began, "we affirm that the following regulations pertinent to extracurricular activities in our school system should be adopted." The document demanded school officials update parents on the characteristics of extracurricular groups, provide consent forms, ensure dues collected remain accountable to the principal, inform parents of the groups' activities, allow only students averaging a C or better and with a good record to participate, and provide parents the right to formally protest the presence of any group within the school, "which he believes might be injurious to the welfare of his child and home."[42]

The group reprinted the High School Bill of Rights with its own scathing commentary, highlighting sentences and adding its own alarming interpretations. In response to the section stating that students may form political and social organizations, including those that champion "unpopular causes," it wrote, "including: violent overthrow of our government, confiscation of private property, restraint of the rights of others?" It posed hyperbolic questions in response to the section on due process, which asserted that students should not be penalized for any political or moral beliefs, by asking, "Sexual intercourse in the corridors? Burning down the building?" It twisted the section advocating for student influence in curriculum by suggesting "courses in the making of Molotov cocktails, administration of concentration camps for nonbelievers, the gymnastics of sex, making effigies for burning, composition of snappy slogans. Perhaps invite exchange professors such as Fidel Castro? Fire teachers who won't give straight A's to revolutionaries?" The group acknowledged that "perhaps some of the comments sound flippant and you will believe that there is no danger here." But it claimed that many such activities had already occurred in Cleveland schools. "Shall we make them legal by permitting the presence of a group in our schools which has told us in their own publication what plans they have in store for us?" it asked.[43]

The community swiftly rallied against the SMC. Nearly 500 people packed the school board meeting, breaking attendance records and forcing officials to relocate the gathering from the cafeteria to the auditorium. Representatives of the Heights Women's Republican Club arrived to voice their grievances, labeling the SMC as an "extremist group with connections to drug traffickers." Students from both schools opposed the club's accusations. One teenage girl pointedly remarked, "I can't think of anything that is more disruptive than a football rally." Still, the board members steadfastly supported Superintendent Frank Gerhardt's decision to suspend SMC's activities in the district. However, their victory was fleeting. A month later, the board reversed its decision after SMC's local attorney delivered a thirty-minute address, prompting the board to rescind the suspension.[44]

In May 1971, a similar attempt to ban SMC occurred in Bedford, a suburb south of Cleveland. After students sought to establish a chapter at the local high school, a group of parents invoked Hoover's testimony from the previous year, alleging that the SMC was Communist controlled. Unlike Cleveland Heights, the Bedford Board of Education responded by adopting new guidelines on extracurricular organizations. Principal Edward Estok introduced rules that prohibited assembly programs on controversial issues and banned the distribution of political literature during school hours. Meetings of any group had to be held after school, receive administrative approval, and serve an educational purpose where "all viewpoints, both pro and con, can be educationally discussed."[45] Cleveland's SMC Coordinator, Duncan Williams, countered these developments, challenging the assertion that the SMC targeted affluent areas where students are "'generally more liberal.'" He argued that antiwar sentiment in Cleveland's middle-class suburbs had the same fervor as its working-class areas. "The allegation that students are being duped by outside forces into joining the SMC is both an insult to students' intelligence and flies in the face of the Constitutional right of the American people to speak out against government policies which are not in their interest," he contended.[46]

Similar to episodes in Cleveland's suburbs, high school antiwar activism and the struggle against repression persisted across the country well into 1971. In May of that year, "two pistol-packing sheriffs stalked the halls" of Peary High School in Rockville, Maryland, to serve papers banning two teenage girls from speaking at a student seminar. The day before, Judge Joseph M. Mathias had signed a court order at his home near midnight to bar the two SMC representatives. The students were stunned. They had begun planning the seminar back in September and had received approval from the school board. "I was kind of wondering why no one came to hear me and then someone said, 'there's a court order forbidding you to speak,'" stated speaker Dale Brown. The Montgomery County Civil Liberties Union chair, John Risher, said the group would seek to have the injunction dissolved.[47]

Despite the persistent repression, high school outreach became one of the most remarkable achievements of the SMC. "High school students have become the most consistent and active builders and organizers of the antiwar movement," the *Student Mobilizer* proclaimed in 1972. Undeterred by obstacles, these students continued to organize rallies and appear en masse, often forming the majority of demonstrators.[48] In its February issue, the *Student Mobilizer* underscored the pivotal role high school students played in the antiwar movement. Three writers asserted, "Over the past few years high school students have been the backbone of the antiwar movement." Through distributing leaflets, working after school in offices, organizing meetings, and participating in demonstrations, they declared, "We have become a national movement." They recognized that protesting the war was also a fight "for our *right* to organize politically in the schools," and that "organizing seriously against the war has meant fighting for our *rights* to do that." They designated April 19 as a National High School Speak-Out Against the War, with proposed activities ranging from strikes and rallies to teach-ins and picket lines. While many high schools operated as usual that day, some students came out in droves. On April 22, about 100,000 people marched in New York City amid the cold and rainy weather.[49]

High school antiwar activism waned as the war officially ended in January 1973, but the high school movement itself pressed on. The antiwar campaigns had morphed into broader struggles for student rights, with students filing lawsuits and challenging officials over violations of their First Amendment rights. The landmark *Tinker* case provided a legal framework for these grievances, yet it did not fully guarantee their rights. The vague judicial interpretations and ambiguous definitions of "disruption" ensured that the struggle for student rights continued, likely bolstering the SMC's appeal among teenagers.

However, another development in the high school political scene reached even more students and outlived the antiwar movement by nearly two years. Underground newspapers, which began proliferating in the mid-1960s, became a more visible sign of youth rebellion than the antiwar protests. These publications, more than any other trend, connected the high school movement and informed students about their peers' actions nationwide and across the globe. This network of underground newspapers became the lifeblood of the high school movement, ensuring its continuity and impact well beyond the Vietnam War era.

5 The Voice of the Movement
The High School Underground Press

"This issue had a lot of national high school shit to show high skhool [sic] students the fact that there is a national hi[gh] skhool [sic] movement." It was a brief message from the editors of Portland's *South West Sun* to the Cooperative High School Independent Press Syndicate (CHIPS), accompanied by copies of their latest newspaper. This undated issue front-page headline read, "Revolution in the High Schools," and featured political cartoons from HIPS. Stories about high school protests in cities such as Houston, San Francisco, and Los Angeles appeared in the paper.[1] Another note from an editor introduced himself and requested, "I could really dig it if you could send me some news articles from other high school[s]. We can't help with money right now, but we can later. We will send you copies of our newspaper and information about the high school collective."[2]

This letter was just one out of hundreds, if not thousands, that CHIPS received over the course of six years. From Aberdeen, South Dakota, to Brook Mountain, Alabama, students shared their developmental stage plans or relayed information about a publication they currently had in operation. Others asked how to start one. Impressively, this teenage press syndicate started as a solo gig, run by a teenager from his suburban Chicago home in 1969. What began as a local initiative soon caught the attention of aspiring writers far beyond the Chicago area. Requests poured in from places like New Orleans, Los Angeles, and Barre, Vermont. After several relocations and collaborations, notably with a group based in Ann Arbor, Michigan, called Youth Liberation, by the early 1970s, CHIPS connected teenagers across North America, spanning over forty states, the territory of Puerto Rico, and Canadian provinces as far north as Yellowknife, Northwest Territories. The buzz even went global, with eager students from England, Australia, and New Zealand sending letters to learn more about CHIPS. Jenny Lavelle, a high school student from Sydney, Australia, for example, mailed a letter to the group about the strict environment at her school and how the headmistress thwarted her friend's attempt to create a newsletter. "This does not deter us one bit," she wrote. "In fact, it makes us more determined." Lavelle asked CHIPS to send US-based underground student papers and weekly news packets. "I would be very grateful if you would do this for me as I am very interested in overseas underground student papers and the things they write about, activities, etc.," she urged.[3] For underground newspaper subscribers, it was clear: the rumblings of dissent in secondary schools were occurring nationwide and abroad.

Much like how the underground press chronicled the sixties, the high school underground press documented the high school movement. It captured the actions and ideas of teenage activists with a depth seldom matched by mainstream newspapers and even adult-run alternative publications. While the latter covered high school news, their coverage varied widely. Some community underground newspapers had adolescent contributors and devoted special editions to the high school scene; others did not cover teenage activists at all.[4] But make no mistake, the high school underground press was not a response to this neglect. Instead, students formed these papers in response to censorship in school newspapers or to have a publication that served as the mouthpiece of an independent student organization or as an outlet for youth in the community. It became the most ubiquitous countercultural presence on campuses across urban, suburban, and rural areas for about a decade. These publications, brimming with poetry, cartoons, advertisements, and commentary on student issues and national problems, offered a radical alternative to the mainstream narrative about school reform. The true number of these underground publications remains elusive, but they proliferated like wildfire. Though these underground papers lacked the hallmarks of traditional journalistic accuracy and objectivity, some strove for higher standards. They instituted stringent application processes, required contributors to disclose their grades and spelling proficiency, and welcomed criticisms from across the political spectrum.[5] When administrators infringed upon their First Amendment rights, some student journalists took their grievances to federal court, with mixed outcomes.

No organization achieved the longevity and reach in serving as a depository for the high school underground press of CHIPS. Founded in 1969, it operated from various locations: Naperville, Illinois; Houston, Texas; Washington, DC; and finally, Ann Arbor, Michigan. This syndicate lasted five years before its decline in 1974, officially closing in 1979. But before we delve into CHIPS, it's important to highlight the efforts of high school students in the South, who also created a regional underground newspaper. The Southern Student Organizing Committee (SSOC), a progressive white student organization supporting civil rights, sought to organize high school students. Activists found an ideal candidate whose recent misfortune presented an opportunity of a lifetime.

Grant Cooper and the Southern High School Underground Press

"There was no better time to grow up," former SSOC member Grant Cooper told me at the end of our interview. Our two separate conversations, which lasted nearly four hours, explain why he felt this way. Born in New Orleans, Louisiana, in 1952, Cooper was raised in a family of five. His mother, from Covington, Louisiana, graduated as valedictorian of her high school. After finishing, she joined the Women's Army Corps during World War II and worked as a librarian. She soon met his father, Arthur Cooper, a Jewish man (she was a French Catholic). After the war, she persuaded Arthur to move back to Louisiana, where they settled in New Orleans, both attending Tulane University and living in the married student dorms. Both of his parents held liberal worldviews. They participated in voter registration drives and supported racial integration, civil rights, and various other causes. "I grew up in that milieu," Cooper recalls. His father worked as a psychotherapist, and his mother later became a social worker. "What some people called a red diaper baby," Cooper reflects, "but my parents, they were kind of socialists when they were in college, but they became more just mainstream liberals when I was growing up." He was raised Catholic and had no idea about his Jewish heritage until he was fourteen when his mother told him, "If Nazis ever took over in America, they would come to get you." For a brief period, Grant's family lived in New York for Arthur's job. "I got both worlds of the Yankee, Northeastern culture and education, and New Orleans." Yet, Grant often felt different. Up North, his friends said he had a Southern accent, but when he returned to Louisiana, his friends told him he sounded like a Yankee.[6]

Grant excelled in school, consistently earning A's, but he felt rebellious as his teachers could not match his intellectual thirst. He questioned them on various subjects, and "my teachers didn't seem to have the answers." By junior high school, he had read numerous books about Vietnam, civil rights, and political science. His political activities led to his expulsion from the Orleans Parish Schools. His father met with the superintendent to negotiate a way for

Headshot of Grant Cooper at seventeen when he was the high school organizer for SSOC. Courtesy of Grant Cooper.

his son to make up the missed time from his dismissal. The only school his father could get him admitted to was Booker T. Washington High School, where he became the only white student there. "It was a great experience," he remembers. "I made a lot of friends, and I really enjoyed the summer."[7]

After completing summer school, he re-enrolled at Fortier High School, where he frequently clashed with school officials and students who opposed his political views. He refused to pledge allegiance to the flag, citing a founding father's assertion that people should neither worship flags nor make oaths. Wearing a black armband to school after the assassination of Dr. Martin Luther King Jr. sparked a confrontation with a group of working-class students known as greasers or hoods. They surrounded him and demanded he remove the armband by the end of the day. Cooper refused, narrowly avoiding a beating thanks to a muscular Black student who offered him protection. "It was just like in the Ten Commandments when Moses parts the Red Sea," he recalls. "When he walked up to me, put his arm around my shoulder, and all the other white kids backed off." Fortier High had its own underground newspaper, *The Finger*, in the fall of 1968. In its first issue, the paper highlighted how both Black and white students questioned hair and dress regulations and the presence of military recruiters on campus. It

The Voice of the Movement 117

demanded a voice in school policy, stating, "It would be very nice of them to hand over this right, but . . . we are dealing with people who run the schools like their own personal kingdoms . . . so the power must be taken." Cooper's friends also expressed certainty that some substitute teachers were actually undercover police officers. "We knew it," Cooper asserts. "We could tell them because they wore a certain type of dress shoe that police wore that was always shined. No other teacher or no other substitute teacher or anybody wore those shoes."[8] There is validity to the claim. The New Orleans Police Department Intelligence Division had indeed been monitoring Cooper and the Fortier High School SDS as early as August 1968. That month, an informant published a memo about a meeting with member Robert Berschinski, who reportedly discussed committing disruptive acts. In addition, the police had confiscated a leaflet the group published in September 1968, which demanded "the immediate removal of all undercover and uniformed police from the campus and vicinity of our school."[9]

Cooper organized off campus as well. After learning about SDS, he discovered that interested individuals could form local chapters. He found the SDS address in the library, sent a letter and money, and formed a chapter at Fortier High.[10] But he likely had no idea about the FBI's anxiety over high school SDS chapters. In May 1968, the New Orleans field office noted that New Left organizations had expanded in the city over the past six months and warned Hoover, "an attempt to organize SDS chapters in two high schools in New Orleans was imminent." The office recommended counterintelligence measures, including anonymous phone calls to students' parents. It's unclear whether Hoover approved this, but by October, the office reported the existence of these chapters. It believed neither the students nor their parents "understand the true goals and aims of the SDS." It again suggested anonymous calls and letters to parents, "advising them of their child's affiliation with SDS may help to curtail their success in building SDS chapters in the high schools." By year's end, the FBI had four high school SDS chapters under investigation.[11] Contrary to the FBI's suspicions of the New Orleans Citywide High School SDS's alleged sinister nature, it aimed to empower students against repression. "United into a strong and working organization," member Berschinski stated, "we students can stand up and let our voices be heard."[12]

Cooper stumbled upon a fortuitous opportunity when he met a member of SSOC. Founded in 1964 by young white students who had been part of SNCC and striving for progressive change in the South, SSOC operated out of Nashville, Tennessee. Initially focused on civil rights, the organization expanded its agenda to include opposing the Vietnam War and the draft, challenging in loco parentis policies on Southern campuses, supporting women's liberation, and fostering interracial organizing campaigns among Southern industrial workers. It formed on the belief that white Southerners would join its cause if approached by fellow Southerners, emphasizing Southern distinctiveness. Over time, SSOC gained more traction on Southern campuses than SNCC or SDS. But most Southern whites opposed its mission, and many who might have shared its values chose not to get involved. Attacks from SDS, a lack of "sharp analytical focus," and internal factions led SSOC to disband in June 1969.[13]

Grant eventually became a paid staff organizer with SSOC in 1968 and 1969, its final two years of existence. One night in the French Quarter, while partying with two friends, he crossed paths with Jim Rumley, a union organizer and "super radical kind of guy," according to Cooper. Their conversation left quite an impression on Rumley, who, upon returning home, informed SSOC organizer Lynn Wells about his new acquaintance. Wells, who had a "fiery personality, a passion for white organizing, and an unrivaled ability to motivate young whites to support SSOC," wanted to expand the group's reach to high schools. In 1968, SSOC had published a leaflet titled "High School Organizing in the South," declaring, "In nearly everywhere except the South, a raging battle is being fought and won against the high school administration." Although this statement somewhat ignored the long history of Black teenage activism in the region, it did signal SSOC's awareness of the high school movement. Seeing Cooper's promise, Wells reached out to him. Cooper, recently expelled from school, sought permission from his father, Arthur, who had grown tired of picking him up from juvenile detention. Wells and Rumley traveled to New Orleans to meet Arthur. Cooper recalls, "They apparently impressed him that they would take care of me and keep me out of trouble." They had limited success in that avenue, but "it was infinitely better than just staying in New Orleans." Arthur gave them his blessing, and Cooper became a paid SSOC staffer, complete with a salary, a vehicle, and a gasoline credit card.[14]

He headed to SSOC's headquarters in Nashville. There, he received informal training, mainly absorbing information and meeting people. The staff wanted to publish a South-wide high school newsletter, which Cooper eventually named *Iceberg*. It was the first, and likely the only, regional underground newspaper geared toward high school students in the South. "It's kind of a weird name because we're in the South and there's no icebergs," he remembers. But the name symbolized the visible fraction of the activism occurring in Southern high schools, hinting at the larger movement beneath the surface. Unlike HIPS, *Iceberg* was not a syndicate. Instead, it sought to inform Southern students about their peers' activities throughout the South. Cooper used an IBM electric typewriter in the office to publish the document.[15]

Cooper also traveled for SSOC. He drove "an old, beat-up Volkswagen or something. And they wanted me to go to different cities." SSOC's various chapter houses reached out to him whenever local high school students sought assistance. His first assignment took him to Richmond, Virginia, where he met with students eager to organize. "I helped them start their own little underground newspaper, helped them learn how to organize, how to try to work on things, how to attract membership, all that kind of stuff," he recalls.[16] In Hermitage, a suburb northwest of the city, students at Hermitage High School formed the Hermitage Student Union. This off-campus group advocated for higher teacher salaries, protection for minority groups, and more emphasis on Afro-American history. School officials viewed it as suspicious. In October 1968, Principal Paul G. Watson told reporters, "There was evidence that indicated the possibility of outside influence that could have been contradictory to the best interest of the school." Sources pointed to the ACLU. The principal addressed the student body, later claiming the unrest was settled.[17] Cooper's report in *Iceberg*, however, painted a grimmer picture. With intimate knowledge of the situation, he described the group's "unbelievable" repression. He wrote—perhaps with some exaggeration, given the lack of verification—that several leaders had been expelled, physically disciplined by their parents, and that "the FBI cooperated with local authorities in harassing one guy, and one student was shot, not badly, in the back by local right-wingers." "More than anything," he added, "this group needs moral support." He then provided its mailing address.[18]

SSOC chapters listed Cooper as a contact in their newsletters. In December 1968, the North Carolina SSOC acknowledged that "the high school is the next arena in North Carolina." It briefly reported on racially charged incidents in Durham and Chapel Hill, as well as the creation of underground newspapers in Greensboro and Charlotte, *Kaleidoscope Eye* and *Inquisition*, respectively. The group had contact with high school students in eight cities across the state. It informed readers that "Grant Cooper . . . will be around for a while helping the folks get together."[19] Cooper had visited various communities throughout the South: Charlottesville, Virginia; Fayetteville, Arkansas; Birmingham, Alabama; and others. "I was like a celebrity," he remembers, but he did not think of himself that way at the time. "A lot of teenagers would have happily signed up for doing what I was doing. It was fun, it was really fun."[20] By February 1969, the Georgia SSOC chapter mentioned *Iceberg*, noting "two thirds of its mass below the surface, the high-school movement continues to grow at a phenomenal rate."[21]

The first issue of *Iceberg* appeared in January 1969. Its front cover declared "CONFORM OR ELSE!" in bold letters, accompanied by an image of police in riot gear wielding batons. In his introduction, Cooper wrote, "First, you're going to want to know who puts it out. I do. Who am I? I'm the high school organizer for the Southern Student Organizing Committee." He emphasized that he was not "some old cat trying to stir up trouble in the high school," but rather someone who recently "got kicked out of high school in Ole' New Orleans, and now I'm doing some organizing." The paper aimed to "help all high school students throughout the South relate their own experiences and accomplishments." Cooper highlighted the growing number of students "getting kicked out of school, using drugs, refusing to comply with the harsh Southern dress codes, and standing up against the racism which is prevalent in Southern 'educational policies." He made it clear: "It is those students who refuse to conform to a society in which war and racism are integral parts that this newspaper is for."[22]

Iceberg reported on news involving Southern high school students. Some accounts were firsthand reporting from Cooper's trips, and others were wire stories. In Oak Ridge, Tennessee, Cooper observed 150 students, along with "twenty-five concerned parents and about twenty-five hecklers," discussing district problems. He noted that about fifteen members expressed interest in creating a paper. They came from largely upper-middle-class liberal households, and their parents allowed the group to hold meetings in their homes. "I'll never forget, they gave me a check" for $50, he remembers, "a lot of money back then, to help me with my expenses." Writing in the *Iceberg*, he concluded with, "If you want to know more about the Oak Ridge High School Movement, the person to write is David Levy." Other stories included the formation of a citywide SDS high school chapter in New Orleans, underground newspapers in Charlotte and Atlanta, and independent student organizations in Nashville and Lakeland, Florida. One story, reprinted from HIPS, covered 800 Black students in Swan Quarter, North Carolina, who were boycotting classes to protest the county's integration plan, which "would utilize only the white schools."[23]

Though *Iceberg* did not declare itself a syndicate, it functioned similarly. It reprinted a review of Malcolm X's autobiography from the *Inquisition*, and a story about the student strike in New York City from *A Lump of Sugar*. The paper asked readers to "send in articles, poems, letters, ideas, pictures, subscriptions, and threats" to the post office box, charging $1 a year for students and teachers, and more for "people who can afford it."[24]

By the second issue, *Iceberg* had slightly expanded its operations with another contributor, Bonye Jacobs, "who was 'forced' out of high school in Atlanta." Cooper and Jacobs reported a strong response to the first issue, stating they were "up to our ears in mail." They were surprised by the level of political activity in major Southern cities and "never dreamed there was so much happening in so-called 'isolated places.'"[25] While the publication's reach remains unknowable due to its brief existence and lack of archived data, it had tremendous reach. In April 1969, the San Antonio FBI field office received inquiries from the Intelligence Community of the Armed Forces about *Iceberg*. Military officials received the publication unsolicited because their children had copies. The San Antonio office viewed this as "a golden opportunity to institute a counter-intelligence program to thwart this publication," and suggested to the Memphis field office that it establish a liaison with the postal inspector in Nashville to "see if a counter-intelligence program is feasible." But no such operation likely occurred since the publication no longer existed by then.[26]

Cooper and the SSOC staff often served as field correspondents. On February 7, 200 students at Jonesboro High School in Jonesboro, Georgia, walked out of school to protest various grievances, from the right to smoke on campus to the lack of basic amenities like toilet tissue, paper towels, and doors on the girls' restroom stalls. *Iceberg* covered this story, arguing that protests could occur anywhere. "People reading the article about the walkout in New Orleans probably read it and said, 'That's really something, but it can't happen here,'" it wrote. But "before the walkout, nobody thought it would happen." A few days later, a group of SSOC staffers visited Jonesboro High to interview the principal. "As we walked in, the few students who were left noticed our freakiness, and asked us if we were from SDS," they recounted. "We said some of us were in SDS[;] . . . most of them cheered us on, and some gave us peace signs." The principal, wary of further unrest, did not want to attract attention. However, the reporters learned that students were planning to start an underground newspaper and Black history courses. They concluded, "Maybe this article will show some of us that if it happened in Jonesboro, with its one main street, 'It can happen here.'"[27]

By March 1969, Cooper articulated the evolution of the Southern high school movement in an SSOC newsletter. "No longer do we have to talk about how New York and West Coast high school students are moving," he argued, highlighting the "unbelievable progress" made in the South across college, GI, and labor organizing, as well as in Black and women's liberation. "Instead of rejecting our Southern heritage, . . . we are learning that we have a common struggle with that of our militant ancestors—the struggle for self-determination," he contended. "And self-determination is exactly what we as high school students don't have." He listed numerous rights and privileges that students lacked and announced an upcoming conference.[28]

Traveling and organizing consumed much of Cooper's time, leaving little for producing the *Iceberg* beyond three issues. Yet, Cooper played a pivotal role in planning a South-wide high school conference in Atlanta over Easter weekend, April 5–6.[29] Although antiwar conferences had long united geographically distant high school students, few such events had taken place in the South by 1969. The Church of the Master hosted the conference. Expected speakers included SSOC members, former SDS president Carl Oglesby, and others. The agenda featured film showings from Newsreel and workshops covering "radical Southern history," women's liberation, Black Power, high school organizing, underground media, the university, and other topics. Attendees would be fed and housed, with expectations for a "large number of high school students from every Southern state."[30]

About seventy students gathered in Atlanta. Registration began on Friday night at the office of the *Great Speckled Bird*, followed by informal discussions. Saturday morning commenced with Southern Newsreel's films on the Black Panthers, a Berkeley demonstration, and other political events. Attendees then debated the films' political content, nonviolent tactics, and the "question of class struggles in the United States." Afternoon workshops focused on Black Liberation, the draft, and Marxism. Jacobs noted the students' "interest and enthusiasm," which indicated they sought more than just "fun and games." SDS National Secretary Mike Klonsky addressed topics ranging from high school repression to the Chinese revolution. Students shared stories about activities at their local high schools, learning new approaches to common problems. Cooper recalls all the workshops, including one where a Black artist had young Black women pose, drawing them to showcase their beauty. Sunday morning discussions centered on women's liberation and a conference critique. Attendees voted on motions, and Jacobs felt satisfied. "The conference proved the growing political awareness of high school students and the people who attended went back to their schools and homes better prepared to deal with local situations," she reported. "And everyone agreed, 'We're going to get together more often.'"[31]

The collapse of the SSOC in June 1969 marked the end of its high school organizing efforts. On April 9, police arrested Cooper and two others for loitering while picketing in front of Fortier High in support of striking teachers. Taken to the Juvenile Bureau, police and FBI officials interrogated him about his activities with SSOC. Unbeknownst to Cooper, Hoover had informed the New Orleans field office in March about his involvement with SSOC, an activity permitted by his parents following his December arrest. Hoover's directive stated that if Cooper were arrested out of state, the division should "discreetly alert Orleans Parish juvenile authorities who could then arrange" his transfer to Orleans Parish. Cooper was held on a $2,500 bond, a sum his family struggled to raise for two weeks. Tragically, during this incarceration, Cooper's mother passed away. Upon release, he faced charges for a forgotten vagrancy arrest, being a "'neglected child without parental supervision,'" and congregating on the street without lawful reason. A writer for the *Finger* reported that Cooper "believes that the entire encounter with the law was nothing but an attempt on their part to put an end to his expression of political and social beliefs." The writer concurred with this assessment.[32]

Despite these challenges, Cooper eventually obtained his GED and later, a bachelor's degree from Louisiana State University. Meanwhile, SSOC's dream of a united Southern high school movement had ended.[33] By 1969, HIPS, *Iceberg*, and FRED (the acronym stood for nothing), a Chicago-based syndicate, had all folded. The absence of any regional or national syndicate or publication left a void in the growing movement. But one student in a Chicago suburb saw this absence as a golden opportunity. What began as a local venture soon snowballed into a national syndicate, continuing well into the mid-1970s.

Cooperative High School Independent Press Syndicate

When John Schaller first set up his press syndicate, he simply wanted to link high school underground papers across the Chicago area. He could hardly have imagined that he was laying the groundwork for what would become the largest and longest-running newspaper exchange for teenagers in the country. Born in rural Wisconsin in 1952, he grew up with a father who was a small-town minister, later transitioning into consulting, and a mother who managed responsibilities outside the home. The couple had six children, and Schaller's mother worked as her husband's secretary. The family moved frequently when Schaller was a child to various cities and suburbs. At fifteen, he lived in Berea, Ohio, and later in Naperville, Illinois, a predominantly white enclave on the outskirts of Chicago. Schaller recalls knowing of only one Black family in the area. The casual racism of the townspeople jarred him as he naively believed that such attitudes did not exist. On the other side of the world, the escalating Vietnam War politicized him further, and he campaigned for Democratic candidate Eugene McCarthy.[34]

In September 1968, at the start of his junior year, Schaller developed an interest in underground high school newspapers. He joined a group of students who had already established an alternative publication the previous year. In December, Schaller and his friends discussed their own venture, and by January, they had launched a paper called *Alternative*. Like many other student-run publications, it focused on campus life, tackling issues such as the draft, racism, and contemporary social concerns. However, their efforts soon drew the ire of the school administration, leading to an attempt to ban the newsletter and a brief suspension for Schaller. "All of that got me involved in politics, and I sort of moved away from science and math interests and decided I wanted to spend my time doing political work," he recalls.[35] In an article documenting the history of CHIPS, he wrote, "It wasn't long before we started feeling the isolation that nearly every similar paper seems to feel." The isolation inherent to many underground papers soon set in. Maintaining contact with like-minded peers proved challenging for him. Schaller sought to bridge this communication gap. By April, he envisioned creating a syndicate connecting papers in nearby suburbs. It took weeks of searching, but he eventually found three other papers with accessible addresses, though he knew more existed. In May, the Chicago Area Draft Resisters hosted a one-day conference for high school newspaper staff. Several members of *Alternative* attended and conceived the idea to start a regional syndicate.[36]

CHIPS sought to fill a void. The high school underground press underwent a significant evolution after the formation of HIPS in 1968. When its editors ceased operations in 1969, new regional press syndicates filled the void. In Chicago, high school students launched FRED in February of that year, aiming to "upgrade the writing in Chicago's many high school underground sheets." By July 1969, FRED had garnered 250 subscribers and operated out of a rundown second-story apartment, churning out content on a mimeograph machine. It achieved a dedicated following, but financial difficulties led to FRED's closure in the fall of 1969.[37] In June 1970, teenage writers in Indianapolis created the Indianapolis High School Press Service to "help out all High School alternate papers." It had "arranged for exchange subscriptions among papers," but likely had a short run.[38]

The summer proved uneventful, but things soon changed. By September, CHIPS counted only six members and had sporadic contact with a few other papers. Slowly, though, the network began to expand. Students from outside the Chicago area reached out to ask about membership. With HIPS having ceased operations, CHIPS inadvertently stepped into the role as the de facto national organization for the high school underground press. Over time, its influence grew, with an average of four or five papers joining each month.[39] Recognizing the financial constraints faced by most high school papers, CHIPS adopted a policy of inclusivity. "It will not cost anything to join CHIPS and there will not be any kind of fee to be a member," it declared. The only expense was postage—each member would send a copy of their paper to every other member and subscriber, along with five copies to CHIPS.[40] However, by April 1970, this system proved unsustainable. The cost of postage and the logistical challenge of distributing copies to every member became a significant burden. In response, CHIPS devised a new approach. Each paper would send enough copies of their issues to CHIPS, which would then compile them into monthly exchange packets. Each packet, containing one copy of every participating paper, would be sent to all members and subscribers, with additional copies stored at CHIPS headquarters—Schaller's home in Naperville.[41]

With assistance from two underground press writers, he published a six-page booklet on how to start a high school underground newspaper. It was a necessary document that addressed many of the logistical hurdles students encountered. Many students simply had no idea where to begin. What type of paper should they use? How could they access printing machinery, fund ongoing circulation, and recruit writers?[42] Communication posed another issue. Most students had no awareness of the existence of teenage-oriented underground newspapers beyond their own schools or communities. Repression was the final issue. Unlike community-oriented publications, which publishers distributed publicly and attracted dedicated readerships, administrators deemed high school underground newspapers as unlawful for simply existing on campus. They feared losing control over the students would reflect poorly on the broader community. A high school principal from a Cleveland suburb explained, "The paper has to represent the school and the community . . . If the paper gets in the hands of students with extreme views, [the] parents will start asking what's happening at that school."⁴³ Consequently, publishers, restricted to reaching their audience before, during, and after school, faced the constant threat of suspension and expulsion, leading many to write articles anonymously.

The booklet offered a step-by-step instruction manual on how to assemble staff, the mechanics of ditto and mimeograph machines, cost of production, distribution advice, and other subjects. "A paper that's hard to read loses much of its appeal immediately," the booklet read. The guide offered students clever hacks for accessing printing machines, suggesting "any church in the area with sympathetic pastors; your school office[,] . . . a sympathetic teacher[,] . . . organizations in the area," and other institutions. For financial advice, it told readers that they likely would not get their return on investment, but asking for donations could give them better circulation. It also recommended grabbing a copy of the ACLU pamphlet, *Academic Freedom in the Secondary School*, to be prepared to "defend yourselves" at board meetings. Beginners were encouraged to team up with UPS or affiliated papers to reach a wide audience, blend diverse writing styles and subjects, and obtain a post office box if they began to receive "large out-of-town circulation."⁴⁴

Someone in the Chicago Area Draft Resisters saw the guide and offered to reprint it into something more aesthetically pleasing. "So, I typed it nicer and he put it in a very nice little booklet," he recalls. Afterward, a short blurb on how to get copies of the booklet appeared in various underground newspapers in many major cities across the country. Students began contacting him. "I don't remember; there were probably half a dozen letters in my bed every day when I came home from school. Mostly people requesting that [booklet]," he said. Schaller expanded his one-man operation and created the Chicago Area High School Independent Press Syndicate, which, akin to HIPS and FRED, exchanged copies of student publications with other affiliate members so editors "could see what other kids were doing, reprint articles if they wanted to, and just generally feel like a part of a bigger movement, which may have been the most valuable contribution made."⁴⁵

It took time for writers to realize that CHIPS was the sole remaining high school-oriented press syndicate in the country. With its name sharing four letters with HIPS, many students often conflated the two groups. A group of students from Bloomington, Indiana, who published the *New Amerikan Mercury*, reached out to CHIPS in April 1969. They stated, "We've written to HIPS, and haven't gotten a reply—do you know if there [sic] still in business."⁴⁶ For others, the news took even longer to reach. Beverly Hills High

School student Eric M. Berg wrote to Schaller in January 1970, expressing his confusion. In his letter, he relayed:

> I just tried calling New York HIPS at their [sic] old phone number. Really weird. It turns out that the # has been reassigned to a private phone in a dorm at Columbia University. The guy who answered said that he never heard of them, but that he's been getting all kinds of calls from places like Iowa, etc.
>
> Then I called Liberation News Service, whose offices HIPS used to share. The guy in the office there said that HIPS is defunct, hasn't published for about a year. He said that they put out about 10 packets (I have #9) and then ran out of money. He gave me the phone # where the people from HIPS are; I gave him my address, and he is going to send me their address.
>
> Anyway, now we know: they're dead.[47]

Schaller graduated from high school in 1970 and found himself adrift. He "had no idea how to get by and wanted to continue doing trips at that point, but I was sort of floundering." Seeking direction, Schaller moved first to Chicago and then to Houston, Texas, spurred by a chance meeting with Harrell Graham at the National High School Conference in Chicago that June. Graham, who had published an underground newspaper called *Plain Brown Watermelon* at his school, faced suspension and saw a federal judge uphold the administration's ban on unauthorized publications in 1969.[48] Schaller had "no particular reason" for relocating to Houston, except a desire to leave Chicago and the Midwest behind. "Some friends from Houston were up in Chicago for a high school conference there, and I just decided to go back with them," he wrote.[49]

In Houston, Schaller began *FPS*. He had long envisioned a news service akin to HIPS but intended for high school organizers more broadly, including underground papers. He noticed there "seemed to be a very definite need, and the people who I had talked to about it seemed enthusiastic." Over the summer, he mapped out his plans, wrestling with what to name the publication. Should it be High School News Service? It was not "extremely catchy, you must admit." Perhaps DALE or FISH? "We would then have CHIPS 'n' DALE" or "FISH and CHIPS," but "who is going to take an organization seriously if its initials are Fish and Chips?" He eventually took three letters and placed them on the cover, settling on "FPS." The initials did not stand for anything specific and could "stand for anything you want them to stand for."[50] Operating out of the office of *Space City News*, a citywide alternative publication in Houston, Schaller found enough financial support to sustain himself by selling the newspaper on the street. Intended to be a biweekly publication, *FPS* managed to come out about once a month.[51]

With the help of two collaborators, Schaller launched the first issue of *FPS* on September 11, 1970. At this time, CHIPS boasted thirty-six official members. Schaller informed readers that his relocation to Houston had delayed the distribution of CHIPS packets and that the summer lull had reduced the volume of incoming mail, as most high school underground papers typically did not publish during the summer break. They distributed the first issue for free, and updated readers on subscription rates, with high school papers and groups being charged $4 for six packets. *FPS*, described as an "off-shoot of CHIPS," solicited "all kinds of underground papers and leaflets . . . clippings from magazines and papers about things that are happening in high schools, arts, drawings, comics, and photos."[52]

Although the newsletter lacked the visual flair of more prominent underground publications, it became a vital source of information, keeping readers informed about the activities of high school students nationwide. Its cover conveyed a clear antiestablishment sentiment, declaring, "Public school is not healthy for children and other living things." An article titled "Screw Your School" argued that public schools were "slowly killing every kid in them" and provided suggestions on how to "fight back." Though disclaiming endorsement of these actions, the article advised students on disruptive tactics such as spray-painting, forging teachers' signatures, making stink bombs, and spitting gum onto floors. Other brief pieces in the newsletter referred to public schools as "military prisons" and included statements like, "if you want to get brain-washed let me tell you what to do. Got to get your education in a public school." The first issue also featured a review of the National High School Conference in Chicago, noting that most attendees felt "too much importance has been given to things like dress codes and similar students'-rights issues." It remarked, "We simply cannot spend all our time hassling about length of sideburns while Black Panthers are systematically shot down in the street." Aligning itself with pro-Leftist movements, *FPS* proclaimed that its next issue would aim to "combat the distortions and lies that the straight media has consistently been presenting" about the Black Panther Party.[53]

Schaller stayed in Houston for about six months. By November, he realized that *FPS* had fallen short of its potential. The second issue largely recycled articles from the Liberation News Service (LNS). Publishers lamented, "We still haven't gotten as many actual subscribers as we'd like." The third issue featured only eleven pages, compared to seventeen in the first two newsletters. Schaller, the sole person working on it, struggled with time and financial constraints. Subscription costs barely covered production and mailing expenses. "I had to spend much of my time earning outside income," he admitted. In December 1970, he moved to Washington, DC, to work with the Student Information Center (SIC), an initiative launched in 1969 by the United States Office of Education. The program aimed to provide technical and financial support for student-run programs, offer a national overview of school tensions, and maintain a staff of local students. Schaller had prior contact with its members and recognized the synergies. Soon after, he met them when a group from Houston drove to DC for a convention. Schaller initially had no plans to stay in DC, but after an interview with the staff, he remained for about six months. The center, located in the Georgetown neighborhood, offered him a salary, office space, and equipment for *FPS*. Paul Davies, editor of the *South Dakota Seditionist Monthly*, came to DC for two months to assist with operations. Schaller also received several inquiries after notices appeared in LNS and *Vocations for Social Change*. "Things are running more smoothly now," he noted from DC.[54]

The optimism was short-lived. "Funding ran out," he recalls. "Also, I was proving a little bit too radical for their funders."[55] His assessment was not far off the mark. The antiestablishment politics of *FPS* persisted even as he collaborated with the SIC. The fourth issue of *FPS*, published shortly after his move to DC, included a satirical article about Nixon's press conference with high school students at the White House. "I agree that the public school system is a tool of the pig imperialist United States government," it quoted Nixon as saying.[56] While it's hard to gauge the exact attitudes of the SIC staff, Schaller continued to use deliberate misspellings like "skool," referred to police as "pigs," and featured wire stories from LNS alongside recycled articles from subscribers about high school uprisings.[57] He even described his new home as "the heart of the federal monster," and Georgetown as "the belly of the hip capitalist beast."[58]

Despite SIC's support, Schaller's one-man show was a hefty load. He continued to place ads from the office in DC, which appeared in community-based, underground newspapers across the country. In Cleveland's *Great Swamp Erie da da Boom*, a small sample read: "(FPS) High school students, and anyone of pre-high school age, can receive a packet of 12 high school underground papers for 50 cents from CHIPS. . . . Copies of a 64-page pamphlet 'How to Publish a High School Underground' are available to the same people for 25 cents." It encouraged readers to "send your pennies and nickels to: CHIPS, 3210 Grace St. NW. Washington, DC 20007."[59] But the ad soon became obsolete. Due to growing differences, Schaller left DC in the summer of 1971. Where would he go next? Fortunately, he had stayed in touch with a group of students from Ann Arbor, Michigan, whom he had met at a conference in DC during his initial visit. These young activists had long been organized in their schools and had created an organization poised to absorb CHIPS and *FPS*, thereby saving it from collapse. Still a young man navigating his path in life, Schaller decided to move back to the Midwest and continue his operations from there.[60]

Ann Arbor's Youth Liberation

In Ann Arbor, Schaller became close friends with a group of high school student activists who had long sought to enact reform at both their schools and district wide. Among these fervent youngsters was Keith Hefner, born in 1954 to parents who were both pursuing PhDs in psychology. As the eldest of four, Hefner witnessed his mother's struggle against the entrenched sexism at the medical school where she worked, eventually pushing her toward a career in clinical psychology. But his father remained within the academy.[61]

Hefner's early political awakening began in eighth grade, catalyzed by two events. In 1959, his parents purchased a duplex in a predominantly white neighborhood and rented the other half to a Black woman and her three children. This act of integration did not go unnoticed. They were harassed, threatened with the revocation of city building permits, and even faced a stop-work order after erecting a fence to protect their children from street traffic. The city's snowplow tore down part of the fence, which his parents repaired without a permit. Eventually, the family moved away, ending the sense of camaraderie Hefner shared with them.[62]

Those formative years stayed with Hefner. As he matured, the disparaging stereotypes and depictions of Black people he encountered clashed with his personal experiences. "It was like cognitive dissonance because, well, that wasn't my experience," he recalls. Peers would make racist comments, and he would think, "What are you talking about? I don't think you've ever met a Black person and you're saying this stuff. I didn't consciously think that, but I unconsciously thought that." Furthermore, his parents subscribed to *Ebony* magazine. Hefner often read stories about the civil rights movement, Black middle-class life, entertainers, and athletes. These narratives presented a stark contrast to the negative portrayals of Black men in local news and media. He also found in *Ebony* images of prom queens from Historical Black Colleges and Universities, an acknowledgment of Black beauty that mainstream culture ignored. "I'm just a ten-year-old kid starting to be interested in girls. And I'm like, well, yes, these girls are pretty, but they're not being portrayed as pretty anywhere else," he reflects.[63]

Ann Arbor itself was a hotbed of youth activism. In May and June 1968, Ann Arbor High School experienced a week of racial tensions sparked by a curriculum questionnaire that Black students found discriminatory. The unrest led to suspensions and the cancellation of classes for several days.[64] The district saw further protests in September 1968 over dress codes, with students at Pioneer High School threatening a walkout after officials suspended three male students for violating the school's long hair policy.[65] One particular controversy spurred Hefner to create alternative literature. A school newspaper reporter wrote a story about the football coach's refusal to let a Black player be quarterback. Culturally, coaches believed that Black players lacked the intelligence and leadership capabilities to play key positions such as quarterback, middle linebacker, and center, a stereotype pervasive from the collegiate to the professional levels.[66] But Hefner recognized a broader issue: "But that builds up into a larger issue. It's not just football players. Where were the Black teachers or the Black administrators? Where are the Black football coaches on and on? Fighting racism on the football team became a set of broader demands that were supported both by students and by the larger community."[67]

Youth Liberation emerged from a loose collective of young activists who published an underground newspaper, discussing national movements such as Black, Women's, and Gay Liberation, as well as the war in Vietnam. They soon realized their own disenfranchisement: they lacked voting rights, were subjected to dress codes, and were dissatisfied with the curriculum. Thus, Youth Liberation formed in 1970, advocating for public schools in Ann Arbor to be run in the interests of the students. It aimed to build a nationwide movement for youth civil rights, akin to Black Power and women's liberation. Additionally, it created a fifteen-point platform modeled after the Black Panther Party's ten-point program. In a bold move, the group even ran a fifteen-year-old ninth grader for the school board in 1972.[68]

Hefner and Schaller did not always see eye to eye. Hefner remembers Schaller as "more of an anarchist or libertarian; he really just thought adults were wrong. He just hated the structure of schools." Although Schaller wrote that *FPS*'s initials stood for anything people wanted it to stand for, it unofficially became known as "Fuck Public Schools." Hefner opposed this incendiary moniker. "To me," he reflects, "public schools have problems," but "public schools [are] also the answer to a lot of problems." When Schaller joined Youth Liberation, the group rebranded the acronym officially to stand for "Freedom, Peace, and Solidarity."[69]

Much like the SIC, Youth Liberation revitalized CHIPS and *FPS*. Despite Hefner's and Schaller's differences, they shared a common vision of youth voice. With an expanded staff and a stable headquarters, CHIPS achieved longevity, avoiding the fate of past high school press syndicates. Youth Liberation published *FPS* as a monthly magazine on children's rights and youth organizing, along with booklets like Schaller's "How to Start a High School Underground Newspaper" and Youth Liberation's "Student and Youth Organizing." Reflecting on its influence, Hefner hoped it "would give young people around the country information and inspiration they needed to fight back against unjust authority."[70]

CHIPS and the High School Underground Press

"We've Moved!" announced the front cover of FPS in its first publication in three months. The October 1971 issue detailed that Youth Liberation had taken over *FPS*, relocating it to Ann Arbor, where it would remain until its end. The issue explained to readers the "political and other differences" with SIC and reported how the staff had spent their time setting up the new office. Youth Liberation, having absorbed both CHIPS and *FPS*, aimed to "develop an extensive literature list." The publication introduced new changes, including yearly subscriptions for $5 for youth and movement groups, and $8 for others—a strategic move given the past challenges that had led Schaller to consider abolishing CHIPS. Now, writers interested in joining CHIPS had to fill out a questionnaire. To receive other papers, editors had to send either fifty copies of their paper or $1 if they did not publish that month.[71]

Frequent moves, however, irritated some subscribers. High school students in Chapel Hill, North Carolina, aiming to start an underground newspaper, voiced their frustration over *FPS*'s various relocations. "You sure are hard to get a hold of. First Wash[ington], then N.Y., now Ann Arbor. What's the deal?" they asked. They shared their plans, noting how a local underground publication had provided *FPS* contact information. "We'd all be real interested to hear what that is about because we have very little money but want to know what is going on in other H.S. across the country," they wrote.[72]

From its new Ann Arbor base, CHIPS engaged in about four years of correspondence with high school students nationwide and abroad. Collecting around 700 publications, the surviving correspondence reveals the diversity yet shared struggles of high school underground newspapers. Some were campus-based, while others had citywide circulation. Inspiring editors sought feedback for improvement. "Please, please send comments and criticism as we want to improve the paper," pleaded a writer from the *Reynolds Bridge*, based in Thomaston, Connecticut. They mentioned learning about CHIPS through communication with other high school newspapers and hoped any information would help their paper.[73] A group of students from Vancouver, British Columbia, expressed, "We'd like to find out how other underground newspapers are funded, financed, and technical hassles like that. Also, about their philosophy and how they're received by the general student population."[74] Meanwhile, a brief note from a student in Stanmore, England, simply requested CHIPS to "send us your weekly news packet to help us with the printing of our school (unofficial) sheet."[75]

CHIPS staffers collected hundreds of high school underground newspapers but had no clue how many such publications existed. Estimates of their prevalence varied. HIPS suggested that around 500 high school underground newspapers circulated, albeit irregularly, on or near campuses in 1969. Meanwhile, UCLA journalism professor Samuel Feldman, after surveying 400 high schools in Southern California during the 1968 to 1969 academic year, discovered that fifty-two schools produced underground publications. Based on Feldman's findings, author Robert J. Glessing extrapolated that if 12.5 percent of the schools in the study had underground papers, then nationwide, with 26,098 institutions listed in the *1968 Digest of Secondary Schools*, the number "would indicate closer to 3,250 such papers than HIPS's estimate of 500." However, Glessing acknowledged that urban areas likely skewed this figure. Regardless of the official count, no one could deny how widespread underground newspapers had become on high school campuses.[76]

CHIPS often required prospective members to complete a detailed questionnaire. This application sought comprehensive information about each publication, including its mailing address, office number, length, circulation, printing methods, and paper size. It also inquired about the publication's inception date, cost, subscription rate, future operational plans, and authorization status for distribution at school.[77] In May 1974, the publishers of the *Chronicle of Current Events* in Covington, Kentucky, sent a $2 money order for the Youth Liberation Student Organizing Kit and requested the addresses of other high school alternative publications and information on joining other press syndicates.[78]

Some of the papers CHIPS received found themselves entangled in legal battles. The outcomes, however, varied significantly. In San Diego, the publishers of *Asian Face* reported that the president of the Asian Club took the principal to small claims court to reclaim the funds the Morse High School Student Government had earned from selling the publication. The question of whether student funds could be used to publish underground newspapers remained unresolved.[79] Another publication CHIPS received, *Corn Cob Curtain*, based in Indianapolis, became embroiled in a legal controversy. After its fifth issue, the school district banned it from all city schools in 1971. Six publishers, with the support of two legal groups, filed a lawsuit in federal court. The case climbed all the way to the US Supreme Court in 1974, propelled by appeals from the school district's attorneys. However, the Court ruled the case moot because, by that time, the publication had ceased to exist, and the publishers had graduated from high school.[80]

CHIPS amassed a robust collection of high school publications, yet this trove only scratched the surface of the underground press scene. Most publishers operated without any correspondence with the organization. Notably absent were publications from conservative students. The underground press, predominantly left leaning, likely held scant appeal for conservatives, who instead created their own underground outlets in reaction to prevailing liberal causes and viewpoints. Akin to conservative activists on college campuses, these writers rarely, if ever, sincerely engaged with their peers' ideas.[81] These publications were typically campus-based, often featuring titles that inverted the names of the newspapers they opposed. In September 1969, during a period of racially charged clashes at Classen High School in Oklahoma City, a group of students published an underground newspaper titled *Get Smart*. This one-page newsletter criticized Black students' afros and attire, as well as the administration's "permissive" stance toward Black students. *Get Smart* positioned itself as a counterpoint to another alternative publication, *Get Down*, and formed to "protect the Classen High School student body from racist extremists who stand in the way of good education at Classen." Unlike *Get Down*, which Principal Wayne Earnest disparaged for its "Black Panther terminology" and critiques of administrators, *Get Smart* evaded scrutiny from school officials. "It'll probably fold up like the other one did," argued one spokesman. *Get Smart*'s mission statement underscored a desire for "student power—the power that comes through education. As long as our halls are infested with those who refuse to obey the common rules of courtesy and traffic, we are glad to have someone in authority in the halls to check incipient riots." One sophomore believed *Get Smart* represented the majority of student opinion, citing, "There are a few race extremists who want to stir up trouble at the rest of the students' expense."[82]

Conservative underground newspapers also garnered support from adults. In June 1970, students at Shawnee-Mission East High School in Prairie Village, Kansas, launched *The Demobilizer*. This publication, created by the debate team, formed in response to *The Mobilizer*, published by the Kansas City High School SMC. The editors felt that *The Mobilizer* presented a one-sided narrative. With 2,600 copies printed and 700 sold, *The Demobilizer's* initial costs were underwritten by editor Ginny Braun's father, vice president of the Heart of America Conservative Club. Such a move was far from unusual. Conservative benefactors have long provided generous financial support to right-wing causes on college campuses, and in this particular case, the high school scene was no different. The publication featured articles critical of campus violence, the women's liberation movement, efforts to ban ROTC on college campuses, and calls for the elimination of the draft. It earned praise from adult supporters.[83]

While CHIPS did receive some publications from Latino, Asian American, and Black students, white writers constituted the majority of the underground press. Additionally, CHIPS ads often ran in community newspapers penned by white radicals. Nonetheless, nonwhite youth created their own newsletters and community publications, which served as outlets for grievances and tools for organizing. An underground newspaper by Asian American high school students in San Francisco in 1971 declared, "This newspaper has been put together by a group of Third World students who feel the oppressions of [George] Washington High and this society and who wish to voice their ideas and opinions."[84] These publications, while often disconnected from national networks like CHIPS, addressed immediate and pressing concerns. In St. Louis, Missouri, students produced an underground newspaper in 1970 called *Street Sheet* that circulated in north-side schools. It critiqued local issues and urged students to "seize control of the schools from the hands of the man and determine our own destiny and curriculum that is relevant to black and not white society."[85]

By 1975, the correspondence between CHIPS and high school student publishers had dwindled. "We weren't getting that many" publications anymore, Hefner recalls. The group continued to publish *FPS* and received some papers, but the economic infeasibility of exchanging them led to a decline in this practice. *FPS* had evolved into a magazine, featuring letters from readers and long-form articles about youth rights and political movements. Nonetheless, its run was impressive: by its final publication in 1979, *FPS* had produced sixty-two issues over nine years, a feat unmatched in the high school alternative press scene.[86]

The underground press did more than any other political development to alert students and other observers to the existence of a national student movement brewing in high schools. Before 1968, no syndicate sought to exclusively gather high school underground papers, and most of these newsletters remained campus-based or citywide. The high school underground press owes much of its success to adult-run syndicates, which provided teenagers with a model to build their own operations. These efforts rose and fell, but nearly all aimed to educate readers about teenagers' political activism in distant communities. While antiwar activism connected isolated students, the high school underground press established robust citywide and national communication networks. Not all readers shared radical views, but many sought a platform to voice their opinions and discuss topics many school officials deemed inappropriate for minors.

While free speech campaigns, antiwar activism, and the underground press were primarily arenas dominated by white youth, the most significant and contentious issues in the high school movement during this period revolved around race. White radicals managed to create citywide and national networks, but these efforts materialized gradually, and participation varied. In stark contrast, when students mobilized around racial issues, they swiftly established citywide coordinating efforts, recruited hundreds, thousands, and eventually over 10,000 participants, and provoked intense reactions from various city institutions.

Part II **Race**

....

She did not speak with anyone from the Black Student Liberation Front or any other Black student organization. Are the only high school radicals white middle class kids?

—Dave Watson, "The Real Radicals in the High Schools,"
  Fifth Estate, no. 83, July 10 to 23, 1969

6 Blowouts, Sit-Ins, and Walkouts
High School Student Uprisings

....

Walnut High School senior Ron Pennington stayed home in Cincinnati, Ohio, during his ten-day suspension from school. On April 30, 1968, he and over 1,400 Black and white students conducted a citywide sit-in that spanned six high schools. They filled hallways, blocked entrances, and handed out fliers, which called for action on a range of grievances affecting Black students. This seemingly sudden act of defiance emerged out of a series of violent and nonviolent incidents in city schools in March. Dr. Martin Luther King Jr.'s assassination on April 4 sparked further unrest, leading schools to close until April 16 as a cooling period. To improve race relations, the biracial Inner-City Council discussed a set of issues with Superintendent Paul Miller. Pennington was there. In a letter to the *Cincinnati Post*, he wrote that Miller "artfully evaded all demands and sidestepped all questions." Little was achieved. Fueling the anger was Miller's refusal to remove School Resource Officers from the high schools, where they had been stationed since October after racial violence struck two schools. The issue was so divisive that school board member Virginia Griffin urged Miller to replace the police with student-led efforts to maintain peace. But Miller dismissed the idea. Meanwhile, other students faced penalties for their activism. Four seniors who had protested the arrest of two Withrow High students were transferred to Guilford School for "guidance and counseling regarding their educational future."[1]

Frustrated by these developments, the Black Student Union outlined a set of demands. It wanted BSUs in every city school, mandatory Black history courses taught by Black instructors, the removal of security forces, and a range of improvements to school facilities and policies.[2] On April 29, leaflets appeared that advertised for a demonstration at the schools. Miller balked at the prospect of this protest. He met with school, police, and city officials and issued a "policy of containment" statement, permitting the demonstration as long as it remained peaceful.[3]

Though the sit-in stayed nonviolent, school and city officials responded with force. Miller ordered ten-day suspensions for 1,306 students across the

Sit-in at Woodward High School, Cincinnati, Ohio. Courtesy of Cincinnati & Hamilton County Public Library, Genealogy & Local History Department.

six schools involved.[4] The Juvenile Court stationed a court referee at each school with orders to place suspended students under house arrest for the duration of their suspension, and to cite any of them who refused to leave campus. At Woodward High, police loaded students who refused to vacate into wagons and took them to Juvenile Court for immediate hearings. Judge Benjamin Schwartz issued a stern warning to parents: failure to keep their children under house arrest would result in contempt charges. The crackdown on a nonviolent protest outraged some residents. A group of adults picketed the Board of Education while carrying signs that read "Listen," "Reinstate All Students," and "Let's Have a Full Hearing."[5]

Pennington was bewildered by the district's heavy-handed response. "Instead of praise for following the American tradition which they learned in school, they were suspended from school for up to two weeks or were arrested," he wrote. To him, the administration's crackdown reeked of hypocrisy. He pointed out that the recent Cincinnati Teacher Union strike had caused more disruption than the sit-ins. "There has been growing discontent with Dr. Miller's policies," he continued. Students "resent having a police officer in every school building," dress codes, and underrepresentation of Black students.[6] Pennington rejected Miller's claim that outsiders organized the sit-ins, noting that "a certain amount of discontent was prevalent" for the demonstration to occur. "Many students feel Dr. Miller is trying to stave off any racial incidents for a month and a half," Pennington noted, "it will be up to the community and the law enforcers to find the solutions to the problems he has caused." In the end, the district yielded to the demands. After Miller met with students and their parents, the school district reinstated the four reassigned pupils and convicted only three persons for trespassing during the sit-ins. More significantly, it agreed to formalize the BSU, create a Black history course in all city schools, and observe Black holidays.[7]

Cincinnati was one of many communities to experience a student uprising that confronted the city's educational system. Across the country, nonwhite students organized some of the largest and most impactful protests for school reform during the late 1960s and early 1970s. As Black Power advocates called for self-determination and community control, Black and Latino students in cities like Boston, Chicago, and Los Angeles led demonstrations that sometimes drew tens of thousands.[8] While the high school movement was multiracial and multiethnic, journalists largely focused on middle- and upper-middle-class white students. One reason for this oversight dealt with reporters overemphasizing the underground press, which remained a majority white domain.[9] Another reason came from the fact that most profile pieces written by journalists focused on white students.[10] Nonwhite students, however, were at the heart of this movement, often organizing around shared issues while addressing unique challenges within their communities. Latino and Asian students, for instance, fought for bilingual education and cultural representation in school curricula. They often gained public support from their families and the community at large. Although many protests were local, smaller actions could trigger vigorous responses from public officials, and uprisings sometimes forced schools to close for extended periods. The ripple effects were felt for months afterward.

There were hundreds, if not thousands, of racially charged high school uprisings across the nation in the late 1960s and early 1970s. Given that the undergraduate population was 95 percent white in 1969, racially-charged protests were far more prevalent in secondary schools than on college campuses. One contemporary study reported 132 racial incidents in twenty-seven states within a four-month period. Another report found that 85 percent of 700 junior high and high schools examined in the study experienced "some type of disruption" between 1967 and 1970.[11] "The high school principal is replacing the college president as the most embattled American," observed a National Education Association official in June 1969.[12] It is difficult to know how many "disruptions" occurred. But by examining one community that experienced multiple student uprisings, we can uncover the issues that ignited them, the varying and intersecting demands of the students, and the community's reaction. This story takes us back to San Francisco, a city with a student population more diverse than many districts across the country. At Mission High School, Black and Latino students came together to organize a unified strike after police brutalized them during a brawl between the two groups. It occurred amid broader unrest in city schools and galvanized the entire community. However, long-standing, local grievances shaped the controversy.

San Francisco's Mission District

Francisco Flores was just an ordinary kid who would emerge as a leader in one of San Francisco's largest high school uprisings. He was born on October 17, 1951, in Stockton, California. His father, from Mexicali, Mexico, and his mother, Carmen, eventually settled in French Camp, San Joaquin County. The relentless heat of Northern California's Central Valley never escaped him. He recalled the midday ritual of darting from one shadow to the next to avoid burning the soles of his bare feet. Cooler evenings brought the barrio alive, a vibrant contrast to the oppressive daytime heat. When Flores was about eleven, his father passed away, prompting Carmen to move him and his two brothers to San Francisco's Mission District. The neighborhood, the city's sole barrio, posed new challenges.[13]

In the early 1960s, the Mission District was the city's poorest community. It had transitioned from its European immigrant roots to a largely Latino population. By 1960, Latinos made up 25 percent of the area's residents, growing to 45 percent by 1970. This diverse community, with ties to Mexico, Puerto Rico, Nicaragua, El Salvador, Chile, and Peru, fostered a sense of *Latinidad*—a shared identity built on unity and commonality. The Mission also housed Black, Native American, Filipino, and American Samoan residents, along with white ethnics, mainly Irish and Italian Americans. Manufacturing jobs disappeared and severely impacted the neighborhood, leading to an 18 percent unemployment rate by 1969. Many residents found work in the service industry, while disillusioned youth often abandoned the job search altogether. Mission High School, where Flores would later enroll, mirrored the area's struggles. The school faced a 35 percent push-out rate, with 25 percent of students absent daily. Only 5 percent of graduates went on to four-year universities, and students' families had the lowest average income in the city, under $5,000 annually. Moreover, 39 percent of the students were bilingual but lacked adequate support beyond basic remedial language programs. In 1969, out of 2,050 students, about 25 percent were consistently absent, with the average student missing eighty-two days a year.[14]

Mission High had also had a history of racial tensions. In the aftermath of the Hunter Point riots in September 1966, where many Black students lived, fistfights between them and white students broke out, which led school officials to dismiss classes midday. On April 16, 1968, these tensions flared violently when unidentified assailants attacked two youths with a pipe, resulting in hospitalization. A second incident occurred shortly after, with four more students beaten and sent home. Police linked these unprovoked attacks to the heightened racial discord following Dr. King's assassination, suspecting involvement from non-student dropouts. The next day, parents, school officials, teachers, police, and students held a meeting to devise strategies to curb the violence. They recommended that the Recreation and Park Department relinquish all or a part of the adjacent Dolores Park to deter "out-of-town troublemakers," install a swimming pool, pave streetcar tracks to prevent students from picking up rocks during altercations, increase campus meetings, conduct police sweeps, involve Police Community Relations workers, and foster greater camaraderie among students. Most of these recommendations likely went unanswered.[15]

Flores began to lay the groundwork for raising awareness about the issues facing his community. For his US History class, he wrote a report on Mexican American history and the social conditions that Latinos in the United States confronted. "I didn't have proper research and writing training," he recalled, but he tackled the assignment with determination. He pulled data from the census, the Economic Opportunity Council—a component of the War on Poverty—demographic information from the San Francisco Unified School District, and he referenced *North from Mexico* by Carey McWilliams. Mrs. Barranco, his teacher, was impressed—so impressed she used his paper as teaching material in her classes. "I was unaware of how that paper would set me up as a student leader," he noted. In another class, an assignment asked students about their inspirations or contemporary sympathies. Flores wrote that he sympathized with SDS. The teacher, intrigued by his response, pulled him aside to ask why. He explained that his sympathy stemmed from watching news reports on SDS and their actions at UC Berkeley. Such sympathy, he admitted, was based on "carnal instinct" rather than "intellectual knowledge." Like many Chicano youth in the late 1960s, Flores developed a deeper sense of ethnic identity and pride. He admired the Brown Berets and their militant stance. As the son of a farmworker, he supported the United Farm Workers Union and its quest for union recognition and labor contracts.[16]

Flores did not need statistical data to grasp the depth of Mission High's troubles. He recalled how, despite the invisibility of the high dropout rate, a return visit years later brought to light the harsh reality. He looked "at the graduation pictures that hang in the main hallway," and to his surprise, "in the year of my graduating class or the years before or after, I did not see anyone I knew." Fridays after lunch morphed into chaotic scenes reminiscent of a party, with students high on drugs populating the hallways. Hall guards, overwhelmed, spent their time chasing down kids for hall passes. "Frequently we would run away from them, and they would chase us," he remembered.[17] Despite the school's diverse student body—450 Black, 680 white, 750 Latino, and 75 Asian students—communication barriers only exacerbated tensions. Edgar Morales, a former student, noted that pupils remained isolated in their respective racial and ethnic groups.[18] Tensions between Black and Latino students were common. Marta Estrella, another former student, admitted to befriending Samoan students out of fear of aggression from some Black youth, seeking their protection due to their physicality.[19]

Flores and his peers wanted to improve the plight of Latinos at Mission High. One morning in gym class, a conversation with a fellow student named Neftali about the Mexican and Mexican American experience sparked a desire to act. They first approached the Spanish student club with their ideas. "To my amazement and disappointment," he recalled, "the group would have none of it; we were turned down." The club's sponsor, Mrs. Buchard, a conservative Latina teacher, dismissed their initiatives with typical belittlement. "We were too young, we didn't know what we were talking about, it was a waste of time, we're being duped by outside agitators," he stated. However, another teacher, Mrs. Barranco, quietly supported them from the background. The club, dominated by recent immigrants, clung to traditional cultural activities like tacos, tostadas, and the jarabe tapatío, which Flores respected but deemed insufficient for addressing issues like high dropout rates, discrimination, and alienation. Realizing their naïveté in expecting unanimous support, Flores and his friends formed an ad hoc group, drafting four demands: relevant education, Latino history classes, Latino teachers, and Latino food in the cafeteria. They had no inkling that their actions at Mission High would spiral beyond their control.[20]

San Francisco's High School Uprisings

The Mission High strike would not happen in a vacuum. From 1968 to 1969, Black and Latino students across the country protested racial injustices and educational inequity. Prior to these uprisings, racially charged student protests had long been centered around segregation and equal access to resources. By the late 1960s, however, protests increasingly called for self-determination and community control. One of the largest uprisings occurred in East Los Angeles in March 1968. Years of inequalities in education and hostile attitudes from school officials led Mexican American students to walk out of school. These walkouts, later called blowouts, involved anywhere from 15,000 to 20,000 Latino and Black youth. Another major school boycott occurred in Chicago. In September 1968, a walkout at Harrison Technical High School sparked additional protests at other city schools. Latino students soon joined their Black counterparts, and about 35,000 students across the city boycotted school on October 14, 1968. Student uprisings, though on a smaller scale, also took place in cities such as Asheville, North Carolina; Denver, Colorado; Seattle, Washington; and elsewhere.[21]

San Francisco's city schools joined the fray in October 1968. Although most people remember the San Francisco State College strike, where a four-month student protest led to nearly 800 arrests from December 1968 to March 1969 and resulted in the creation of a School of Ethnic Studies and a Department of Black Studies, the city's junior high and high schools experienced significant social unrest during this period.[22] The spark occurred at Balboa High School, where racial clashes soon spilled over to the adjacent Denman Junior High School. Fueled by rumors that a Black student had been shot to death, fights between Black and white students erupted. In response, the Board of Education pledged $3,500 to station extra police at Denman Junior High to keep the school operational.[23]

The unrest continued at two schools. On October 23, district headquarters dispatched police to Poly High School after students reacted fiercely to a report their teachers had submitted to the Board of Education. Poly High had undergone significant demographic changes. It hired its first Black principal in the fall of 1968. Black and Filipino students comprised 51 percent of the student body. This change caused concern among some white faculty members over the dwindling number of white students, who had begun transferring to a neighboring school.[24] Around twenty teachers penned a letter to the school board, lamenting what they saw as the decline of Poly High. They criticized the students for drug abuse, on-campus prostitution, low graduation rates, and poor attendance. The letter declared that the school, "continues to decline as an educational institution to the point where it is no longer viable as currently constituted." This incendiary letter enraged about 1,000 Black students, along with some white and Filipino youth, prompting them to walk out of school and march to the school district headquarters. The students met with two school board members, presenting demands for a more inclusive curriculum, improved school facilities, and access to the adjacent Kezar Stadium for recreational use during school hours. The district conceded, agreeing to establish Black history courses, grant students access to the stadium, and strive to hire more Black and Latino teachers. While the immediate fervor subsided, the students chose to drop their demand for the dismissal of the twenty teachers. Still, they remained committed to ongoing negotiations with the school administration.[25]

On the same day as the student walkouts at Poly High, the George Washington High Black Student Union took a stand against murals depicting President George Washington with slaves, which many Black students found deeply offensive. Instead of staging a protest, the students engaged in discussions with administrators to propose an alternative mural. Opinions on the art varied widely. Several teachers insisted that the existing mural remain uncovered.[26] Frustrated by the slow pace of change, some students placed images of Black Panther cofounder Huey Newton and other political revolutionaries over the image, which school officials swiftly removed. After a month of deliberations, both parties reached a compromise: the mural would stay, but a contest would be held for students to create plaques to hang beneath it.[27]

Each incident at these schools differed, but the growing reliance of school administrators on police presence emerged as a common thread. The emerging modern security apparatus in public schools grew rapidly due to the modernization of police departments. School Resource Officers were first introduced in schools in the 1950s and expanded drastically in the 1990s. But there was a spike in the 1960s.[28] This evolution, driven by urban uprisings and the Johnson administration's war on crime declared in March 1965, led to an influx of military-grade weapons and technologies to local law enforcement. The Omnibus Crime Control and Safe Streets Act of June 1968 further empowered police departments with riot-control training and equipment like AR-15s, M4 carbines, steel helmets, batons, masks, armed vehicles, two-way radios, and tear gas.[29] This militarization of police created a pathway for administrators to implement new, intensive security measures, implicitly framing schools—especially those with significant Black student populations—as dangerous. The war on crime targeted schools as federal law enforcement grants supported the creation of school security forces. Over time, school buses and campuses would have electronic surveillance equipment.[30] Justification given by public officials dealt with the framing of school violence and student uprisings as matters of school safety rather than racial justice. This portrayal allowed officials to adopt punitive crime control measures. Furthermore, dialogues about criminality were "reestablished as a racial problem that would continue to face more punitive state responses influenced by broader discourse on youth, race, and crime."[31]

Many of these security measures would expand significantly in the decades that followed, but in the late 1960s and early 1970s, some schools opted to bring in police and security guards. In March 1969, Newark, New Jersey, introduced security guards in eight schools to deter intruders and address student disorder. Many of these guards lacked law enforcement backgrounds but were trained at the Newark Police Academy. School administrators anticipated expanding the program to include 180 full-time employees along with a reserve force.[32] The mere presence of police in schools led to troubling consequences over minor infractions. At Franklin K. Lane High School in Brooklyn, for instance, three students were removed from study hall and arrested after one grabbed a piece of paper from another. They were charged with disorderly conduct, and one youth spent the night in Rikers Island Penitentiary.[33] By 1972, Chicago public schools employed 490 armed guards, 90 percent of whom were off-duty police officers. Their duties included preventing intrusions, curbing potential violence, reporting assaults, and slowing the spread of drug trafficking. A majority of teachers and staff supported their presence on campus.[34]

In San Francisco, the deployment of police in schools also received support from some parents. The guardians of children in Catholic schools petitioned Police Chief Thomas Cahill, the superintendent, and the Municipal Railway to increase law enforcement around their children's schools. They demanded protection from students at Everett Junior High and Mission High, "who consistently 'cut' classes." Calling for the hiring of truant officers, the parents wrote, "At the times when it has been necessary to call the police, we have seen that their presence is a deterrent to the physical molesting of our girls. . . . This problem," they continued, "is immediate as daily danger to our girls is unpredictable due to the freedom these truant students have on the streets." They also requested more streetcars to transport their children before the troubled schools dismissed. "Immediate action is imperative because of the daily dangers to our daughters," they urged.[35]

On October 24, 1968, San Francisco Mayor Joseph L. Alioto addressed the escalating unrest in the city's high schools. After initially urging everyone to "cool it," Alioto's speech mirrored those of many liberal politicians of the era who dismissed urban uprisings as mere hooliganism or the work of outside agitators. "Every generation of Americans . . . has had its quota of punks," the mayor declared. Demonstrating a posture of toughness, Alioto called for schools and police officials to "segregate those who are provocateurs," based on the belief that a few troublemakers caused the disturbances. He insisted that schools remain open and that officials should not hesitate to call in the police if needed. Although he acknowledged that students had legitimate grievances, he overlooked the fact that little had been done to address these issues. "So, we're telling the school department that it's their business to keep the schools open and to call upon the police department for all the help they need," he said.[36]

The diversity of protests notwithstanding, school authorities grew increasingly alarmed about the growing unrest in the city's schools. Incidents like the walkout at Poly High, the protest over the mural at George Washington High, a failed student boycott at Lincoln High, and Black students at Balboa High demanding the removal of their principal led Superintendent Robert Jenkins to vow a crackdown on student agitators. Reflecting the schools' escalating dependence on law enforcement, Jenkins stated, "Those who incite students or threaten teachers will be turned over to the police to be prosecuted under the full provisions of the law." He also pledged to allocate funds for additional security guards and to have school entrances monitored to prevent unauthorized access.[37] Jenkins attributed the social unrest in high schools to outside agitators and refused to acknowledge the district's failure to address long-standing grievances about racial equality among students and their parents. The presence of police officers and security guards did little to quell the protests and violence.

The get-tough measures seemed to make rebellion in the schools even more likely. In November, violence in San Francisco's high schools deteriorated. Random acts of violence erupted at several schools. On November 1, a minor explosion in a garbage can at Balboa High injured one student and shattered two windows. The next day, a teenager fired a gun at the principal's office at Galileo High School. In mid-November, arsonists targeted both Galileo High and Woodrow Wilson High Schools, causing thousands of dollars in damage.[38] These incidents went unsolved, making it difficult to ascertain their motive. "Authorities often describe vandalism as a wanton act, making it seem both purposeful and purposeless," noted education scholar Campbell F. Scribner.[39] Whether it was hooliganism or alienated youth rebelling against a society that schools represented as racially and socially inequitable, these incidents followed a period of constant campus disorder, prompting school officials to take emergency measures.

In mid-November, the Board of Education voted to establish security forces to protect the city's schools, a move that ignited controversy. Critics argued that principals were better suited to handle disciplinary issues and that police presence should be reserved for emergencies only. Supporters of the new security measures believed that radicals intent on disrupting the schools had orchestrated much of the unrest. One member of the Service Committee on Public Education cited the lack of evidence of outside agitators. In the end, the school district approved the deployment of security guards. Administrators insisted that the guards would protect schools from unauthorized guests.[40]

School officials remained resolute in their crackdown on disorder. In December, Superintendent Jenkins issued a memo to all school principals and assistant principals. The memo declared that the primary issue facing schools was "unauthorized personnel." Jenkins mandated that all doors remain locked, with custodial staff periodically checking them. He claimed that "marches and demonstrations" were "unnecessary" because proper channels already existed for students to voice their concerns. The memo also announced the hiring of ten school patrol aides to safeguard the schools and respond to emergencies.[41] Jenkins continued to ignore the underlying issues that fueled campus unrest, and these get-tough policies failed to break the cycle of rebellion in San Francisco schools. In December 1968, Black students at Lincoln High organized a sympathy strike with San Francisco State, demanding the creation of a Black studies program. However, the principal thwarted their efforts and accused them of being influenced by leaflets distributed by members of the Third World Liberation Front.[42]

City residents had mixed reactions to the violence. In December, obstetrician and gynecologist Paul Scholten, who also edited the San Francisco Medical Society's monthly publication, observed, "Almost every doctor who cares for adolescents has seen victims of beatings on school property, and physicians who staff emergency rooms have treated many such patients." He noted that real estate agents struggled to sell homes near troubled schools, and concerned parents were increasingly enrolling their children in private schools.[43] Some Black parents vehemently opposed the growing police presence in and around campuses. In March 1969, the Concerned Black Parents organization, representing families of George Washington High students, sent a letter to the district superintendent demanding an end to Tactical Squad harassment and urging the principal not to call the police for juvenile issues.[44]

The racial turmoil in city schools galvanized Asian American students, whom school officials had long regarded as docile. In 1968, during a meeting where Black parents discussed community control over the schools, PhD candidate Ling-Chi Wang from UC Berkeley highlighted that Chinese students were also getting the short end of the stick.[45] But broader discussions of racial inequality in public schools overlooked the challenges faced by these students. Wang testified before the US Senate Select Committee on Equal Educational Opportunity on March 5, 1971. He reported that some teachers mocked Chinese accents, while others, particularly older ones, flocked to schools with predominantly Chinese student bodies, viewing these students as submissive, hardworking, and unlikely to challenge authority. At Galileo High, where the student body was 64.8 percent Chinese, the faculty was over 95 percent white, with a mere 3 percent representation of Chinese people. Wang noted that the school's issues with absenteeism, suspensions, disciplinary problems, disciplinary transfers, dropouts, and delinquent behavior stemmed from the unheeded demands to recruit more Chinese teachers.[46]

Asian American activism took a visible turn in February 1969, months after Black students had challenged the mural at George Washington High. Chinese students at the same school asked the assistant principal to recognize Chinese New Year as a regular school holiday. When the assistant principal deferred the decision to the Board of Education, the students raised the Chinese, Japanese, and North Vietnamese flags on the school's flagpole and sprayed "Yellow Power" on the front of the school auditorium. This bold statement marked a significant shift, as Asian students began to voice their demands more forcefully at other high schools as well. At Lowell High, an editorial argued that the Asian population, which constituted 30 percent of the student body, deserved to "hold significant standing within the school's power structure."[47] Parents of Chinese students also demanded that the school district cater to the needs of their children. In late February 1969, about 150 members of the Concerned Chinese for Action and Change picketed the district headquarters, demanding Asian studies, Asian American history, increased adult education, and the hiring of faculty who could "understand and identify with the Chinese community."[48]

Within this national and local context, Flores and his peers would launch the city's most significant high school student uprising. Catalyzed by an incident of police violence, Black and Latino students united to confront racial inequity and the increasing security measures at their school.

Mission High School Strike

The Mission High strike unfolded against a backdrop of social unrest in San Francisco's schools and the militarization of the police department. Unlike the other student uprisings, the controversy at Mission High extended for months. The initial spark ignited in late January when a group of Black students attacked Flores's friend, Edy Morales, following a confrontation during lunch in the cafeteria. Morales, an immigrant from Managua, Nicaragua, had arrived in the United States in 1963 with his five siblings and mother. He spoke only Spanish in an English-dominated elementary school environment, an experience that left him feeling "very lonely" and isolated. By the time Morales started at Mission High in 1966, he gravitated toward others who shared his cultural background. Typically, students hurried to get lunch early to secure a spot at the adjacent park. Morales and others noticed that if a Black student stood in line first, they would allow others to cut in front of them to get free lunch. On January 23, Morales's brother attempted to cut the line. A Black boy shoved him, to which Morales replied by calling him a "stupid nigger." The situation escalated as the two boys agreed to fight outside but backed down when weapons were drawn.[49]

Later that day, as Flores, Morales, and their friends sat at their usual lunch spot by the stairway, fifteen Black teenagers approached them, including the boy Morales's brother had confronted earlier, now joined by his two older brothers. Tensions quickly flared. One student shouted in Spanish, "¿Qué es esta mierda? A darles en la madre" ("What is this shit? Let's beat their ass"). "It just became a rumble," Morales recalled. "Hit who you can, while you can; there were more of them than there were of us. It was a little frightening." The fight, though brief, rapidly escalated as more Latino students and some white students—nicknamed "white shoes" for their distinctive two-tone Catholic school shoes—joined the fray. The Black students regrouped near the girls' gym, preparing for another clash. Meanwhile, trouble brewed elsewhere at Dolores Park. Estrella and a friend watched from a hill as some Black students approached, cursing and throwing a bottle at them.[50]

Police arrived to control the escalating situation. Principal Harry Krytzer reported that 250 to 300 of the school's 2,000 students had been involved in the unrest. To defuse tensions, he invited twenty-five students into his office, but his efforts proved futile. Inside the office, one youth lunged at another, sparking a fight among twelve students who began throwing punches. Observers outside the glass enclosure pounded on the windows until they feared the panes might shatter. The school remained relatively calm the next day despite expectations of further violence. However, reports circulated of students roaming the hallways, committing acts of vandalism, and setting trash cans on fire in the bathrooms. A portion of the Tactical Squad guarded the main entrance as Black students on the steps chanted, "Police off campus." Nonetheless, the police remained on campus until 5:00 p.m. Krytzer, visibly disappointed by the situation, seemed oblivious to its underlying causes. "Some of the young people do not keep their heads in a time of crisis," he lamented. "They follow rather than lead and get caught up in the emotion of the moment."[51]

The Tactical Squad, shortly known as Tac Squad, formed out of the 1966 Hunter's Point riot. Prior to its development, the San Francisco Police Department reluctantly created the Community Relations Unit (CRU) in response to stories in the city's Black newspaper, *The Sun-Reporter*, which frequently reported on police brutality. Police Chief Cahill selected Lieutenant Dante Andreotti to head the CRU and instructed him to go into the community and "teach respect for law and order." But Andreotti had a different vision. He sought to build positive relationships with the community and became quite popular. CRU members attended various social functions, sponsored dances, parties, movies, and sporting events with minority youth. In all, it challenged the conventional wisdom held by San Francisco police that criminals were "social deviants in need of punishment." But most rank-and-file police officers "detested the liberal CRU." Some officers referred to its members as "nigger lovers" or the "commie relations unit." The 1966 Hunter's Point riots provided Chief Cahill with the pretext to undermine the CRU's influence. He pushed for the creation of a special elite unit modeled after Los Angeles's Special Weapons and Tactical Team, which had been formed in response to the Watts riots of 1965. In 1967, Andreotti resigned from the CRU, citing his inability to continue working in what he described as a "general white racist atmosphere." The election of Mayor Alioto marked a turning point. Chief Cahill seized the opportunity to sign General Order 105, establishing the paramilitary Tac Squad. Although initially intended to combat crime and quell urban riots, the Tac Squad increasingly found itself deployed against political activists in the city.[52]

This paramilitary unit famously intervened in many political demonstrations, but school officials had little hesitation in summoning it to campus. In February 1969, a fight broke out in Lincoln High's cafeteria between Black and white students, spurred by false rumors, leaving four students injured, one with a serious stab wound. Principal Reginald Y. Alexander called the Tac Squad to campus and dismissed school early. He attributed the violence to outside agitators.[53] In another incident on March 18, the school board voted to investigate the Tac Squad's conduct after parents and faculty lambasted its actions. Earlier that month, a riot occurred after a basketball game between Woodrow Wilson and Sacred Heart High Schools. But two board members defended the decision to summon riot police. Educators were not completely opposed to police quelling disorder; they just felt the Tac Squad was unnecessary. Additionally, student body president Brenda McArthur accused the unit of beating handcuffed students and hurling degrading and profane language toward Black youth. "We felt it should have been handled by the regular police," she told board members. Another teacher commented that the riot police called teachers "nigger lovers" for trying to protect the students. However, some faculty felt that the riot would have been exacerbated if the Tac Squad had not been summoned.[54]

Throughout the week, an organization called the Mission High Parents Group petitioned Chief Cahill for police protection at schools afflicted by violence. Their formal request sought protection for students both within the school and in the surrounding areas. "We are confident that our Police Department will help to restore order out of the chaos which now exists in our school," the letter read. However, Cahill informed Superintendent Jenkins that he lacked the workers to staff the school on a day-to-day basis. Jenkins responded by saying that the school district was training security agents under a $70,000-a-year plan, assigning one agent to each school.[55]

Violence erupted again on Monday, January 27, at Mission High. The conflict spilled over into Dolores Park, where Black youths wrecked a nearby snack bar, grabbed money from the cash register, overturned tables, and smashed windows in the school cafeteria. School officials called the police to the campus. Dressed in riot gear, the Tac Squad forcefully dispersed about 500 students who were fighting in the park. The youth retaliated by pelting officers with rocks and bottles. As police cleared the small crowds from the streets around the school, they found the windows of Go-Getters Market smashed and some items looted from the display. The police blocked off streets around the school and assisted faculty members and parents in separating the students. Officers reported arresting ten teenagers during the three-hour incident. The *San Francisco Chronicle* captured the chaos with a front-page headline: "Mission Rampage: High School Trouble."[56]

Having endured police violence, the students realized their collective grievances. "We got ourselves together last week to fight the Blacks," read a leaflet distributed by Latino youth. "Now it's time to fight the real enemy."[57] In the days that followed, Black and Latino students presented the principal with two sets of seventeen demands. While school administrators might have perceived these requests as spontaneous, they were deeply rooted in long-standing grievances and previous failed reform efforts. The demands called for a range of reforms, which included curriculum reform, the creation of an Ethnic Studies program, Black and Latino faculty and staff, improved school facilities and food quality, elimination of IQ tests, ID cards and hall monitors, removal of police from around campus, and a stronger voice in student government.[58]

Like many racially charged protests, the students garnered support from community members. Strikers at San Francisco State and others voiced their concerns about the fighting between Black and Latino students and backed their grievances. The strikers believed that the two groups had a common enemy, the capitalist system, and should unite rather than divide. Interestingly, Flores agreed to settle differences through a scheduled fight with a handpicked Black student. "He wasn't much of a fighter[;] neither was I; we wound up entangled, wrapped up around each other, all tired out before the stupid fight was stopped," he recalled. This fight, intended to end interethnic conflict, led to Black and Latino students forming a united front and developing a joint list of seventeen unconditional demands. Not all Latino students supported this. Neftali and his group withdrew from the organizing effort after seeing Flores and his group collaborating with Black classmates. But Flores persisted.[59]

On February 4, student representatives from Mission High delivered their seventeen unconditional demands to the school board. "Polite but fervent" is how education reporter Jim Wood described their presentation. Speaker after speaker warned the board that conditions at the school were intolerable and that they held it responsible. If it did not act, then there would be consequences. The students wore Brown Berets or Third World Liberation

Front pins, with adult leaders from the Mission District in attendance. Principal Krytzer, in a weary voice, defended his administration as he read the demands one by one. As he spoke, shouts erupted from the hall. "Shut it down," some yelled. "Burn it down," and "All 17." Flores, unaware of how he ended up on the agenda, attended the meeting and spoke. He expressed his belief that the school did not care for its students. Furthermore, he highlighted the absurdity of students who spent half the semester in the park still managing to pass. "Most of our people don't get nothing, nothing out of high school," he asserted. While most speakers were Latino, some Black youth also voiced their concerns. One student opposed the use of identification cards, saying, "It's like walking into a prison. You flash your ID, yeah, I'm in cell 2, cell 302, English class." The board stated it would discuss the reforms on March 1. Krytzer conceded that the students had legitimate grievances regarding the cafeteria and lavatories, but he firmly stated that hall monitors would not be removed, viewing them as a necessary measure following the unrest in the fall.[60]

The Mission High strike coincided with the student strike at San Francisco State. The event had its roots in California's three-tiered higher education system. During the mid-1960s, the state reorganized this system, introducing the SAT and tightening admissions criteria at state colleges. Consequently, Black student enrollment at San Francisco State College plummeted just as the children of southern migrants reached college age. These students found themselves disproportionately placed in junior colleges, the lowest rung in California's educational hierarchy. Originally, state colleges admitted the top 70 percent of high school graduates, but the master plan reduced this to the top 33 percent. As a result, the Black student population at San Francisco State dropped from 10 percent to 4 percent, even though it had previously boasted the highest number of Black students in the state. With a conservative state government in power, cuts to funding for state colleges and financial aid loomed large. Governor Ronald Reagan's administration slashed $250,000 from the Educational Opportunity Program and excluded $2.5 million for the program from the next budget.[61]

In this fraught context, the BSU announced a strike for November 6, presenting ten demands. The strike led to nearly 800 arrests, attracted intensive local and national media coverage, and brought the Reagan administration, university administrators, and activists into direct conflict. The Third World Liberation Front soon endorsed the strike, adding five more demands. The violence inflicted by police on protesters galvanized moderate students to side with the radicals. Eventually, university president Robert

Smith resigned, and Reagan appointed professor S. I. Hayakawa, a hardliner who swiftly declared a "state of emergency." The Tac Squad intervened, and the unrest, which escalated in violence, continued until March, when committees negotiated an end to the strike on March 20, 1969. In the aftermath, the college established a School of Ethnic Studies, consolidating all Black studies courses into the new Department of Black Studies. The college also agreed to increase minority enrollment and remove police from the campus. While most strikers received amnesty, many leaders were jailed and banned from campus.[62]

The event prompted some educators and reporters to allege the presence of outside influences at Mission High, stoking fears that the unrest on college campuses had spilled over into high schools. On February 5, police arrested thirty-three individuals—both students and non-students—on truancy charges when they refused to return to afternoon classes and protested outside the school. Officers apprehended non-students for loitering on school property. Flores took issue with the *Chronicle*'s coverage of the arrests. Reporters claimed that the Third World Liberation Front had incited Mission High students to strike, but Flores recalled that the demonstrators were off school grounds. They had read from a mimeographed document titled "Mission Strike Directions," which called for a "mass rally" at the bell at Dolores Park.[63] On the same day, Claire Salop, an activities counselor in student affairs, addressed about 250 educators at a meeting of the California Association of School Administrators. She warned, "Within 18 months or two years, the focus of revolution will not be on the colleges, but on your high schools. This thrust can't be stopped. The students want an education that has meaning."[64] Around the same time, a document allegedly outlining a blueprint for a Black student group to take over a high school surfaced in San Francisco schools. It had originally appeared mysteriously on the desk of a Peninsula school principal, who then showed it to the administrators' association. The group decided to distribute the sheet to its members as a warning. Some school officials, however, recognized the absurdity of the document. The assistant principal at Mission High dismissed it as "ridiculous" to think any organization would draft secret plans and distribute them on high school campuses.[65]

The Mission High strike captivated the city and its institutions more than any previous high school student uprising in San Francisco. The *San Francisco Examiner*'s editorial board weighed in, offering a sympathetic yet patronizing analysis of the situation. The editorial argued that although Mission High had problems, the students' ultimatum would only worsen the situation. "Uncompromising demands described as 'non-negotiable' almost invariably are met with uncompromising resistance," it stated. The editorial acknowledged some issues, noting the need for experienced teachers in "disadvantaged area schools" and bilingual education. However, it also argued "a good deal of the weakness must be laid on the elementary schools and indifferent families who fail to provide the encouraging spark that ignites that student's scholastic ambitions." "Meanwhile we urge the rebellious Mission students to cool it for their own good," the editorial board urged. "Mission High School isn't all this bad. It continues to graduate sound scholars—those who attentively take advantage of what it has to offer."[66]

The school district did attempt to address issues affecting Latino youth. Around 170 people attended a conference titled "Latinos Speak Out: A Community Plans for Action" at Mission High. Sponsored by the school district and the State Department of Education, the meeting allowed attendees to outline grievances and propose solutions to educational and community problems, as well as to appoint groups to follow through on these plans. However, not all educators supported this move. The San Francisco Classroom Teachers Association sent a letter to Superintendent Jenkins, accusing the district of treating teachers like second-class citizens. The letter cited the recent speak-out, claiming that Principal Krytzer had been pressured to hold the event despite opposition from himself, the faculty, the teachers' association, and some parents.[67]

On March 18, the Mission Coalition Organization, representing community members and teenagers, announced its intention to present several demands to the Board of Education on behalf of the Mission High students. The organization aimed to secure the board's support for students' rights to organize and to appoint a central administrator to unite various interest groups in developing a relevant educational program at Mission High. Ben Martinez, the group's president, referred to the school administration as a "dictatorship" and held it responsible for the recent unrest. On April 1, the group appeared at a board meeting, calling for improvements in Mission District schools, the removal of Principal Krytzer, an end to current busing practices, and the expansion of the Marshall School Annex. They felt the board had been inactive since the students submitted their demands in January.[68]

However, in June, the board reassigned Krytzer to Presidio Junior High School, along with the two assistant principals. At another board meeting, youth opposing Krytzer's transfer disrupted the proceedings, prompting helmeted police officers with riot sticks to restore order. One student denounced the Mission Coalition Organization as "dirt," praised Krytzer as a leader of law and order, and warned of potential violence the following year if he transferred. Several youths formed Students for Mission High and allied with the conservative Young Americans for Freedom to investigate ties between radical groups and the school board, which they believed "has so often acquiesced." With support from various conservative community organizations, they also sought a referendum for the September ballot to allow elective rather than appointive school board members and to let the public decide on the quality-equality school integration plan partially approved by the board. Rising senior Cathy Garcia headed the group. Flores knew her well. He had mistakenly allowed her onto a reconciliation committee after the last major incident of ethnic tensions at the school. "She used her sexuality and sensuality on me," he recalled. "She flirted with me and was so nice," even inviting him to her home for dinner, where "the whole family picked my brain." The group she led claimed that students who spoke out against "political" teachers were penalized with low grades. This 200-member group demonstrated to school officials that a strong minority opposed their activist peers' actions and rejected Krytzer's transfer in favor of a Spanish-speaking principal.[69]

Despite administrators' reluctance to address most of the seventeen demands, the Mission High Strike became a symbol of resistance and a model for other students engaged in acts of rebellion. Newsreel's film *High School Rising* captured this sentiment, featuring a sixteen-minute black-and-white documentary showcasing student voices and unidentified individuals discussing the problems at Mission High. The film began with snapshots and clips of students outside the school, followed by a still image of an official confronting a Black youth, repeatedly telling him to "get into class." "They don't teach us nothing but yet still expect us to be in class all the time. And then as soon we [sic] try to better the school, they're ready to throw all of us in school," one girl said. Several students critiqued the police presence. "If you was a student around the school, you wouldn't want to have police coming around here, coming harassing you all the time. . . . That ain't for nobody," one remarked. Another student likened the school to a "concentration camp." The film highlighted the daily frustrations and disillusionment students felt, with another voice-over citing the lack of relevance in the education system:

> The ways your studies are directed are isolated. You learn about English and English grammar. And then over here you learn about

mathematics. And over here you learn about some crazy psychology who doesn't have a damn thing to do with what your mind works like. Then you get into high school, it isolates you from what's happening in the world. While you're reading about the lies of the Declaration of Independence. While you're reading about George Washington. You know what's going down outside. You know about the war that's going on in Vietnam. You know about what's going down in Latin America. You know about what's going down in Africa. But you don't know this from what's going on inside that school. Then you're isolated into a trap.[70]

Throughout the documentary, students argued that school is inherently divisive, forcing them to compete in IQ tests, grades, sports, and student body offices. "It makes us compete and act alone because they know that individuals are easier to control than groups," one student asserted. The film featured numerous clips of students appearing disengaged and bored. Other voice-overs contended that schools primarily served corporate interests and that the tracking system placed privileged students on a college track while relegating Black, Brown, and white working-class students to vocational programs. More importantly, the film emphasized that these disadvantaged groups should not fight against each other, noting, "it helps the man. See, it keeps us apart and makes us much easier to control than if we were to fight together against the things that hold all of us back and keep us separated."[71]

The film unapologetically aligned with the student strike. At one point, a school official claimed that the strike was nonexistent because it is illegal for high school students to strike. The same official then alleged, "I'm sure that the demands as they are written do not reflect entirely young people's thinking. There is obviously adult direction." A student promptly shot back, "They talk this shit about, they putting stuff in our head. They ain't put nothing in our head. We wrote the seventeen demands. . . . we were just getting outside support." Other students claimed they had been threatened with suspension or jail time if they continued striking, and others decried administrators' willingness to call the police on them. Toward the end of the film, students expressed the urgency of having their demands met and the importance of educating themselves. The "best way to start moving on the system is to learn from the struggles of the Black and Brown kids," one girl argued. "They're getting it on because they got it worse than any of us. And we gotta support them. We gotta unite with them against the shit that's keeping all of us down." In all, the film portrayed Mission High as an emblem of defiance for the marginalized fighting their oppressor.[72]

Over the summer lull, the urgency of the seventeen demands seemed to wane as the school board remained nonresponsive and Flores's tenure as an activist reverted. In August, he appeared on the program for the Bay Area High School Liberation Conference. Alongside Bruce Trigg of the New York High School Student Union and various radical organizations, Flores spoke about the strife at Mission High and the Los Siete de la Raza, a group of seven young Latinos who were on trial for an altercation with police that left one officer dead.[73] Flores observed that the organizing fervor at Mission High had dissipated by the following school year. As a prominent student leader, he found himself under the tutelage of a Latino police officer who took him on trips to San Quentin to speak with prisoners. He also attended the Upward Bound Program at the University of San Francisco. Reflecting on that period, Flores felt he had been "plucked out of the community so I couldn't have contact with the other student organizers." When he returned to school the next semester, he noticed, "We were disconnected. The isolation had cooled us off on being organizers. The tactic worked." He also recalled the presence of the Concerned Mission Parents, who served as hall guards and "constantly tried to convince me of the 'errors of my views' and, of course, how correct they were." Personal distractions also played a role in his waning political engagement. He became heavily involved in partying, "doing drugs and drinking, mostly LSD at the time," which, along with other habits, "had a detrimental effect on me and my activities." Additionally, he invested a lot of his energy in a relationship with a girl at his school. This former political radical had, in many ways, transformed into a typical rebellious teenager.[74]

Flores believed these efforts dampened the spirit of activism, but Chicano activism persisted at Mission High into the fall of 1969. He participated in a demonstration in September when nearly 100 students walked out of school in solidarity with the United Farm Workers Union grape boycott. During the November Moratorium to End the War in Vietnam, Mission High reported the largest number of absences, with 700 students out of school. A girl unsuccessfully challenged the school district in court to distribute leaflets for the event, but the district liberalized its policy just days before the ruling.[75]

The Mission High strike and the student uprisings in San Francisco's junior high and high schools mirrored a national wave of activism from the late 1960s to the early 1970s. Black and Latino students orchestrated various demonstrations to reform their schools. Their demands often overlapped, but local circumstances shaped specific grievances and community responses. Moreover, racial protests mobilized communities to a far greater extent than antiwar activism. The uprisings in San Francisco drew various people and institutions into the crisis: the police department, city hall, community organizations, medical institutions, private school parents, and even the real estate market. Each uprising had its own catalyst. School officials summoning police to handle the disturbances and institutionalizing security measures tied them together. Black students and their parents spoke out against these trends, challenging the prevailing notions of criminality that underpinned anti-riot and anti-crime legislation.[76] Administrators' insistence on cracking down on troublemakers by employing security guards sparked debates over who was better suited to handle disciplinary issues: school officials or police.

Although racially charged protests at high schools represented the most significant episodes of collective student activism, they had mixed outcomes. Some students achieved immediate success, while others saw their demands fade as momentum dissipated. Administrators, under pressure to act, could easily sidestep issues by postponing action until the summer months. In response, some students began to adopt written documents, often called bills of rights, to affirm their entitlements. These rights campaigns emerged as a remedy to the shortcomings of student uprisings. By campaigning for a bill of rights, students aimed to compel school districts to amend their policies and ensure the protection of student privileges. These campaigns occurred nationwide and stirred controversy, even though they were less disruptive than other forms of protest. In Philadelphia, a racially diverse coalition of students banded together to enact change across the district. Unbeknownst to them, their successful campaign resonated with teenage activists far beyond the city's borders.

7 Student Rights as Civil Rights
Philadelphia's Student Bill of Rights Campaign

Philadelphia Board of Education member William Ross once dismissed student rights as "a middle-class issue." That presumption changed when he found himself arguing with a student rights advocate from North Philadelphia's Benjamin Franklin High School in January 1972. The argument dealt with the proposed renaming of the school, which many students and teachers preferred to rename Malcolm X. The student presence at the meeting belonged to a citywide organization that confronted the Board of Education, which sought to amplify and implement the nearly two-year-old Student Bill of Rights and Responsibilities. They presented a list of negotiable proposals, which included a review of dress codes, the elimination of arbitrary discipline, the use of impartial hearing examination cases, and student and parent access to their personal files. The meeting featured typical accusations of outside agitators. Principal Odette Harris of William Penn High School believed "the students are being told what to think and do." She elaborated, explaining, "The students are getting involved in emotional issues and not seeing the total picture. They are not developing their intellect." But the young attendees disagreed. Susan Bailey, a senior at Philadelphia High School for Girls, or Girls High School for short, and President of the Union of Student Governments, replied, "If the schools were working so well, there wouldn't be so many students who are reading way below the national norm. Our major purpose is to change the schools so that students will come out of them with some knowledge." The group felt that the bill had given pupils the power to deal with other power blocs in the school district. One youth commented, "What's happening right now is that the teachers and administrators are afraid students will realize they have a chance to speak out against things they don't like."[1]

Many school officials and even journalists who covered teenage activists shared Ross's sentiment that student rights were a "middle-class issue," hence, a white, middle-class concern. But throughout the high school movement, Black, Latino, Asian, and Native American youth made demands that often overlapped with those of their white peers, but they possessed a broader definition of the term. White youth who advocated for student rights emerged from administrative repression on antiwar activities and First Amendment rights. Nonwhite youth organized around these issues as well. But rather than merely viewing schools as oppressive institutions that suppressed their constitutional rights, they first and foremost viewed them as institutions that reinforced racial inequality and adhered to white social norms. "There should be no limitation on a Brother's hair," read one demand from Lincoln High School in Los Angeles in March 1968. "The Natural symbolizes pride in one's Blackness. Also, there is a growing need for Black identity."[2] These students critiqued systemic policies that perpetuated racial disparities, such as the tracking system, the absence of bilingual courses, and the pervasive predominance of white faculty and staff, some of whom they charged with harboring racist attitudes. Additionally, they called for ethnic studies, better school facilities, more minority faculty and staff, curriculum reform, and freedom from police harassment on campus. All these demands constituted their vision of student rights.

But when young activists in San Francisco and elsewhere advocated for these rights through direct actions, they received mixed results. Many school boards and administrators responded promptly, but others provided empty promises. Therefore, young activists sought permanent measures. As early as 1967, teenagers led numerous campaigns for district-wide or school-based declarations of rights, often called high school or student bills of rights.[3] They were far more practical and less radical than the SMC's 1970 document and mostly emerged independently from the group. These campaigns encouraged school officials to affirm their commitment to school reform and amend long-standing grievances. Initially resistant, many administrators eventually conceded, demonstrating that student rights were achieved not only through the judicial system but also through local school boards.

These efforts occurred across the nation in communities large and small, like New York City and Jeffersonville, Indiana.[4] In Massachusetts, the effort advanced to the governor's desk in 1974 after being passed by the state legislature as a bill.[5] However, the Philadelphia Student Bill of Rights stands out as an impressive story with unique characteristics. First, the idea for such a document arose from the fallout of a protest in November 1967 that turned into a police riot, followed by numerous other disturbances in city schools. Second, the campaign featured a diverse cast of activists. In a city marked by stark racial polarization in its neighborhoods and schools, this coalition's diversity was not just notable but extraordinary. Many of the movement's leaders hailed from Mount Airy in Northwest Philadelphia, the

One of the largest high school bill of rights campaigns occurred in New York City. This photograph was taken on April 15, 1970, and features a student on a stage with a banner that reads, "Full Rights for High School Students! High School Student Rights Coalition." The *Militant* Photographic Collection, box 2, Folder 12, Hoover Institution Library & Archives.

city's only intentionally integrated neighborhood. Third, the campaign reveals that animus over waning administrative authority was hotly contested with school boards. Numerous groups—administrators, teachers, board members, and even the mayor-elect—routinely sought to undermine and dismantle the initiative. Last, many of these activists had no direct connection to any national networks in the high school movement. But the success of their campaign reverberated well beyond Philadelphia.

Susan Bailey and Black Philadelphia

Susan Bailey knew that Philadelphia schools had problems. Though she lived in a middle-class, integrated neighborhood and attended a magnet school that shielded her from many of the challenges facing the city, she was keenly knowledgeable of the struggles her peers endured. Driven by this awareness, she became a strong advocate for the high school bill of rights and built an interracial coalition in the process.

She was born in 1955 in Philadelphia. Her grandfather, George Bailey Sr., was the first in his family to be born free in Lincolnton, Georgia, in 1905. Like many Blacks in the South, George worked as a sharecropper, but he desired more out of life. At thirteen, he fled to Philadelphia, where his older sister lived. George found work during the day assisting a Jewish grocer and spent his nights on the assembly line at Campbell Soup Company in Camden, New Jersey. By 1920, he had saved enough to open his own store, Bailey's Grocery. During a visit back home, George met his future wife, Mattie Lou Andrews. The two married and returned to Philadelphia, running the grocery store together at 813 West Oxford Street on the north side. George became the first Black member of the Frankford-Quaker Grocers Association, and Bailey's Grocery was store number five. They had one son, George Bailey Jr., who preferred to go by his middle name, Dallas. Dallas would achieve more success than his parents could have dreamed. A gifted athlete, his skills placed him as one of the top 100 high school football players in Pennsylvania. He went on to attend Temple College, the first in his family to do so. However, football was still a segregated sport, and Dallas's parents paid his tuition because no scholarships were available to him. Through a connection with Mattie's pastor, William H. Gray Sr. of Bright Hope Baptist Church, whose son, Rev. Dr. William H. Gray Jr., was president of Florida A&M College, Dallas attended Florida A&M on a football scholarship. There, he met Martha Ann George during his senior year. Martha, hailing from Paducah, Kentucky, had attended the University of Arkansas at Pine Bluff and earned her master's from Indiana University in Bloomington. When she met Dallas, she worked as a teaching assistant.[6]

The couple married in 1948 and moved to Fort Lauderdale, Florida, where they both began their careers as teachers and soon started a family. Their life in Florida was idyllic but short-lived. After the birth of their second child, George Sr. fell ill and asked Dallas to return to Philadelphia to take over the family business. Dallas obliged, and under his stewardship, the store became a cornerstone of the North Philadelphia community. Dallas became a board member of the Frankford Grocers' Association Federal Credit Union. Known for his good humor and keen interest in civic affairs, he turned the store into a hub where locals could learn about community events and find resources. His engagement in local politics led him to become a Democratic Committeeman, and the store served as a neighborhood polling place. Martha, equally engaged, served as a troop leader and board member for the Philadelphia District Girl Scouts of America, president of the Germantown YWCA board of directors, an officer of the C.W. Henry Home and School Association, and an active member of Delta Sigma Theta Sorority. Both Dallas and Martha were generous benefactors to Bright Hope. If a church member needed help, the pastor would send them to the store for a box of food. The respect the community had for the Baileys preserved the business during the 1964 Philadelphia riots. Amid the violence, Dallas rushed to his store to check for damage. He found the spot unscathed under the protection of neighborhood gang members.[7]

As their family grew, Dallas and Martha moved from an apartment over the store to the West Mount Airy neighborhood in 1952, a community in the northwest corner of Philadelphia. By 1950, the area had a population of nearly 20,000. While some white residents feared the neighborhood's changing demographics, others embraced integration. The Baileys' social standing as well-educated, politically active, and liberal-minded individuals, combined with the neighborhood's diverse housing and proximity to Fairmount Park and the Wissahickon Gorge, made it an attractive place for similarly upwardly mobile Black families and made white residents more resistant to leaving. Dallas purchased the family home at an ideal time. In 1953, community leaders in West Mount Airy, including clergy from four local religious institutions, conducted extensive research and concluded that a racially mixed neighborhood was "both sustainable and, just maybe, even desirable." They launched a "sell your neighborhood" campaign and encouraged residents to support integration through education, persuasion, and community events. The high cost of living meant that only the most financially stable families could afford homes in the area.[8]

Dinner conversations in the Baileys' household nurtured their children's intellectual curiosity. Dallas and Martha discussed current events and asked about their daughters' school days. "They never dumbed down their conversations for us, and we all had good communication skills," Susan recalls. "An interest in people and politics was ingrained in us." Dallas had a firm belief, reinforced by Martha's readings of YWCA studies, that socially active girls delayed relationships and sex. Therefore, he encouraged engagement in "all worthy pursuits." Of course, the shotgun he possessed and made sure all neighborhood boys knew he kept under his bed did not hurt either. Susan became politically active at a young age. She worked with the Philadelphia Resistance, an antiwar organization that emerged from the Vietnam

Summer Committee with the mission to educate Philadelphians about the Vietnam War. Along with a friend from elementary school whose father was involved in the group, she helped organize several demonstrations.[9]

The Baileys provided Susan with a middle-class comfort that shielded her from many of the harsher realities experienced by her peers in other parts of the city. Her elementary school, C. W. Henry, had a Jewish principal and an integrated staff. Her kindergarten teacher was a Black woman, and Susan sat between two white students, as pupils sat alphabetically. Her first brush with racism came in eighth grade, during a dispute with a teacher over not receiving an A in sewing despite helping other students who did receive A's. Susan went on to attend the Girls High, a college-prep public magnet school known for its diverse student body. Many of the most visible leaders in the city's Student Bill of Rights campaign attended the school. There, Bailey collaborated with people like Laura Punnett, a white girl who lived one mile away from her and who would become a leader in the movement.[10]

The November 1967 Philadelphia Student Demonstration

Unlike Bailey, many Black high school students in Philadelphia contended with not only predominantly white faculty and administrations but also with the realities of a shrinking white student population. By 1967, Germantown High School, once diverse, had become 99 percent Black, a shift driven by gerrymandering and the exodus of white families to parochial and private schools. Violence plagued many campuses. South Philadelphia High School became notorious for the racial tensions that erupted into fights after a teacher claimed Black students were inferior and had "smaller brains." The same teacher suggested that offering whiskey to Black parents would boost parental involvement. At Bok Vocational High School, Black students endured daily harassment during their commute, which involved navigating ten blocks of a working-class Italian neighborhood. They faced verbal abuse, with residents calling girls "black bitches" and hurling trash at them as they walked to school. Some white residents, however, claimed they were the ones victimized.[11] Across the city in 1967, disturbances and interracial violence spilled from the hallways of schools to the streets outside.[12]

The genesis of the Philadelphia Student Bill of Rights can be traced back to a series of student uprisings and disturbances, with the most significant incident occurring on November 17, 1967. On that day, about 3,500 Black students from at least twelve high and junior high schools converged on the Philadelphia Board of Education building at Twenty-First Street and

Parkway. This demonstration represented the culmination of a three-month organizing campaign spearheaded by the Black People's Unity Movement's (BPUM) education committee and a network of student activists it had cultivated. BPUM's efforts were twofold: it advocated for greater community input from Black parents and teachers in public schools while also promoting self-love and intraracial solidarity among young people. By 1967, Black youth in Philadelphia had developed a keen interest in Black Nationalism. BPUM positioned racial unity as a counter to gang affiliation. It held street rallies where youth listened to speakers condemn racism from police and white-owned businesses in their neighborhoods. Adult activists organized workshops and rallies for teenagers, encouraging them to bring lessons of racial pride, Black history, and Africanist practices back to their schools. When the school year resumed in September, BPUM student activists had established a council with representatives from various secondary schools. Throughout the fall, the council met to develop their demands, strategize for increasing support for each school's BSU, and spread its message through word of mouth and leafleting in corners and housing projects. By the end of October, the council was primed for action.[13]

In the lead-up to the November demonstration, activists at Simon Gratz High School in North Philadelphia pulled a fire alarm and broke a door chain. About 350 students walked out and attended a Black Power rally in front of the school. A week later, a walkout occurred at Bok Vocational in South Philadelphia, where racial tensions simmered due to shifting demographics. Other high schools organized demonstrations in front of their buildings, where they advocated for Black history courses, relief from overcrowding, and physical improvements to the buildings.[14]

On November 17, the day of the sit-in, Police Commissioner Frank Rizzo called in his mounted police. Some youth in the crowd reported that they heard Rizzo shout, "get their Black asses." Officers and horses moved in and began arresting students at the scene while teachers deliberated with Superintendent Mark Shedd about new courses. The situation escalated when students started to flee the charging horses and police batons. Police swung nightsticks at youth who resisted arrest. What began as a protest quickly turned into a full-scale riot, instigated by the police, that spilled into Center City and the downtown area. In the chaos, fleeing students shattered store windows and vandalized cars. By the end of the day, twenty-two people were injured, and police arrested fifty-seven students. The incident did not pass without significant fallout. School board president Richardson Dilworth pointed the finger squarely at Rizzo, accusing him of inciting the violence. The image of police officers attacking unarmed youth sparked outrage and condemnation from both Black and white parents, teachers, and community leaders.[15] Susan, a would-be participant in the protest, recounted how her godfather, a subordinate of Lieutenant George Fencil, sensed trouble. He "called my father as soon as he found out that there was going to be a problem on November 17 and told him to make sure I stayed at home," she recalls.[16]

Another cause for the push for a student bill of rights emerged out of the school district's alignment with the police. In response to racial clashes in October 1968, Mayor James Tate, Rizzo, and the city council urged the school board to ratify a proposal that would grant the Philadelphia Police Department jurisdiction inside every school in the city. This plan aimed to integrate the 330 non-teaching aides already stationed in schools into the department's ranks, create parental watchdog groups, and establish detention centers for unruly youth to "isolate rebellion from the rest of the student body." It also called for the "vigorous prosecution" of trespassers and mandated identification cards for students. The school board rejected Tate's proposal. Black parents praised the board for maintaining its independence and lambasted the ID cards as the city's attempt to "resemble South Africa." But the veto angered City Council President Paul D'Ortona, who threatened to withhold an additional $30 million from the school district. The racial unrest, to him, justified upgrading security. Board members tried to compromise, but in the end, Dilworth and Rizzo agreed in a closed-door meeting in mid-November to deploy uniformed police in schools under the principal's direction. The new policy allowed police to patrol the areas around twelve campuses the school board labeled as "troubled schools." It placated white parents' demands for punitive policing and undermined Black voices who called for social services.[17]

Philadelphia's Student Bill of Rights

For several years, student unrest simmered to the point that school officials recognized the urgent need for a solution. By spring 1970, discussions about a high school bill of rights began to gain traction. The concept did not emerge out of thin air. Philadelphia school officials knew about the bill of rights campaign that occurred in New York City earlier in the year. Superintendent Shedd, a figure whom activists would come to see as an ally, took action by forming a committee of twenty-one members, comprising students, parents, teachers, and administrators. Shedd's reputation preceded him. He arrived in Philadelphia in 1967 from Englewood, New Jersey, where he had earned a reputation for racial liberalism for his role in desegregating public schools. Assuming the position of superintendent on September 1, Shedd made an immediate impression on Black residents by enrolling his four children in predominantly Black public schools near his Germantown home. The committee Shedd assembled came out of the aftermath of a student boycott at West Philadelphia High School in November 1969. Sparked by dissatisfaction with a particular instructor's teaching methods, the protesting students demanded the teacher's transfer. The teachers' union threatened to strike, and the school board ultimately decided to retain the educator. However, this incident brought to light a myriad of long-standing grievances that demanded attention.[18]

Mark Lloyd, the former chair of the Student-Faculty Advisory Committee and a recent Central High School graduate, articulated these grievances in a statement to the Board of Education and Superintendent Shedd. Lloyd's speech cataloged past events, underscoring the necessity of the proposed document, including the November 1967 demonstration and a May 1970 protest at Olney High School, where students occupied the auditorium to voice various complaints. The school board's response, which was a legal injunction against the students, did little to address the underlying issues. Therefore, the committee championed the adoption of a nine-point bill of rights for students. This proposal sought to enshrine several rights: legal counsel and due process, a say in curriculum and disciplinary matters, freedom from degrading or corporal punishment, and the right to First Amendment activities. Additionally, the committee called for the election of a student "ombudsman"—a Swedish term for advocate—for every 1,000 students. This role would help address grievances, defined as complaints arising from "personal loss, injury, or inconvenience because of a violation, misinterpretation, or inequitable application of an established policy governing students."[19]

In July 1970, Bailey, along with four other student leaders, spoke with *The Philadelphia Inquirer* during a series of education forums that tackled the myriad problems plaguing city schools. The students charged that their peers were not learning properly, citing systemic suppression and neglect. "The students are frustrated because they are coming to a place called 'the school,' and they're not getting anything out of it," declared Robert A. Schenkman, student president of George Washington High School. They criticized disciplinary practices that denied students due process, the rote memorization prioritized over critical thinking, pervasive racism within schools, and the abundance of administrative frills and unused equipment. Bailey offered a candid assessment of what she perceived as subpar standards. She noted that at her high school, students were confined to a prescribed book list for their grade. "Even if you had already read all the books you were interested in on the 9th-grade list, you couldn't read a book from another grade for credit," she stated. "You're limited to what 'they' think your ability is. They won't let you make your own mistake. How are you going to learn anything when you're always right?" The conversation also touched on the proposed student bill of rights. When a reporter asked Bailey why the document stated the only criterion "for a student's grade is his work," she responded, "Because if the teacher doesn't like you because you're opinionated, he might lower your grade. Sometimes he just can't stand your guts."[20]

Throughout the spring and summer, the school board held meetings that diluted the proposal originally submitted by activists. On July 27, thirty-seven people testified before the Board of Education on whether the Student Bill of Rights should be implemented in its original or revised form. Speaker after speaker shared their views as board members listened attentively, though they remained mostly silent. Some speakers endorsed the original version, while others opposed the document entirely. "In our view," began a representative of the Philadelphia Fellowship Commission, a human rights organization, the document "can be such a mechanism because they build in a systematic structure which will involve students more effectively in real situations which affect them." Other parties shared concerns or opposed it completely. The Philadelphia Federation of Teachers (PFT) expressed qualms about writing materials that could expose school personnel and students to "unfair censure or ridicule," privacy matters, and other issues. It urged the Board to "postpone consideration of the resolution until after the schools reopen."[21] One presenter completely opposed it, stating, "It is the first step to allowing the students to run their own education." The *Inquirer* commended the school board, its president, former mayor and senior partner of one of the city's most powerful law firms, Richardson Dilworth, and Superintendent Shedd for their deliberative approach. The paper largely praised the students for their civility and reasonableness.[22]

One person named Robert Lee Williams submitted a written statement to the Board of Education. He accused it of wielding more power than the US Congress. Holding two documents—one a duplicate of the students' proposed Bill of Rights and the other "an imitation" from the Board—Williams cited specific examples to illustrate his point. Regarding First Amendment rights, he noted that the students had originally requested these rights on campus. He then read from the Board's revision, which stated that freedom of expression shall "be governed by the First Amendment to the United States Constitution and the policies of the Board of Education." He followed with, "Now let me explain how you have insulted our intelligence." Then, he asked, "Why did you honorable men assume the authority to change 'shall be in accord with' and substitute 'shall be governed by?' A minor change but an unnecessary infringement on us." Williams also pointed out that the Board had removed the word 'picket' from its revisions. "Tell me, does the word 'picketing' frighten you so much that you feel a burning desire to remove it?" he asked. His biggest grievance dealt with the Board aligning its policies to the First Amendment. "Are you telling us and the public at large that you reserve the power to deny students of their First Amendment rights under the United States?" He suggested that if the Board felt students were too inept for these privileges, "you should change your title and one should address you as the infamous board of public indoctrination." He concluded his speech with a witty call to action: "Adopt our duplication, not your imitation."[23]

On November 9, the school board reconvened for another public hearing, marking a full year since the student boycott at West Philadelphia High. However, by this second public hearing, little had changed. Only two Black members sat on the school board. All city schools had a Black instructor who taught Black history, but it remained a minor subject. Police presence had increased, as had the number of non-teaching assistants. While efforts were made to assign Black principals to schools, the Director of the School District's Office of Community Affairs, Oliver Lancaster, noted that both Black and white students were increasingly dissatisfied with conditions. Black students felt their demands for equality were ignored, while white students felt they were not receiving their rights. During the second public hearing, fifteen individuals spoke, including students and parents, offering comments either supporting or opposing the implementation of the Bill of Rights. Backing came from external organizations such as the ACLU, the Philadelphia Principals Association, and the Northeast Health and Welfare Council. The PFT opposed it. Dissenters cited concerns about student immaturity and cognitive limitations. Mrs. Ken Murray, president of the Hancock Home & School Association, offered a scenario: "If I were a cartoonist, I'd draw a child standing in front of a lawyer. He would be asking the lawyer: 'Read me my rights because I can't make out the big words.'" The audience booed. Most groups in attendance supported the bill, but the primary concerns among opponents dealt with the role of the "student advocate." Parents viewed it as a replacement for adult authority, and teachers saw it as a threat to their control.[24]

On December 21, the Board of Education passed the Student Bill of Rights by a narrow five-to-three vote. Leading up to the vote, one district official expressed concern that the Board might delay the decision until January. "If that happens," he warned, "we may be faced with a student strike sometime in January." External organizations, including the SMC and the Philadelphia Bar Association, which sponsored a Youth Forum to discuss "The Bill of Rights in Today's Society," backed the students. The Board's decision, however, averted the feared strike. Now, the Bill of Rights would remain in effect until June 1972, at which point it would be re-evaluated.[25] The Board's version of the Bill of Rights was a succinct two-page document. It opened with a preamble stating that it was "established in order to achieve a greater cooperative effort in shaping the structure and direction of the Philadelphia public school system." The document outlined twelve rights and responsibilities for high school students, including First Amendment "rights and limits"; genuinely representative student government; an elected ombudsman "trained to offer counsel on students' rights"; the right to counsel and due process in matters of suspension, transfer, and expulsion; the right to participate in decisions affecting the curriculum and discipline; grading based solely on performance; and protection from "unreasonable or excessive punishment." Pupils were also required to avoid disrupting the school and behave appropriately. Last, it declared that no rule or regulation "shall be established which diminishes the right of any students as set forth in Student Bill of Rights and Responsibilities."[26]

This document granted students power in matters of discipline and curriculum. However, it did not satisfy all parties. Administrators feared it went too far. Even during the vote, Board member William Ross objected on financial grounds, citing concerns that the grievance procedure and other provisions could cost the district up to $200,000. Superintendent Shedd estimated that the ombudsmen would cost around $1,000 for the current fiscal period.[27] On January 18, 1971, school officials convened to address questions and concerns raised by the Philadelphia Principals Association, which had submitted a document with thirteen critiques. The group agreed that principals should have the right to appeal the selection of the ombudsman and have more control over their training and responsibilities. The meeting resulted in modifications to certain sentences and phrases throughout the document. Most importantly, officials agreed to empower principals to exercise local discretion on matters of free speech and student government, making them "responsible for the implementation" of the Bill of Rights.[28]

If administrators felt that the original Bill of Rights went too far, students believed it did not go far enough. In the citywide underground high school newspaper, *Red Army*, editors penned a column under the headline, "High School 'Bill of Rights'—Bullshit!" The publication, with its unclear origins, carried a strong antiestablishment stance laced with Marxist analysis. "They think they can satisfy us with some meaningless words on a piece of paper stamped 'Bill of Rights,'" the article began. "Well, they're wrong!" The editors lamented that the Board provided no copies of its document to students due to logistical purposes, "yet they did print up copies for Shedd and other pigs to use at a meeting last week." While they acknowledged the inclusion of an ombudsman, "the bureaucrats always win out so what difference does it make?" Freedom of speech and press seemed insignificant because "we have to put our names on everything we give out or post up (and every name goes into Rizzo's files)."[29]

The column also highlighted recent incidents that coincided with the passage of the Bill of Rights. At Edison High School, around one hundred students and a substitute teacher stormed the principal's office after he refused to allow the showing of a Viet Cong propaganda film. Meanwhile, West Philadelphia High officials suspended student leader Robert "Bobby" Stewart and transferred him to Bartram High School. The editors argued that suppressing the film kept Black, Puerto Rican, and poor white students from learning "how to deal with their common oppressor at home." The piece also noted, "Catholic school students don't even have the bullshit rights that public school students have." It cited the suspension of Mark Canty from Cardinal Dougherty High School for leafletting about a student rights demonstration on January 14. "The day the 'Bill of Rights' was passed," it concluded, "marked just another day of oppression for Phila. High School students."[30]

Others who believed the document lacked muscle engaged in direct action. A group of teenagers calling themselves the Students' Rights Coalition organized a demonstration in front of the school board and the Catholic Archdiocese building. In a statement to the Black-owned *Philadelphia Tribune*, it declared: "High school students have won a victory with the passage of the Student Bill of Rights. However, this is merely the beginning of our struggle. The Bill is vague and inadequate. Also, no Bill of Rights has been passed for elementary, junior high, parochial, private, or suburban high school students." Shelli Sonstein, a Girls High student, relayed that the

Bill of Rights "is not being implemented in most schools, and the principals still hold the power." She recounted how Principal Dr. Ruth Klein "will not honor the Bill of Rights, so we must continue to put pressure on the Board of Education." Others saw it as a "good start," but felt it did not "go far enough." On the day of the rally, students from public, private, parochial, and suburban schools gathered to demonstrate and speak to reporters. Bobby Stewart recounted his suspension for intervening when a nonteaching assistant reprimanded a student. He told the pupil they had the right to remain silent, leading to his suspension by Principal Walter Scott. "As it is now," he said, "you don't get to tell your side of the story. If you're suspended or transferred, you can't do anything about it." Sonstein demanded, "We must end the victimization of political activists in schools, get all cops out of schools, and implement the Bill of Rights for all students." Recent events of student rights violations led these activists to feel that "many rallies will be needed before all these things are attained, and we must continue to put pressure on the Board of Education."[31]

Bailey's recollection was different. School administrators knew that student government officers truly represented students, so "they came to us when there was a question and encouraged other students to bring their ideas to Student Governments too." The first Girls High School Ombudsman, Leah Vaughan, she remembers, "worked very hard. She believed grievances should be confidential." On several occasions, the school board members called Dr. Klein to rein her in. Klein would then call her into the office and let her know she was supposed to have a conversation with her. Instead, she winked and said, "'Keep up the good work' and we had our talk if anyone asks. I know a few other principals weren't as encouraging but, Girls' High wasn't just about teaching academics but, also about empowering women."[32]

Attitudes likely varied among school officials, but the tragic murder of a junior high school teacher reignited fierce opposition to the Student Bill of Rights.

The Slaying of Samson L. Freedman

On February 1, 1971, just before 3:00 p.m., Samson L. Freedman, a fifty-six-year-old ceramics teacher, exited Leeds Junior High School in Mount Airy. His routine departure from work soon turned fatal. Without warning, an assassin fired a .45-caliber bullet that struck Freedman in the back of the neck, splitting and embedding itself in his skull. He succumbed to his injuries an hour later at Chestnut Hill Hospital. The police mobilized quickly and searched for the shooter. By 7:00 p.m., they apprehended fourteen-year-old Kevin Simmons at his home. Simmons revealed to investigators that he had been suspended from school on Friday. Freedman had overheard him cursing another student and mistakenly thought Simmons had hurled profanity at him. The school administration instructed Simmons to return on Monday with his mother. He returned, but without her, carrying instead his father's .45-caliber gun, kept at home for protection against gang members. Simmons placed it in his locker. As classes ended, he stood in a doorway on the Mount Pleasant side of the building, adjusting his belt where he had tucked the gun. Simmons's account of what happened next conflicted with those of eyewitnesses. He claimed that as Freedman passed him, he stumbled, and the weapon accidentally discharged. However, witnesses insisted that Simmons deliberately aimed at Freedman before pulling the trigger. Some even recounted that Simmons had threatened to "get" Freedman earlier. "Kevin opened his coat," reported one witness. "I saw the gun in his belt and heard Kevin say he was going to shoot Mr. Freedman. Then Mr. Freedman came out. I heard a shot and saw him fall."[33] The tragedy prompted a citywide shutdown of schools for a day. Around 5,000 people gathered to pay their respects. Mourners surrounded the solid oak casket, adorned with the Star of David, as tiny shovelfuls of dirt marked their final farewell to the fallen educator.[34]

Though seemingly unrelated, the PFT seized upon the tragedy to launch an attack against the Bill of Rights. PFT President Frank Sullivan attributed the breakdown of discipline to what he termed "permissiveness," arguing that measures like locker searches were necessary. "Is that an invasion of privacy?" he asked. "The Student Bill of Rights would frown on that as an indignity." Going against students' prior demands, the PFT also called for more non-teaching assistants and security personnel, as well as enhanced facilities and programs for students with learning difficulties.[35] Bailey, though residing in West Mount Airy, noted the shooting took place on the east side, an area she viewed as vastly different from her own. "East Mount Airy was as far from West Mount Airy as Kensington was from Chestnut Hill culturally and socially," she states. She had no personal contact with anyone connected to the shooting. When several school board members cited the incident in their attempts to undermine the Bill of Rights, her group expressed their sorrow for Freedman and reminded the board that the shooter was not a high school student. They suggested a more thoughtful approach, advocating for measures that would provide outlets for frustrated students and prevent such tragedies, rather than simply eroding student rights.[36]

The PFT remained steadfast in its attempt to overhaul the Bill of Rights. Just four days after the murder of Freedman, Sullivan publicly condemned the text, claiming it violated the union's contract with the school board and called for Superintendent Shedd's dismissal. The union viewed Shedd's proposed twenty-point discipline program as futile, criticizing his refusal to retract the Bill of Rights. PFT's chief negotiator, John Ryan, articulated the union's fears: "When teachers do try to enforce any of these disciplinary rules, no matter how minor, they'll be subject to being brought up on charges, confronted with an experienced trial lawyer and maybe even face counter-charges from the kids." A poll taken shortly after Freedman's slaying revealed that one-fifth of the city's teacher union members wanted Shedd to resign. Sullivan argued that teachers deserved "the same freedom of speech the students enjoy in their bill of rights."[37] The editorial board of the *Philadelphia Inquirer* dismissed the PFT's accusations against Shedd, calling the notion that he was responsible for Freedman's death "one of those exaggerations which only heighten fear and hatred." To the editors, Shedd was a "very convenient scapegoat" because he publicly supported the Bill of Rights, which made him an "easy mark for those who cry 'permissiveness' loudest."[38]

Preserving the Student Bill of Rights

The fate of the Student Bill of Rights came into peril in the fall of 1971. On December 9, the Board of Education unanimously voted to formally accept Shedd's resignation as superintendent at a cost of $58,500 or more. "I have no regrets," said Shedd to a jammed press conference in his office two hours later. "I have had a great many frustrations, but one of the great rewards was the opportunity to associate with deeply committed people." Board member George Hutt relayed that the acceptance of Shedd's resignation did not reflect each member's views on his performance.[39]

But one person who likely cheered privately was Mayor-elect Frank Rizzo. Shedd and Rizzo had "one of the longest-running political vendettas" Philadelphia had seen for quite some time, according to the *Daily News*. Their feud began on the day of the November 17, 1967, demonstration when Shedd criticized Rizzo for the police riot. "If there is one thing Frank Rizzo never does," the *Daily News* claimed, "it is forget. Frank Rizzo never forgets." He ran on an "I'll fire Shedd" platform and made Shedd a campaign issue. In fact, Rizzo attacked the superintendent indirectly by claiming in one of his first campaign statements that parochial schools had less violence than public schools because of stronger discipline. Coincidentally, a small race riot occurred at Roman Catholic High School the next day, which required police to arrive on the campus after fights between Black and white students broke out in the cafeteria. The school remained closed the following day. But Rizzo refused to take credit for Shedd's resignation. "It wasn't my decision to get rid of Dr. Shedd. The people made that decision," he claimed. "The people realized that Mark Shedd had destroyed a fine school system."[40]

With Shedd gone and Rizzo as mayor, the Student Bill of Rights came under renewed scrutiny. Freedman's murder was tragic, but observers saw through the veneer of political opportunists who tried to link two unrelated events. But Rizzo himself opposed the document. Newly appointed board member Dolores Oberholtzer also objected to it. She and Rizzo advocated for altering it. Many opponents of the document cited that high schools in the city were unsafe and said that student license had gone too far. Sympathizers argued that young people lacked self-esteem and brought gang wars off the street and into school or refused to show up at all. In January, School Board president William Ross hinted that he might abolish the Bill of Rights since the text, he argued, provided students' rights without spelling out their responsibilities. "Students didn't want a Student Bill of Rights," he contended. "The superintendent's office asked them to ask for it." But as time passed, most educators became more accepting of the program and felt that it had opened new lines of communication between students and administrators and averted confrontations. Dr. James T. Lytle, a school district administrator who supervised the program, stated, "My feeling is that there's a lot of misinformation on the Bill of Rights." He admitted that it cannot solve all problems, but "it's been relatively successful considering the obstacles." Not all school officials agreed. Abraham Lincoln High School Principal Bernard Rafferty, who also headed the Philadelphia Association of School Administrators, felt that the document did nothing to cut down on incidents. But he concurred with Lytle that it has helped principals become more aware of students' needs and anxieties and solve problems before they erupt. Nonetheless, the district intended to review it at the end of the present school year before continuing it.[41]

To preserve the Bill of Rights, Bailey and several of her peers expanded the Board of the Union of Student Government (USG). The group was previously composed of all the elected student government presidents in the city's public high schools. USG claimed to represent 59,000 students, even though it had about 100 active members. It opened its meetings to all students, but only presidents could vote on matters. Rather than small collective efforts, the members realized there was strength in numbers and invited all other officers. Since Bailey and her friends came from a well-integrated community, they all "believed it was necessary and kept it in mind when involving people." One of her friends, preceding Girls' High President and USG co-founder, Laura Punnett, was Jewish. The president and vice president of Central High School (the academic magnet for boys) were Black; the new Student Government president of Germantown High School, Emily Rice, was white; and the president of South Philadelphia High was an Italian girl, "although she was afraid to leave her neighborhood sometimes." "It was important to have diverse thoughts and opinions in all conversations and decisions," Bailey says. "All of these student leaders were thoughtful and great communicators so, I always felt confident in our decisions and direction." They received assistance from sympathetic adults. One of Bailey's neighbors allowed the group to hold gatherings in her home and arranged meeting spaces for them in the school district building. They also received advice from a member of the Fellowship Commission and a Community Legal Service attorney, Steve Gold, who assisted in strategy sessions and educated them about contemporary law for them to cite, if necessary, when discussing issues.[42]

Bailey's involvement in USG captured the attention of the *Daily News*, which published a profile piece about her in February 1972, a rare occurrence in the high school movement, as most journalists wrote in-depth pieces about white youth. The article published a portrait image of Bailey with an afro and allowed her to explain the purpose and goals of the USG. She recanted the prevailing argument about the breakdown of discipline in the city's schools. "The biggest problem isn't discipline, absenteeism, or fighting," she argued. "The biggest problem is that the schools don't entice students to want to go to school." Formed in June, the USG sought to work within the system and pressed a ten-point student rights program on the administration. Working with attorney Gold, it had filed a suit in Common Pleas Court charging that the school district had no rights under state code to suspend or expel students for absenteeism or tardiness. The group had succeeded in implementing the Bill of Rights in most of the city's high schools. Local officials admired the members' dedication. "What impresses me is their political sophistication," uttered Lytle. "They are meeting with city councilmen, board members, principals, etc. . . . they are lobbying in the true sense of the word." Bailey felt, "High schools today are too methodical and planned. If we can change some of the reasons why a student dislikes the school, then we can change some of the basic attitudes about education and life in general."[43]

The USG had an uphill battle. In February 1972, the new superintendent, Matthew Costanzo, outlined a new get-tough policy on permissiveness in the public schools and said before a crowd of 2,000 teachers and administrators at South Philadelphia High that "anarchic behavior" would not be treated with "impunity." Bailey saw Costanzo as "no Einstein," but he was honest with her group. She, along with many Philadelphians, saw him as unqualified and "just another Rizzo supporter."[44] Speaking before more than 250 members of the Association for Supervision and Curriculum Development in March 1972, members of USG accused the school system of failing city students because it was nonresponsive to their educational needs and ignored their rights as human beings. Bailey, who spoke, accused school officials of ignoring the bill. Gary Baker, student president of Edison High, backed her. "When we lost Dr. Mark Shedd, we lost our Bill of Rights," he followed. "Many of our seniors, who are graduating, are reading on a sixth-grade level." Counterarguing pathological arguments about urban minorities, other members in attendance cited apathy and graffiti as an indication of low morale on the part of the students and accused teachers of "miseducation."[45]

Despite assurances to either eliminate or alter the Bill of Rights, Costanzo agreed that it should be retained in June 1972. He had received the results of a school survey on the bill that polled 1,000 students, student leaders, principals, and teachers, conducted by the School District's Office of Research and Evaluation. Only one in five students responded, but most other groups completed it. Half of department heads and 40 percent of teachers wanted the document terminated. However, 69 percent of principals and 55 percent of vice principals wanted the bill retained but with modifications on students' responsibilities. A reported 92 percent of student presidents, ombudsmen, and students wanted the bill to continue. Around 41 percent of students wanted changes in the methods provided for solving problems. Ross, who originally wanted the document terminated, modified his previous opinion and concurred with Costanzo in favor of revising the code. Thus, on July 17, the school board unanimously approved retaining the Bill of Rights with some modifications. Suggestions to improve the bill included explicit dress and discipline codes; annual distribution of the document; monthly meetings between students, faculty, and parents to ensure better implementation and understanding of the bill; better communication on school activities; and an obligation by students to keep informed and exercise their rights.[46]

The Student Bill of Rights remained intact for at least six years. Yet by October 1975, the passage of time had sown confusion among a new cohort of pupils, disconnected from the original campaign's fervor. Many ombudsmen noted that students were unaware of their roles, while teachers and administrators dismissed them as inept, seldom viewing them with the same responsibility as adults.[47] By December 1976, the *Daily News* observed a stark shift in student unions' strength compared to the radical energy of the late 1960s. "We're not radical anymore," asserted Dale Grundy, the Philadelphia Student Union's first executive director. "That image hurt us in the past. Now we're trying to teach students to negotiate effectively for their rights." Internal disputes, financial constraints, weak leadership, and accusations of racial and geographic dominance plagued the organization. During the previous school year, white students from three schools seceded to form their own "District 8" group, distancing themselves from issues like gang violence and homicides, which they felt were irrelevant to their concerns. Grundy lamented that school officials frequently violated the Student Bill of Rights and Responsibilities, opened student leaders' mail, controlled their funds, censored publications, and barred ombudsmen from grievance hearings.[48]

The ineffectiveness of the Student Bill of Rights cannot be pinned solely on student disorganization. From the outset, a significant faction of teachers and administrators harbored deep-seated opposition to its implementation. The document endured largely because of the efforts of student activists who labored tirelessly to draft and promote it. They maintained pressure on school officials to adhere to its tenets. These young advocates did not rest on their laurels; they kept organizing and mobilizing even during the summer months, a period when student activism typically waned. By 1976, the document remained intact, but the original champions had moved on, leaving behind a cohort less capable of ensuring its enforcement.

The Philadelphia Student Bill of Rights was predominantly a local matter, resonating through some nearby suburbs, but its influence extended far beyond the metropolitan area. In Indianapolis, the publishers of an underground newspaper at North Central High School reprinted it in their newsletter after the local daily, the *Indianapolis News*, in 1969 featured it following a disturbance at Shortridge High School. The reprint opened by acknowledging that the document emerged from disturbances in city schools, mirroring issues in Indianapolis. "Something should be done to have a policy of real students' rights before school is disrupted," they argued. In January 1972, North Central High adopted its own Statement of

Students' Rights and Responsibilities.[49] In 1971, the Kentucky Civil Liberties Union presented the Philadelphia Student Bill of Rights at its Students' Rights Conference.[50] However, students in Jefferson County public schools did not propose their own similar document until May 1975.[51] Most notably, activists from the Intermountain Indian School in Utah incorporated the Philadelphia document into Section A, 3731, when they presented the Indian Student Bill of Rights before the Senate Appropriations Committee on April 11, 1972. They also integrated similar texts from Arlington, Virginia, and Albuquerque, New Mexico, to outline the rights of Native American youth in both public and boarding schools. The document addressed First Amendment concerns regarding speech, religion, and privacy, relevant education, and strong student government, along with other concerns for Native youth in public and boarding schools.[52]

High school bills of rights campaigns, while less theatrical than student uprisings, played a crucial role in bolstering students' calls for school reform. These campaigns forced school boards and administrators to negotiate each proposal in detail, rather than offering empty promises. Although these documents could be overturned by a vote or a federal court case, young activists were often aware of impending changes. They used the allotted time given to public meetings to voice their dissent effectively. Local circumstances significantly influenced which issues students considered most urgent. In Philadelphia, youth criticized the placement and expansion of police in schools. But in many suburban white communities that had their own bill of rights campaigns, rarely did this concern emerge.

Not all students driven to activism were directly motivated by the civil rights or antiwar movements. School violence also shaped the high school movement, prompting teenagers with no prior experience in formal politics to become political actors. In newly integrated schools or neighborhoods with shifting racial demographics, Black students and their parents often demanded reforms to address racial conflict, revise curricula, and change disciplinary policies. They also sometimes sought police protection against white resistance, which frequently involved physical assaults and intimidation. School violence was a nationwide issue, but one institution in Cleveland, Ohio, faced an overwhelming amount of communal violence for a decade.

8 Violence and Reform
Cleveland's Collinwood High School Race Riots

On April 7, 1970, Cleveland's Mayor Carl Stokes was at home on Tuesday night watching the David Frost Show. The featured guest, actor Harry Belafonte, provided a brief relaxation until urgent news shattered the peace. Reports came in about the sheer magnitude of the violence that had occurred at Collinwood High School the previous day. On Monday, around 8:00 a.m., an unruly crowd of 350 to 400 individuals gathered outside and began shattering windows—fifty-six in all. "We don't want to go to school with the niggers," spat one demonstrator when questioned about why he stood outside the building. Inside, staff hurried nearly 200 Black students into a third-floor cafeteria. At 10:30 a.m., the crowd breached the building through a side entrance. They smashed more windows, destroyed furniture, and wreaked havoc. Music director George Stone confronted the mob with a chair, but rioters retaliated by hurling clubs at him. Panic seized the cafeteria as the chaos continued. In a desperate bid for survival, Black youth hurled tables and chairs down the stairs to form a barricade. They snapped the legs off tubular metal chairs to use as makeshift weapons in case the mob broke through. But the worst-case scenario was avoided. An hour later, rioters cleared the building. Officials then escorted Black students downstairs and safely evacuated them onto chartered buses. Fifteen mounted police and a few adults protected them from the crowd, which included parents clutching umbrellas and baseball bats. They shouted, "Get the animals," and "Nigger blood." Several people hurled rocks as the buses departed the area.[1]

Upon hearing the news, Stokes sprang into action. Having little to no power over the school system, he had previously been reluctant to intervene when student uprisings erupted in the city's predominantly Black high schools during the previous academic year. But the Collinwood riot was too severe to ignore. With tension mounting, he dispatched a police detective to summon Superintendent Paul Briggs to City Hall, gathering school board members and councilmen from the Collinwood area for an emergency meeting. Stokes strode into City Hall at 8:30 p.m. He adamantly opposed closing the school, believing a minority of lawbreakers had caused the riot. Briggs initially decided to close the school, but the late-night discussion with the school board around 10:30 p.m. saw the mayor's stance prevail. By 11:00 p.m., Briggs, board members, and Safety Director Benjamin O. Davis Jr. made a televised announcement on three different stations that the school would remain open. As the midnight hour approached, Stokes contacted Adjutant General Sylvester T. Del Corso, commander of the Ohio National Guard, to notify him of the potential need for deployment. Del Corso assured him that his men would be prepared by dawn. Just after midnight, at 12:20 a.m., Stokes fired off a telegram to Governor James A. Rhodes:

> This is to inform you that a state of emergency exists in the City of Cleveland relative to the Collinwood High School at 15210 St. Clair Avenue. The school has been closed due to extreme violence. We are reopening the school at 8:30 A.M. today, Wednesday April 8. We anticipate the strong probability of a violent reaction which may be beyond the ability of our Cleveland police to adequately handle. I hereby formally request that you alert the Ohio National Guard and have their assistance and presence readily available in the Cleveland area should the necessity for help materialize later today.[2]

The school reopened the following day, flanked by 166 policemen tasked with maintaining order. Nearby, in the suburbs of Cleveland Heights and Shaker Heights, stood about 700 members of the Ohio National Guard. As the day progressed, the police presence gradually diminished, but a contingent stayed throughout the night to remain vigilant against a recurrence of the previous day's violence at both Collinwood and the nearby junior high school. Despite these precautions, the impact of the previous day's unrest lingered. About 30 percent of students stayed home. Outside the school, Davis conversed with anxious parents. When asked if he could ensure their children's safety, Davis responded candidly, stating, "There are no guarantees."[3] He was right. By 1970, Collinwood had endured five years of race riots. Although many parents desired peace, the violence at Collinwood High would continue for five more years. The school and surrounding area would resemble a battleground, where residents witnessed regular police calls, school closures, possession of weaponry, physical assaults, stabbings, hospitalizations, and even a murder.

The students at Collinwood High were not directly connected to the high school movement, nor did they participate in antiwar protests or student rights campaigns in any significant manner. But racial violence within school settings frequently thrust students into roles as activists, even if they had not previously engaged in formal politics.[4] In the aftermath of the April 1970 riot, Black students launched a boycott against nonacademic activities.[5] This action occurred regularly. After various racial clashes, both Black and white students, along with their parents, drafted a list of demands and met with school officials to advocate for policies they believed would mitigate racial tensions. Akin to nonviolent protests, Black students demanded greater representation among faculty and staff, the removal of racist teachers, Black history courses, and questioned the deployment of police, noting its discriminatory use of force and apparent indifference to white antagonists. But some demands were completely opposite from those of their peers in the high school movement. Rather than demanding the removal of police officers from campus, Black students and their parents called for police protection on and off campus to shield them from white violence. Although their counterparts called for amending suspensions and expulsions, Collinwood students demanded stronger disciplinary policies to punish agitators. These efforts, coupled with shifting neighborhood demographics, ignited a strong white backlash. White youth and their parents, adopting reactionary and retaliatory rhetoric, claimed that the mere presence of Black students exacerbated racial tensions and demanded their removal. They wanted police to closely monitor Black students, whom they accused of lawless behavior.

Despite efforts to mitigate racial tensions, the clashes persisted for ten consecutive years from 1965 to 1975. It fit the broader pattern of school violence. As Black and Latino students found themselves in newly desegregated environments or in schools with shifting neighborhood demographics, they faced white resistance from students and parents. The sparks varied widely, from small fights that morphed into large brawls to off-campus racial violence and the sight of interracial dating. In urban, suburban, and rural areas, schools reported an average of roughly one serious incident of "personal violence" per school each month. From September to November 18, 1970, there were over 225 "disorders and disruptions" reported. Nearly 900 arrests were made, and 200 people were injured, including twenty policemen and twelve teachers. School and law enforcement officials failed to identify the underlying causes or context and instead targeted Black students for punishment, expanded police presence, and enacted harsher disciplinary rules.[6]

But what set Collinwood apart from many other episodes across the country dealt with the pervasive nature of clashes involving both students *and* adults, occurring both on *and* off campus. Elected officials and parents became perplexed and debated what drove the persistent violence. Did it come from bad parenting? Adults corrupting youth by sharing their racist beliefs? Outside agitators? Some even adopted inertia, saying, "That's just the way it is." These questions came up regularly in newspaper editorials, school board meetings, and discussions with public officials. Cultural explanations appealed to emotions. The reality was rooted in political, economic, and social trends in the greater Cleveland area and the Collinwood neighborhood.

Cleveland's School Desegregation Campaign

On March 19, 1965, a routine trip for a father to pick up his fifteen-year-old son and fourteen-year-old daughter quickly spiraled into chaos. "As I drove down E. 152 St., a gang of white hoodlums swarmed out of a pool room with cue sticks and cue balls and started throwing and smashing against my car," he told *Call and Post* reporters. The Black teens at the Northeast branch of the YMCA had been attending a well-supervised social event, an unusual occurrence in a center that Black social groups had traditionally avoided. Outside the building, a group of "white hoodlums" harassed and threatened the teens. YMCA officials called the police multiple times, to no avail. No witnesses reported the exact reason teens congregated outside the center, but there had been reports of a minor clash in the area. A white youth had been struck in the head, and another was cut or stabbed. However, the recent racial conflict at Collinwood High likely loomed large in everyone's minds. Sensing the escalating tensions, the supervisors decided to end the dance early to allow the teens to leave and avoid a potential conflict. Their decision came too late. The gang turned their aggression toward Black motorists, creating a terrifying situation for the father and his children. "I was so surprised I automatically stopped and stalled the engine," the father recalled. "My children were screaming—the boys outside were howling and calling names—I was scared to death and didn't know what to do." The reporter who wrote about the incident, appearing perplexed, asked, "What happened? Nobody knows just what, or why the uneasiness."[7] This seemingly random act of chaos, however, was rooted in Collinwood's recent history of demographic shifts, a backlash to civil rights activism, and a concerted effort by some residents to maintain the neighborhood's white majority.

Situated about seven miles northeast of downtown Cleveland, Collinwood is bordered to the north by Lake Erie, with rail yards dividing the neighborhood into North and South Collinwood for statistical purposes. Originally part of East Cleveland Township, Collinwood was known as Collamer when it existed as a separate village before the city of Cleveland annexed it in 1910. Throughout much of its history, the neighborhood was predominantly white, home to Irish, Italian, Slovenian, and other white ethnic groups.[8] People of modest means lived in the area, with residents owning their homes and maintaining strong ethnic, religious, and economic ties. However, during the 1950s, Collinwood found itself adjacent to increasingly Black neighborhoods, particularly the former majority Jewish neighborhood of Glenville to its west. While there had been a small Black community in Collinwood for years, the western fringes of the neighborhood had seen an influx of Black residents seeking relief from the overcrowded conditions in Glenville.[9] Additionally, white migrants from southern Appalachia began settling in "shabbier residential areas" like Collinwood Railroad Yards, known as Five Points.[10]

The slow but visible Black presence increased as the civil rights movement sought to desegregate schools, and Collinwood was ground zero. Cleveland's Black population expanded during the Second Great Migration, growing from 147,808 to 279,352 from 1950 to 1965. By 1965, Black children made up about 54 percent of the public school population, and 99.1 percent of Black residents lived on the East Side. Consequently, majority Black schools became severely overcrowded. Kindergarten students had been placed on a waiting list. Parents had long complained about subpar teachers, a lack of remedial instruction, low expectations from faculty, few Black administrators, high student-teacher ratios, poor physical conditions, inadequate social services, and a severe lack of vocational courses. But on the predominately white west side, schools had better teachers, services, buildings, and low student-to-teacher ratios. To alleviate the issue, administrators converted auditoriums, gymnasiums, libraries, storerooms, playrooms, dispensaries, basements, and attics into classrooms and began constructing mobile classrooms in schoolyards. In 1957, the Ohio Department of Education intervened and authorized the city to establish a relay program. Applying only to all-Black schools, the policy bused one group of pupils to school in the morning, sent them home, and bused another group in the afternoon. Schoolchildren attended school for three and a half hours, which was below the state standard of a five-hour school day.[11]

Black mothers objected to this policy. In September 1961, activist Daisy Craggett and other Black parents organized the Parents' Against Relay Classes and picketed the board of education administration building to demand full-day sessions. More importantly, the parents had discovered that there were 165 empty classrooms in public schools in white communities. The negative publicity of the relay program led school administrators to abolish the program in Spring 1962. Seeking another solution, the school board adopted an even more controversial busing plan for the 1962 to 1963 school year. Black students and their teachers were to be bused to underutilized white schools on the East Side to save money and commute time. Black parents approved of the policy but opposed the plans to minimize contact between Black and white schoolchildren that sought to appease white parents. In these "integrated" environments, Black students could not eat lunch in the cafeteria or participate in assemblies, physical education classes, and school-wide extracurricular activities. They could only access the bathroom once at a designated time per day and could not see the in-school nurse.[12]

The school board engaged in a juggling act with school desegregation to placate Black demands and simultaneously not upset their base. Board President Ralph McCallister's base lay in white ethnics who resided in various pockets of the East Side. These parents desired that schools remain segregated. Some of these residents said that children from Glenville were welcome to use the school premises, but demands for integration went too far. Those who adamantly opposed integration formed the Collinwood Improvement Association and the North American Alliance for White People to resist integration. They viewed Black youngsters as socially pathological and intellectually inferior and feared miscegenation. Certainly, not all white politicians held these views, but the strength of the white ethnic blocs ensured they walked a fine line to avoid antagonizing them.[13]

Opposed to the segregated practices their children experienced in white schools, the Relay Parents changed their name to the Hazeldell Parents Association (HPA). Later, the NAACP, Urban League, CORE, and other Black and white civic organizations formed an interracial coalition called the United Freedom Movement (UFM) in December 1962 to challenge the school board. UFM negotiated with Superintendent William Levenson and McCallister and eventually delivered an ultimatum in response to inaction: Black students bused to schools must be fully integrated by September 1963. School officials did not budge. Intact busing continued. In response, the UFM held a rally at Cory Methodist Church in the Glenville neighborhood and voted to pursue nonviolent direct-action protests. Picketing at the board began, and protesters returned each day of the week, beginning on September 30. The publicity the picketers received led the school board to create the Human Relations Committee to oversee the integration of bused students. But the plan did not suffice. The committee sought to have about 20 percent of bused students engage with white pupils for about forty minutes each day and remain separate for the rest of the school day.[14]

UFM members were outraged, and white residents in Collinwood now confronted the civil rights movement in their neighborhood. After the school board passed a resolution to address UFM's demand by using the "fullest possible incorporation of transported students into receiving school organizations," white residents immediately opposed the plan. The UFM decided to picket the receiving schools. On January 29, 1964, UFM and HPA activists arrived at William H. Brett Elementary and began protesting and picketing. White parents and other residents hurled objects at them. The event coincided with a sit-in at the Superintendent's office, where protesters stayed for several hours, but he never appeared. The next day, activists went to Memorial Elementary, where a mob of about 1,400 residents attacked them and two *Call and Post* reporters. Police stood by and watched. Collinwood's Brett and Memorial Elementary schools eventually integrated the bused students, but only a small number remained. The board eventually placated white parents by announcing the construction of three new schools on the East Side on February 26, 1964. Civil rights protests at receiving schools continued, culminating in another sit-in at the board of education, where police violently removed protesters, and the death of a white minister and CORE activist, Bruce Klunder, when a bulldozer accidentally ran over him as he lay in a shallow ditch to protest the construction of an elementary school. Activists organized a system-wide school boycott on April 20, 1964, coinciding with actions across the nation. But the school board continued construction. McCallister resigned in 1964, replaced by Paul Briggs, the former chair of the Ohio Commission on Civil Rights. Briggs inherited a school system that had seen little desegregation and would experience some of the most violent racial clashes in one neighborhood for ten consecutive years.[15]

Collinwood residents had been catapulted into civil rights battles, upending what had been for decades a lily-white community buffered by other majority-white areas. Discriminatory housing policies and slumlords produced overcrowded conditions and served as the catalyst for Black families to leave Glenville. As the Black population in the city increased, integrated living seemed all but inevitable. Collinwood residents used civic organizations and even collective violence to oppose school integration. They would continue to do so as Black families migrated into the area. White opposition to integration manifested itself in three ways. The first was flight. Middle- and upper-middle-class families who could afford to leave had departed. But the ones left behind had mortgages too burdensome to abandon, and some lived on fixed incomes.[16] The second option was advocacy. Civic organizations harbored overt racism but rarely espoused those ideas publicly. Instead, these parents demanded meetings with district officials to outline their complaints and demand the removal of Black students. The last option was to fight. The most extreme opponents of integration resorted to threats, intimidation, and physical assaults. No matter what action or inaction they decided to take, many white residents feared ongoing racial transition in the community, civil rights activism, and losing neighborhood homogeneity. The local press regularly referred to the "Collinwood School Crisis" as a riot, melee, disturbance, and various other phrases that portrayed it as cyclical, routine conflicts between students. In actuality, the school served as a proxy for a systematic campaign among white residents to terrorize Black children and drive Black families out of the neighborhood, thereby maintaining its previous racial makeup. For the next ten years, Collinwood was at war.

Linda Rae Murray and the 1965 Collinwood High Riots

Akin to her peers, Linda Rae Murray attended Collinwood High for an education. But she had no idea she would be a spokesperson to highlight the neighborhood's growing racial tensions. She was born on August 25, 1948, in Cleveland, Ohio. Her mother, Ruth Childress, attended the majority-white Glenville High and dropped out to marry Linda's father, Raymond, who enlisted in the Army during World War II. Raymond had been a well-read child, but during his tenure at East Technical High School, a counselor discouraged him from applying to college. "You're going to shine shoes," is what he remembered the counselor telling him. Neither of Linda's parents was politically active. Yet their political views influenced her. While watching the evening news, segments appeared about the Soviet Union, and her parents reminded the kids how the Soviets helped achieve victory in World War II. They would then ask them their thoughts about socialism. The family lived in housing projects in the Central neighborhood when her parents separated, but Murray did not attend school in the area. In the fourth grade, she was enrolled in an academically talented program after taking an IQ test, which required her to take three buses to a white neighborhood to Boulevard Elementary School in the suburb of Shaker Heights. She remembered her classes including about half Black students and half white, and white parents feeling uneasy about their children attending class with Black kids. However, the education was better. "We read actual novels and books," compared to little, short snippets. "And we learned how to discuss them. And we might spend . . . a month on a book." The school also taught her research and presentation skills.[17]

As a child, Linda and her brother joined Student CORE. As a member, she participated in organizing a rent strike in the Hough neighborhood and joined the 1964 citywide school boycott. She eventually found herself in Marxist circles when she joined a study group after the Cleveland Public Schools terminated a popular junior high school teacher. The small group met with him every Saturday to read history, *The Communist Manifesto*, and works by Vladimir Lenin. "It allowed us to analyze the Civil Rights Movement," she remembered. Through the group, she realized "that the problems that existed for the Civil Rights Movement wasn't just segregation or . . . that white folks didn't like us[;] . . . there were some structural problems, deep-seated problems that existed in the United States." She assisted Student CORE's rent strike in the Hough neighborhood. "We were involved in it, in whatever way high school students can be," she recalled. Murray initially disliked reading because the librarian recommended books to her that were well below her reading level. When she selected her own books one day, she found a new passion.[18]

Her family moved away from housing projects and relocated to Glenville, where she attended Collinwood High beginning in the seventh grade. The Black student population hovered around 20 percent with a student body of 3,200 students, containing both junior and high school students. Most of her Black peers resided in the Glenville neighborhood and attended the school's academically talented program, referred to as the enrichment program for gifted students taking college-prep courses. Several of her peers shared experiences they had with assistant principals who told them that it was a privilege to attend Collinwood High. If they continued to misbehave, the officials warned, then they would have to leave the school. Student life was segregated. Black pupils separated themselves in the lunchroom. Interestingly, they measured the growth of the Black population by how many tables they occupied in the cafeteria. In gym, white students dominated playtime. When Black youth tried to participate, their white peers pushed them away.[19]

The beginning of impending racial violence at the school emerged in 1964. As the school year ended, a group of young adults, all in their twenties, attacked Black students as they exited the building. The tension only escalated with the dawn of the new academic year. On September 10, 1964, vandals defaced the entrance steps with graffiti. The racist messages read, "No Niggers," "Dark Man Go," and were accompanied by two large KKK symbols. Principal John Lee, attempting to downplay the severity, attributed the vandalism to local troublemakers "probably in their early 20s and likely school drop-outs." He lamented, "We just wish we'd be let alone by these outsiders who believe in trouble and want trouble. They are trying to make the school a neighborhood battleground." His concern proved prophetic. Neither Lee nor the community could foresee that the 1964–65 school year would herald a relentless era of violence and unrest.[20]

The first major riot at Collinwood High occurred on March 18, 1965. On the previous day, Murray arrived early to school, as she usually did, around 7:30 a.m. Upon arriving, she saw pickets of white students chanting around the school grounds. Her status as a "civil rights veteran" led her to initially admire the organization and discipline of the demonstrators. However, as she drew closer, she realized the chants were far from benign. "Two, four, six, eight, we don't want to integrate," the crowd shouted. Inside the school, chaos ensued. White girls were running, screaming, and crying, desperate to leave. "The school was like two square blocks. . . . Every entrance was covered," Murray recalled. Concerned for her sister's safety, Murray searched for her, but she refused to leave the school. Murray, however, left. Later, school officials arranged a meeting between Black and white student council leaders. Both sides agreed to disarm and avoid further trouble. Murray's classmates reassured her that everything had been resolved. "Oh Linda, everything's worked out. We're going to have this truce," they asserted.[21]

However, the truce was short-lived and built on shaky ground. Unbeknownst to Murray's peers, adults had orchestrated the picket and held secret community meetings. The following morning, March 18, Murray arrived at school to find an even larger crowd gathered outside. She saw no white girls running around inside the school. This time, it was eerily empty, devoid of any white students. "So, then I get scared again[;] . . . now there are like hundreds of parents surrounding the school," Murray recalled. "I'm saying I can't get out; I can't leave the school. It's fifteen or twenty minutes later, my colleagues who are coming later than me are having to fight their way through the crowds, run through the crowd to get into the school." Crowds of white boys circled the building as white girls left campus grounds. The boys warned the girls, "You'd better leave, there's going to be trouble." Several teachers who had arrived early tried to induce the students to go to class, but the crowd mocked them, including assistant principal Howard

Scene capture on the steps of Collinwood High School on March 18, 1965, by Cleveland Press photographer Herman Seid. Courtesy of Michael Schwartz Library Special Collections, Cleveland State University.

Lawrence. Black students soon found themselves trapped as the crowd's number swelled. Principal Lee and some teachers locked themselves in the main office. The situation escalated rapidly. Murray and others attempted to move the schoolchildren into the auditorium for safety, but many remained in their homerooms, with teachers refusing to let them leave. Like déjà vu, Murray once again feared for her sister's safety, assuming she had perished in the chaos outside. Luckily, some Black parents who lived nearby had formed a caravan and covertly rescued as many children as possible by sneaking underneath the building. But most students knew nothing about this effort. Most remained locked inside the building. Murray joined a delegation that confronted Lee and demanded he do something. "You have to call the police," they implored. "You have to find some way to escort us out of here." But the mob outside made it impossible for them to leave safely.[22]

The first four police units to arrive began confiscating clubs, sticks, and other weapons with which the students had armed themselves. "Send everyone and everything you can," officials called over the police emergency radio broadcast as more students arrived for classes and joined the milling pupils. A police helicopter, hovering above, offered a bird's eye view of the chaos below, estimating the crowd at 700 to 800 people, disrupting traffic. Dozens of fights broke out among small groups, making it impossible for even the most observant person to keep up with the chaos. Athletes assisted mounted and foot policemen as they pushed through the crowds. During the clashes, Associated Press photographer Julian Wilson fell. Councilman John Banko tried to stop a fight, and someone pushed him to the ground. He entered the building in tears and pleaded with Lee to close the school for the day. Teachers who watched cried. At one moment, white youths charged at fifty Black students who had just exited from the front entrance. Senior James Carlson later reported that six or seven boys attacked him, and one hit him with a club. Seventh grader Larry Richard relayed that as he tried to enter the building, he heard seven white boys scream, "Let's get him." Both boys later had X-rays taken. Those trapped inside had limited communication. They relied on transit radios scavenged by students for information. Even the act of self-preservation took on a desperate tone as some resorted to breaking chairs in a basement classroom to use as improvised weapons. Eventually, buses arrived at the campus to transport students back to the Glenville area. The crowd continued its rage. They hurled projectiles at the departing vehicles, which shattered the windows. The violence had lasted for about three hours, and two white youths required hospital treatment.[23]

The news reached Glenville High, where Murray's brother Randall attended. "They're killing people at Collinwood," shouted people at the school. The rumor was inaccurate, but many Glenville residents knew the threats of violence that could occur if they walked into an all-white neighborhood. Most likely, they were aware of the city's two race riots in the previous years. In June 1963, in an area near the Rockefeller Park system called Sowinski Park, which was to the west of Glenville, incendiary media coverage of a young couple allegedly attacked by Black youth ignited a race riot. White rioters threw stones at Black motorists and burned two Black-owned businesses. In Little Italy in January 1964, white rioters attacked civil rights demonstrators. Urged by Collinwood students, Randall joined around 200 youth who began marching to the neighborhood. However, police halted them when they were still over thirty city blocks away from their destination.[24]

As the school day ended at 3:30 p.m., large groups of white students and adults began to congregate, moving from street corner to street corner, hurling rocks and bricks, even damaging a police cruiser in their anger. The police eventually managed to disperse the crowd by 5:00 p.m. But the unrest did not end there, as individuals within the crowd targeted a zone car, shattering its window with a brick. Additionally, the crowd converged near Forest Hill playground, adjacent to Patrick Henry Junior High School, where they ignited a short-lived hay fire.[25]

Rather than viewing the violence as an extension of communal violence that had plagued the area since the school desegregation protests, police and school officials saw it as the byproduct of bad-faith actors who, if brought to justice, would settle the issue. Inspector Michael J. Blackwell promised to find the ringleaders responsible and stated, "I hope this can be settled quietly. The sooner it's over, the sooner we can get back to being an orderly community." Briggs wanted order. In a telecast, he cast doubt that the disorder would have occurred without the "backing and approval of some adults." Deputy Superintendent of Schools, Alva R. Dittrick, believed a "small hard core" group of people of both races caused the violence. Principal Lee attributed the violence to the incident that happened at the YMCA the previous Friday night, and the fight that occurred between white and Black youth by the building that required two white youths to seek medical care for cuts. Lee also cited other incidents that had occurred over the weekend, including minor scuffles on Monday that teachers broke up. On Tuesday, he said a group of white students held a meeting near the school and decided to try to calm the ringleaders. And on the previous day, according to Lee, words passed around among some white students to "keep the girls out of school tomorrow."[26] Privately, he felt differently. He told FBI agents tasked with investigating the incident that "there is a hard-core group of white parents who keep their kids stirred up against the Negroes." He also believed the recent publicity concerning the civil rights demonstration in Selma, Alabama, had done much to increase tensions. But he still felt certain that outside influences or professional agitators were nonexistent.[27]

Murray felt differently. She departed on the buses that took the students back to Glenville and witnessed objects hurled at them. "What were we trying to do with this desegregation stuff?" she asked. Why would people "take off of work, bring their babies in the buggies to throw bricks at a bunch of kids, half of whom were . . . seventh, eighth, [and] ninth graders?" She understood the advantages that the school provided, but why attend school with people "that are going to throw bricks at you?" She could not wait to leave Collinwood, and by the time she went off to college, "I was enraged."[28]

In the aftermath of the riot, parents tried to mitigate racial tensions. Collinwood High alumni Rufus Pierce went to the school to attend a meeting for parents to help solve the school's racial problem. He grossly miscalculated the situation. Mistakenly, he walked into the auditorium, thinking the meeting was in that part of the building. "Of course, I never realized my mistake until I got into the meeting and some young hoodlums—their faces filled with anger, looked back at where we sat, and demanded to know—what are you niggers doing here?" Pierce knew he was in danger. Some people in the auditorium told the youth to leave him alone. But others urged the teens to attack him. "I looked around as they rushed towards me, realized the meeting was all white, and that I was in a dangerous situation." One white man tried to protect Pierce but got knocked down and was later questioned by police as to why he was fighting. The youth then set their sights on Pierce's wife, who ran to the police for help. Pierce expressed confusion about what transpired. He had lived in Collinwood for thirty years, graduated from the high school, and had six children enrolled in school. "For many years there was no trouble out here at all, but in recent years there has been a gradual deterioration of race relations so long and so well established." Of course, Pierce seemed to be oblivious to the fact that for most of his time in the area, white residents viewed their Black neighbors as nonthreatening given their small percentages.[29]

The conflict led school officials to engage with students and hear their proposals to mitigate racial tensions. Students now had the opportunity to propose reforms. A reported twenty-five Black and white students met with assistant principals Lawrence and Joseph Lesko on March 19. They recommended strict enforcement and penalties for misbehavior. Carrying weapons would carry a five-day suspension; pushing, shoving, and fighting in the halls would result in a one-day suspension; and students who used obscene language would be punished. Lawrence left the meeting feeling optimistic and thought it had a "real conciliatory atmosphere." But on the same day, 200 policemen stayed in the area throughout the day, and police arrested twenty-four people, juveniles and adults, who continued to roam through the neighborhood well into the evening with homemade weapons. Many students stayed home, with only about 975 pupils in class the previous day.[30]

Riots, as historian Lana Barber noted, "are one of the few occasions in which journalists, academics, and government officials converge to actively seek out and record the opinions of ordinary people on the state of their city." Additionally, these large-scale conflicts "create a unique archive that allows historians unparalleled access to the views, thoughts, and frustrations of regular city residents, beyond oft-quoted politicians and media-savvy activists."[31] While high school violence sometimes spilled off campus, it seldom reached the scale of urban uprisings, though it shared similarities. They had political undertones. Journalists flocked to scenes, interviewing school administrators, police, elected officials, and occasionally students, who critiqued the state of the schools and proposed solutions.[32] A study by Urban American Inc. discovered that racial violence in high schools escalated during the 1968–69 school year. White students and their parents reacted to changing demographics in newly desegregated schools or those affected by neighborhood transitions. In response, Black students engaged in self-defense. The triggers for violence varied and evolved over time, including white student hostility, the firing of Black teachers, police violence, student safety concerns, and discriminatory discipline.[33]

Although local papers often reduced students' interviews to soundbites, Cleveland's Black newspaper, the *Call and Post*, and a 1966 Congressional Testimony provided them with a platform to discuss what happened. One *Call and Post* reporter interviewed three Collinwood students: Murray, Robbie Hamilton, and David Mathis, who all sat on the Human Relations Council. All three hoped that the recent riot would not be forgotten and sought to use it to foster change and improve race relations at the school. "School officials were continuing to say there was nothing wrong," claimed Murray. The trio cited the superficiality of their white peers' friendliness, as Black students faced exclusion from social clubs and felt unwanted. Even if a white member of a club nominated a Black pupil, it would likely create enemies within the club. Teachers remained "hush-hush" about the civil rights movement whenever someone mentioned it. All three students recognized the ineffectiveness of the human relations club since previous white members had graduated, and there had been no replacements. The group almost lost the right to be associated with the school and had to take over lost and found duties to qualify as a service club since it currently lacked recognition as a social group. On race relations, Murray stated, "The actual problem lies in the community; there's not really much we can do about it."[34]

In April 1966, Murray and white student Howard Birdsong testified in front of a US Civil Rights Commission hearing in Cleveland. Collinwood had not experienced a major riot since March 1965. But the lack of a newsworthy incident certainly did not mean it could not occur again. Briggs spoke at the hearing and discussed the challenges of integration. "If you run out of whites, you run out of chances for integrated education," he stated, referencing how residential patterns complicated matters. He believed, "If these youngsters could divorce themselves from the prejudice of their parents, they would be a lot better off." Murray and Birdsong were more pessimistic. Both felt no progress had been made since the 1965 riots. The students had drafted a paper to help the situation, but it got filed away. Murray and Birdsong differed on what they thought were the root causes. She admitted that she believed the riots were nothing more than an extension of "Collinwood's attempt to remove Negroes from schools." Furthermore, she believed that most "white students at Collinwood resent the presence of Negro students." Birdsong agreed with her latter statement but attributed it to the climax of built-up tensions between Black and white students, with white students resenting Black students being bused to the area. He also stated that prior to the riot, Black boys had chased a white girl, and white students retaliated.[35]

School Reform Efforts

Besides unreported daily harassment and intimidation, Collinwood High had no major reported racial incidents until 1969. On March 13, police arrested six youths for smashing forty windows and placed extra officers on duty. Spurred by rumors of two white teenagers suspended for fighting a Black youth three weeks ago, on the next day, about 150 white students and adults paraded around the building and threatened to boycott school until they could have a meeting with Briggs. "If he wants time, we'll give him time," yelled Dennis DiGiacomo, a student elected spokesman for the group. "We'll give him all day. We want to meet with Briggs." School officials called the police around 11:00 a.m., and the protesters scattered. The students distributed leaflets that bore the name of the United Citizens' Council of America, National Headquarters. In big letters, the leaflet asked readers, "Special rights for black savages?" Hawking conservative critiques of urban uprisings, the leaflets continued, "Do you believe that law enforcement should be relaxed so blacks can murder, rape, loot and burn without fear of punishment?" One white kid had a handkerchief tied around his head and claimed it "symbolizes white power, baby." Around 2:00 p.m., the same day, the crowd regrouped and demanded Briggs come to the school and talk with them.[36]

When Principal L. Barrett Smith informed them that Briggs refused to do so, they began shattering about thirty windows and hurling bricks and rocks at several cars. The crowd cornered one Black motorist and hit his car with a brick. Police arrested the brick thrower and nine other students. *Cleveland*

Press reporter Dick Feagler was at the scene. When he spoke to Principal Smith, he noticed that he looked exhausted as he sat behind his desk. Smith told Feagler, "I know it sounds trite, but I wish you'd try to put in the paper that only a small percentage of the students were on the street here today." Although the crowd pale in comparison to the 1965 riot, Feagler's reporting revealed that racial tensions had persisted. He strolled into a neighborhood center called Open End, where the boy who screamed "white power" went after the demonstration. There, he saw a big sign on the door that read "Brotherhood" and young people shooting pool. He spoke to a "big husky youth," who relayed, "We've let these people go too far. They broke my window last week. They spit on you." "Who?" Feagler asked. "The [racial epithet]. That's who," the youth replied. Feagler reported that he spoke to Albert Ballew, president of the Collinwood Improvement Association, who watched the demonstration as he stood across from the high school. "I don't know if you could call this a racially tense community," he claimed. "This is the only community where black[s] and white[s] live together. There is no other community in Cleveland to compare this to." Ballew might have been unaware of the Ludlow neighborhood, which sat on the border of Cleveland and its suburb Shaker Heights. Coinciding with racial tensions in Collinwood, middle- and upper-middle class residents there pioneered harmonious racial integration and had received national recognition.[37]

Although less severe than the 1965 riot, the recent violence allowed students to air grievances, even though white participants proposed policies that not only sought to reduce Black enrollment but also endorsed notions of Black criminality. A reporter from the *Call and Post* observed a meeting parents and community leaders had with school officials and recognized "that their major grievances arise from the steadily-increasing Negro population at the once 'lily-white' East Side school." The Collinwood Area Police Citizen Committee held a meeting that evening where students and parents expressed racist allegations that referenced stereotypes about Black people's propensity toward violence, sexual proclivities, intelligence, and drug use. The reporter noted that attitudes expressed were "glaringly anti-Negro, with charges of beatings, carrying concealed weapons, and 'molestings' (of white girl students) were aired before Principal Smith." Interestingly, the crowd did not mention any forms of white violence. Yet, at one meeting that occurred that weekend, one speaker opened with, "If there are any n——r lovers here, let's get them out right now."[38]

Briggs and Smith had a separate and secret meeting with small groups of white and Black students in the morning and evening, respectively.

Spokesmen for white students and parents attributed the worsening racial tension to the growing Black enrollment. They alleged that marijuana use had increased with the Black population. Others accused Black students of "molesting" white girls in the hallways and that Black boys were "getting too familiar" with them. The white students demanded frequent locker searches for drugs and weapons. Their parents even demanded a probe of eligible Black students attending the school and accused them of receiving favoritism in assignments, transfers, and from teachers. The meeting with Black parents and students, on the other hand, painted a reverse picture. The same teachers whites accused of showing Black students favoritism were cited in the meeting as displaying anti-Black prejudices. Black students complained about the stepped-up harassment, racial slurs, and physical attacks targeted at them outside the building. The students suggested that school officials improve communication between them and white students through a series of joint meetings.[39]

At the heart of these two contrasting meetings were white grievances over the changing demographics of the neighborhood and a deliberate forgetfulness of white violence and racism. In contrast to the early part of the decade, Black students attending the school came from families that had settled in the area. The balance was 70 percent white and 30 percent Black. Well-off whites fled to the suburbs, leaving their low-income counterparts behind. A *Call and Post* columnist attributed white fears to the success of the John Hay High School student revolt, which "must have given him [Ballew] a grand and glorious idea for a vehicle around which to rally this latest anti-Black crusade." Additionally, rising Black Nationalism, demands for community control, and the 1968 Glenville shootout might have stoked additional fears of Black militancy. Therefore, white parents and students tried to justify their actions by blaming Black criminality as a justification to reduce enrollment. Because both sides liked Principal Smith and agreed that a small minority of the student body caused the revolt, false optimism emerged. "All the parties were satisfied that we are moving in the right direction," summarized Smith of the weekend event. Nonetheless, he told parents that twelve additional attendance officers had been assigned to patrol the school corridors and lavatories.[40]

The campus might have remained calm, but racial terrorism persisted in the neighborhood. Prior to Collinwood's largest riot in April 1970, residents reported various complaints of physical assaults and intimidation. The *Call and Post* received complaints in June 1969 after white youth and adults attacked Black students attempting to enter the high school. A mother had to take her twelve-year-old son to the hospital for X-rays after attackers stomped his leg. Two girls reported that whites began to chase Black students as they headed to school. The students ran up to the doors only to find some of them locked. Parents complained that police did nothing to stop the attacks. The day-to-day violence became so chaotic that rumors began circulating that a Black boy and girl had died as a result of an attack. About 300 students met at a vacant lot at Glenville High to protest the plight of Black students at Collinwood.[41]

Persistent Violence and Reform Efforts

Nothing seemed to improve in the 1969–70 school year. City, police, and school officials routinely downplayed the violence. Black mothers reported that since school had opened in the fall, their children had been "ducking through alleys" in fear of attacks by white youth while heading to school. Attackers cut one student with a dagger. One mother reported that white students harassed her thirteen-year-old son on his way home, and the principal once rebuked him for entering a door restricted to whites. Numerous Black parents reported a black limousine driven by white individuals parking in front of Spellacy Junior High. They observed rifles sticking out of the windows pointed at Black children as they left the school. The daily violence and intimidation led one mother to report that her two daughters' grades declined. "We are trying to organize parents to do something about the situation. All we want is for our children to go to school in peace," uttered one mother.[42] Black parents and students had long recognized what drove the persistent violence and intimidation. The *Call and Post* reported that mothers it interviewed after the storming of the school in April 1970 felt that "the attacks are an attempt by whites to get Negroes to move out of the area."[43]

White parents and their children likely engaged in "perpetrator trauma," whereby those who inflict violence engage in deliberate amnesia about their actions to reduce guilt, shame, or distress.[44] But Black parents could not engage in this cognitive dissonance. Prior to the April 1970 riot, Mrs. Louella Harvey said that before Easter vacation, a seventeen-year-old white youth hit her thirteen-year-old son Elton in the face with a chain. In September, an assailant reportedly threw a rock from a bus window at a girl as she walked home from school. Some Black parents admitted that they feared letting their children stay at school for detention because they routinely got attacked on their way home. Some mothers drove their children to school each day to avoid physical assaults. "The whites are using an intimidation tactic, and the police say that since there are no injuries, it is not necessary to take action," stated one mother. Many parents complained that police were "rather congenial" with white violence. Collinwood mother Naomi Donerson provided the *Call and Post* with a copy of a letter she sent to various state and local officials.[45] In it, she outlined how her fifteen-year-old son, who attended Collinwood, had been attacked, almost losing his left eye. She questioned the validity of him and others serving in Vietnam and being law-abiding citizens while being denied the fundamental right to attend school:

> Since my own son was attacked, beaten and kicked by a gang of Collinwood hoodlums last Friday morning, December 12, 1969, upon deboarding a bus for school. I have moved from the ranks of that silent majority to the open and public defense of my son and other black pupils who wish to attend school peacefully, lawfully and without interference, to graduate from high school, to enter college and prepare for a life's occupation, and to become a useful and productive citizen.
>
> On Friday morning, December 12, 1969, I was called and reported to Collinwood High School. I know from my own experience what some of the needs are to keep school attractive to a youngster. Only time will tell what traumatic effect that Friday morning will have upon my son and other black pupils who have become victims of hoodlums. It would be interesting to know how many hundreds of black students have been intimidated and beaten out of the opportunity to obtain an education.
>
> Is it any wonder these same Black youngsters have raised the question in so many minds about the validity of being called upon to protect their community in time of strife or their country in time of war. Especially, since this same country and city that obligates them by law to defend it in time of war has refused to extend to him the rudimentary protection of the law enforcement agency in order to attend high school.
>
> I cannot guarantee that my son will graduate from high school and be willing, if called upon, to move into defense of his community if that community has not given him the ordinary protection due [to] all citizens. I cannot guarantee that I would want or encourage my son to think in terms of protecting a community that has refused or failed to protect him and his black neighbors. . . .

> My action, I know, is somewhat unusual. I am not a member of any organized militant group. I am not a black nationalist. But today I am able to understand more fully what they mean by their talk of self-determination and defense of their own community.

She informed the recipients of her letter that her son did not retaliate, but he was "neither a sissy nor a coward." Instead, he identified his attackers within two hours and filed charges. But she wondered, "What are the affected officials and agencies going to do about this to make certain it won't happen again?"[46]

In April 1970, *Cleveland Press* reporter Paul Stein went on an undercover assignment by posing as a substitute teacher to observe Cleveland schools for a month. His first report focused on Collinwood High just before a mob stormed the building, which showed little had changed and exposed white readers to the racism in the area. Upon his arrival, Stein noticed two police cars parked outside and a uniformed officer stationed in the doorway. "I had heard, of course, about racial tension in Collinwood High and, unfortunately, nothing I saw that day dispelled the report," he wrote. Throughout the day, Stein taught six groups of approximately twenty-five students each and engaged with about 150 students in total. During a study period, he attempted to privately converse with Black students about school issues, but they gave vague responses, implying that "things aren't so bad." In stark contrast, the white students "exhibited no such shyness. They indicated dislike for Black students." When he asked a group of white youths about guns in school, one replied, "There ain't many guns in the school. . . . But I know plenty of people who have them in the neighborhood. When trouble comes, they'll be ready." Stein noted the ominous certainty in the student's words, emphasizing the "'when'—not 'if.'" At one point during the day, Stein rushed into the hallway to find a Black and a white student "slugging it out, right in front of an elderly woman teacher on hall guard duty." "What happened?" he asked a Black teacher nearby. "Nothing out of the ordinary," came the reply. "Just a little skirmish." The altercation had erupted after a white pupil shoved a Black peer against a locker. Students informed Stein that such scenes were "almost daily occurrences."[47]

Black students still tried to reduce violence and proposed reforms before and after the storming of the building. In November 1969, about fifty Black youth walked out of classes and charged school officials with discrimination. Principal Joseph A. DiZinno denied the allegations and blamed outsiders for recent troubles. The students wanted to eliminate segregated entrances at the school, terminate teacher assistants and an assistant principal who used racist words and manhandled Black students, ensure police protection on the bus and while walking home from school, have Black history taught by Black educators, and ensure that no student who walked out should be punished. The *Call and Post* attributed the boycott to a leaflet distributed by Larry Thomas of the Black Unity Recreation Center. Thomas said students would hold classes at the Black Unity Recreation Center every day until the demands were met.[48]

The demand for police protection on the bus and while Black youth walked home from school echoed similar sentiments elsewhere. Throughout the high school movement, students routinely organized against the growing police presence in and around campuses. But in some instances, students and their parents wanted a police presence. In Irvington, New Jersey, in September 1971, a group of Black parents proposed sixteen demands in response to racial violence at the high school. They demanded that local officials station Black security guards in the high school and hire more Black policemen and teachers. It is likely that such demands occurred elsewhere.[49]

After the storming of the building in April 1970, Black students launched a boycott against nonacademic activities to protest the attitudes that "Collinwood High School belongs to whites alone." Students circulated a leaflet calling on Black classmates not to participate in various activities. Prior to the boycott, several members of the student council sought to remove the council president, Gary Meglich, who had participated in the demonstration that closed the school on April 6. A white student introduced the impeachment motion, but it failed by forty to twenty-three votes. Black council members constituted twenty-two of the impeachment votes. One nonvoting member, Marcla Mendez, noted that only a minority of whites caused the disruption. But she discussed the racial problems at the school: "Everyday [sic] white students tell the blacks that they don't want us in their school. They tell us to go back to Africa, to go back to our own neighborhood. The whites feel that Collinwood is their school and theirs alone."[50] Neither boycott solicited concrete policies.

Parents continued to mobilize to stifle violence after the April riot, but racial divisions still influenced demands. The Collinwood Improvement Council demanded improvement in safety in hallways and at sporting events and dances. It also called for transfers from Glenville High to be removed and for student conduct to be enforced equally. Notably, its president, Clyde Madison, led the class boycott of white students prior to the school's closing. The Collinwood Committee of Black Concerns, on the other hand, sent a letter to Secretary of Health, Education, and Welfare Robert Finch asking that federal funds be withheld from the Cleveland Board of Education. The parents also criticized zoning policies. They charged that gerrymandering had led to maintaining overcrowded conditions in Glenville schools and that the number of Black teachers and staff was disproportionate to that of Black students at Collinwood High and Spellacy Junior High schools. They also charged that disciplinary transfers of Black students out of Collinwood constituted discrimination. Furthermore, the administration had failed to conduct human relations sessions or create policies on attitude changes of prejudiced staff. Some parents established rumor clinics for the summer to work on racial harmony, but the Committee of Black Concerns cited Madison's involvement and charged the organization as unrepresentative of all interest groups.[51]

Five More Years of Violence

School and elected officials might have wished the April storming of Collinwood High marked an end to tensions, but the school continued to experience routine riots until 1975. The Black population continued to grow, and with seventh and eighth graders moved to junior high school, the school's population hovered around 2,100 students in the 1970 to 1971 school year. Black students constituted one-third of the population. In September 1970, a mob of 300 white students rushed Black students at the school entrance at 8:20 a.m. The incident left one student with a stab wound in the left hip, and another needed treatment for facial lacerations from being hit with an umbrella. Rumors of a stabbing, violence, and arrests of Black and white students on opposite corners outside the school contributed to the incident. "We're sitting on a powder keg. It's deep-rooted hatred by ethnic groups, and we can't do much about it," decried DiZinno, recanting previous optimistic statements uttered by school officials in the past. A police officer followed this sentiment with, "Today is nothing special. It happens almost daily at Collinwood."[52]

In one of the last documented efforts for school reform, about 1,000 white and Black students staged a sit-in in the cafeteria to pressure DiZinno to address their twenty demands. Among them were his removal, a soda machine, a student lounge, the removal of security guards in the halls, an open lunch period, student evaluation of teachers, and abolishing ID cards. "We believe that since the students are in the majority at the school, they should therefore have a voice in setting school policies," stated one demonstrator.

The group had lost faith in DiZinno's ability to resolve racial tensions. One participant accused him of solving problems by simply crushing them. They pointed out how officials suspended no students during the storming of the building in April 1970.[53] The action was notable, but the demands likely fizzled. Police routinely arrived at Collinwood to break up racial clashes.[54] By September 1972, Black parents still reported their children as young as eleven were being chased home by "bigger boys coming down from another school," and children told stories of Black students "getting their heads busted." "When we moved here in March," began Mrs. Emma Thomas, who had three children attending Spellacy, "they told me this stuff had died down. I don't want my children getting beat up."[55]

In the fall of 1974, the turmoil at Collinwood reached a tragic crescendo. The violence began with a racial clash at a football game in September, where two Black youngsters and two others were stabbed. Amid conflicting accounts of the incident, simmering anger on campus escalated. One Black youth, caught in the heat of the moment, yelled, "Blacks are no longer 10 percent out here; it's more like 50–50 now, and that means war!" Despite the incident failing to galvanize calls for reform, it did draw attention to discriminatory police tactics. As police targeted Black students, one youth shouted: "Why don't you talk to them over there; they do the stabbing and you stop us." Another exclaimed, "Four people get stabbed and all you do is tell us to go across the street; I guess that's 'nigger territory.'"[56]

The following month brought tragedy. On October 6, a red and white 1965 Chevy Malibu pulled up to the court as Black youth played together. No one would have thought much about it. That was until a presumed twenty-year-old white man suddenly exited the car with a revolver and pointed at his intended targets. Earlier that day, a group of about five Black youth allegedly harassed a sixteen-year-old white boy. They jumped him on his way from school, to which the boy vowed, "I'll get you." According to twenty-five witnesses, sixteen-year-old David Britton was playing with eleven of his friends when a man standing at five feet eight inches with a heavy build approached them carrying a handgun. All the youth fled, except Britton. The man fired four shots, one of which struck Britton in the right side of his chest. He then calmly walked back to the car, where three white youths waited inside, and drove off. Medical officials pronounced Britton dead fifteen minutes later. His mother mourned, "I think they were just out to get any Black person." Police later identified two minors in the vehicle as brothers who attended Collinwood High. At a trial later that month, witnesses identified sixteen-year-old David Deaton as the shooter. Seventeen-year-old Michael Weaver testified that he, Britton, and three others saw Deaton walk past them, and someone in the group suggested he was in the wrong neighborhood. Weaver and the others began assaulting him, but Britton did not participate. Deaton retaliated five to ten minutes later by firing at the boys who had attacked him.[57]

The slaying of David Britton represented a turning point in how the press covered the violence at the school. The *Cleveland Press* admitted that it had underreported many incidents because it felt it "had an obligation not to aggravate matters." But the tactic failed. The violence had disrupted business activity in the area and forced the school system and the city to cover the bill for property damage and extra police security.[58] With a renewed focus, it reported on the frequent episodes of violence that continued for the remainder of the school year. In October 1974, 500 students bolted out of the school when they heard police sirens arriving to break up a fight.[59] The community mobilized afterward to find solutions. About twenty-five residents and officials convened to analyze problems in the area, but nothing concrete came of it. Some residents urged that security guards at Collinwood High be replaced with persons from the community since students "respect people they know." But Cleveland secondary schools Director James H. Mirsch reported that no decision had been made on relieving guards who had been at the school since September 25.[60]

Yet some security guards committed criminal acts. In October 1974, a Collinwood High security guard forced a fourteen-year-old girl into his car around 11:30 a.m. after she chased him to get her coat back that he had taken from the auditorium. Jimmie L. Jones Jr. then transported her to a house in East Cleveland and raped her. He then returned her to the school, and she immediately notified school officials. The police apprehended him. Immediately afterward, the incidents posed questions about guards' qualifications. Jones had been employed for two months and worked at the school for five weeks through a contract agency. Briggs said most guards were hired by the school system, but some were contracted with an outside agency to increase security at various schools.[61]

The ceaseless violence wore down Principal DiZinno. "I'm 64, I've given 40 years of my life to schools in Cleveland. I've had enough. I can't take any more," he confided to a reporter. The challenges became overburdensome: six arson indictments, two guns confiscated, twenty-five students arrested for assault, and he personally transported twelve students to the hospital for injuries, and six others for drug overdoses. Just from December 1974 to February 1975, the school reported a knifing, multiple police interventions, a second school closure, and $5,000 in damages from arson. A brawl in April sent three students to the hospital. On top of that, he endured threatening phone calls targeting him and his family, which strained his home life. "My wife saw changes in my behavior. I was becoming short-tempered, irritable," he admitted. DiZinno had hoped to remain for another year or more, "but I don't see things changing much in the future." He still remained proud of his students. Nearly 50 percent went on to college, many with scholarships. "We just don't get enough publicity on the good kids at the school," he lamented. He marked July 25 as his official departure date and planned a trip to Italy with his wife.[62]

But the situation at Collinwood eventually did change. The hiring of a new principal and renovations at the school offered a glimmer of hope. Roy Maye, a business teacher who had witnessed the tumultuous years, reflected on the positive changes: "I came during the riots and everything was going downhill, and then it started to turn for the better. This is the best year I have witnessed."[63] Ultimately, the racial tensions at Collinwood High faded as the Black population grew, making it increasingly difficult and ill-advised for white students to maintain their aggressor role.

The ten years of race riots at Collinwood High School might appear as an outlier in the high school movement. All the activism that occurred at the school responded to an abnormal amount of violence rather than the usual rights violations. But the protests it spurred revealed that not all teenage activists in this period were propelled to action by the same factors. With little to no formal experience in politics, Black students and their parents demanded the right to receive an education free from violence and intimidation. Violence at Collinwood and other schools routinely led Black youth to demand curriculum reform and increased faculty representation. But Collinwood High students, first and foremost, were seeking a safe educational environment. While some Black and Latino students elsewhere called for the removal of campus police, the violence at Collinwood High made the idea infeasible to some students and parents. However, Black youth and their parents' demands for police protection rarely translated into how they envisioned its implementation. White officers were indifferent to white violence and rarely provided adequate protection to Black youth. School officials insisted that the presence of law enforcement produced safety. But it provided a false sense of security, effective mostly in the aftermath of conflicts. Additionally, Black students and parents persisted in their efforts to implement reform but often came up short. They could not overcome the vehement white resistance among residents and the indifference, and later fatigue, from school and elected officials. White parents and their children, on the other hand, overlooked what drove demographic shifts and sought to reverse Black migration through policy, intimidation, and violence, which amounted to an organized terroristic campaign. Tragically, the ten years of violence at Collinwood High fit within a cycle of urban uprisings: unresolved grievances erupted into violence, prompting individuals and institutions to examine the root causes, make recommendations, and ultimately, do nothing substantial.

But the story of the high school movement does not end on this sober note. Throughout this political development, a different form of policing shadowed teenage activists, often with the cooperation of school officials, parents, and students. This surveillance occurred even in areas without vibrant youth activism or a campus police presence.

Postscript

Silence speaks volumes. Although the Collinwood High School riots lasted ten years, they were poorly documented. Aside from a brief blog post with several mislabeled photographs, a sentence in a book, and three paragraphs in an anthology, there is virtually no secondary material on the subject. A handful of oral histories exist, but only one of them provides any real depth.

I first learned about this story as the lead historian for the Cleveland Civil Rights Trail and decided to return to the subject for this book. I have had many informal conversations with residents about the event. Interestingly, I discovered that memories of the riots divided along racial lines. White Clevelanders, in general, recall with clarity the 1966 Hough riots and the 1968 Glenville shootout, but were oblivious to the white-on-Black violence that unfolded in Collinwood. In some cases, they seemed indifferent to learning about it. On the other hand, Black Clevelanders, even those who did not grow up in Collinwood or were not alive at the time, knew about the violence. But few wanted to talk about it. Of all the people I reached out to, only one agreed to an interview, and even then, it was conducted via email, after a friend of his turned me down. "Is this guy serious? Why does he want to write about this?" the friend asked.

"Everybody knows about Hough, everybody knows about Glenville, but few people remember Collinwood," uttered journalist Phillip Morris, who worked for the *Plain Dealer* for thirty years. He told me this over the phone when he heard about my interest from a school district official. Another acquaintance of mine uttered the same sentiment. The fact that two unrelated people shared the same words signals a pattern I noticed during my time in Cleveland: although the city celebrates its immigrant and industrial heritage, it had long omitted the experiences and perspectives of its Black residents. Furthermore, the silence surrounding Collinwood is not just a gap in the historical record, but a deliberate forgetfulness of white violence against Black progress. In this matter, Cleveland is not sui generis among other communities.

Part III **Surveillance**

··

Within the last several weeks, a number of young, bearded individuals, purporting to be "freedom-loving" pacifists, have been distributing *Right On*, a copy of which is enclosed, in front of our son's high school in Medford [Massachusetts].

—F. J. von Merling to J. Edgar Hoover, October 1969

9 Troublemakers

School Administrators and the FBI

Principal R. F. Michalak of Custer High School in Milwaukee, Wisconsin, seemed perturbed about a new youth group. In December 1968, several teenagers established a citywide organization called the Milwaukee Student Alliance. Likely suspicious of its origins, Michalak dispatched a package containing the group's documents to the city's FBI field office. Agents received the envelope, which revealed a leaflet titled "Is Student Protest Spreading to the High School?" and the Alliance's underground newspaper titled *The Open Door*. "The Milwaukee Student Alliance," the leaflet began, "is an attempt on the part of high school students from all over Milwaukee to come together to discuss our mutual problems and act as a force for social change." Agents forwarded the documents to FBI Director J. Edgar Hoover, who, in turn, authorized an investigation into the organization.[1]

Michalak did not act alone in his approach. Other city school officials acted similarly, with some fearing student radicalism "might overrun their and other Milwaukee schools during the forthcoming school year." The Milwaukee School Board designated a faculty member as a liaison with the police department regarding "high school radical matters." Individual schools reported instances of suspicious activities to the police. Officials at Washington High School informed authorities about political literature being distributed on campus. Michalak himself shared the address of *The Open Door* and provided the names of contributors to the police. Administrators at the Catholic school Pius XI High requested a meeting with the police chief and officers in the Special Assignment Squad in October to "discuss methods to forestall any widespread high school radical movement."[2]

In a bid to undermine the group's aspirations, the FBI incorporated it into its counterintelligence program (COINTELPRO). Placing high schoolers in this project, the agency believed, would thwart students' efforts to radicalize their peers. The culmination of this strategy occurred in February 1969, when the FBI discreetly mailed a package to Lauren Dixon, the principal of Homestead High School in Mequon, a suburb north of Milwaukee. Enclosed within the envelope were copies of *The Open Door* and *Kaleidoscope*; the latter was a more prominent citywide underground newspaper. Confronted with highlighted "objectionable statements and pictures" marked in red pencil, Dixon braced herself for the worst. She believed that if students read these publications, their fragile psyches would suffer, as she firmly believed they lacked the maturity necessary to make informed decisions.[3]

Her conviction propelled her to action. She voiced her concerns in front of the Board of Education, invoking the newspapers as a justifiable cause for implementing a more stringent code of conduct. About a dozen students attended the meeting to dissent. The board was unpersuaded. It passed Dixon's proposal unanimously. Under the new rule, any student found in possession of either publication would be suspended or expelled from school. For FBI officials, this development proved to be efficacious. Their elation, however, overshadowed the reality that as the investigation progressed, no concrete connections to outside agitators emerged. Soon after, in March, the Bureau closed the case. Nonetheless, FBI informants were instructed to remain vigilant should the group exhibit any signs of aligning with radical organizations.[4]

The event that unfolded in Milwaukee was far from unusual. FBI surveillance operations on the high school movement occurred across the United States in major cities, suburbs, and even rural areas like Aberdeen, South Dakota. They occurred within a widespread pattern that was diverse in intrusiveness, scope, and duration. Field offices opened dozens of case files on individual teenagers as young as fourteen. Agents saved newspaper clippings, listened to radio broadcasts, and watched television programs to remain updated on students' activities. Some of these investigations lasted for just one month, and some continued for five years. Often, ordinary people solicited the FBI and volunteered as informants. They were parents suspicious about political materials their children brought home, dodging questions when pressed; school administrators who believed adults were brainwashing students; community members concerned about the countercultural tone of publications and public demands deemed too sophisticated to be made by teenagers; and, in rare instances, the students themselves who spied on their classmates. The campus became an origin point for some FBI operations. A network of individuals, ranging from district-level officials, administrators, faculty, and staff to individual students, served as conduits for information. Motivated largely by a variety of factors, they informed the FBI about the political activities among factions of the student body. Regularly, they confiscated documents from activists, forwarded them to Bureau offices, and shared intimate information about students.

School officials' collaboration with intelligence operations coincided with the punitive turn in public education. Police were "everywhere and becoming part of the daily operations of schools."[5] But these developments occurred in the public eye and largely in urban centers that experienced widespread unrest. Few people knew that high school campuses were also the site of surveillance operations set to discredit and undermine teenage activists. Some youth organizers suspected it, but even they had no idea that school administrators had enlisted as informants. No matter how modest activists were in their demands, school officials believed they were being led by adult radicals. Almost no location illustrates this dynamic more than Albuquerque, New Mexico. Even though the city experienced no major social unrest fomenting from the high schools, administrators collaborated with the FBI and local police department for a full school year to discredit a citywide student rights group called the Youth for Radical Progress. Furthermore, in Minnesota, surveillance of a student rights organization in the Twin Cities began after a fellow classmate secretly expressed concerns about her activist peers.

Albuquerque

Albuquerque teen Barbara Voldahl was a self-identified moderate, but little did she know that her involvement in a youth rights group would come under scrutiny. Her family arrived in New Mexico in 1966. The oldest of five, she was born into a military family in Monticello, Minnesota, on February 7, 1952. Her father, Lowell, served his entire career in the Army while her mother remained a stay-at-home mom. Lowell's tenure in the army uprooted the family numerous times, causing them to live in various locations: Germany, Sacramento, San Francisco, San Diego, Maryland, New Jersey, Arizona, and New Mexico. Barbara had moved almost every year before she reached the ninth grade. The family relocated to New Mexico for a third time, and Barbara stayed until she graduated from high school. By then, she had become accustomed to meeting new people, but one of her sisters struggled to make friends, while the other, like her, was an extrovert. After finishing ninth grade at James Monroe Junior High School, she matriculated into Sandia High School. Established in 1958, Sandia High reflected the district's efforts to accommodate the city's expanding student population.

Voldahl found the campus culture academically focused. Any attempts on her part to rally students around political causes went unanswered unless they included transforming dress codes. "It was not a hotbed of revolutionaries," she remembers.[6]

Although Albuquerque's high schools were not centers of radicalism, they eventually did change, even if only slightly. The lack of a visible political scene certainly did not mean teenagers were apolitical. In 1967, a large crowd of students at Albuquerque High School attacked a group of about twenty-five college students who passed out anti-draft leaflets on campus.[7] Dress codes became a flashpoint. By the late 1960s, debates over dress, hair, and self-presentation became intertwined with larger cultural and political struggles. Social movements adopted various hair and dress styles for their political activism. Long hair, beards, colorful dresses, blue jeans, and other styles became symbols of fighting racism, sexism, imperialism, materialism, and conformism. Changes in fashion fueled cultural anxieties about gender, race, class, and notions of respectability.[8] Albuquerque, like school districts across the country, had restricted students' appearances. As a site of respectability, schools forbade boys from wearing their hair at a certain length and girls from wearing slacks. Culturally, women wore jeans and pants for casual gatherings or the outdoors, while dresses and skirts served for professional and fancy occasions.[9] By the mid-1960s, students began challenging dress code policies. Some turned to the courts: more than 100 cases over hair length were appealed to the US Circuit Court of Appeals, and nine reached the US Supreme Court in the 1960s and 1970s.[10] In 1969, Albuquerque experienced several dress controversies involving hair length, slacks, and bell-bottoms, as students and even their parents confronted the school district's dress policies, which lacked uniformity across schools.[11]

Within this environment, Voldahl could not help but notice how kids at her school who gravitated toward hippie culture or political activities received different treatment. Even though Sandia High had cliques like any other high school, she herself avoided any bullying or ostracism. She maintained a group of friends and made fair grades. Yet, she became curious about the wider world beyond her high school, beyond the Sandia and Manzano mountains, as hippies, racial inequality, politics, and the Vietnam War dominated civic discourse. Dress codes initially interested her as she sought "fairness for all students regarding personal choices of haircuts and clothing and opinions." Voldahl shared her dislike of dress codes alongside her peers, but her interest in political activities included other issues as well.[12]

Two encounters nourished her curiosity. First, she met Walt Dickerson. He served as a church pastor and opened a coffeehouse for youth called Knowplace. Nicknamed Tartarus, Knowplace operated as a nonprofit venue on the part of the Albuquerque Christian Youth Council. Dickerson explained its purpose as "a place to get young people off the street. It serves as a place where young people can exchange ideas[;] . . . all in all, it is a vehicle of expression for our young people." The coffee shop had hosted a speaker from the California-based grape-strike movement, a draft counselor, and musical performers.[13] After finishing her regular volunteering hours at the American Red Cross, Voldahl happened to pass by the establishment during its development phase. Observing people cleaning up the storefront, she approached them to learn more about the project. "Remember," she states, "I already said, it's not hard for me to talk to people." She became intrigued and eventually assumed the role of "manager," in which she crafted the business model. "We had bands who performed for free or in exchange for rehearsal space during the week. Between sets, there were poetry readings, political speeches, and other discourse," she recalled. As a coffee shop, the establishment, ironically, did not serve coffee but opted for soda and chips. It attracted a more diverse crowd than Voldahl had encountered at Sandia High. The atmosphere fostered a free speech environment on any subject, with Dick endorsing everyone as long as there was no advocacy for violence. Opinions flowed freely from a diverse range of individuals, including many college or post-high school students. No one, for the most part, encountered censorship for expressing their thoughts.[14]

Second, she met fellow Sandia High student John Paul, who would become the target of the ire of school administrators. Through him, she eventually got involved with a group called the Active Students for Democracy (ASD). Sandia High students formed ASD in 1968. In a leaflet, the group explained its purpose was to "bring about changes . . . that will make high school correspond to the world instead of being a small fake society in itself."[15] It promoted itself as a student power organization that sought to democratize schools and portrayed schools as having "degenerated into a state of unawareness, closed off to the truth of the outside world." It viewed schools as too sheltering, administrators as too traditional, and student councils as ineffective. The group also demanded First Amendment rights, the abolishment of dress codes, student power, and a designated smoking area. "Although we do not encourage smoking," it began, the group felt smoking students should have a place to do so and learn about its hazards.[16] Paul and David Fadley were best friends who embraced national issues and tried to motivate their fellow classmates into activism but often came up short. Voldahl remembers Paul as passionate and charismatic, who naturally drew people to him. Fadley, on the other hand, was calmer but fiery in his beliefs. She herself was nowhere near as militant as the two of them. Thus, she contributed in other ways. She edited documents for ASD by using the mimeograph machine at the Red Cross office where she volunteered. She sold them and passed out free flyers. Occasionally, she attended ASD meetings at Paul's house or Knowplace. On campus, she supported the group by joining meetings with school administrators and researching themes for debates. In one episode, she chained herself to the flagpole in protest of the ROTC on campus, but the incident did not make local news.[17]

The FBI became interested in the ASD as soon as it made its presence known in November 1968. Other student rights groups existed that year, but ASD aggressively disseminated its message. An informant noted that the group had distributed leaflets "surreptitiously at Sandia High" and forwarded them to the FBI. These leaflets—nearly a dozen—posed questions to passersby, touching upon themes of self-determination, free speech, dress codes, and student power that echoed throughout the high school movement. "Is this school really yours?" read one. "Your ideas are needed to change this school," read another that also provided a meeting time and location for ASD. Others asked readers: "If this is your education, why don't you have a say in it?"; "Are you mature enough to determine your own dress code?"; and "Support a campus student smoking area." Signaling free speech, two flyers read, "School is to prepare us for society—not to protect us. Support an uncensored newspaper," and "Ready to read both sides of the news? Support an uncensored newspaper."[18]

ASD did not foment a vigorous youth movement in the city, but rumblings on campuses led *Albuquerque Journal* education reporter Frankie McCarty to write a week-long series on high school student activism in the city in March 1969. In contrast to other cities across the country, Albuquerque's secondary campuses remained relatively calm. The 1968–69 school year witnessed no strikes or demonstrations. Superintendent Robert L. Chisholm acknowledged the limited activity, stating, "One suspects it's like an iceberg. There hasn't been a whole lot appear yet, but there have been some efforts on the part of some students to do some things." The series covered students' desires for a more significant role in determining curriculum and exercising constitutional rights, contrasting with the perspectives of administrators.[19]

Notably, McCarty covered a meeting held by a rights group called the Students Open Forum with the executive assistant to the superintendent,

Daryl Harrell. It asked him to hear the group's complaints. Harrell accepted the invite and brought along two other administrators: Ralph Dixon, director of secondary education, and Dave Smoker, information director. The two-hour discussion covered students' grievances about school policies and the issue of harassment. Harrell agreed to arrange a face-to-face conversation with principals to address some of the issues and encouraged the students to attend the meeting with positive suggestions. Voldahl told a reporter, "I think we accomplished something. At least they listened."[20]

Little did Voldahl know that Harrell carefully curated a public persona where he aligned himself as an ally with students. He told McCarty about his efforts to persuade school principals toward more progressive policies on dress codes and publications. But the principals, he claimed, showed no enthusiasm for reforming the policies. However, beneath this facade, Harrell had ulterior motives.[21]

About a month before the *Albuquerque Journal* published its special series on high school activism, two juniors from Highland High School contacted Harrell about an underground newspaper they wanted to distribute called the *Joint Effort*. The two students clarified their reasons for wanting to publish the paper and disavowed any association with SDS. In response, Harrell cited the district's policy on unauthorized publications and asked for copies of the newspaper to review before making a decision. Harrell deceived them, for he himself was a former special agent of the FBI. Hailing from New Mexico, Harrell served in the Air Force with a role in military police and later taught at community colleges and public schools in Carlsbad before his stint with the Bureau. He later returned to the field of education. Therefore, instead of presenting the copies to the superintendent or principal, he handed them over to the field office. Many of the documents Voldahl had printed for the ASD had been confiscated by him and others and forwarded to the FBI[22]

Harrell began working as an informant as early as November 1968, when he furnished flyers to the agency that the ASD posted at Sandia High. He even informed agents about the details of his meeting with the Students Open Forum. Recounting that gathering, he relayed that Ken Sanchez, a student at Valley High School, had contacted him to receive permission to address a special session of the Albuquerque School Board. Harrell claimed he talked Sanchez out of the idea and opted for the scheduled meeting he had at San Felipe Church in Old Town on March 15. One of the students likely provided him copies of leaflets because he furnished them to the agent and told them he would keep them updated about developments and also provided a booklet published by the ACLU titled *Academic Freedom in the Secondary Schools*.[23]

The inaction among school officials led ASD to change its name to Youth for Radical Progress (YRP). Explaining the name change, it defined youth as "any person who is young in spirit and not fearful of change." Radical Progress, it continued, meant "forward movement in the . . . cultural aspect of our society and our lives." Most people witnessed injustice, it argued, but felt disempowered to make a difference. "Only we the people, the youth, the educators, the workers, can change this troubled world." In listing its goals, it stated that it sought to gain students and teachers a stronger voice in curriculum, desired a judicial board for each high school to have a check and balance model for disciplinary matters, freedom of speech and expression, more public services such as draft counselors for senior males, and free classes during non-school hours. "YRP seeks freedom and pure justice for our brothers here at school and throughout the world," the leaflet concluded.[24]

The summer lull provided time for school administrators and federal and local law enforcement officials to prepare for potential unrest. In September, Superintendent Dr. Tom Wiley received a memo on "potential militant student activity," which named several members of YRP. It claimed the group had "infiltrated the school-sponsored cinema club and is meeting with them on Wednesday evenings." Additionally, Wiley learned about YRP's intentions to film a picture entitled "Grotesque Fascism on Sandia Campus." The film, the memo reported, called for armed guards in the hallways with a scene of a student being given a haircut while tied to a chair. About a week later, another informant, likely Harrell, advised FBI agents that they believed that thirty members of YRP at Manzano High "could possibly be a source of trouble." The informant went on to list all of the goals of the group and provided the names of alleged leaders and the possible faculty sponsor. But the agent concluded that the group did not warrant an investigation. Instead, the FBI kept it in the index.[25]

In the fall of 1969, YRP largely strategized plans to organize high school students. During the upcoming October Moratorium, a nationwide antiwar demonstration to show middle-class objection to the war in Vietnam, the group distributed leaflets at nearly half a dozen schools urging peers to wear black armbands and walk out on October 15. The group failed in fomenting a district-wide student walkout. Yet, school officials reported that about 3,500 students were absent. Other schools reported on activities. The West Mesa High School student council passed a resolution calling for an end to the war. Many students wore armbands to demonstrate support for or opposition to the war. At Sandia High, the school hosted hourly assemblies, and other schools held class discussions or invited guest speakers to speak about Vietnam. The only reported walkout occurred at Rio Grande High School, where an estimated 100 students walked out to attend moratorium activities.[26]

Although the Albuquerque FBI office concluded that the YRP did not yet warrant an official investigation, both it and Army intelligence agents routinely monitored the group's activities. The 901st Military Intelligence Detachment (MID) counterintelligence operation branch called the group "a radical high school organization sired by the SDS." It noted that Fadley "exhorted high school students to take over their schools" during the October Moratorium.[27] The 901st MID provided Special Agent Condon with a handwritten report on a meeting held by the YRP. An informant attended a weekly meeting held at a private residence and informed his superior that the group discussed its upcoming participation in the November 15 moratorium. They wrote that it intended to present a skit or play in support of the event, and outlined the themes of the plan. "As other details concerning the future activities of YRP become known, they will also be reported," the memo concluded.[28]

The Albuquerque FBI field office had declared that no official investigation existed, but Hoover sent a memo in November stating that he received a spot report from the US Army Counterintelligence regarding YRP. He then ordered the field office to "handle your investigation in accordance with Bureau instructions." The report labeled YRP as a group "who model themselves after the Students for a Democratic Society participated in the rally/demonstration at the armed forces entrance and examining station" during the November 15 moratorium. Intelligence officials saw a banner that featured a black clenched fist on a field of red with the word "unite" on it.[29] The Albuquerque office responded in December that it still believed that current activities did not warrant an active investigation. But it noted it had four informants, two of whom were at the 901st MID and the 112th MID. The other two were Harrell and someone "who was furnished the information by [John] Paul's mother and who requested that his identity be protected."[30]

Hoover, COINTELPRO, and the SDS Threat

FBI officials had long accused adult-led political organizations of indoctrinating teenagers, but for Hoover, SDS was the worst culprit. He believed it deliberately targeted high school students. The belief had some merit. SDS viewed youngsters as an oppressed group, and campus chapters in secondary schools had existed as early as 1963. However, school and government officials largely overlooked the distinct tensions between high school and college students. While some concerns overlapped, high school SDS chapters prioritized issues specific to their schools—issues that college organizers often ignored. The belief that the group was radicalizing high school students cemented itself after the Columbia University protest in April 1968. A coalition of various student groups began a nonviolent building occupation where students called for the university to cut ties to research for the Vietnam War and end its construction of a gym in adjacent Morningside Park. SDS emerged as the most visible group during the week-long demonstration. Soon after, more high school students formed or sought to organize SDS chapters. From 1968 to 1969, new chapters sprang up in cities such as New Orleans, Los Angeles, St. Louis, and Honolulu, and in several suburbs of Cleveland.[31]

In the months following the Columbia University uprising, a three-year-old pamphlet titled *High School Reform: Towards a Student Movement*, originally published in December 1965, resurfaced and drew renewed scrutiny from federal officials. Written by then-high school student Mark Kleiman from Southern California, the pamphlet portrayed high schools as oppressive institutions. Kleiman described schools where "many have some form of police-squad with students being recruited to guard building entrances and inform on their peers." He criticized irrelevant courses, strict dress codes, attendance policies, and instructors, ultimately concluding that "high school is not worth the time we spend there." Kleiman's pamphlet also offered practical advice on how SDS could "communicate meaningfully with segments of the student population with which we have had little previous contact." His suggestions included supporting underground newspapers, assisting student protests, organizing teenagers, reforming student government, and building alliances outside of schools. Much of this advice reflected activities that high school students were already undertaking independently.[32] Nevertheless, in 1969, the US House Committee on Internal Security dubbed the pamphlet the "blueprint for the radicalization of high school students." In its report, Congress painted a dire picture of SDS's efforts, claiming the group was actively working to win over teenagers and had entered the "staging grounds" for this campaign. The report cited Kleiman's pamphlet as evidence and accused SDS of inciting disturbances. "The high schools in the United States are clearly targeted by the radical left, and particularly SDS, for 'activism,'" the report stated. It concluded that a coalition of nonstudent adults—educators, local political officials, and others—would be essential in thwarting SDS's efforts. "School officials must be prepared to wield firm and effective authority in dealing with young activists who seek to create chaos in our educational system," the report warned.[33]

Some school officials adhered to the warnings. The principal of Shaker Heights High School in Shaker Heights, Ohio, expressed hesitancy toward approving the school's SDS chapter as a recognized activity in February 1969. Principal William Greenham knew the FBI investigated the group and other "subversive" organizations. He shared concerns that students might become entangled with groups already under federal investigation. Officials in California took a firmer stance. In September 1969, the State Board of Education voted eight to two to deem SDS as "unfit to be recognized as a student organization by any California public school or public school district."[34]

Hoover extended the paranoia about SDS when he published an article in *PTA Magazine* in January 1970. It encapsulated his view on the threat the group posed to teenagers. In "The SDS and the High Schools," Hoover began by narrating three likely fictionalized incidents. Highly detailed, all three stories dealt with students holding private meetings on how to disrupt schools, appearing on campus to distribute leaflets and encourage meeting attendance, and discovering underground newspapers "smuggled in by a sympathetic student or faculty member." "High schools are today being specifically targeted for New Left attack," he wrote, "the downward thrust from the college level of student turbulence." He proceeded to tell the FBI's perspective on the history of SDS and its goals, warning that the organization saw high schools as part of the establishment. To Hoover, teenagers were impressionable. Despite the difficulties students encountered when seeking to form chapters, SDS reached out to them by creating a nucleus of a few SDS-motivated students and leafleting; holding seminars, conferences, and workshops; assisting in underground newspapers; encouraging students to participate in demonstrations; receiving speaker invitations; and working with faculty members who were past members or sympathizers.[35]

The article contained conflations, mischaracterizations, and myopic analysis. First, Hoover parroted a popular yet erroneous claim from newspapers, suggesting that college protests had spilled over into high school campuses. In reality, high school student activism had coincided with college protests since the civil rights movement. In some locations, teenagers even led the student movement.³⁶ Second, he asserted, "The key emphasis of SDS is extremism, violence, and revolution." This reflected the FBI's skewed perspective on a national organization whose goals and methods varied locally. Last, he misinterpreted the organic issues young activists addressed as the by-products of SDS recruitment. He included two photographs on the first and second pages depicting a scuffle between high school students and an alleged group of SDS members, describing the latter as having been dragged to safety after their "unsuccessful attempt at infiltration."³⁷

After the Columbia University protests, the FBI established COINTELPRO–New Left. COINTELPRO, initiated in 1956, aimed to discredit and neutralize organizations perceived as subversive, including the Socialist Workers Party and the Communist Party of the United States of America. During the late 1960s, the FBI focused its efforts on New Left and "Black Extremists" groups.³⁸ The origins of COINTELPRO–New Left can be traced to William Sullivan, a senior FBI official and staunch advocate for counterintelligence measures against suspected radicals. On May 9, 1968, one of Sullivan's top aides outlined the initiative to Hoover, stating that its purpose was to "expose, disrupt, and otherwise neutralize the activities of this group and persons connected with it." Hoover approved the program the following day. Two weeks later, he issued a memo to fifty-nine field offices, instructing them to provide headquarters with the names of New Left groups, their leaders, and proposed strategies to undermine their activities. Among the organizations identified as part of the New Left was SDS. Field office proposals included spreading propaganda and misinformation, leaking damaging information, or sending anonymous criticisms of activists to family members, school officials, and sympathetic journalists. Efforts also focused on sowing discord within and between groups. Hoover's directive was clear: criticize, mock, and humiliate the targets.³⁹

Although COINTELPRO primarily targeted suspected adult radicals, the high school movement became an indirect focus. The FBI sought to disrupt what it perceived as efforts by SDS and the Black Panthers to organize teenage activists. Hoover initially felt hesitant about taking this approach. After the Washington, DC, field office suggested mailing information about SDS to local high school principals in September 1968, based on the group's declaration to organize school chapters the previous month, Hoover rejected the plan. He feared it "could create a source of possible embarrassment to the Bureau." At the time, the FBI had no confidential sources at the high school level to safely funnel information and had no knowledge of principals' attitudes about SDS. He did instruct the office, however, that if it discovered information regarding the organization's effort to organize at a particular school, it could consider such a measure with his authorization.[40]

But by winter 1968, his attitude changed. From then to 1970, FBI field offices continuously warned school districts about the dangers SDS posed to high school students through COINTELPRO operations. In Los Angeles, in January 1969, the FBI asked for permission to furnish materials to local high school administrators to make them "aware of the evils" of SDS. A source who visited many school districts "found that in most cases the principals of these schools are totally unaware of the SDS and its aims and objectives." The FBI drafted a list of fifty-two high schools and received permission from Hoover to receive seventy copies to fulfill its commitment.[41] In Sacramento, California, in April 1970, the FBI furnished Hoover's "The SDS and the High Schools" article to seven school districts within its jurisdiction and encouraged administrators to send copies to each junior high and high school principal within their district. The following October, the field office furnished more copies to two school districts. It also sent copies of a local underground newspaper called *Capital Outrage* and a high school publication called *Downwind* that it believed "members and sympathizers of the off-campus SDS in Sacramento" published. It furnished the material to a friendly source on the Board of Directors, which later resulted in the Board and district's legal department concluding that the distribution of the paper on school grounds violated an existing state statute.[42]

Counterintelligence operations sought not only to influence the opinion of school officials but also to persuade them to take actions that thwarted students' ability to organize. In October 1968, the St. Louis field office received information that SDS had announced its intention "to make in-roads in local high schools." The FBI contacted a friendly media source at the *St. Louis Globe-Democrat*, which published an article about the announcement. Shortly after, school officials at Lindbergh High School canceled a speaking engagement that featured SDS representatives. In the same city, at Webster Groves High School, the FBI furnished materials about SDS to administrators, which led officials to block students' attempts to form a chapter at the school.[43]

But not all school officials were passive participants in counterintelligence operations. In November 1970, seven students at Central High School in Davenport, Iowa, sought to create an SDS chapter on campus. "Some of us decided we needed an effective voice for the left," said Bob Marion, a student spokesman for the group. "We decided to hook up with SDS because they best described our ideals." They viewed the group as providing "an effective political alternative" to the Teenage Democrats, Teen-Age Republicans, and Young Americans for Freedom, which formed in response to the student body presidential election.⁴⁴ One school official became alarmed by the development. They contacted the FBI office in Omaha, Nebraska, and sought information to influence the faculty vote. The Bureau furnished four documents, one of which included Hoover's article on SDS and the high schools. Agents had no idea what the official did with the material, but it appeared likely that they distributed it immediately to their colleagues. History teacher Al Simmons told a local reporter that the faculty voted against the proposal forty-one to ten after hearing one coworker link SDS with disturbances on college campuses.⁴⁵

COINTELPRO also targeted "Black Extremist" organizations, particularly the Black Panther Party and other Black Nationalists, who bore the brunt of these operations when the FBI believed both groups were seeking to organize high school students. The hesitation Hoover showed to white youth was nonexistent when it came to Black youngsters.⁴⁶ But the methods were similar. In February 1969, the FBI learned about a proposed appearance by a Black Panther Party spokesperson at Woodlawn High School in Woodlawn, Maryland. Hoover then granted the office permission to contact an established news source and sources in the Baltimore County Police Department and the Department of Education. The contact scheduled meetings with the police chief and deputy superintendent to discuss what methods could be implemented to curtail any appearances of Black Panther members. When Panther representatives arrived at Woodlawn High, police escorted them to the vice principal's office, and they summarily left campus after facing possible arrest for trespassing. The FBI remained in daily contact with the Inspectional Service of the Baltimore City Police Department, which placed pressure on the City School superintendent to ban the Panthers. Eventually, the school district banned representatives of the Panthers from speaking in the city's schools. The FBI cited the news as favorable because it "reflects results from the above efforts."⁴⁷

The FBI sought to marginalize perceived Black radicals, aiming to prevent them from engaging in activism or influencing young people. In April and May 1968, the Columbia, South Carolina, field office reported to headquarters that it had two contacts at Dreher High School who were "willing to cooperate." One contact had disrupted a plan by Black students to march to the state capitol, while the other monitored suspected militants. Interestingly, the FBI expressed concern that integrated schools could become "explosive," not due to white hostility, but because "as many of the young Negro militants are expected to cause trouble in the high schools."[48] Field offices adopted precautionary measures elsewhere as well. In October 1968, the Sacramento field office requested approval to distribute copies of a speech by Eldridge Cleaver to local school officials and PTA groups. The speech, described as "filled with obscenities and numerous derogatory remarks" about Governor Ronald Reagan and other officials, was accompanied by a provocative question: "Is this who you want your children exposed to???????"[49] Similarly, in Seattle in March 1969, the FBI learned that the Black Panther film *Off the Pigs* had been screened for junior high school students. The agency reported that the school principal had been pressured by extremists into closing the school to ensure "this inflammatory film could be shown to students." The office suggested showing the film to people engaged in public communications and later received authorization to show the film on a strictly conditional basis and not to "suggest any course of action upon the individuals viewing the film."[50]

Hoover certainly wielded the most power to turn his beliefs into action, but many institutions and people, including police, politicians, school administrators, and journalists, accused SDS of fomenting high school unrest. Amid national paranoia over the SDS's alleged intention to infiltrate the high schools, an official of the National Association of Secondary School Principals warned in June 1968 that SDS would try to create dissension in the public schools in the coming fall.[51] This climate of fear persisted throughout 1969. "Don't think it can't happen," cautioned Kathie Ilene Tanner, vice chair of the Tennessee Chapter of Young Americans for Freedom, in April 1969. Speaking about SDS, she told an audience at the Lions Club in Memphis, Tennessee, "The organization is spreading to high schools in New York now. There's nothing to stop its spread here except positive action from responsible people."[52] Around the same time, California officials blamed "outside agitators" and the SDS for high school protests. Governor Ronald Reagan claimed these groups "think they can create anarchy and chaos if they get to the younger people."[53]

Similar warnings appeared in congressional testimonies and various newspaper editorials. The US Congress held hearings that featured various speakers who reported SDS's efforts to organize high school students.[54] In November 1969, Ohio Congressman John Ashbrook observed the presence of SDS member Mark Rudd in Columbus, Ohio, and commented, "From the ranting of this budding Hitler, we can learn much of what SDS plans for our high school age youth."[55] This apprehension extended to places as remote as Jefferson City, Missouri. Acknowledging that schools in central Missouri had been "free of any major disruptive activities or SDS recruiting activities," the editorial board of the city's *Post-Tribune* in December 1969 expressed confidence that Congressman Richard Ichord's report on radicalization in high schools would "be of 'paramount importance' to every high school superintendent, principal and school board across the nation."[56]

Warnings about SDS causing disorder on high school campuses were wildly overstated. A nationwide Associated Press survey revealed that the group was active in only a small number of high schools, with its overall impact described as "minimal." While some college SDS chapters expressed interest in recruiting high school students, others had no such plans. SDS chapters emerged in certain cities but were reportedly absent in others. Tensions occasionally flared when college-aged persons engaged with high school students. For instance, in October 1969, about a dozen college-age individuals arrived at Lincoln High School in Seattle to distribute materials. Their visit led to heated exchanges that often devolved into shouting matches laced with profanity. Some students burned the pamphlets, and one Black girl dismissed a speaker advocating for wealth redistribution as "crazy." These limited and mixed interactions did little to nothing to mitigate the conspiracy about SDS organizing high school students. It persisted into the following year.[57]

FBI Surveillance Continues in Albuquerque

The debate over SDS's effectiveness in organizing high school students played out in Albuquerque. Back when reporter McCarty published his week-long series on high school unrest, one reader, M. W. Wildin, wrote a letter to the editors to argue that by quoting UNM professor Roger Y. Anderson the series created a "false impression of the level of activity of the SDS among high school students and of the degree of success achieved so far through that activity." Wildin cited an article from the *Christian Science Monitor* that reported SDS had established units in eleven high schools and noted it had appointed a secondary-school coordinator.[58] Professor Anderson responded to the letter and highlighted a factor many skeptics overlooked. He acknowledged the national SDS had responded to a "flood of appeals," but those appeals were initiated by the students themselves because of the group's "notoriety and not because of any carefully organized national campaign. . . . It is too easy, Mr. Wildin," he continued, "to escape responsibility and reality by believing that young people's disenchantment is caused by outsiders." Students are, instead, he argued, "suspicious of, and hostile to, outsiders who try to organize them." "It is much more difficult to accept that the reasons for discontent might lie much closer to home—with the parents and the schools," he concluded.[59]

But few people shared Anderson's views. His letter did not sway school officials who were committed to tying YRP to SDS. One FBI memo reported that in November 1968, two sources reported that John Paul and someone named Bernard "were attempting to organize a Students for a Democratic Society type group at Sandia High."[60] In another memo from the 901 MID, Sandia Base, an informant who attended a meeting held at Knowplace Coffeehouse noted that the meeting concerned December moratorium activities. The handwritten memo noted "there is some indication that the YRP and the SDS are jointly coordinating the December activities."[61] In one notable incident on December 22, 1969, an administrator from the Albuquerque Public Schools heard an interview on the local radio station KOB while driving in their vehicle. The listener identified the young man speaking as John Paul and recalled that he mentioned the group began as an SDS chapter but had since changed its name. Some of its members still belonged to the national SDS, but the group had fragmented. As the interview continued, the listener remembered Paul asserting, "It's patterned after the Students for a Democratic Society as a high school counterpart," and aimed to promote "student involvement and freedom of the press and speech in the local school system." One month later, the official ordered his secretary to contact the station to see if the recording could be retrieved. She proceeded and informed him that it had been destroyed.[62]

The YRP continued its activities the next semester and so did school officials' collaboration with the FBI. Sources within the school district continued to furnish materials distributed by the YRP monthly to the FBI well into June. Interestingly, new individuals contributed to the investigation.[63] The nationwide reaction to Kent State represented one of YRP's last major actions before its eventual demise. On May 5, seven Manzano High students attempted to raise a black banner to replace the American flag to mourn the students shot dead and wounded by the Ohio National Guard. Manzano High students Bonnie Bank and her sister Nancy were among the participants. As the group sought to raise the flag, Bonnie realized she had no idea how to hoist it. The moment of confusion attracted a crowd, where some students began hurling rocks and threats toward them. Principal Brown, in a letter to Superintendent Wiley, reported that the incident caused a verbal confrontation as the "majority of students on the scene interpreted this action as being a willful desecration of the American flag." Brown noted, "a large number of students today are still incensed at the action of the seven." School officials then called a conference with the students' parents. Bank's father opposed any motion to expel the demonstrators. Thus, officials agreed to remove all the participants for the remaining school year "for their own protection." "These students will not lose grades, credits, nor diplomas," Brown informed Wiley. Summarily, the seven suspended students distributed a leaflet that explained their reasons behind the incident. "We feel this was an American tragedy," they began. "This was not an attempt to desecrate the American flag." Highlighting a conundrum, they stated, "If there is no room in America for differing opinions and freedom of expression, then there is no such thing as a democratic America."[64] The suspension of seven Manzano High students put an end to the YRP's activities on campus. But one educator's private anguish summarized school administrators' frustrations with one member of the group.

On June 14, Sandia High teacher Colonel W. Jack Atkins penned a letter to his pal Cary Carlton, an FBI agent in the Albuquerque field office:

Some time ago when we were chatting, you told me to let you know of anyone who really seemed dedicated to doing harm to our government. I have thought this one for some time and feel you should have the name of one of our Sandia High School students—John Paul. Should you want [his] home address, etc. I'll have to go to the files. I wouldn't be surprised if you already have a file on him! He is almost politically masochistic in his desire and efforts to create trouble for the school and fellow students. I've only had one run-in with him this far but I think every teacher he has had has had trouble with him. My experience was when he was trying to take down the school flag to 'throw it on Rounds (the principal) desk to show I don't approve of Cambodia.' He makes it an issue of refusing to accept adult authority—I had to restrain myself to keep from clobbering him that day. From what the kids tell me, he will go to any end to distort and disrupt, i.e., he believes he could live in harmony with a Communist regime in this country. Personally, I think he is probably too naïve to be accepted by hard-core types but would be used by them.

I assume you know that Sandia HS has had sheets plastered to windows during the night—one was signed by the SDS, Black Panthers and Weatherman—if you wish, I can search my files for a copy.[65]

Although Atkins deeply despised Paul, his letter demonstrated that he had little knowledge about YRP and its ideology. He was not alone. Most school officials cared little to understand the group's positions. Instead, they immediately labeled it as subversive and regularly disseminated published material to the FBI. Their efforts eventually ceased once the YRP ended operations. But the FBI continued its investigation into political dissidents in the city. In one memo, the Albuquerque office confirmed to Hoover that it was taking advantage of the summer lull by "strengthening and enlarging our contacts with school authorities and other sources of information." The office had previously engaged in a few counterintelligence operations that resulted in the withdrawal of a job offer to a part-time teacher whom it identified as a member of SDS. In June, the field office distributed literature to high schools and colleges in the area to "enable them to better understand the true menace represented by SDS."[66]

Albuquerque's short-lived high school movement appeared to no longer exist at the start of the next school year. Almost one year removed, in February 1971, Robert Smith of the *New Mexico Lobo* revisited some of the characters. He noted that despite a small group of Chicano students fighting against apathy, "high school radical activities" seemed to have come to an end. Liberalized dress codes and smoking rules delivered a blow to the movement, as did the liberal attitudes among some principals regarding student involvement in policymaking.[67]

Interestingly, some of YRP's goals and ideology influenced the district's reevaluation of student rights. In November 1971, the Board of Education proposed a "Statement of Rights and Responsibilities of Senior High School Students." The documents stirred various opinions, with some labeling it as weak and others claiming it provoked student power and unrest.[68] Nonetheless, in May 1972, the Board adopted the statement as policy. "Schools are communities within our democratic society," the document began. "They have as one of their primary functions that of educating the young to the fullest extent possible to exercise their rights and to assume their responsibilities of citizenship." Acknowledging *Tinker*, the document covered a variety of areas, but most notably it allowed students to exercise free speech that was non-disruptive, which included wearing buttons, armbands, or other symbolic expressions; permitted the distribution of newspapers, leaflets, and other literature on school premises that did not interfere with normal school activities; and stated that students have a right to a relevant education.[69] Ironically, the same group that school officials and the FBI deemed subversive left an imprint on district policy.

Voldahl and Bank had graduated from school before the district adopted its new policy. A new job opportunity led Bank's family to relocate to Tucson, Arizona, where she completed her senior year. Before YRP's demise, Voldahl's own activism took a back seat when her father received a call from his Commanding Officer's office informing him about her activities and associates. Afterward, she had limited freedoms, with little ability to leave the house, and restrictions on who she kept as company. Her father then went on to do another tour in Vietnam. Examining the FBI file, Voldahl states, "I now believe that the Military Intelligence unit passed the information along to the CO [commanding officer]." Along with other members of YRP, she graduated from high school that spring. She last saw Paul in August 1970 at a place called His House near the University of New Mexico. Having grown up in a secular household, he berated her for "never telling him about God." After seeing him for a final time, she learned a year later that he entered a seminary to become a Catholic priest.[70]

On-Campus Informants

While Albuquerque's school officials extensively collaborated with the FBI, such actions were commonplace. Throughout the nation, school administrators and staff acted as informants, passing on information upon request to the FBI and local police. Together, they all aimed to stymie student activism and restore order on campus. Unlike Atkins, they seldom documented their concerns in writing. Yet, their consistent actions demonstrated their refusal to acknowledge students' ability to act independently. In April 1969, Principal Robert Ferrell of Robbinsdale High School in Robbinsdale, Minnesota, confiscated twenty leaflets calling for an antiwar rally and furnished them to the Minneapolis FBI office.[71] In Philadelphia, in February 1971, Morris Fineberg, who did electrical work for the Board of Education, sent a copy of *Red Army* with a note that asked, "Please look into this matter as this [is] not the only piece of literature being circulated" at Northeast High School.[72] School officials also volunteered to be informants. In Kalamazoo, Michigan, during a probe into the High School Liberation Front in 1970, at least two school officials, Secretary Amy Young from Kalamazoo Central High School, upon request, and Assistant Principal Richard Loney from Portage Northern High School, as a source, served as informants. Loney shared details about the group's meeting locations and its precarious financial situation.[73]

The FBI frequently reached out to school officials to gather intel on political groups and underground publications or to confirm the cessation of public demonstrations. While many officials cooperated, they often confessed they were unfamiliar with the group or that it had long been defunct. In January 1972, the FBI's Minneapolis office contacted four individuals in Aberdeen, South Dakota, regarding an underground newspaper, the *South Dakota Whippersnapper*. Principal Willard Ellis and others stated they had no knowledge of the publication. Shortly after, the office closed its investigation.[74] Conversely, when the El Paso, Texas, FBI office contacted two assistant superintendents regarding the Organization for Student Rights and its publication, *The Word*, both claimed ignorance. But they pledged to stay vigilant for any information and assured they would inform the Bureau if they came across relevant details.[75] However, in numerous correspondences with school administrators, officials reported achieving peace after recent disturbances. High school officials in locations such as Charlottesville, Virginia, and Jackson and Laurel, Mississippi, all confirmed that protests at their respective schools had ended when contacted by agents.[76]

School administrators also bypassed the FBI and collaborated directly with police. State and local police departments in major cities, suburbs, and small towns established their own intelligence divisions collectively referred to as Red Squads. These units operated with broad discretion and targeted protests, dissents, and any activity they interpreted as threatening to the status quo.[77] In most circumstances, Red Squads conducted their own investigations into teenage activists without assistance from school officials. But there are some instances where administrators sought their help. The New York State Red Squad, which opened investigations on numerous organizations and demonstrations throughout the state, received a report from a school principal in Union Springs about a rumored sit-in demonstration by students over the dismissal of a teacher.[78] In August 1969, school board members in Akron, Ohio, provided materials published by the Student Coalition for Constructive Social Reform—a local student rights and antiwar group that publicly opposed Junior ROTC—to the police intelligence unit.[79] And in Cincinnati, Ohio, in November 1971, Principal Richard Wagner of Aiken High School notified Detective Bill Simpkins of a planned march originating from the school. Student Evelyn Hatcher organized a group to protest a nuclear test scheduled on November 6 on Amchitka Island and wanted to meet the mayor. After an authorized gathering, some of the pupils left campus and tried to commandeer a city bus. Police intercepted the youth and charged them with unlawful pedestrian assembly.[80]

School officials played a significant role in cooperating with government operations against the high school movement. But some skeptics hovered around the same age as activists. Their involvement was not as prolonged as that of administrators, but their actions triggered the same results and show how pervasive fear was on campuses.

Minnesota Student Union

In September 1969, high school student Don Vagstad spoke to an education reporter about the youth group he led as chair. It was called the Minnesota Student Union (MSU). Founded in October 1968, the MSU functioned as a state-wide organization focused on education reform and pursuing constitutional rights for students. It also addressed dress codes, the Vietnam War, and the juvenile justice system. Its members mostly consisted of middle-class white students who, according to Vagstad, had "a middle-class sense of guilt." By March 1969, the MSU reportedly had forty-five chapters throughout the Twin Cities, and by October of that year, it had grown to over 100 chapters across the metropolitan area with anywhere from 1,000 to 1,500 members. Each chapter operated autonomously and formed when students contacted central headquarters, which served as "an advisory group." Public reactions to the organization were mixed. Vagstad claimed the MSU's discussions with school boards often fostered understanding, but some administrators viewed it as a threat and sought to suppress its activities. He dismissed allegations of outside influences. "We have formed no political alliances and have received no funds from the government," he declared. "Although I suspect they spend quite a bit keeping an eye on us."[81]

Vagstad's suspicions of being spied on were accurate. By the fall of 1969, school administrators across the state had publicly and privately questioned the group's origins and activities. They refused to believe the students were completely independent. But what sets this surveillance operation apart from others throughout the high school movement—most of which began by administrators forwarding documents to the FBI—was something far more unexpected. It was someone much closer, someone MSU members likely could not have conceived of.

In April 1969, MSU member Leah Rutchick attempted to gain approval from the student council to establish the group as an official organization at Alexander Ramsey High School in Rosewood. Rutchick herself sat on the council. Reflecting on her days at the school, she remembered the student body as "kind of conservative," but a great location for her because "it allowed increased artistic expression." She eventually became the leader of the MSU at her high school. That decision brought unwanted scrutiny. One day, the principal called her into his office and asked, "Leah, are you the head of the Minnesota Student Union?" She confirmed, which led him to ask her about a student who invoked the group's name to smoke in the bathroom. She denied that the MSU endorsed such a right. Other than this incident, Rutchick could not recall any open public opposition to her group.[82]

But there was someone on campus who strongly opposed the organization. When Rutchick proposed to the council her motion to sanction the MSU, she also requested the council to pass a resolution opposing the Hennepin County Grand Jury's indictment of three University of Minnesota students who had occupied Morrill Hall in January 1969. The council took no action on the requests. But fellow council member Mary Jean Shreve harbored reservations. Without her peers' knowledge, she acquired nine pages of documents provided by Rutchick to the council and forwarded them to FBI Special Agent H. Clifford Miller. Shreve's relationship to Miller is unclear. He could have been a relative or a family friend, or someone directed her toward him. But what is certain is that Shreve informed Miller of the student council meeting and shared that she was "concerned and suspicious of this group."[83]

Shreve's reservations about the organization reflected the community at large. The MSU had engaged in nonviolent civil disobedience since its inception, but quickly gained notoriety among school officials and fellow students. In November 1968, students at Marshall-University High School distributed a petition that opposed the formation of a union and rejected the idea that it represented all students. The petition received 316 signatures. At that same school, two members of the MSU had been suspended for participating in an anti-draft demonstration.[84]

A series of public actions increased the group's notoriety. In January 1969, the group helped organize a demonstration at the Blake School. School officials there had expelled a student for wearing long hair. A reported fifty students from the MSU staged a demonstration against the decision. In February, officials at Robbinsdale High School suspended 115 students for wearing blue jeans and other clothing that violated the school's dress code. Robbinsdale High Principal Robert B. Ferrell dismissed the protest as disingenuous. Even though a MSU member denied being involved with the protest, Ferrell believed the MSU "has set as their goal to disruption of the orderly processes of education . . . until the faculty and administration capitulate to their demands of a change or abolishment of the presently existing dress code." To him, the demonstration "was a well-organized resistance with information and help forthcoming from not only student union members but outside influences as well." But he admitted, "I don't have facts to back it up that I can make public." Some students shared their views in the editorial section. Four Robbinsdale students wrote a letter explaining that the ineffectiveness of the Student Council was why the MSU was being formed on campus. But another student at the same school, although sympathetic to the protest, felt the demonstration "became an effort by rebellious students to break the authority of the administration."[85]

Teenage Informants

Given this context, it is not surprising that a fellow student would take the time to report the group to the FBI. But Shreve's actions were atypical. There are likely only a handful of incidents where teenagers took the lead in launching an investigation against their activist peers. After a small group of SDS members distributed literature at several high schools in Seattle, Washington, in 1970, two students, in separate occurrences, offered to assist federal authorities. On February 11, 1970, student Carl Greninger called the FBI after catching wind about "a group of radical students currently attempting to get a SDS chapter started at Nathan Hale [High School]." Greninger opposed the group and declared he "would like to assist this office in every way possible, especially furnishing information . . . if the chapter is started."[86] A parallel episode occurred at Queen Anne High School two days later. Charles Taulbee Jr. joined his father in a telephone call with the FBI after Taulbee Sr. expressed concern about his son's safety. Taulbee Jr. had signed a complaint with the Seattle Police Department regarding individuals distributing SDS literature at the school. The boy informed the FBI that he had not been threatened but wanted to curtail SDS activities. He complained to the principal about a teacher with the group's literature in their portable classroom, which he claimed served as the organization's headquarters. But the principal told him it was a matter for the school board.[87]

Some students appeared more than willing to assist various government agencies. In Skokie, Illinois, in March 1971, former US Army intelligence officer John O'Brien revealed that the Army had been monitoring dozens of high schools in the northern suburbs of Chicago. He claimed the Army targeted schools in affluent suburbs, particularly those with significant Jewish populations, because "it is those schools in which most of the anti-war activity occurred." When the principal at one school repeatedly refused to cooperate, intelligence officials bypassed the administration and established relationships with staff members who had access to students' academic and personal records. These efforts also included working with student informants. Both Red Squad and Army intelligence, according to O'Brien, recruited numerous teenagers in the area. These young spies received small payments in exchange for information about their classmates.[88]

Teenage informants sometimes played an indirect role in surveillance operations. In July 1972, two FBI agents arrived at John Lundstrom's home to interview his son Richard, who was a rising junior at Custer High School in Milwaukee, Wisconsin. Richard informed the agents that in May, he received a leaflet from a man named Phillip Shamalie, who was active in the Milwaukee chapter of the Youth Against the War and Fascism. Richard read the leaflet, but the "pro-Communist articles" led him to hand it over to his father. A few days later, a peer of his approached him and asked if he was interested in attending a meeting in connection with the leaflet he received. He decided to attend the meeting since he was curious as to who was behind the document. A middle-aged woman picked him up in a red '64 or '65 Oldsmobile and drove him to the location. Once Richard arrived, he noted that approximately fifty people were in attendance. He saw posters festooning the meeting hall and left early out of disgust. He told agents he was "'fed up'" with the pro-Communist slogans and speeches. Little came out of his testimony, but the FBI recommended that the girl Richard mentioned have a case file opened to "fully identify her and determine the extent of her activities with the YAWF or the WWP."[89]

Most teenagers disapproving of their activist peers' actions resorted to verbal or physical bullying, penned op-eds in local or school newspapers, or simply chose to ignore them. In response to an article in Cleveland's *Plain Dealer*, which documented teenage activists in the metropolitan area, one student at the suburban Cleveland Heights High School responded in the school newspaper. "Do we, what I believe to be the majority of Heights kids, have to let the activities of this minority of students ruin our school and our reputation?" they asked. "We aren't all Michael's People or SDS'ers and it is about time that we let people know it."[90]

But for those who chose a different route, they rarely left behind a motive explaining their actions. In September 1968, a student at Downers Grove North High School, located in an outer suburb west of Chicago, furnished a leaflet published by the Suburban Liberation Front that he obtained at school.[91] At least in one incident, an adult explained a student's motive. In Portland, Oregon, in September 1970, an anonymous individual typed a letter to the local FBI office and reported "one of our fine high school students" collected a leaflet in the downtown area. "He was quite concerned about the effect this material may or may not have upon high school students throughout the city of Portland." The author agreed to send "such information to you when we find it within our schools."[92]

School Administrators and the MSU

Shreve's involvement in the investigation of the MSU ceased after her contact with Special Agent Miller, but surveillance of the group continued. The MSU likely exacerbated fear among skeptics when a member wrote a letter to the editor in response to a previous editorial in April 1969. MSU member Gordon Raup challenged the Cottonwood County Citizen of Windom's claim that long hair was actually "simply a rebellion against authority." If students can challenge rules they dislike, the organization pondered, "then it would be difficult to argue that a girl coming to school in a bikini—or topless—would have her educational opportunities curtailed, either." Raup said he could not agree more. In what could be interpreted as a threat, he wrote, "Student unrest will continue until students can determine their own destinies by controlling the institutions which affect them, namely the schools."[93] His statement raised alarm bells and confirmed what many skeptics had already believed about the group. They felt inclined to act. Almost nobody tried to delegitimize the group more than educator David Meade.

Meade worked as a school principal for fifteen years and served as the Executive Secretary of the Minnesota Association of Secondary School Principals, a private, nonprofit organization supported by dues from principals. All principals and assistant principals from public, private, and parochial schools, as well as junior colleges, had membership. Meade, along with many administrators, harbored suspicions about the MSU. An attendee at the Minnesota Education Association assembly mentioned Raup's editorial to Meade and later made a Xerox copy of the editorial with a note, "This is the article that I mentioned to you at MEA Del. Assembly." On his own accord, he provided copies of literature on the union and clippings on SDS to various school principals. Administrators were appreciative of his actions. One special agent informed the Bureau that he had a conversation with Superintendent De Floren Rude of Red Lake, who relayed that Meade had substantial information on SDS's and the MSU's attempts to "organize and influence high school students in the Minnesota area." Rude himself was "concerned about the possible threat of SDS and the Minnesota Student Union" and recommended that the agent contact Meade.[94]

Meade finally got his wish. In May 1969, an agent arranged a meeting with him to discuss the MSU. Meade talked up his efforts to keep local school principals in the loop about the group's activities. The FBI appreciated his dedication but declined to provide him with intelligence it did not possess on the potential link between SDS and the MSU. Meade, undeterred, kept rattling off stories. He told the agent that an SDS recruiter from Chicago was active in the Red Lake area and had attempted to instigate a student strike at Stillwater High School the previous year. But the FBI could not corroborate the claim. Meade shared a few more tales of failed attempts by outside agitators to stir unrest in high schools, but again, the FBI could not confirm them. Still, Meade was on a mission. The absence of a conspiracy, to him, only confirmed it further. He mentioned his plans to get someone to attend MSU's weekly Saturday meetings because, in his mind, there "must be a tie-in between" MSU and SDS—though he admitted to being "unable to establish one to date." Meade asked for help connecting the dots, but the FBI politely passed, citing its own limitations. The meeting ended with Meade no closer to cracking the case, though he vowed to stay in touch with the Bureau. The investigation, however, came to an immediate halt after the meeting with Meade. The MSU remained active until 1970, but the FBI made only passing references to it in July 1970 and April 1973, even though the group had disbanded three years earlier.[95]

What occurred in Albuquerque and the Twin Cities occurred with varying degrees of intensity across the nation. Given that the FBI protected the identities of many of its informants, the full extent of school officials' involvement will forever remain unknown. Reporters, parents, and teenage activists remained completely oblivious to their actions. These school officials viewed politically active students as troublemakers and tried to connect them to SDS, the Black Panthers, or whatever local political group operated within their communities. High schools were not just the site of new security features and procedures in response to activism and racial violence, they were also the location of clandestine investigations conducted by federal law enforcement agencies. Administrators remained skeptical about the originality of students' ideas that appeared in printed materials and their ability to organize direct actions. But school officials represent only one of several groups who served as informants. Mothers and fathers also contacted the FBI. They kept their actions secret from school officials and their own children. Although they acted on the same set of beliefs about outside agitators, they were not as interested in discrediting teenage activists. Rather, they saw the FBI as the best line of defense to protect their children's innocence.

10 To Save the Children
Parents and the FBI

In the early hours of March 22, 1969, Warren Bauer called the FBI office in Baltimore, Maryland. The clock had just struck 12:15 a.m. when Clerk William J. Herr answered the phone. Bauer, although polite throughout the conversation, "was critical of the fact he was talking to a night clerk and deems this matter should be handled by a higher authority." He relayed his concern about his son, a student at Towson Senior High School, who had received a copy of an underground newspaper called the *Spark*, published by the High School Student Union of Baltimore. Herr noted the details of the call: "Mr. Bauer stated the paper contains numerous vulgar statements which he feels represents a militant negro and communistic trend which should be looked into by the FBI." Bauer suggested that "it would be in the best interest if a special agent of the FBI would telephonically contact him" by noon. Responding promptly, Special Agent Arthur S. Hamilton called Bauer at 1:20 p.m. the same day, arranging for his wife to drop off the newspaper at the FBI office since she worked downtown. Mrs. Bauer delivered the document later that day. She brought a newspaper clipping from the *Baltimore Sun* concerning *Spark*, a copy of the publication itself, and a letter from her husband.[1] Addressed to Special Agent Hamilton, the letter revealed the father's deep-seated concerns:

> I personally think that the attached edition of *Spark* is subversive in essence and is an extension of what seems to be a phenomena currently occurring in the Colleges and Universities recently throughout the United States.
>
> Although the material seems to be shoddy and poorly constructed, it is quite evident that the editorial construction of this paper must be a deliberate effort by an intelligent, mature person or persons to undermine the Government of the United States.
>
> I am sure you are quite aware of the seriousness of such methods being used on our college students; however, when such methods are used on the more ammature [sic] minds of High School students, the situation is obviously becoming much more critical.

If you do not believe that this subject is within the jurisdiction of the Federal Bureau of Investigation, please return the attached paper stating reasons and what branch of government that does have jurisdiction.[2]

The FBI had no reason to return the documents to Bauer. The group had already been under investigation for a month prior to his call and would remain so for the remainder of the year. But Bauer was far from the only parent to contact federal law enforcement regarding his child's political activities.

School administrators who collaborated with the FBI and local police departments often saw teenage activists as troublemakers. Parents, on the other hand, saw their children as needing to be *rescued* from some sinister off-campus influence. They saw the FBI as the best line of defense. In the realm of popular culture, the FBI under Hoover is often portrayed as an all-seeing behemoth of surveillance. But alongside schools, the origins of some of these investigations into the high school movement lay within the confines of the most intimate sphere: the home. In white middle- and upper-middle-class households, parents began to harbor suspicions about their children's phone conversations and the materials they brought home from school. Their sons and daughters often refused to answer questions. When pressed, some parents successfully relayed information they extracted from their children to the FBI. Interestingly, the Bureau's own special agents were not immune to these intimate episodes. Some of these officials had children enrolled in school or maintained friendships with families whose children participated in political activities. These connections made them a minority among parents. Most who disapproved of their children's actions expressed their grievances through more conventional means, such as contacting school officials, writing editorials in local newspapers, or asserting their authority by grounding their child. They forwarded documents they confiscated, voiced their concerns in writing or orally, and the FBI often obliged. The motivations behind contacting the Bureau varied. Some had previously assisted the FBI, others had friends who were current or former agents, and many held a deep admiration for Hoover. However, most kept their reasons and connections discreet.

Through their letters and phone calls, these parents often praised the FBI, expressing admiration for its agents and Director Hoover. This reverence reflected the era in which they came of age, when popular culture lionized the Bureau. The FBI officially adopted its current name in March 1935, a change that occurred quietly amid a wave of government agency rebranding. Around the same time, Hollywood began producing violent, graphic crime films that were acceptable under the Hays Code if the authorities triumphed in the end. In April 1935, Warner Bros. released *G-Men*, a film that depicted a "heroic corps of detective-lawyers hell-bent on stemming the nation's violent crime epidemic." Although produced without FBI cooperation or approval, the movie became a powerful propaganda tool. It sparked a wave of "G-Men" films that cemented the image of federal crime-fighters as cultural icons. Comic books, radio shows, newspapers, and magazines eagerly joined the craze. NBC radio conducted live tours of Bureau offices, and a pulp magazine called *G-Men* featured "Famous Cases of J. Edgar Hoover" alongside his speeches in every issue. Hoover himself capitalized on this popularity, organizing free daily public tours of FBI headquarters and collaborating with Universal Studios on a new *G-Men* film, this time with official Bureau involvement. For many adults of this generation, the FBI symbolized a heroic force in the fight against crime.[3]

Much like school officials, parents who acted as informants could be found across the nation. They, too, agonized over the causes of high school unrest and how to address the problem. The societal turmoil of 1960s America fostered a climate of law-and-order politics, fueled by a pervasive sense that the moral fabric of society was unraveling. These parents did not interpret their children's defiance as typical adolescent rebellion but rather as part of a larger conspiracy, one in which off-campus influences were indoctrinating students with malicious intent.[4] However, two communities stand out as particularly illustrative examples of parental involvement. In Palo Alto, California, a small, middle-class suburb in the San Francisco Bay Area, the FBI investigated several student organizations for nearly six years. Numerous parents, in what is today referred to as the Silicon Valley, contacted agents about their children's participation in two political groups. Similarly, in Charlotte, North Carolina, parental involvement took a direct route. A mother penned a letter directly to Hoover himself to express concerns about her son's involvement in the Charlotte Student Union. This letter prompted an investigation. Soon after, several other parents in the area began to assist the FBI with their concerns about their own children in the same group.

FBI Surveillance in the Silicon Valley

Situated in the Silicon Valley region of the San Francisco Bay Area, Palo Alto—Spanish for "tall tree"—was a small city of around 50,000 people in the 1960s and primarily consisted of middle-class white families. The Ohlone tribes originally inhabited the land, with Spanish explorer Gaspar de Portolá among the first Europeans to lead an expedition to the Bay Area, giving permanent names to the region's natural features.[5] One of the most significant institutions to arise in Palo Alto was Leland Stanford Junior University. It is named after Leland and Jane Stanford's only child, who died of typhoid fever during a family trip in Europe. Devastated by the loss, the parents established a university to preserve their son's memory and serve the children of California. Stanford University officially opened its doors in 1891.[6]

Following World War II, Palo Alto experienced significant population growth. The opening of Stanford Industrial Park drew thousands of new residents and commuters. Additionally, the Stanford Medical Center relocated from San Francisco to Palo Alto in 1959. New housing developments emerged, featuring residential neighborhoods with elegant mid-century modern homes and contemporary designs. The population soared from 25,000 to 55,000 by 1960. To accommodate this growth, the city opened a new elementary school each year during the 1950s, along with two junior high schools and two new high schools, Gunn and Cubberley.[7] Within this small-town milieu, spurred by recent population growth and a burgeoning countercultural scene, a small group of teenage radicals would go on to rally against the Vietnam War and gradually critique society and their schools at large.

Since 1965, an unorganized group of teenagers in Palo Alto had been engaging in antiwar activities. It began when students at Palo Alto High School, known as Paly High, attended an after-school debate on the war featuring folk singer Joan Baez and antiwar activist Ira Sandperl.[8] Antiwar activists did not reflect the overall sentiment of the student body. An editorial in the school's newspaper asserted that, regarding the war, "Marches, sit-ins, and other methods of civil disobedience only antagonize, and rarely offer realistic suggestions." The writer contended that the army could bring peace.[9] While most students remained indifferent to antiwar activities, the activists faced ridicule from their peers. After witnessing verbal and physical harassment by pro-war students, Cubberley High student Matt Stahl called for tolerance toward antiwar activists, stating, "Logic, not a fist, changes a person's mind." He urged both groups to respect each other's views.[10]

The emergence of the United Student Movement (USM) birthed the student rights struggle in Palo Alto. Organized loosely in 1966 among teenagers from the city's three high schools, the group addressed civil rights, peace, and students' rights. According to the group's newsletter, it sought to unite high school students, raise awareness about US policies, and challenge the "arbitrary dissemination of information that is biased in favor of Washington policy." "We respect the tenets of a democratic society, and we look for a more perfect society," it stated. "We view with trepidation the trend of the people to disassociate itself from the issues, and we wish to end this apathetic silence."[11] The overall makeup of the group fluctuated. Participation increased during upcoming antiwar demonstrations and declined during lulls. The group formed as teenagers contacted schools throughout the mid-Peninsula to create peace clubs and report on the activities of other students throughout the region.[12] Coming together, the group proclaimed to have representatives from each high school and establish a central senate where members would strategize actions, philosophies, and organizational change. It opened its meetings to all students. Anyone could submit writings to the newsletter. Ideologically, the group objected "to the fact that the American public is not receiving the truthful information." It sought to make the student body more informed on issues and create a dialogue about US policies and its opponents "without prejudgment as to truth or falsehood." To educate its peers and the larger community about politics, it sought to invite speakers, establish weekend seminars, form discussion groups, compile Vietnam kits, and show films. It also sought to "determine our rights as high school students," create new classes on subjects like "non-violent defense," and establish open debates.[13]

Within its first six months of existence, a handful of parents in various surrounding suburbs acted swiftly when they captured their children in possession of materials published by the USM. In December 1966, a mother from Los Altos called the FBI field office in San Francisco. E. E. Spitzer's daughter, who attended Homestead High School in Cupertino, had received a leaflet distributed by the group. Spitzer informed the agency that although she did not want her daughter to know she had contacted the FBI, she would notify the Bureau again if the girl came home with more materials. FBI agents also contacted Frederic O'Glover, executive assistant to the president of Stanford, who informed them what the acronym meant. Because the group held meetings on Stanford's campus, Bureau officials assumed university students were behind the organization. In another incident, an "unknown male" gave a special agent a leaflet distributed by the USM at an anti-napalm rally.[14]

The intellectual sophistication of its members raised eyebrows among adults. The group called for revolutionary change and aligned itself with anti-imperialism and leftist political theorists. Its members had upbringings that led them to align with progressive causes. David Jacobs was born in

Palo Alto as a third-generation Californian. During his childhood, his parents moved often, going from Palo Alto to England to Ohio, before finally resettling in California when he was ten years old. He had long developed an interest in politics, and in high school, he created a group called the Fabian Society, named after the British socialist organization. On his own accord, he studied Stalinism, Trotskyism, and Maoism. His political outlook changed dramatically one day when he stumbled on a book titled *The Anarchists* by James Joll, a well-known British historian. From that point, he began to self-identify as an anarchist.[15]

The group's first major action occurred in Redwood City in March 1967 when its members marched in solidarity with the community against the Dow Chemical napalm plant. Clergy in the area launched a campaign to halt the production of napalm. Protesters received national attention from media outlets, but the event also revealed a class divide in the community. Most nonstudent anti-napalm demonstrators were among the most affluent and educated members of the community and held liberal views on military conflicts and race relations. On the other hand, poorer and less educated white residents balked at dissent and had concerns about demographic shifts. The protest had "not in my backyard" characteristics. Cubberley High teacher Sylvia Williams recalled that journalists reported many members of the community feared the proximity of napalm to their homes more than its usage in Vietnam.[16]

But demonstrators were diverse. The high school students, on the other hand, expressed sympathy for the plight of the Vietnamese people and sought to move beyond consciousness raising and discussions. During spring break, USM members passed out leaflets that read, "Ashamed? Congress—Your Silence Kills. . . . Vigil to protest mass murder in Viet Nam and fast in praise of life." Putting their bodies on the line, they organized a weeklong fast by giving up at least one meal a day to build up for the march and received support from students at several area schools. The students pledged to use the money saved from fasting and donate it to Vietnamese children through the Committee of Responsibility. Over Easter weekend, about twenty-five students participated in the demonstration and brought along sleeping bags, guitars, and juice. After the plant closed from community pressure shortly after Easter in April 1967, the youngsters felt that they had helped the cause, and it possibly provided them with momentum to pursue other goals.[17]

Although USM had yet to gain notoriety among school officials and the student body, parents still expressed qualms over its existence. In May 1967,

Los Altos resident James Hale became suspicious when his daughter Sally became interested in the USM. He likely relayed his concerns to his coworker at Lockheed Martin, Gene Greer, who worked in the security section. As a former FBI agent, Greer advised Hale to contact the field office in San Francisco. Hale obliged. He called the Bureau and reported that Sally had received phone calls from the group and had a mimeographed pamphlet in her possession. Additionally, he told the person who published his complaint form that the group had requested permission to set up an anti-draft table at his daughter's school, Homestead High. School officials declined the request; thus, as Hale claimed, USM considered setting up a table in the school's parking lot. He wanted to press Sally for more information, but "didn't think it [was] wise at this time" because of upcoming final exams. However, he eventually intended to "question her further about USM support, financial resources, officers, etc." Hale pledged to Bureau officials that he would forward any USM literature and information to the agency.[18] His cooperation with the FBI might have ceased for unclear reasons, but one informant eventually provided the Bureau with a membership list that included 159 names of active and inactive members, and Sally appeared on the list.[19]

Parents as Informants

The concerns of parents in Palo Alto captured the prevailing sentiment that permeated countless investigations. Many mothers and fathers sincerely believed that adult radicals had their children in their sights. The identities of these external entities varied geographically and temporally, and in some cases, were never identified at all. While the media spotlight often fixated on college campus uprisings, parents had expressed qualms about high school political activities as early as 1965. In December that year, two informants alerted the FBI to the activities of a group known as the High School Activist League, operating across several Cleveland, Ohio, suburbs. Merely three days later, Cleveland's *Plain Dealer* printed a headline that thundered, "Antiwar Forces Infiltrate High Schools." The article shed light on the origins of the group in Washington, DC, and its ambitious plan to recruit high school students nationwide. At least two parents relayed information to the FBI. One mother acknowledged her son's affiliation with its members while vehemently disapproving of their actions, viewing them as "un-American." Meanwhile, another source, having previously infiltrated the Communist Party, declared he wanted to expose the group's true motives and "prevent innocent students from becoming involved with it." Moreover, a father, who divulged having a nonparticipating daughter in high school, relayed the intelligence she shared about the League and the previous protest to the FBI. Even after closing the file on the group, the FBI still sought to find any remnants of "communist infiltration."[20]

Parents who contacted the FBI viewed the institution as the best line of defense against ideologies they perceived as threatening to their children's innocence. In Providence, Rhode Island, in June 1968, father Ernest Trudelle mailed an envelope containing copies of two pamphlets and a short letter to the Bureau. "I have a son, age 16, who is going [to] Providence Hope High," he began. "I'm afraid he is getting involved with a subversive group called RIHSSFP—[Rhode Island] High School Students for Peace." He provided the group's address and concluded the letter with, "Please inform me as to whether it is or not, and also advise a very concerned father."[21] Similar concerns echoed time and again. In October 1969, a married couple in Medford, Massachusetts, wrote a letter to Hoover after an underground newspaper titled *Right On* appeared on their son's high school campus. "My wife and I are terribly distressed by the ominous message these persons are trying to convey to impressionable youth," he fretted. Placing faith in Hoover's ability to tackle this "real threat in our community at large," he pleaded for him to be "unrelenting in exposing publicly the unsavory characters hiding behind their bushy-haired mouthpiece."[22] Some parents identified the group they fretted about. In September 1969, in Wellesley, Massachusetts, Teuvo Lanen called the FBI to report that his son had been recently elected coordinator of the Viet Nam Peace Action of Wellesley High School. "He does not believe his son is in SDS," summarized the writer, "but thinks this organization is SDS connected." Lanen added he would forward any literature or names he comes across pertaining to the group.[23]

Akin to school officials, parents found it inconceivable that high school students could organize independently and felt a sense of patriotic duty to act. In March 1969, a woman named Clyde Sorrell contacted the FBI after listening to the demands made by the Maryland-based Montgomery County Student Alliance at a school board meeting. She "suspected that it was Communist controlled and dominated." As a member of the Daughters of the American Revolution and the Women's Republican Club of Gaithersburg, her civic engagement convinced her that "she could not feel that she was a good citizen unless she reported her feelings toward the organization." She expressed a willingness to work with the FBI if the agency requested her assistance.[24]

Most parents likely concealed their communications with the FBI from their children, but some aggressively used their sons and daughters as conduits to extract information, whether the children realized it or not. In September 1968, a father in the Chicago suburb of Arlington Heights, and an active member of the ultraconservative John Birch Society, sent his son to a meeting held at a private residence by a youth group called the Suburban Liberation Front. The boy informed him about what the attendees discussed at the meeting and provided him with license plate numbers and documents he received. In response, the father furnished the material to the FBI and police and promised he would have his son attend future gatherings.[25] Other parents were not as discreet. In December 1973, a father in Chesterland, Ohio, reacted assertively when his son received a pamphlet from Youth Liberation. Seeking clarity, the father asked an FBI agent to interrogate his child. With the father present, the official conducted an interview with the boy, who refuted any affiliation with the organization and claimed he did not understand why he received the pamphlet.[26]

Akin to school administrators, the FBI sought to influence parents' actions through COINTELPRO operations. But the Bureau had no method of measuring its success. Noting the development of SDS chapters in high schools in the New Orleans area in October 1968, the field office felt that "anonymous letters or telephone calls to the parents . . . may help to curtail their success in building SDS chapters in the high schools."[27] In December of that same year, Hoover took note of an incident in Washington, DC, where police apprehended a seventeen-year-old girl during a demonstration against the House Committee on Un-American Activities. The student had worn a hat that featured the provocative phrase "Fuck the Draft," accompanied by the words "resistance," "anarchy," and "NYHSU-Andrew Jackson." The latter denoted the New York High School Student Union. Seizing upon this opportunity, Hoover authorized the New York field office to dispatch an anonymous letter. Posing as a concerned mother of a young activist, the author warned the girl's parents that if they continued allowing their daughter to associate with "her Yippee friends, she will surely end where my poor daughter is now—under psychiatric care."[28]

USM and Parents' Public Complaints

Parents who contacted the FBI and local law enforcement represented a minority during the high school movement. Most suspicious parents publicly condemned youth activism, and the community of Palo Alto was no different. In 1967, school officials placed USM on probation for sponsoring an upcoming antiwar demonstration in Oakland. On probationary status, about forty Cubberley High students and twenty students from other area high schools rode buses from Stanford to Oakland and demonstrated for two days in Stop the Draft Week protests.[29] In December, the group decided to show a film on the Armed Forces of National Liberation in Venezuela. But Cubberly High's school policy required the group to provide a counterargument within three days to have a balanced presentation. Administrators, overlooking the impracticability of teenagers finding a representative to speak in favor of the Venezuelan government, suspended the group for its failure to produce anyone, as well as for its distribution of an unauthorized newsletter. After Principal Thomson suspended the group from campus, he sent out a letter to parents in December 1967 to detail why he had made the decision and to counteract what he saw as watered-down portrayals of the group in the local press. He tied the group to the New Left and adult-led organizations' intentions to organize high school students. "I am not suggesting by these facts that a huge conspiracy exists with a Total Leader who pulls all the strings and whom everyone obeys," he claimed. The school board later backed Thomson, and one local attorney thanked board president Bernard M. Oliver for acting against "certain minority extreme elements of our community."[30]

Parents praised the administration's action. A married couple sent Oliver a letter and stated that, as parents, they were "very concerned" with the USM's activities in the school and supported Principal Thomson's actions. They believed that a "small group of dissidents want[ed] to change [their] educational system to suit their own purposes" and were insistent on using school facilities to "further the insidious goals of extreme left wing special interest groups."[31] Another parent appreciated Thomson but argued that outside influences were present in all groups and that it was not in people's best interests for "every organization to become a consensus, non-value-oriented organization." Thomson sent him a three-page response, thanking him for his "thoughtful letter."[32] One resident directed a letter to the liberal member on the school board, Agnes Robinson, and stated his support for the administration. "History has proven again and again that revolutionary groups flourish" in periods of turmoil, and "whither when an informed and active citizenry vigorously defend their rights and institutions," he stated. He affirmed his belief that "this group is clearly totalitarian in nature." These attitudes among residents only strengthened charges of outside agitators.[33]

Thomson stood as one of the most vocal and powerful opponents of the USM in the school district, but the FBI had no verifiable correspondence with him. Other school officials assisted in the investigation. Agents had confidential informants who relayed information to the Bureau on students who were active and inactive in the group in the fall of 1967. One named informant was A. Blaine Huntsman, the superintendent of the Mountain View–Los Altos Union High School District in nearby Mountain View.[34] The FBI also worked in conjunction with the Palo Alto Police Department, which relayed information about the organization's activities.[35] By April 1969, the USM admitted to knowing that FBI agents had been prowling the high schools and that agents had investigated certain members of the group and questioned administrators. Undeterred, the group viewed the investigation as a positive because it "shows only that they are running scared, that they don't know what to do."[36] But little did the organization know that parents and concerned residents largely initiated the investigation. These contacts continued to interact with the FBI well into 1969 regarding the USM. In June that year, a Los Altos resident alerted the FBI that the USM appeared as a sponsor of an Election Night People's Party in downtown Palo Alto that sought to fight for the right of peaceful assembly.[37] Furthermore, an official at Paly High forwarded six pieces of material to an FBI agent back in March of the same year.[38]

As with all youth groups, the USM declined as its core membership graduated from high school. Jacobs witnessed the decline firsthand. He saw the Maoist contingent take over the group, and they soon excommunicated him. His exclusion led him to lose many of his close friends and even his girlfriend at the time. But the student movement continued in Palo Alto, and so did FBI surveillance. After the Maoists graduated from high school in 1969, Jacobs and others developed the Radical Student Union (RSU). Unlike the USM, whose primary concerns had originally been about the war and US policies abroad, the RSU acknowledged that it had to broaden its appeal and address issues that most students could relate to on an individual level.[39]

The FBI continued to monitor high school students in Palo Alto well into 1972, but high school principals emerged as the primary informants. After the USM declined, the RSU raised alarm bells. In February 1970, the San Francisco field office established three informants but noted, "several parents have shown concern about captioned organization and have contacted the FBI." The office pledged to follow the group's activities and remain "alert for any acts which could result in violence."[40] But as the investigation commenced, parents' involvement is shrouded in mystery. In August 2009, the

FBI reported the field office file on the RSU had been destroyed. But the headquarters file revealed that Principal George Millar and, later, newly appointed Paly High principal Lawrence Lynch enlisted as informants.[41] The two officials, along with other confidential sources, provided agents with their analysis of certain suspects' continued involvement in radical activities as well as their physical appearances, addresses, and parents' names. However, the Bureau failed to arrive at a definitive conclusion on whether teenage activists were under the guidance of outside agitators.

The parents who served as informants in Palo Alto were largely unaffiliated with the FBI, and others did not disclose any networks they might have had. However, in Charlotte, North Carolina, a few parents who had previously worked with the FBI or had friends who did so took an active role in surveilling a student organization. One mother provided intimate details about the fractures within her seemingly idyllic home life.

FBI Surveillance in Charlotte, North Carolina

Laura Mackay Irwin and her husband Basil epitomized the American Dream. Laura was born one year before the Great Depression in July 1928 in Camden, South Carolina, but had long considered Orangeburg home. She completed her education at the all-women's institution, Winthrop College in Rock Hill, before joining the FBI's Charlotte, North Carolina, office in 1948 as a stenographer. Meanwhile, Basil, born in January 1926 in Knoxville, Tennessee, served in the Navy during World War II. Subsequently, he pursued a bachelor's degree in chemistry at the University of Chattanooga (as it was then known) in 1949 and worked as a technical representative for various regional textile chemical companies. Together, the couple had three children. The family spent multiple summers at Edisto Beach, South Carolina, a family-oriented community on the eastern coastline, where they fished for shrimp and canned and pickled vegetables. Both Laura and Basil actively participated in their church. Basil took on multiple roles as a deacon and elder. Laura contributed to the community through her membership in the Charity League, an organization dedicated to promoting community service among mothers and daughters. By all accounts, the Irwins were an all-American family. But things soon changed. The idyllic, middle-class comfort the Irwins enjoyed began to fracture when one of their children became involved in radical politics.[42]

The Irwins' son Basil Jr. had begun to participate in a group called the Charlotte Student Union. It formed in 1968 as an effort to "achieve a greater understanding of our problems through free expression and full participation by each high school student." Like many independent student organizations, it sought to make the curriculum more relevant and defend the rights of students as citizens. Individual actions, the group realized, were futile. Thus, it was "necessary to have a mass student support created by [the] awakening of each high school student to his present alienation from the decision-making processes and his right to participation."[43] Its initial membership hovered around an estimated 100 active members from four city schools.[44]

Laura and Basil Sr. had suspicions about this organization. Both had tried to dissuade Basil Jr. from attending the group's meetings, but he did not listen. Laura's frustration obviously hit a crossroads. So, as a former typist for the FBI, she drafted a letter and mailed it directly to Hoover himself. "This letter may seem unimportant," she began writing in March 1968. "It is, however, of deep concern to me and others in our city and even perhaps in other parts of our country." Her tenure with the Charlotte FBI office led her to develop a "deep admiration for the Agents and their dedication to duty and to our country and to the Bureau." Recently, she discovered the existence of a group she mistakenly identified as the Student Leadership Union, Southern Branch, which she claimed operated within the school district. She expressed distress over her son's involvement in its meetings, recounting the futile attempts made by both her and Basil Sr. to keep him from participating, all of which fell on deaf ears. "At his age, 17, parents do not tell their sons or daughters positively they cannot attend meetings," she explained. "It would only be human nature to do so just in spite." She contended that teenagers lacked the mental resilience necessary to discern and resist propaganda. "Even adults have fallen into this trap, so how can children understand or cope with problems like the subtle way Communism works?" she asked.[45]

Irwin recounted how she had conversed with administrators about the situation in the schools but deemed them too inept to resolve the problem. In response, she proposed a countermeasure. She suggested a special agent knowledgeable about communism "set up a program by which they could be allowed by the Bureau to go into high schools and give talks." Likely influenced by misleading media accounts, Irwin fretted that sinister forces were seeking to "destroy our educational system" on the collegiate level and were now "beginning to operate in the high schools." She concluded the letter with an attachment on the statement of purpose of the Charlotte Student Union and insisted her son was "an intelligent child," and touted his credentials. "He is a Junior Marshal in his school which means he is in the top 13 in a class of around 500, and most of the courses in which he participates are the advanced classes," she explained. "Of all the agencies, I feel that the Bureau would be the one which could help the most. Naturally, I am biased in my feelings."[46]

Hoover responded to her letter one year later. He empathetically stated, "I certainly understand the concern which prompted you to write and give me the benefit of your view and suggestion relative to the problems confronting our students today." He then prompted agents in Charlotte to contact Irwin for more information on the group. Acknowledging that she resigned from the Bureau under "satisfactory conditions," Hoover advised the Charlotte office that she could be used as a potential security informant with specific Bureau authority.[47]

Irwin was fortunate that Hoover responded, as the FBI did not always honor parents' concerns. Officials deemed some groups as too small or insignificant to launch a full-scale investigation. In Rochester, New York, in 1968, a father who served as a former potential security informant mailed a copy of an underground newspaper his daughter received at Brighton High School. The girl provided him with the names of the distributors of the *Nickel Bag*, but the FBI labeled it a dead file and launched no investigation.[48] Further south in San Antonio, Texas, in September 1970, a woman mailed copies of an underground pamphlet and an outline of a high school bill of rights to a special agent. She noted that John Jay High School students received them across the street from the school and at a shopping mall. In addition, she mailed several copies to PTA council presidents because "I felt parents should be made aware of it." Given its minuscule membership, the FBI launched no formal investigation into the San Antonio High School Student Union.[49] In Bronxville, New York, in 1972, a woman named Jean Mill sent a note to the FBI with copies of an underground newspaper titled *Renegade*. "We have never had anything like this before in Bronxville," she claimed after relaying that the publication had been sold on street corners. "It worries me to have such literature distributed by teenagers and sold to innocent bystanders." Yet again, the Bureau did not open an investigation despite having a copy of a sixteen-page underground newspaper.[50]

The Charlotte Student Union existed within a milieu that balked at its mere existence. During and after the dismantling of Jim Crow, the political climate in the South remained inhospitable to radical organizing, mass civil disobedience, and progressive political demonstrations. Southern student movement leaders were a "prophetic minority" that went up against a "recalcitrant majority" of rightward-leaning white students.[51] Charlotte residents, like many Southern communities, saw liberalism as a "threat to the innocence of youth and the overall safety of the community."[52] Throughout the South, the mere presence of underground newspapers threatened the social order. White Southerners deemed the promotion of racial equality, Black culture, and interracial relationships as radical.[53] In fact, a high school underground newspaper called the *Inquisition* was under investigation. Charles H. Crutchfield, president of the Jefferson Standard Broadcasting Company, which owned and operated a television station in Charlotte, furnished a copy of the publication to the police chief after "one of our people brought me a copy."[54]

Neal Hoyman was one of the founders of the Charlotte Student Union. Like many teenage activists, he came from a politically active family. His father, Scott Hoyman, was an organizer and bargainer with the Textile Workers Union of America and later served as its Southern Regional Director. Founded in 1939, the organization actively sought to organize Southern textile plants to help workers achieve higher wages, health insurance, and other benefits to ensure fair labor practices. The family moved to Charlotte in 1967, having previously resided in Greensboro. They became convinced they were monitored by law enforcement when one of their neighbors, who worked for the phone company, informed them their phone had been tapped. Rather than receiving outside help, as many adults insisted, Neal printed leaflets on his father's mimeograph machine. He held a meeting in his basement that had a sizable attendance, which included his next-door neighbor.[55]

School officials avoided making any public statements about the group but knew of its existence. Privately, they opposed having an off-campus organization outflank the school-sponsored student government. Predictably, they feared that the Union belonged to the Southern Student Organizing Committee. Students denied this allegation. Cary Chenoweth, a senior at Myers Park High School, told local reporters that the Union "may get influence from SSOC . . . but I think any group of this type is going to have influence from SSOC." Nevertheless, he insisted, "We're completely on our own." Likely unaware of SSOC's high school outreach efforts, Chenoweth saw the group's membership as "too far away from high school to know what's going on," given their ages. School officials were unconvinced by his statement. They believed the Union denied affiliation to shed its unfavorable publicity. They also cited the fact that Chenoweth had a brother in SSOC, a fact that he confirmed. Still, Chenoweth denied the claims. SSOC, he insisted, would take credit for any student group, "whether you're a chapter of the Communist party, SDS, SSOC, or the PTA," he said. The group largely engaged in organizing, albeit mostly unsuccessfully.[56]

Yet, its small membership and rough patches in its organizing efforts failed to quell parents' fears about its alleged subversiveness. Other parents in the Charlotte area communicated with the FBI via phone concerning the Union. One mother, Margaret Sanders, reported telephonically that she learned about the group after her stepson informed her that an underground newspaper had been in development at South Mecklenburg High School. He refused to elaborate when she pressed him for more information. For unclear reasons, he summarily ran away from home to stay with his grandmother, only to return six weeks later when he needed his father's signature for college admission. Sanders carried on with her inquiry. She sought more information from other sources, but nobody shared her concerns. A school counselor and principal at South Mecklenburg High, who both knew about the group, seemed uninterested in investigating its ranks. In another instance, she contacted Hoyman's mother, who saw nothing wrong with the Union and cited the presence of a clergy member at all meetings held in her home.

Not all parent informants were as persistent as Sanders, but they acted on their own accord around the same time. Mrs. D.W. Ford furnished a leaflet to the FBI after expressing concerns about the group's activities. She had learned about it after attending a film showing on the Columbia University uprising. Afterward, she called the Charlotte office and asked for an agent to contact her via telephone. Special Agents George Koons and Cox called her around the time she had furnished a leaflet that read, "Are Myers Park [High School] Students ready to unite?" The leaflet called for a meeting to begin a dialogue about what students "must do to attain a status as free individuals in a high school situation." Echoing a fear of Northern agitators, she claimed that a similar organization had been created in Chicago and that these groups had formed to organize students in all of Charlotte's high schools.[57] A special agent received information from an acquaintance when Mrs. Henry Bryant advised that her daughter, Jane, received information about attempts to organize high school students.[58] David Rasmussen, an engineer at the Catalytic Construction Company, called the FBI to report that his son had attended meetings sponsored by the Union and that he was "extremely concerned" regarding his son's activities. In various conversations with his boy, he gathered that the organization was "definitely anti-American" and shared his fear that his son would be "eventually convinced to participate in student riots and 'hippy' activities."

Although he knew none of the names of the leaders or the group's plans, should such information come to his attention, he would "immediately notify the Charlotte Office."[59] But the investigation of the Union ended in April 1969. The field office reported to Hoover that the high school students had no known affiliation with SSOC or any other New Left group.[60]

Parents' involvement with FBI investigations into the high school movement preceded and succeeded that of school officials. Whether they were concerned about the actions of their own children or others, they saw the FBI as protectors of childhood innocence. They had far more intimate interactions with teenage activists than school officials, as they had access to their children's living spaces and did not have to respect their privacy. Race and class certainly influenced their perspectives and provided them with the social capital to conceive the idea to contact the Bureau. Interestingly, none of the nearly 400 investigations into the high school movement revealed that outside agitators were manipulating children. Yet, these operations continued unabatedly for at least fifteen years. The absence of a conspiracy strengthened the accusation of one existing.

Furthermore, the FBI had only minimal success in weakening the movement. School administrators and parents were far more effective in undermining the high school movement through mundane actions such as verbal disapproval, narrow readings of judicial decisions, suspensions and expulsions, or exercising parental and administrative authority. Ironically, as students achieved piecemeal victories in education reform, they also experienced increased surveillance as schools began to rely increasingly on law enforcement to handle disciplinary issues. The records reveal the widespread paranoia among government and school officials, parents, and fellow teenagers about their placid community being invaded by outside forces—not necessarily those physically present but ones who, to them, promoted insidious ideas that galvanized an otherwise obedient population. Parents of high schoolers drew attention to groups that most likely would have slipped from the FBI's radar. They sincerely believed that outside agitators had indoctrinated their children with countercultural messages. Although the allegation lacked credible evidence, they remained committed to the conspiracy rather than viewing it as a genuine expression of students wanting political freedoms. Ultimately, teenage activists were in the middle of a growing paradox: as they received expanded constitutional rights, they also faced intrusions on their privacy as school and police officials passed along their private information.

Epilogue
High School Student Activists in Adulthood and Memory

When I met Steve Wasserman in person for the second time in August 2023, I could not help but notice the connection between his intellectual curiosity and his youthful activism, both of which have shaped his career as a publisher. His office in Berkeley held a treasure trove of books, which rivaled any public library. I first encountered his name while conducting interviews for an undergraduate research project on how high school students, teachers, and administrators grappled with the anti-Vietnam War movement. Several interviewees strongly urged that I speak to him. Over the years, we conducted three interviews and remain in touch.

Wasserman's adulthood represents a broader pattern: countless former teenage political activists whose early engagement with politics and organizing significantly influenced their adult lives. Many remained quite politically active, and others retreated from the scene and found meaning in other ventures. Several stated that they lost interest in organizing only to find themselves in some sort of activist role.

Members of SOEAL ventured into diverse careers. Jesse Tepper reminisced fondly about his post-high school years. "I think I'm one of the luckiest guys in the world," he said. Despite graduating near the bottom of his class, he enrolled at Saint John's College in Santa Fe, New Mexico, and "was bored out of my mind." He returned to San Francisco and worked for the Service Center Program, which aimed to consolidate various state agencies. Tepper remained in San Francisco, doing community organizing in the Fillmore and Haight neighborhoods, establishing a freedom school, creating a newspaper called *Dead Center*, and later earning a master's degree from the State University of New York, Stony Brook, in 1972. He ran for supervisor in 1975 and 1977, got involved in Little League, and had a field named after him.[1]

Other former members of SOEAL shared Tepper's trajectory of continued activism. Jonathan Bennett remained "a political activist for all of my life." He dedicated himself to political journalism, focusing on occupational safety and health. Carol Pittman, after earning the equivalent of a master's degree in anthropology, devoted herself to organizing, forging coalitions, and eventually working within the labor movement, even serving as Association Director of the New York State Nurses Association. Betsy Brown became an electrician in the Pacific Northwest and reunited with Frank McMurray upon returning to San Francisco, where both worked in unions and published a newspaper called *Art and News*. Kate Northcott got involved with the hippy movement, enrolled in art school, dropped out, and later earned a degree in art from Sonoma State and an MFA from San Francisco State. She worked in the arts until her mid-thirties and then became a therapist, following in her parents' footsteps. "I think of myself as an activist, but I'm really not," she states. Peter Shapiro attended San Francisco State and became involved in the strike there. He abandoned his "cavalier attitudes about the Communist Party" and enrolled in graduate school at UC, but he later dropped out and worked for the US Postal Service, where he stayed until he retired. During this period, he taught labor history at a storefront on Market Street in San Francisco called Liberation School. He also had a foothold in journalism, serving as the labor editor of *Unity*, published by the League of Revolutionary Struggle, and editing his local union paper in Portland for six years. In 1990, he became active in a union at a post office, moved to Portland, Oregon, served on the executive board for six years, retired, and co-chaired the Portland chapter of Jobs with Justice, a nationwide labor-affiliated solidarity and mutual aid organization. After retiring, he published a historical account of the eighteen-month strike by Mexicana frozen food workers in Watsonville, California, in the mid-1980s.[2]

Two former SOEAL members entered academia. Elisabeth Semel graduated from high school at sixteen and took a year off before going to college. She got accepted into several state universities, but did not know what she wanted to do. "So, I stayed out and worked a bunch of different jobs during which my parents flipped out that I was never going to go to college," she said. She eventually enrolled at Bard College in New York, remaining politically active, participating in antiwar protests in Washington, DC, where she was "tear-gassed again." Semel then attended law school, became a public defender in Solano County and later in San Diego County. She then went into private practice as a criminal defense lawyer and later directed the American Bar Association Death Penalty Representation Project in Washington, DC. Semel returned to the Bay Area in 2001 to join the faculty at UC Berkeley Law and launch its Death Penalty Clinic. Semel still co-directs the clinic, which represents people facing capital punishment in California and the Deep South. After living in Moscow, disillusioned with the Soviet Union, Paula Garb returned to the United

States in 1990, having met a Jewish Russian immigrant in Irvine, California, while speaking on tour about Mikhail Gorbachev's reforms at the Yorba Linda Library. "That's how I got to Irvine, pretty much the same way I got to Moscow," she states. She earned her PhD in anthropology in 1990, taught at UC Irvine, co-founded the Center for Citizen Peacebuilding, and served as its co-director for twenty years. We last communicated in 2024 when I provided her documents to help her complete her memoir. She passed away in August that year.[3]

Mark Citret distanced himself from activism and focused on photojournalism. He recalls an indelible image embedded in his memory from the student strike at San Francisco State College: a puppy that had wandered into the crowd. "And this big, tacky police sergeant picked up this puppy and was protecting it. Holding it. And that's the picture I wish I made," he admits. After a pause, he confesses. "But I didn't." He feared the officer might have seized his camera, but more importantly, he knew his peers would have condemned him "for making this enemy look human. That's part of why I lost interest in political activism," he reflects. He found photography to be a safer, more relaxing, and apolitical pursuit. "There's just no ideology to it," he says. "By and large, I just photograph what grabs me."[4]

The former teenage antiwar activists shared similarities with the members of SOEAL. Katharine Harer, for instance, did political work at San Francisco State before heading off for a summer hitchhiking through Europe that turned into a year. Upon her return, she said, "I wasn't interested in being political anymore." She got involved in creative writing and the arts, trading her activism for a different kind of expression. Although she stopped organizing, she remained engaged, earning a Master's in English and joining the California Poets in the Schools program, teaching kindergarten to twelfth-grade students creative writing. "At that point, I decided that was the most radical thing I could do," she explains. Harer ran a small bookstore, Small Press Traffic, dedicated to small press publications for seven years, became deeply involved in the teachers' union at the community college district where she taught, and served as its co-president and negotiator, representing all three colleges in the district, for over a decade. In later years, she served as co-vice president for the teachers' union and as a leader of organizers. She taught both part-time and full-time at Skyline Colleges in San Mateo County for over forty years. Gordon Fox graduated from high school in June 1970 and briefly attended Case Western Reserve University in Cleveland before transferring to UC Berkeley, where he finished his degree. He remained a professional activist until he was twenty-eight, when

"I concluded that wasn't the best for me." He enrolled in graduate school at thirty and worked in ecology and evolutionary biology.[5]

Kipp Dawson, whose teenage activism preceded the high school movement, remained active well after her time with the SMC. She helped plan the Women's Strike for Equality in New York City and the early anniversary Christopher Street Liberation Day celebrations after Stonewall, worked as a fundraiser for abortion rights, ran for office under the Socialist Workers Party, organized workers underground as a coal miner, and retired as a public-school teacher in Pittsburgh. Geoff Mirelowitz, after graduating from high school, moved to New York and became the national staff coordinator of the National SMC. He later joined the National Executive Committee of the Young Socialist Alliance. "After high school, I was involved in every single big national action against the war," he said. As the war ended, he became more involved in the socialist movement and worked as an industrial worker until his retirement. When we last spoke in 2017, he was involved in a lawsuit against the Burlington Northern Santa Fe Railroad, defending long-tenured workers with clean records who had been terminated. "That's the last political activity I've been involved in," he said, "defending safety on the job at the railroad."[6]

The former members of the New York High School Student Union also followed diverse paths. Trigg fulfilled his parents' wishes and became a doctor. He remained active in the movement after high school, attending City College of New York and the University of Buffalo, where he stayed involved with the student Left. He began medical school in 1977 at George Washington University, met his future wife at Jacobi Hospital in the Bronx, and moved to a Navajo reservation to work for the Indian Health Service in 1983. As of 2009, he resided in Albuquerque, New Mexico, where he worked as a public health physician focusing on sexually transmitted diseases and opiate addiction and was active in Physicians for a National Health Program. Estelle Schneider attended the University of Wisconsin at Madison and joined SDS, leveraging her New York HSSU skills. She remains a proud feminist, shaped by the sexism she faced as a youth. Elk Gene pursued history at UC Davis but found academia too dull, opting instead to become a labor union president. Wendy Friar, after working on the New York Stock Exchange, became a nurse and vice president of a Catholic Community Hospital, dedicated to serving the poor and working with community outreach programs for underserved women. She met her husband Jamie Friar when they were both members of the Union. Jamie followed his childhood passion for journalism and worked for the Associated Press for twenty-five years as of 2009. Jeffrey Schwartz went to Woodstock and spent time in the first aid tent, "talking people down from bad trips." The experience inspired him to apply to every psychiatric hospital in New York City in 1974. He went on to work at South Beach Psychiatric Center in Staten Island for 33 years, serving as union president for the last twenty and continuing as director for ten years after retirement.[7]

Josh Kiok graduated and enrolled in the State University of New York, Stony Brook, and got involved in the Independent Caucus of SDS, which eventually changed its name to the Red Balloon Collective. The group aligned itself with various progressive causes and unsuccessfully organized a national conference on campus in 1972 to create a new nationwide radical youth organization. After college, Kiok went to medical school and today is a practicing clinician. "I am not a member of any organized group, but still go to demonstrations in support of Palestine, against police brutality, against the American invasion of Afghanistan, Iran, etc.," he states. Robert Newton dropped out of school to travel and connect with the movement. He worked in the printing trade, eventually settling in Buffalo, where he organized youth involved in gangs and worked on school desegregation. He returned to New York City, running several small print shops focused on progressive causes. At twenty-five, he went to college and graduate school to study mathematics and today is an oceanographer at Columbia University. After high school, Maxine Orris left the city and remained involved in the antiwar movement. She joined an organization that formed a union in the hospital. Today, she leads a medical practice in New York City. Howard Swerdloff, after graduating early, became a full-time high school student activist. He eventually succumbed to parental pressure to attend college and enrolled in the State University of New York Old Westbury. There, he continued his activism and later became involved in a unionization effort at a printing company. By the 1980s, he had settled down, working seventy hours a week, raising a family, and, after thirty years, returned to school for a master's degree, eventually teaching at Rutgers University in New Jersey.[8]

The individuals who helped build the high school underground press remained active in various ways. After Youth Liberation ended in 1979, Keith Hefner founded Youth Communication in 1980 and received numerous awards, including the Luther P. Jackson Award for Educational Excellence from the New York Association of Black Journalists. As executive editor or coauthor of several dozen books and programs, he assists editors and staff with editorial quality control and collaborates with the management team on strategy and fundraising. After Youth Liberation, John Schaller worked in book publishing and ran a travel company for seven years, which eventually led him to Laos. There, he noticed a lack of books and published materials. Drawing on his publishing and business experience, he began producing children's books and delivering them to rural schools for ten years. Grant Cooper distanced himself from activism but remains in touch with former activists from the Southern Students Organizing Committee. He worked various jobs and eventually became an entrepreneur. He founded Strategic Resumes to assist affluent clients and currently sits on the board of directors of the nation's largest resume writing association. He put three children through college, who all have professional careers. "For a little kid who didn't have a pot to piss in, I've done all right," he tells me. Although he took a step back from activism, he remains in contact with former SSOC members. He helped organize the sixtieth reunion of SSOC that took place in Nashville on June 16, 2024.[9]

Interestingly, during our initial contact, Cooper mentioned his absence from the first comprehensive book on the subject, Gregg Michel's *Struggle for a Better South*. According to Cooper's recollection, Michel got sick and did not get a chance to interview him. He tried to reach out but never received a response. Normally, I would have bypassed this story, but Cooper mentioned it when I first contacted him in 2015 and when we reconnected in 2023. I did contact Michel just to get more clarification, as I wanted to know more about the story. He relayed that he did not remember if he had contact with Cooper since this took place over twenty years ago. "I don't question his memory, but I simply don't recall if I knew of him or connected with him before the book." Michel acknowledged the difficulties of conducting oral histories and praised Cooper and former SSOC members for their steadfast support of "racial justice and peace and freedom in the decades since SSOC dissolved. . . . I respect and admire all they have done for a half century now to make the South a better place, a project that is still ongoing," he wrote to me. Nonetheless, both men worked together to organize SSOC's sixtieth anniversary. I hope Cooper's story adds an important element to SSOC's history and the overall high school movement.[10]

The students who rallied their peers on a citywide basis continued to be active. In 1972, former Mission High activist Francisco Flores strolled into an editorial office and asked if the *El Tecolote* needed assistance. From that moment, he began a career as a writer and engaged in work as an amateur historian, writing articles about the Mission District. He passed away in February 2022.[11] Susan Bailey chose to enroll in college after high school, stating, "My options were to get married or work in my father's store." After impressing a recruiter with her organizational work, she chose Barnard College. However, her father objected to her living in Harlem, so she attended George Washington University in Washington, DC. She graduated with a degree in American Studies and worked for Equifax before Keith Hefner, aware of her high school organizing, approached her. Due to limited funds, she left and held various jobs and ultimately became a Community Affairs Manager at Philip Morris Management, overseeing a grant to the Philadelphia Mayor's Commission on Literacy to help adult learners. In 1994, after experiencing a stroke, she retired and moved to Jacksonville, Florida, where she currently serves as a pastor. Her childhood friend, Laura Punnett, received a ScD in Occupational Health Epidemiology and serves as Professor and Chair of Biomedical Engineering at the University of Massachusetts, Lowell. Linda Rae Murray did not organize students, but after she left Collinwood High, she obtained her PhD and went on to become a world-renowned public health champion and spent her career serving the medically underserved in Chicago.[12]

Many of the students who were under government surveillance were surprised by the existence of a file and took different paths in life. Although Barbara Voldahl now identifies as a conservative, she admitted, "The same things that were important to me in high school have been important to me for the last fifty-plus years, though my activities are more low-key." She joined the Army in August 1970 as a Neuropsychiatric Specialist and reenlisted after her daughter was born. She continued holding various jobs and enjoyed working with veterans and soldiers. In retirement, she joined Braver Angels, an organization promoting civil discourse amid political polarization.[13]

Numerous individuals who are not profiled in this book have pursued careers that are closely tied to their youthful activism. As I delved into archival records, I encountered future scholars at prestigious research universities as well as smaller teaching and community colleges. Notable individuals such as historian George Chauncey and architecture scholar Marta Gutman come to mind. Chauncey published an article in a high school underground newspaper in Portland, Oregon, in 1971. Gutman, on the other hand, founded the metro-wide Greater Rochester High School Student Union in Rochester, New York, in 1969.[14] Others include sociologist Annette Laura, Africana Studies professor Wendy Wilson Fall, anthropologist Michael Blakey, historian John French, and nursing professor Phoebe Pollitt. I also had the privilege of interviewing a diverse range of academics, including sociologists Martin Laubach, David Smith, and Joel Andreas, law professor Barry

Kellman, political scientist Miriam Golden, and cinema studies professor Howard Besser. Beyond academia, many activists ventured into various other professions. Jeffrey Henson Scales, now a photograph editor at the *New York Times*, honed his skills by capturing images of the Black Panther Party at just fifteen years old.[15] Leni Schwendinger, who co-founded the Berkeley HSSU with Steve Wasserman, became a renowned lighting artist and designer, owning Leni Schwendinger Light Projects.[16] Anne Finger, the founder of the Rhode Island High School Students for Peace, evolved into an award-winning fiction and creative nonfiction writer. These young activists were not merely passing through a transient phase of youth; they carried the spirit of activism well into their adult lives.[17]

Interestingly, many former activists I interviewed, or at least corresponded with, had either forgotten or had no knowledge of the high school movement. Only a handful could recall it accurately, yet they expressed confusion over the lack of scholarship on the subject. "I'm not widely read in that area," wrote Hefner in our initial contact email. "But I can't ever recall seeing a scholarly review of 1960s high school activism. It was a very decentralized phenomenon, episodic, and often disappeared without a trace in media or memory, which makes it very difficult to study."[18] His assessment is not far off. Most scholarship on this topic has been confined to academic articles, which general audiences rarely read or have access to due to paywalls. The prevalence of articles might suggest that the topic is not substantial enough for a book-length project. Although several scholars have written manuscripts on the subject, these works remain few and far between. Given the advancing age of many former activists, time is running out to capture their stories. And it is important for scholars to know that the experiences of teenagers in Albuquerque are just as meaningful as those in Los Angeles.

The absence of public recognition of this history might also explain why contemporary high school student activism perplexes observers. "It's really unusual," stated sociologist Doug McAdams in reference to the rapid mobilization by the Parkland students. "Young people are typically overrepresented among the ranks of activists, but those are almost always university students or young adults." After a tragic school shooting that claimed the lives of seventeen people on February 14, 2018, in Parkland, Florida, students at Marjory Stoneman Douglas High School spearheaded a national campaign for gun reform. They received praise from admirers and criticism from skeptics. Critics spewed conspiracy theories by labeling the students as "crisis actors" or questioning the plausibility of high school students organizing a nationwide rally. Impressively, March for Our Lives had an estimated 1.2 million participants who held rallies nationwide demanding gun reform.[19]

Drawing parallels to the student protests of the 1960s, the movement's youth leadership was evident. However, most journalists, politicians, and even the activists themselves persisted in comparing these *high school* students to *college* students from half a century ago. Some went as far as to present their movement as a novel phenomenon. I witnessed this misleading comparison firsthand in October 2018 when I attended a book promotion event that featured three Parkland activists at Nicholas Senn High School in Chicago. Although the conversation was enlightening regarding what constitutes activism and the challenges they faced, none of the panelists or the audience members appeared to know that fifty years ago, Nicholas Senn High was a hotbed of political radicalism. Students at that school produced a plethora of underground newspapers where they critiqued administrative policies, racial attitudes, and the placement of policemen on campus.[20]

The persistent obscurity of this history to many Americans is troublesome. Education has been and continues to be a battleground in cultural conflicts and public policy debates. Politicians and parents have sparred over curriculum, permissible books, and often point fingers at students, their families, and teachers for academic underachievement. Having attended eight different high schools in three states, I witnessed firsthand how race and socioeconomic status shaped the educational experiences of schoolchildren. My disadvantaged peers knew quite well whether they had been receiving a quality or subpar education. I will never forget the response I received from a girl after showing her my class schedule during my first day at Farrell Area High School in Farrell, Pennsylvania, a small Rust Belt town. After scanning the document, she pointed to the physical science class and said, "You'll actually *learn* something in that class." She was correct. At my previous school, Liberty High in Bethlehem, Pennsylvania, my Algebra I class had just finished covering speed formulas. When I arrived in Farrell mid-school year, the students had yet to learn about equations. Far too often, the blame for educational shortcomings is directed at students' behavior and perceived indifference, rather than scrutinizing public policies regarding funding and resources. Yet, as this book has outlined, there is a historical record of students advocating for better schools and curriculum reforms, only to face accusations of being manipulated by outside agitators or branded as troublemakers. Ignorance of this history only perpetuates stereotypes that students cannot organize, form independent thoughts, and, worst of all, that disadvantaged minority students do not care about their education.

Historians often follow trends. Before the emergence of March for Our Lives, there was no prominent political activism stemming from high schools unless one followed local newspapers and broadcasts from unfamiliar areas; therefore, there has been little research in the subjects outside of education scholars. Aside from the Parkland students launching a national movement for gun reform, much of contemporary high school student activism remains a local concern. In 2015, students in my hometown of Allentown, Pennsylvania, organized a citywide walkout to protest long-standing grievances within the school system. However, the event only received local coverage and quickly faded from the public eye. I had a personal interest in the walkout, remembering the district's issues that had worsened since I last attended in 2005 as a freshman.[21] Besides a short letter to the editor I wrote, none of the local reporting provided any historical context.[22] Often, these events are viewed in isolation, rarely seen as part of a broader, significant theme in American history. When it is connected, it is usually linked to historic college campus protests or episodic incidents like the *Tinker* decision or the 1968 East Los Angeles High School walkouts. In fact, I have lost count of how many times people tried to link every high school protest I wrote about to the East Los Angeles blowouts.

One might assume that museums, archivists, and both amateur and public historians would have advanced the understanding and urgency of documenting high school student activism, but that has seldom been the case. Aside from notable accounts of Chicano and civil rights activism and movements in major urban centers like New York City and Los Angeles, many institutions remain largely unaware of this youth movement. For example, when I visited the Cincinnati History Library and Archives to research the 1968 citywide sit-in, none of the staff had heard of the event. Some assumed that while youth activism might be expected in the San Francisco Bay Area, such political developments seemed unlikely in their own communities. Countless times, when I mentioned my research topic, archivists thought I misspoke and meant college students. I find it even more frustrating when oral history centers conduct interviews with former college student activists and skim over their high school years.

However, there are signs of improvement. As many former youth activists reach retirement age, they have begun donating their possessions to archives in their local communities. But these contributions are often scattered. For instance, the largest collections of high school underground newspapers published in South Dakota are held at the state capital in Pierre.[23] In 2018, I personally convinced an interviewee to donate her copies of Indianapolis's *Corn Cob Curtain* to the Indiana Historical Society after writing a persuasive email to the staff. I even followed up with a letter to the *Indianapolis Star* to encourage others to do the same (I doubt many people ever read it).[24] I resorted to such methods after being turned down by a committee when I tried to donate a high school underground newspaper from Bloomington, Indiana to a local library. The staffer loved the object, but the board voted against it for reasons unknown to me. Some high schools likely hold records, but like North Central High School in Indianapolis, they have no means of making their collection known to the public. At least one high school, Paly High in Palo Alto, California, recently digitized not only its school newspaper but also underground publications that circulated on campus.[25] Nonetheless, these available records represent only a fraction of what might exist. There are likely thousands, if not tens of thousands, of records sitting in people's homes. As of now, the owners probably do not understand the significance of their possessions. But it is never too late to demonstrate that their campus-based newsletter was part of a larger political development. One that changed American education in profound ways.

Appendix 1

List of Independent High School Student Organizations

The following list is a compilation of independent high school student organizations in the United States that emerged from 1964 to 1975. Most organizations had memberships limited to one school, while others were citywide. Some formed on an ad hoc basis. A few groups existed in junior high school or had college students as members. Although Black Student Unions were the most ubiquitous groups, many eventually became official campus organizations.

State	City/County	Name of Organization
AL	Mobile	United Student Action Movement
AR	Little Rock	Students for Black Culture
AR	Little Rock	Students Rights Coalition
AZ	Mesa	Radical Student Union
AZ	Phoenix	People for Peace
AZ	Phoenix	South Mountain High School SMC
AZ	Phoenix	Students for Peace
AZ	Tucson	High School Committee Against the War
AZ	Tucson	Mexican American Liberation Committee
AZ	Tucson	Student Progress Organization of Tucson
AZ	Tucson	Vox Populi
CA	Berkeley	Berkeley HSSU
CA	Berkeley	Berkeley Young People's Liberation
CA	Berkeley	Student Committee of Concern
CA	Berkeley	Supporters of American Ideas
CA	Berkeley	Youth for Civil Rights
CA	Beverly Hills	Save Our Schools
CA	Culver City	Culver City Students Against the War in Vietnam
CA	El Cerrito	El Cerrito HSSAW
CA	Fresno	Fresno High School Student Alliance to End the War in Vietnam
CA	Fresno	HSSU
CA	Larkspur	Redwood Student Union Co-ordinating Council
CA	Long Beach	Student Underground Press Association
CA	Los Altos	Los Altos High Liberation Front

State	City/County	Name of Organization
CA	Los Angeles	Black Student Alliance, a.k.a. Black Youth Alliance
CA	Los Angeles	BSU
CA	Los Angeles	Garfield High School Strike Committee
CA	Los Angeles	High School SDS of Los Angeles
CA	Los Angeles	High School Union
CA	Los Angeles	Radical Student Union
CA	Los Angeles	Student Coalition for Progressive Change
CA	Los Angeles	Students for a Democratic Campus
CA	Los Angeles	United Asian Students
CA	Los Angeles	United Student Movement
CA	Los Angeles	West Coast HSSAW
CA	Los Angeles	Westside High School Liberation Front
CA	Los Angeles	Young Citizens for Community Action
CA	Marin County	Marin Youth for Social Action
CA	Mill Valley	Tam First Amendment Club
CA	Oakland	Asian Bloc
CA	Oakland	Associated Students Union of Oakland
CA	Oakland	Oakland Student Alliance
CA	Oakland	Students Against the War
CA	Palo Alto	Radical Student Union
CA	Palo Alto	United Student Movement
CA	Richmond	Unified Students
CA	Sacramento	New Student Movement
CA	Sacramento	San Juan Student Union
CA	Sacramento	Students for Peace
CA	San Bernardino	Chicano High School Coalition
CA	San Diego	United Students of Asian Heritage
CA	San Francisco	Asian Alliance
CA	San Francisco	Bay Area HSSU
CA	San Francisco	High School Coalition
CA	San Francisco	High School SMC
CA	San Francisco	HSSAW
CA	San Francisco	Poly Tech Student Peace Union
CA	San Francisco	Students for Mission
CA	San Francisco	Students' Organized Education and Action League
CA	Sunnyvale	Fremont Student Alliance
CA	Sunnyvale	Student Liberation Army Group
CA	Ukiah	Concerned Students Organization
CA	Visalia	Carnales
CO	Denver	Black Beret

State	City/County	Name of Organization
CO	Denver	Black Student Alliance
CO	Denver	Youth Coalition
CO	Lakewood	Alameda Student Union
CT	Bridgeport	Bridgeport HSSU
CT	Bridgeport	Student Revolutionary Movement
CT	East Windsor	Committee of Concerned Students
CT	Fairfield	Fairfield Student Union
CT	Fairfield	Fairfield Students Against the War
CT	Fairfield	Student Union
CT	Hartford	Hartford HSSU
CT	Madison	Students for a Complete Education
CT	New Haven	High School SDS
CT	New Haven	Student Voice
CT	Newtown	Helpful Education about Drugs
CT	Simsbury	Simsbury HSSU
CT	Waterbury	HSSU
CT	Willimantic	Black and Puerto Rican Student Liberation Front
DC	Washington	BSU
DC	Washington	DC Gay Youth
DC	Washington	High School SMC
DC	Washington	High School Student Information Center
DC	Washington	Modern Strivers
DC	Washington	Organization of African Students
DC	Washington	Student Coalition Against Racism
DC	Washington	Student Coalition for Education Now
DC	Washington	Students for Administrative Reform
DE	Dover	Dover HSSU
DE	New Castle	New Castle Student Union
DE	Wilmington	Delaware HSSU
DE	Wilmington	Delaware Students for Peace
DE	Wilmington	High School Youth Against War and Fascism
DE	Wilmington	Student Action Group
FL	Brevard County	Brevard County Student Union
FL	Coral Gables	Dade County Student Union
FL	Fort Lauderdale	Youth for a Better Democracy
FL	Jacksonville	Environmental Action Group
FL	Lakeland	Concerned Student Council
FL	Miami	Dane County Student Union
FL	Orlando	Student Liberation Front
FL	Orlando	Students for Freedom
FL	St. Petersburg	Black Student Coalition
FL	Tallahassee	High School SMC

State	City/County	Name of Organization
FL	Tampa	Youth Emancipation Proclamation
GA	Atlanta	Atlanta High School Student Alliance
GA	Atlanta	High School Mobilization Committee
HI	Honolulu	Hawaii Student Union
HI	Honolulu	Oahu HSSAW
HI	Honolulu	Roosevelt High School SDS
HI	Honolulu	Student Investigation Committee of Student Rights
HI	Honolulu	Student Organizing Committee
HI	Honolulu	Student Rights Organization
HI	Oahu	Hawaii High School Students for Peace
HI	Oahu	Hawaii Student Committee on Student Rights and Responsibilities
IA	Des Moines	Black Committee for Student Power
IA	Des Moines	BSU
IA	Des Moines	Valley HSSU
IA	Iowa City	Student Friends Organization
IL	Carbondale	High School Rights Coalition
IL	Champaign	Student Coalition
IL	Chicago	Black Student Alliance (Farragut High School)
IL	Chicago	Black Student Alliance (Kennedy High School)
IL	Chicago	Black Students for Defense
IL	Chicago	Concerned Black Students
IL	Chicago	Concerned Committee for a Better Education at Clemente High School
IL	Chicago	Concerned Students of Forestville
IL	Chicago	High School Radical Union
IL	Chicago	High School Rights Coalition
IL	Chicago	High School Youth Against War and Fascism
IL	Chicago	HSSAW
IL	Chicago	Lane Students for Democracy
IL	Chicago	Latin Student Coalition
IL	Chicago	Maplewood Student Union
IL	Chicago	Mobilized Citizen Coalition
IL	Chicago	New Breed
IL	Chicago	Students for Freedom
IL	Decatur	Student Coalition
IL	Decatur	Student Union
IL	Des Plaines	Des Plaines Environmental High School Coalition
IL	Evanston	Black Organization for Youth
IL	Evansville	Niles Township Student Coalition

State	City/County	Name of Organization
IL	Highland Park	Students Organization for Survival
IL	Naperville	Cooperative High School Independent Press Service
IL	Naperville	Naperville Alternative Student Coalition
IL	Oak Park	School-Community Council
IL	Rockford	RAMS Student Union
IL	Skokie	HSSAW
IN	Bloomington	Bloomington Student Union
IN	Fort Wayne	Fort Wayne Student Rights Organization
IN	Indianapolis	BSU
IN	Indianapolis	Chicano Associated Youth Organization
IN	Indianapolis	Indianapolis High School Press Service
IN	Indianapolis	Indianapolis Youth Council
IN	Indianapolis	Student Rights Committee Southport High School
IN	Indianapolis	Students for Social Change
IN	Jeffersonville	Committee for the Defense of Student Rights
IN	Jeffersonville	Student Coalition
IN	Kokomo	Black Student Coalition
IN	Muncie	Students for Peace
IN	South Bend	Black Student Alliance
KS	Johnson County	Students for Academic Freedom
KS	Lawrence	Peace Action Coalition
KY	Covington	Student Strike Committee
KY	Dayton	Committee to End Repression at Dayton High School
KY	Louisville	Freedom Associated with Individual Reform
KY	Louisville	Seneca Student Rights Committee
KY	Louisville	Student Rights Committee
KY	Louisville	Students With a Purpose
LA	Baton Rouge	Baton Rouge Student Union
LA	Metairie	Riverdale High School SDS
LA	New Orleans	Benjamin Franklin High School SDS
LA	New Orleans	BSU
LA	New Orleans	Fortier High School SDS
LA	New Orleans	McDonough High School SDS
LA	New Orleans	Newman High School SDS
LA	New Orleans	New Orleans Citywide High School SDS
LA	New Orleans	Teens for Freedom
LA	New Orleans	United Students
MA	Andover	National Prep School Union
MA	Boston	Black Student Federation

State	City/County	Name of Organization
MA	Boston	Black Students Alliance
MA	Boston	Boston High School Rights Committee
MA	Boston	BSU
MA	Boston	Greater Boston High School Rights Coalition/Committee
MA	Boston	Greater Boston High School SMC
MA	Boston	High School Coalition
MA	Boston	High School Radical Action Project
MA	Boston	Massachusetts High School Rights Coalition
MA	Boston	Massachusetts Liberation Front
MA	Lowell	Committee for Concerned Students
MA	Medford	Concerned Students
MA	Pittsfield	Berkshire County HSSU
MA	Salem	United Student Involvement/Alliance
MA	Springfield	BSU
MA	Wellesley	Viet Nam Peace Action of Wellesley High School
MA	Worcester	Worcester Area High School SMC
MD	Baltimore	Baltimore High School Students for Peace
MD	Baltimore	Baltimore HSSU
MD	Baltimore	Baltimore Students' Rights Organization
MD	Baltimore	BSU
MD	Baltimore	Students Concerned About Vietnam
MD	Bethesda	Montgomery County Student Alliance
MD	Bethesda	Student Coalition
MD	Bladensburg	Student Organizing Committee
MD	Montgomery County	Maryland Student Union
MD	Potomac	Political Action Committee
MD	Silver Spring	Concerned Students
MD	Silver Spring	Student Forum
MD	Silver Spring	Student Organizing Committee
MD	Wheaton	Student Coalition
MI	Ann Arbor	Ann Arbor HSSU
MI	Ann Arbor	Student Liberation Front
MI	Ann Arbor	Students to Organize for Peace
MI	Ann Arbor	Tappan Student Union
MI	Ann Arbor	Youth Liberation of Ann Arbor
MI	Battle Creek	Black Student Alliance
MI	Battle Creek	Student Union
MI	Berrien Springs	Students for Peace and Freedom
MI	Dearborn	Dearborn High School Student Coalition
MI	Detroit	Black Student United Front

State	City/County	Name of Organization
MI	Detroit	Concerned Whites Unite to Support the Black Student Demands
MI	Detroit	Cooley HSSU
MI	Detroit	Detroit High School Students for Peace
MI	Detroit	High School Liberation Union
MI	Detroit	High School SMC
MI	Detroit	High School Youth Against War and Fascism
MI	Detroit	Radical Student Association
MI	Detroit	Rebels
MI	Detroit	Revolutionary Student Coalition
MI	Detroit	Young Students for World Peace
MI	Grosse Pointe	Grosse Ponte Student Union
MI	Kalamazoo	Black Action Movement
MI	Kalamazoo	High School Liberation Front
MI	Lansing	League of Valid Existences
MI	Lansing	Student Rights Committee
MI	Livonia	Livonia HSSU
MI	Royal Oak	Youth for Peace, Freedom, and Justice
MI	Union Lake	Environmental Action to Save Our Earth
MN	Bloomington	Metropolitan Student Coalition
MN	Minneapolis	Determined Ebony Council of Youth
MN	Minneapolis	High School SMC
MN	Minneapolis	Minnesota Student Union
MN	Oak Park Heights	Concerned Advocate
MO	Camdenton	Students Tired of Pollution
MO	Kansas City	High School Coalition on Welfare Rights
MO	Kansas City	High School Liberation Front
MO	Kansas City	High School SMC
MO	Kansas City	Save the Environment Please
MO	Kansas City	Student Liberation Party
MO	St. Louis	Beaumont Vanguard Party
MO	St. Louis	High School Liberation Front
MO	St. Louis	Park Action Coalition for Students
MO	St. Louis	SDS Chapters in City Schools
MO	St. Louis	Student Union
MO	University City	University City Vietnam Summer
MS	Hattiesburg	Mississippi Student Union
MS	Pascagoula	Student Coalition
NC	Charlotte	Charlotte Student Union
NC	Raleigh	United Students Association
NE	Omaha	Black Association for Nationalism Through Unity

State	City/County	Name of Organization
NE	Omaha	High School Student Freedom Union
NE	Omaha	Millard Liberation Front
NE	Omaha	Nebraska Student Coalition for Draft Education
NE	Omaha	Students for Constructive Change
NJ	Camden	Concerned Students of Camden High School
NJ	Cherry Hill	South Jersey High School Coalition
NJ	East Brunswick	East Brunswick High School Students for Peace
NJ	Franklin	Black Youth United
NJ	Franklin	Franklin High School Coalition
NJ	Franklin	Together
NJ	Hammonton	High School Aid Committee
NJ	Medford	South Jersey Students Rights Coalition
NJ	Metuchen	Student Coalition
NJ	Middletown Township	Brotherhood
NJ	Middletown Township	Concerned Students for Peace
NJ	Neptune	BSU
NJ	Neptune	Neptune High School Libertarian Alliance
NJ	New Brunswick	New Jersey Student Union
NJ	New Brunswick	Student Coordinating Organization for Peace and Equality
NJ	Newark	Newark Student Federation
NJ	Newark	Newark Student Union
NJ	Oakland	Student Liberties Union
NJ	Plainfield	New Jersey High School Liberation Movement
NJ	Plainfield	Plainfield HSSU
NJ	Plainfield	Plainfield Students Against the War
NJ	Red Bank	Independent Student Union
NJ	Red Bank	Red Bank Student Community Action Group
NJ	Rumson	The People
NJ	Vineland	Student Union
NJ	Warren	Student-Community Service
NM	Albuquerque	Active Youth for Democracy
NM	Albuquerque	Chicano Youth Association
NM	Albuquerque	High School Students for Environmental Reform
NM	Albuquerque	Los Caballeros de Nueva España
NM	Albuquerque	Students for Educational Reform
NM	Albuquerque	Students Open Forum
NM	Albuquerque	Youth for Radical Progress
NV	Reno	Students for Individual Rights
NY	Binghamton	High School Rights Coalition

State	City/County	Name of Organization
NY	Binghamton	United Student Movement
NY	Buffalo	Black Action Movement
NY	Buffalo	United Black Students of East High
NY	Buffalo	United Students
NY	Hewlett	Democratic Students' Coalition
NY	Larchmont	Students for World Peace
NY	Long Island	High School SMC
NY	Long Island	Students for Environmental Quality
NY	Melville	Nassau-Suffolk HSSU
NY	Mount Vernon	Westchester Students for Peace and Civil Rights
NY	New York	African American Cultural Naturalist
NY	New York	Afro-American Student Association
NY	New York	Black and Puerto Rican Citywide High School Council
NY	New York	Black Pioneers
NY	New York	Black Youth Alliance
NY	New York	Black Youth Federation
NY	New York	Bronx Science Comm. For Political Action
NY	New York	BSU
NY	New York	Citywide Student Strike Committee
NY	New York	Clinton Resistance
NY	New York	Committee for Student Action
NY	New York	Dalton Students Against the War
NY	New York	Forest Hills Students for Peace
NY	New York	High School Alliance
NY	New York	High School Coalition
NY	New York	High School Coalition for Student Action
NY	New York	High School Independent Press Service
NY	New York	High School SDS
NY	New York	High School SMC
NY	New York	High School SNCC
NY	New York	High School Women's Coalition
NY	New York	High School Youth Against War and Fascism
NY	New York	HSSAW
NY	New York	John Bowne Students for Peace
NY	New York	Martin Van Buren Students Against Militarism
NY	New York	Monroe Student Action Committee
NY	New York	Music and Art Students Against the War
NY	New York	National High School SMC
NY	New York	New Lincoln Committee for Peace
NY	New York	New York High School Student Rights Coalition

State	City/County	Name of Organization
NY	New York	New York High School Students for Peace in Vietnam
NY	New York	New York HSSU
NY	New York	Radical Zionist High School Union
NY	New York	Student Coalition for Relevant Sex Education
NY	New York	Students Against Social Injustice
NY	New York	Students for Environmental Action
NY	New York	Stuyvesant Committee to End the War in Vietnam
NY	New York	Stuyvesant Radical Coalition
NY	New York	United Federation of Harlem Youth
NY	New York	Waldon Students Against the War
NY	New York	Washington Irwin Students Against the War
NY	Nyack	Rockland County Student Action
NY	Rochester	BSU
NY	Rochester	Concerned Youth
NY	Rochester	Greater Rochester HSSU
NY	Rochester	High School Student Coalition
NY	Rochester	High School Youth Against War and Fascism
NY	Rochester	Puerto Rican Student Union
NY	Syracuse	Black Youth United of Syracuse
NY	Syracuse	High School Alliance
NY	Syracuse	HSSU
NY	White Plains	Ardsley HSSU
NY	White Plains	Student Action Movement
NY	Yonkers	Concerned Black Students of Yonkers
OH	Akron	Student Coalition for Constructive Social Reform
OH	Akron	Zebras
OH	Athens	Free High School
OH	Chillicothe	HSSU
OH	Cincinnati	BSU
OH	Cincinnati	Cincinnati High School Coalition
OH	Cincinnati	HSSAW
OH	Cincinnati	Liberal Students Demarche
OH	Cincinnati	Radical Zebra Party
OH	Cincinnati	Students for Responsible Action
OH	Cleveland	American Political Activism Through Youth
OH	Cleveland	Black Unity Movement
OH	Cleveland	Cleveland Metropolitan Area Student Council
OH	Cleveland	High School SMC
OH	Cleveland	High School Youth Against War and Fascism

State	City/County	Name of Organization
OH	Cleveland	National High School Activist League
OH	Cleveland	United Black Student Alliance (high school & others)
OH	Cleveland	United Students for Action
OH	Cleveland Heights	Heights SDS
OH	Cleveland Heights	Michael's People
OH	Cleveland Heights	Student Interaction Committee
OH	Columbus	Students Rights Organization
OH	Dayton	Concerned High School Students
OH	East Cleveland	Shaw SDS
OH	Kent	Ohio Union of High School Students
OH	Oxford	Concerned Young People
OH	Shaker Heights	Shaker SDS
OH	Springfield	Springfield HSSAW
OH	Upper Arlington	Student Union
OK	Enid	Oklahoma Alternative Student Union
OR	Corvallis	Student Liberation Front
OR	Hood River	Hoover River Valley Student Union
OR	Portland	Black Coalition
OR	Portland	High School Collective
OR	Portland	High School Peace Action Coalition
OR	Portland	High School SMC
OR	Portland	HSSU
OR	Portland	Portland High School Rights Coalition
OR	Salem	Society of Strangers
PA	Allentown	Allentown Community Youth Movement
PA	Chambersburg	Youth Against Pollution
PA	Chester	Congress for the Advancement of Student Rights
PA	Chester	HSSAW and the Draft
PA	Delaware County	Student Action Committee
PA	Hershey	Students for Change
PA	Lehigh Valley	Youth in Action
PA	Media	Penncrest Student Union
PA	Nazareth	Nazareth HSSU
PA	New Castle	Committee of 28 Concerned Students
PA	Philadelphia	Black Catholic Student Union
PA	Philadelphia	Black Student Coalition
PA	Philadelphia	Black United Liberation Front
PA	Philadelphia	BSU
PA	Philadelphia	High School SMC
PA	Philadelphia	Philadelphia High School Coalition
PA	Philadelphia	Philadelphia Parochial Student Union

State	City/County	Name of Organization
PA	Philadelphia	Philadelphia Student Union
PA	Philadelphia	Student Coalition
PA	Philadelphia	Students Concerned
PA	Philadelphia	Students' Rights Coalition
PA	Philadelphia	Union of Student Governments
PA	Philadelphia	United Youth Congress of Metropolitan Philadelphia
PA	Pittsburgh	Black Catholic High School Student Alliance
PA	Pittsburgh	Black Federation of Students
PA	Pittsburgh	Black Student Alliance
PA	Pittsburgh	High School Students for Peace in Vietnam
PA	Pittsburgh	Students for Better Schools aka Allderdice Committee for a Better School
PA	Swarthmore	Swarthmore High School Students for Peace
PA	York	HSSU
PR	San Juan	Federation of Students for Independence
PR	San Juan	High School Students for Independence
RI	Providence	Rhode Island High School Students for Peace
RI	Warwick	Students for Social Change
SD	Sioux Falls	Sioux Falls High School Alliance
TN	Knoxville	Students for a New Birth
TN	Memphis	Invaders (college and high school)
TN	Nashville	Nashville Student Union
TN	Oak Ridge	Citizens for Educational Reform
TX	Austin	High School SMC
TX	Corpus Christi	Student Union
TX	El Paso	Alliance
TX	El Paso	Organization for Student Rights
TX	Houston	Advocating Rights for Mexican American Students
TX	Houston	Afro-American for Black Unity
TX	Houston	Legal Students' Rights
TX	Houston	North Side Student Association
TX	Houston	Student Organization for Free Though
TX	Houston	Student Union for a Democratic Society
TX	Houston	Students for Individual Rights
TX	Houston	Young Revolutionary African People
TX	San Antonio	San Antonio HSSU
UT	Salt Lake City	Intermountain Peace Coalition
UT	Salt Lake City	Utah Student Association
VA	Arlington	Arlington Student Coalition
VA	Arlington	Students for Peace

State	City/County	Name of Organization
VA	Burke	The Ozone Collective
VA	Charlottesville	Student Action Movement
VA	Hermitage	Hermitage Student Union
VA	Portsmouth	United Black Student Association
VA	Richmond	Richmond Area High School Student Committee Against the War in Vietnam
VT	Burlington	Student Organizing Coalition
VT	Rutland	Vermont Student for Peace in Vietnam
WA	Pullman	High School SMC
WA	Pullman	Pullman High School Moratorium Committee
WA	Seattle	Asian Student Coalition (high school chapters)
WA	Seattle	BSU
WA	Seattle	Democratic Student Union
WA	Seattle	High School SMC
WA	Seattle	Queen Anne HSSU
WA	Seattle	SDS Chapters in City Schools
WA	Seattle	Seattle Alliance of BSUs
WA	Seattle	Seattle Student Union
WA	Tacoma	High School Liberation Front
WI	Madison	Concerned Students of West High School
WI	Madison	Dane County HSSU
WI	Madison	High School SMC
WI	Madison	HSSAW
WI	Madison	LINKS#
WI	Madison	Students for Social Justice
WI	Madison	Wisconsin HSSU
WI	Milwaukee	Black Organized Youth
WI	Milwaukee	High School Youth Against War and Fascism
WI	Milwaukee	Milwaukee Educational Alliance
WI	Milwaukee	Milwaukee HSSU
WI	Milwaukee	Milwaukee Student Alliance
WI	Milwaukee	Milwaukee Student Union
WI	Milwaukee	Students for Peace and Freedom
WI	Milwaukee	Teens for Peace
WI	Milwaukee	United Liberation Force
WI	Milwaukee	Wisconsin Student Union
WI	Milwaukee	Wisconsin Youth for Democratic Education
WI	Sheboygan	North HSSU
WI	Shorewood	Shorewood HSSU
WI	Spring Green	River Valley Student Alliance
WI	Stevens Point	Stevens Point High School Coalition
WV	Beckley	Beckley Student Union

Appendix 2

List of High School Underground Newspapers in the United States

The following record is the most comprehensive list of high school underground newspapers in the United States from 1965 to 1975. Although over 1,000 publications are included, this sheet is an undercount due to the brief runs of many newsletters. Many of these publications only came to public attention following a controversy. Some newspapers mentioned the existence of current or previous publications without providing their titles. Those omissions are labeled as "unidentified."

State	City	Name of Publication
AK	Fairbanks	unidentified
AL	Birmingham	*Southside Rag*
AL	Hoover	*Students of Berry*
AL	Mountain Brook	*General Glutz*
AR	Fayetteville	*Common Speech*
AZ	Globe	*Summer's End*
AZ	Phoenix	*Central High Rag*
AZ	Phoenix	*Fruit of the Loom aka Brophy Briefs*
AZ	Phoenix	*Noise*
AZ	Phoenix	*Opinion*
AZ	Phoenix	*Rebel*
AZ	Phoenix	*Scope (The)*
AZ	Tucson	*Mine*
AZ	Tucson	*Off Hand*
AZ	Tucson	*Vox Populi Journal*
CA	Barstow	*An Independent Paper*
CA	Berkeley	*Pack Rat*
CA	Berkeley	*Rag (The)*
CA	Beverly Hills	*Beverly Stash*
CA	Beverly Hills	*Casserole Productions*
CA	Beverly Hills	*Daily Son*
CA	Beverly Hills	*Local Rocks*
CA	Beverly Hills	*Rap*
CA	Beverly Hills	*Strawberry Fields*
CA	Beverly Hills	*Trash*
CA	Citrus Heights	*Surveyor*
CA	Downey	*Dawn*

State	City	Name of Publication
CA	Downey	*Jugendbewegung*
CA	Downey	*Oink!*
CA	El Monte	*Knights Banana*
CA	Encino	*Come Together*
CA	Felton	*Spring Rain*
CA	Fremont	*Brightside*
CA	Fresno	*Alta California*
CA	Fresno	*Valley High Free Press*
CA	Glendora	*Paper (The)*
CA	La Crescenta	*Cheshire Cat*
CA	La Habra	*Catalist (The)*
CA	Lakeside	*Rug Spotting in Amerika*
CA	Lakeside	*Two Week Leak*
CA	La Puente	*Freethinker*
CA	Livermore	*Bull Sheet*
CA	Lompoc	*Energy*
CA	Lompoc	*Genesis II*
CA	Long Beach	*Frox*
CA	Long Beach	*Long Beach Rising Star*
CA	Long Beach	*Loudmouth*
CA	Long Beach	*Paper (The)*
CA	Long Beach	*Rising Sun*
CA	Long Beach	*T.R.I.P.*
CA	Los Angeles	*Censored (The)*
CA	Los Angeles	*Fat Press*
CA	Los Angeles	*Insight*
CA	Los Angeles	*New Improved Tide*
CA	Los Angeles	*Participator*
CA	Los Angeles	*Red Tide*
CA	Los Angeles	*Sir-Press*
CA	Los Angeles	*Third Eye (The)*
CA	Los Angeles	*Vigil (The)*
CA	Los Angeles	*Vista*
CA	Los Angeles	*Worrier (The)*
CA	Manhattan Beach	*Up Against the Wall*
CA	Marin County	*High Times*
CA	Mount Diablo	*Mother Trucker*
CA	Oakland	*Buddy Act-Express*
CA	Oakland	*Dove*
CA	Oakland	*Notes from the Underground*
CA	Orange	*Dog*
CA	Orange	*Planted Seed (The)*
CA	Palo Alto	*Class Struggle*

State	City	Name of Publication
CA	Palo Alto	Radical Rag
CA	Palo Alto	Radio Free Heaven
CA	Palo Alto	Revelator (The)
CA	Palo Alto	Serve the People
CA	Pasadena	Blazing
CA	Pasadena	Doublethink
CA	Pasadena	Headlines
CA	Redwood City	Liberty
CA	Reseda	Open Forum
CA	Rialto	Fourth World Liberator
CA	Rowland Heights	Publick Occurrences
CA	Sacramento	Bull Sheet
CA	Sacramento	Downwind
CA	Sacramento	Excalibur
CA	Sacramento	Floyd
CA	Sacramento	Freedom of the Press
CA	Sacramento	Gap (The)
CA	Sacramento	Grok
CA	Sacramento	New Student Movement
CA	Sacramento	Outlaw
CA	Sacramento	Sadhotchi
CA	Sacramento	Underground Eagle (The)
CA	Sacramento	Volunteers
CA	Sagner	Seeker (The)
CA	Salinas	Rebel (The)
CA	San Diego	Asian Face
CA	San Diego	Four Flights Up
CA	San Diego	Student Voice (The)
CA	San Francisco	Activist Opinion
CA	San Francisco	Bay Area High School Free Press
CA	San Francisco	Dare to Struggle
CA	San Francisco	Seize the Times
CA	San Jose	A Spree
CA	San Juan	Volunteers Newsletter
CA	San Mateo	Free Spirit Party
CA	San Pedro	Burr'd (The)
CA	San Rafael	Free Youth
CA	Santa Barbara	Itch (The)
CA	Santa Barbara	Star Spangled Revolutionary Press
CA	Santa Barbara	Trumpet (The)
CA	Santa Clara	Undergrind (The)
CA	Saratoga	P.O.P. (Pissed Off Paper)
CA	Simi Valley	Underground Pony Express

State	City	Name of Publication
CA	Sunnyvale	*Fail Us*
CA	Torrance	*7 O'Clock News (The)*
CA	Walnut	*People*
CA	Walnut	*Student*
CO	Aurora	*Independent Tribune*
CO	Boulder	*High School Independent—Mass Media*
CO	Boulder	*TIS Newspaper*
CO	Denver	*Activist (The)*
CO	Denver	*NOUS for Free*
CO	Denver	*Student Reprint*
CO	Denver	*Student's Free Press Needs a New Name*
CO	Denver	*Student Underground Chronicle*
CO	Fort Collins	*Iron Tower (The)*
CO	Fort Collins	*Poudre Advocate*
CO	Fort Collins	*Spilled Ink*
CT	Bridgeport	*Glass Onion (The)*
CT	Bridgeport	*Minority (The)*
CT	Bridgeport	*Myth (The)*
CT	Cheshire	*Spark*
CT	East Hartford	*Sheet Son of Rag*
CT	Fairfield	*Glass Onion*
CT	Georgetown	*Nickel Bag*
CT	Guilford	*Startle!*
CT	Hartford	*People's Press*
CT	Manchester	*Pit*
CT	New Haven	*Gadfly Free Press*
CT	New Haven	*Lee Annex Unleashed*
CT	Orange	*Hot Lead*
CT	South Windsor	*Collaboration*
CT	Stamford	*Stamford Free Press*
CT	Storrs	*Midnight Rambler*
CT	Thomaston	*Reynolds Bridge*
CT	Torrington	*Locus*
CT	Torrington	*X-Ray Straight*
CT	Watertown	*Free*
CT	West Haven	*S.P.S.*
CT	Weston	*Unicorn*
CT	Wethersfield	*Pool of Ignorance Press*
CT	Windsor	*Iskra*
CT	Windsor	*Roach*
DC	Washington	*Eastern Free Press*
DC	Washington	*Fly by Night*
DC	Washington	*Free Student*
DC	Washington	*High Western Mirror (The)*

State	City	Name of Publication
DC	Washington	*Resistance*
DC	Washington	*Salt of the Earth*
DC	Washington	*Struggle*
DC	Washington	*Them Changes*
DC	Washington	*Uhuru*
DE	Wilmington	*Acid Flash*
DE	Wilmington	*What's Left*
FL	Boca Raton	*Young People's News Service*
FL	Davie	*Ideoplastos*
FL	Davie	*Nova Free Press*
FL	Eau Gallie	*Brotherhood*
FL	Jacksonville	*Relayer*
FL	Jupiter	*Con-ver-Sation*
FL	Lakeland	*Primer (The)*
FL	Miami	*Street Sheet*
FL	Pensacola	*Ivory Tower*
FL	Pensacola	*Public Eye*
FL	Sarasota	*First Amendment*
FL	St. Petersburg	*Joint Effort*
FL	Tallahassee	*Amazing Grace*
FL	Tallahassee	*Black and Aware*
FL	Tallahassee	*First Edition (The)*
FL	Tampa	*First Amendment*
FL	West Palm Beach	*Hieronymous*
GA	Atlanta	*Grady Grope (The)*
HI	Honolulu	*Chainbreaker*
HI	Honolulu	*Encounter (The)*
HI	Honolulu	*Hemo da Skool*
HI	Honolulu	*Mid-Pacific Poop*
HI	Honolulu	*Occasional Tripe*
HI	Kailua	*Wrapper (The)*
IA	Ames	*Dog's Breath*
IA	Cedar Rapids	*Transmission*
IA	Cedar Rapids	*Trash*
IA	Council Bluff	*United Students for Salvaging America*
IA	Des Moines	*Karma*
IA	Des Moines	*Peace Pipeline*
IA	Elridge	*Sandwich*
IA	Grinnell	*Guernica*
IA	Iowa City	*Crosstown Chronicles*
IA	Iowa City	*Feedback*
IA	Iowa City	*Iowa City Oppressed Citizens*
IA	Iowa City	*Name This Paper Homeground*
IA	West Union	*Milestone*

State	City	Name of Publication
ID	Boise	unidentified
ID	Sandpoint	unidentified
ID	Twin Falls	*Crystal Ship*
ID	Twin Falls	*Yellow Sheet*
IL	Alton	*Common Sense*
IL	Arlington Heights	*Vaseline*
IL	Arlington Heights	*Vulture (The)*
IL	Aurora	*Word (The)*
IL	Batavia	*Spud Tater*
IL	Belleville	*Liberator*
IL	Bensenville	*Chimes of Freedom*
IL	Bensenville	*Da BBA Gazette*
IL	Bensenville	*Student Opinion*
IL	Berwyn	*Key (The)*
IL	Bethalto	*Omega*
IL	Champaign	*Oclupaca*
IL	Chicago	*69 Lane Tech*
IL	Chicago	*Above a Whisper*
IL	Chicago	*Action Bulletin*
IL	Chicago	*Affluent Drool (The)*
IL	Chicago	*Barf*
IL	Chicago	*Decisive Dawn*
IL	Chicago	*Fuge Times*
IL	Chicago	*Grab Hold*
IL	Chicago	*Greater Responsible Action Student Party*
IL	Chicago	*High Ground*
IL	Chicago	*Intercourse (The)*
IL	Chicago	*In Touch*
IL	Chicago	*Looking Glass*
IL	Chicago	*Mau-Mau*
IL	Chicago	*Paper (The)*
IL	Chicago	*Smuff*
IL	Chicago	*Student Action*
IL	Chicago	*Therefore Chose Life*
IL	Chicago	*Young Red (The)*
IL	Des Plaines	*Happy Trails*
IL	Edwardsville	*Clip (The)*
IL	Elgin	*American Revelation*
IL	Evanston	*Gadfly (The)*
IL	Evanston	*Toehold*
IL	Greenville	*Angry Voices*
IL	Harvey	*Herald (The)*
IL	Highland Park	*Derelicked*
IL	Joliet	*Grass High*

State	City	Name of Publication
IL	Joliet	*Leaf*
IL	Joliet	*Subterranean Notes*
IL	Libertyville	*Paralax*
IL	Lincolnwood	*New Free Press*
IL	Lombardi	*Messiah (The)*
IL	Macomb	*Logos*
IL	Mount Morris	*Mt. Morris Revelation*
IL	Naperville	*Alternative*
IL	Naperville	*Chipmunk*
IL	Naperville	*Everyday People*
IL	Naperville	*Free Voice*
IL	Naperville	*Smoke Signals*
IL	Naperville	*Student Free Press*
IL	North Lake	*Student Resistance*
IL	Oak Park	*Fenwick Free Press*
IL	Oak Park	*L'Affiche*
IL	Oak Park	*Means (The)*
IL	Oak Park	*Midnight Special*
IL	Oak Park	*Trapeze*
IL	Oak Park	*Who Says We Can't*
IL	Olympia Fields	*Plot*
IL	Park Forest	*Sum-Times*
IL	Park Ridge	*News and Views*
IL	Rochester	*Rockford Alternative Middle School*
IL	Rock Island	*New Times*
IL	Skokie	*New Free Press*
IL	Skokie	*West Free Press*
IL	Stockton	*RAP*
IL	Streator	*Paper (The)*
IL	Urbana	*Tin Whistle*
IL	Villa Park	*Daily Drudge (The)*
IL	Waukegan	*Minstrel*
IL	Wilmette	*Fifth Estate*
IN	Bloomington	*New Amerikan Mercury*
IN	Brownsburg	*Digger (The)*
IN	Columbus	*Different Drummer (The)*
IN	Elwood	*Head (The)*
IN	Evansville	*Sheet (The)*
IN	Fort Wayne	*Alternative (The)*
IN	Fort Wayne	*Deadringer*
IN	Fort Wayne	*Hotchpotch*
IN	Franklin	*Domiabra*
IN	Gary	*Alternative*
IN	Goshen	*Student Independent Press*

State	City	Name of Publication
IN	Indianapolis	After Breakfast
IN	Indianapolis	Apathetic Majority (The)
IN	Indianapolis	Asylum (The)
IN	Indianapolis	Corn Cob Curtain
IN	Indianapolis	Critique
IN	Indianapolis	Easy Writer
IN	Indianapolis	Indianapolis High School Free Press
IN	Indianapolis	IRA
IN	Indianapolis	Our Paper
IN	Indianapolis	Revelation
IN	Indianapolis	Steeple (The)
IN	Indianapolis	Student Voice (The)
IN	Indianapolis	Terestias
IN	Indianapolis	Warren Goes Underground
IN	Kokomo	Free Press
IN	Mishawaka	Student Supplement
IN	Mishawaka	Voice (The)
IN	Noblesville	Blackhawk Broadcast
IN	Noblesville	Power to the Peaceful
IN	Plainfield	Om
IN	Poseyville	Lone Viking
IN	South Bend	Desiderata
IN	South Bend	Seedling (The)
IN	Terre Haute	Ore 1
IN	Terre Haute	Pride City Dispatch
KS	Hays	Bird
KS	Lawrence	Freed Speak
KS	Maryville	New Society
KS	McPherson	Acid Press
KS	Overland Park	Daily Android
KS	Overland Park	Free Times
KS	Overland Park	Passage
KS	Overland Park	Yzfjolp
KS	Shawnee Mission	Free Press (The)
KS	Wichita	Antithesis
KS	Wichita	Exposition
KS	Wichita	Icom
KS	Wichita	Polemic
KY	Bardstown	Dupont II
KY	Covington	Chronicle of Current Events
KY	Covington	Underground Railroad
KY	Lexington	Lafayette Free Press
KY	Lexington	Porno Smut
KY	Louisville	Ballard Brotherhood

State	City	Name of Publication
KY	Louisville	Good Life
KY	Louisville	Seneca
KY	Louisville	Student Voice
KY	Louisville	Uprising
KY	Louisville	We The People
KY	Paducah	Eulogy (The)
LA	Metairie	Free Press
LA	New Orleans	Common Ground
LA	New Orleans	Finger
LA	New Orleans	Word
LA	Shreveport	Hi Bird Free Press
LA	Shreveport	Thoughts
MA	Bedford	Dean Duck Incarnate
MA	Boston	Beginning of the End (The)
MA	Boston	Eastie First
MA	Boston	Nameless Newsprint
MA	Boston	Right On
MA	Boston	Surgite
MA	Bridgewater	Named and Screaming
MA	Bridgewater	Running Dog
MA	Brockton	Apathy
MA	Burlington	Vision
MA	Cambridge	Disorientation Manual
MA	Cambridge	Time's Up
MA	Chelmsford	Chelmsford Free Press
MA	Chelmsford	Egg (The)
MA	Chelmsford	New Free Press
MA	Chelmsford	When the Leaves Breaks
MA	Cochituate	Brass Tacks
MA	Framingham	Issue (The)
MA	Georgetown	Dancer (The)
MA	Hancock	Odyssey
MA	Haverhill	Lip (The)
MA	Hingham	Graffiti (The)
MA	Leominster	In the Heart of the Beast
MA	Natick	Tannis
MA	Needham	Razir
MA	New Bedford	Iskra
MA	North Adams	Jailbreak
MA	Peabody	Bull (The)
MA	Salem	Liberated Witch
MA	Scituate	Sotyagrana
MA	Sharon	Eye (The)
MA	Somerville	Straight Talk

State	City	Name of Publication
MA	Springfield	*Smash*
MA	Stow	*Wildflowers*
MA	Wellesley	*Searcher (The)*
MA	Winchester	*Focus (The)*
MD	Baltimore	*Ball-Point Banana*
MD	Baltimore	*Expression*
MD	Baltimore	*Lampoon*
MD	Baltimore	*One Nation Underground*
MD	Baltimore	*Spark*
MD	Baltimore	*Strobe (The)*
MD	Baltimore	*Today's World*
MD	Bethesda	*Hysteria*
MD	Bethesda	*Marshmallow Gnus and Whirl Report*
MD	Bethesda	*Maryland Student Union Newsletter*
MD	Colesville	*Outcry*
MD	College Park	*They're Shooting Eagles*
MD	Harwood	*Leak (The)*
MD	Howard County	*Changes*
MD	Kensington	*Bombstead Bullsheet*
MD	Montgomery County	*MCSA Newsletter*
MD	Montgomery County	*Resistance*
MD	Potomac	*Position Paper*
MD	Silver Spring	*First Amendment*
MD	Silver Spring	*Rush*
MD	Towson	*Gaudio*
MD	Towson	*Student Forum*
MD	Wheaton	*Open Door*
ME	Auburn	*Spargent*
ME	Waterville	*Mess*
MI	Albion	*Slave (The)*
MI	Allegan	*Underground Newspaper*
MI	Ann Arbor	*5% Press (The)*
MI	Ann Arbor	*Finally Got the News*
MI	Ann Arbor	*FPS*
MI	Ann Arbor	*Grapevine*
MI	Ann Arbor	*On the Fritz*
MI	Ann Arbor	*Owl (The)*
MI	Ann Arbor	*US*
MI	Ann Arbor	*Venceremos*
MI	Ann Arbor	*Youth Liberation*
MI	Ann Arbor	*Youth Rising*
MI	Belleville	*Liberator (The)*
MI	Berkeley	*Aesthetic*
MI	Berrien Springs	untitled

State	City	Name of Publication
MI	Birmingham	*Spirt (The)*
MI	Clio	*Borealis*
MI	Detroit	*Alternative Media*
MI	Detroit	*Black Student Manifesto*
MI	Detroit	*Black Student Voice*
MI	Detroit	*Cass Commentary (The)*
MI	Detroit	*Cass Student Voice*
MI	Detroit	*Cody Caste*
MI	Detroit	*Combat*
MI	Detroit	*Common Filth*
MI	Detroit	*Daily Planet*
MI	Detroit	*Inter Comm*
MI	Detroit	*Kulchur*
MI	Detroit	*Pregnant Duck*
MI	Detroit	*Rebel (The)*
MI	Detroit	*Rebel's Voice*
MI	Detroit	*South Hampton Illustrated Times (SHIT)*
MI	Detroit	*Student Notebook (The)*
MI	Detroit	*Student Voice*
MI	Detroit	*Truth (The)*
MI	Detroit	*Wasted Ink*
MI	Detroit	*Yellow*
MI	Flint	*Unity*
MI	Hartland	*Hartland School Notebook*
MI	Hibbing	*Underground (The)*
MI	Hibbing	*Underwater*
MI	Highland Park	*Red Tide*
MI	Houghton	*Brook*
MI	Howell	*F.L.I.P. (Fine Little Independent Paper)*
MI	Ionia	*Ripped*
MI	Kalamazoo	*Hope on Pop*
MI	Kalamazoo	*Jailbreak*
MI	Lansing	*Optimist (The)*
MI	Lansing	*Snort*
MI	Livonia	*Liberator (The)*
MI	Livonia	*Lookinglass*
MI	Mount Morris	*Voice (The)*
MI	Muskegon	*Underbird*
MI	New Baltimore	*Student Voice (The)*
MI	Plymouth	*Free Verse*
MI	Rochester	*Rochester's Peoples Paper*
MI	Romulus	*Overground*
MI	Royal Oaks	*Think!*
MI	Royal Oaks	*UN*

State	City	Name of Publication
MI	Saratoga	Pop—Isimizay
MI	Southfield	Hiccup Gazette
MI	St. Clair Shoes	Donald Duck Speaks
MI	Trenton	Fort Street Journal
MI	Troy	Issue (The)
MI	Union Lake	Earth
MI	Warren	Sister Charlotte's Mind Sanctuary
MI	Warren	Star Spangled Bird (The)
MI	Warren	Toke
MN	Alberta Lea	Eclectic
MN	Alberta Lea	Underground Silence
MN	Anoka	Blind Student (The)
MN	Bloomington	Dove (The)
MN	Bloomington	Weatherman
MN	Hopkins	Other Side (The)
MN	Hutchinson	Shaft (The)
MN	La Cresent	File 13
MN	La Cresent	La Cresent High School Free Press
MN	Minneapolis	Blakely Barb
MN	Minneapolis	People (The)
MN	Minneapolis	Side of Beef
MN	Minneapolis	Spaghetti Sandwich
MN	Minneapolis	SubStandard
MN	Minneapolis	Veal Cutlet
MN	St. Cloud	Down the Road
MN	St. Joseph	Finger (The)
MN	St. Joseph	Other (The)
MN	St. Paul	Finger (The)
MN	St. Paul	FREEP
MN	Wayzata	Duck Soup
MN	West St. Paul	Sports Blab
MN	White Bear Lake	Unconscious Power
MN	Windom	Joe's Beans
MO	Carthage	Do It
MO	Clayton	CLAMO
MO	Kansas City	Demobilizer
MO	Kansas City	Embers
MO	Kansas City	Kansas City High School Mobilizer
MO	Kansas City	Kao Krap
MO	Kansas City	Papyrus Populi-The Paper of the People
MO	Long Lane	Buffalo Snout
MO	St. Louis	BullSheet
MO	St. Louis	Discorporate (The)
MO	St. Louis	News (The)

State	City	Name of Publication
MO	St. Louis	*Pioneer (The)*
MO	St. Louis	*Street Sheet*
MO	St. Louis	*Weed (The)*
MS	Jackson	*New Roach*
MS	Pascagoula	*Altogether*
MT	Helena	*Paper Tiger*
NC	Asheville	*Free Voice Press*
NC	Burlington	*Jeweler's Loupe*
NC	Chapel Hill	*Virgin*
NC	Charlotte	*Inquisition*
NC	Charlotte	*Lankentur Subterranean Disgust*
NC	Durham	*Fusion (The)*
NC	Durham	*Pusher (The)*
NC	Durham	*Student Voice*
NC	Durham	*Uprising*
NC	Fayetteville	*Farmer's Gazette*
NC	Greensboro	*Kaleidoscope Eye*
NC	Raleigh	*Ignition*
NC	Wake Forest	*Voice (The)*
ND	Dickinson	*Our Bag*
ND	Fargo	*American Spirit*
NE	Bellevue	unidentified
NE	Fremont	*Open Eye*
NE	Lincoln	*Forum (The)*
NE	Lincoln	*Scrub*
NE	Lincoln	*Subdivision (The)*
NE	McCook	*Fried Dog*
NE	Omaha	*Flashing*
NE	Omaha	*Hiram aka Son of Hiram*
NE	Superior	*Artery*
NE	West Point	*Mess (The)*
NH	Concord	*Bane (The)*
NH	Concord	*Concord Union Leader*
NH	Dover	*Insight Publications*
NH	Durham	*Free*
NH	Lancaster	*Waterfountain*
NH	Manchester	*Arke*
NH	Manchester	*Barnacle (The)*
NH	New London	*Bosheeto (The)*
NH	Peterborough	unidentified
NH	Portsmouth	*Strawberry Grenade*
NH	Salisbury	*Jottings*
NJ	Basking Ridge	*Behind these Walls*
NJ	Bayonne	*Bayonne Free Press*

State	City	Name of Publication
NJ	Bridgewater	*A Salty Dog*
NJ	Camden	*Hypo*
NJ	Dover	*Family*
NJ	East Orange	*Bulletin Board*
NJ	Edison	*Voyce*
NJ	Emerson	*Thorn*
NJ	Fair Lawn	*Red Alert*
NJ	Hackensack	*Common Cense*
NJ	Hackensack	*Smuff*
NJ	Hasbrouck Heights	*Co-Pilot*
NJ	Highland Park	*First Amendment*
NJ	Irvington	*Peaceful Coexistence*
NJ	Keansburg	*Liberator (The)*
NJ	Kearny	*Yes Press*
NJ	Leonia	*Mangled Pigeon (The)*
NJ	Little Silver	*Fourth Floor*
NJ	Livingston	*Coalminer*
NJ	Livingston	*New Livingston News and Broadside*
NJ	Madison	*Arbul*
NJ	Madison	*Conscience*
NJ	Mahwah	*Oracle*
NJ	Maplewood	*Spark II*
NJ	Metuchen	*Underneath Metuchen High*
NJ	Morristown	*Snaf*
NJ	New Brunswick	*Jive Times*
NJ	New Brunswick	*New Jersey Student Union Press Service*
NJ	New Brunswick	*Surgery: The Transit Messenger*
NJ	New Brunswick	*Synergy*
NJ	New Brunswick	*Unity Paper*
NJ	New Brunswick	*Yellow Submarine*
NJ	Newark	*Oh Yes*
NJ	North Plainfield	*PYC Paper*
NJ	Paramus	*Forum (The)*
NJ	Pennsauken Township	*Instead*
NJ	Phillipsburg	*Karot (The)*
NJ	Piscataway	*New Wave (The)*
NJ	Pomona	*Argo*
NJ	Princeton	*Dungeon (The)*
NJ	Princeton	*Friends of Flight—Two Newsletter*
NJ	Red Bank	*Changes*
NJ	River Vale	*Free Word*
NJ	Roselle	*Alternative (The)*
NJ	Rutherford	*Grokk*
NJ	South Brunswick	*Oracle*

State	City	Name of Publication
NJ	Teaneck	Glass Eye
NJ	Teaneck	Paper Tiger
NJ	Ventnor	Common Sense
NJ	Vineland	Probe
NJ	Vineland	Stoneroller
NJ	Wall	Here and Now
NJ	Warren	S.C.S. Paper
NJ	West New York	Stand
NJ	Westfield	Ergo
NJ	Westfield	Synergy
NJ	Weston	We Dare to be Free
NM	Albuquerque	Gauntlet
NM	Albuquerque	Joint Effort
NM	Albuquerque	Probe
NM	Albuquerque	Venceremos
NM	Los Alamos	Free Soul
NM	Los Alamos	Styx
NM	Santa Fe	Stone Heavy
NV	Carson City	Flash
NY	Bay Shore	Old Mole
NY	Bay Shore	Peoples Voice
NY	Bemus Point	Free Corn
NY	Binghamton	Reflection
NY	Brightwater	People's Voice
NY	Bronx	B.L.A.D.A.U.N.
NY	Bronx	Daily Planet
NY	Bronx	Independent News
NY	Bronx	Sphinx's Farrow
NY	Bronxville	Renegade
NY	Brooklyn	Prep Press
NY	Buffalo	Graffiti
NY	Buffalo	Probe
NY	Centereach	Underground Rag
NY	Cheektowaga	unidentified
NY	Clarence	unidentified
NY	Dix Hills	New Morning
NY	East Norwich	Troglodyte
NY	Eastchester	Issue
NY	Fayetteville	Bee-Hive Jive
NY	Fayetteville	Fist (The)
NY	Forest Hills	Neuk
NY	Greene	Kiss-Off
NY	Greenlawn	Dog Breath
NY	Hamburg	Prison Break

State	City	Name of Publication
NY	Harrison	Harrison Free Press
NY	Holmes	Catalyst
NY	Ithaca	School Spirit
NY	Ithaca	Volunteer
NY	Jacksonville	Relayer
NY	Jordan	unidentified
NY	Lakewood	Literary Revelation
NY	Manlius	Fist (The)
NY	Marcellus	Da New Prune
NY	Massapequa	Chief Chat
NY	Massapequa Park	Massapequa Free Press
NY	Melville	New Morning Free Press
NY	Monsey	Rebirth
NY	New Hyde Park	Brick (The)
NY	New Hyde Park	Spectrum
NY	New Morning	Half Hollow Hills High School Free Press
NY	New Rochelle	First Amendment
NY	New Rochelle	Underground
NY	New York	Back Door (The)
NY	New York	Black Youth Alliance Newsletter
NY	New York	Brandeis Brief
NY	New York	Come Out
NY	New York	Enrage
NY	New York	Forth Street (The)
NY	New York	Herald Tribune
NY	New York	Hickory Hog
NY	New York	High School Action
NY	New York	High School Independent Press Service
NY	New York	High School News Service Bureau
NY	New York	High School Raising
NY	New York	Institutional Green
NY	New York	Jail Break
NY	New York	J.H.S. Student Union Voice
NY	New York	John Bowne Was a Pacifist
NY	New York	Kids Unlimited
NY	New York	Lobby (The)
NY	New York	Mama
NY	New York	Midnight Special
NY	New York	Miserable Dictu
NY	New York	New York Herald Tribune
NY	New York	New York High School Free Press
NY	New York	Observed (The)
NY	New York	Paper Tiger
NY	New York	A Rebirth of Wonder

State	City	Name of Publication
NY	New York	*Rip Off*
NY	New York	*Sansculottes*
NY	New York	*Snidely*
NY	New York	*Staten Island Student Union Newspaper*
NY	New York	*Streetfighter*
NY	New York	*Weakly Reader*
NY	New York	*Winter in Amerika*
NY	Onondaga	unidentified
NY	Pelham	*Mindfood*
NY	Penfield	*Experiment*
NY	Penfield	*Upper Story*
NY	Rochester	*Barchester Chronicle*
NY	Rochester	*Bean Soup*
NY	Rochester	*Brighton Free Press*
NY	Rochester	*Erewhon Express*
NY	Rochester	*Fight Back*
NY	Rochester	*Fight Forward*
NY	Rochester	*Nickel Bag*
NY	Rochester	*Union Times*
NY	Roslyn	*Rat*
NY	Schenectady	*Mark and Charlie do it again*
NY	Schenectady	*Out to Lunch*
NY	Shrub Oak	*Mirror Free Press*
NY	Shrub Oak	*More Sugar*
NY	Smithtown	*Nassau-Suffolk High School Free Press*
NY	Smithtown	*Volley High Free Press*
NY	Southampton	*Student Free Press*
NY	Southampton	*Up Against the Wall*
NY	Syracuse	*Cogito: An Independent High School Magazine*
NY	Syracuse	*Fist (The)*
NY	Syracuse	*Gunning*
NY	Troy	*Snafu*
NY	Tully	*Assorted Others*
NY	Utica	*Eclipse (The)*
NY	Utica	*High School Student Press*
NY	Utica	*Scorth*
NY	Utica	*Times They Are a Changin*
NY	Westfield	*Radish*
NY	Westfield	*Wax Paper (The)*
NY	West Seneca	*Strike*
NY	White Plains	*Lost Creek #1 East*
NY	White Plains	*Paper Workshop*
OH	Akron	*Free Press*

State	City	Name of Publication
OH	Akron	*Prole (The)*
OH	Akron	*Shackled Dove (The)*
OH	Beavercreek	*Beaverbullsheet*
OH	Beavercreek	*Student (The)*
OH	Chillicothe	*Roundhead*
OH	Cincinnati	*Act II*
OH	Cincinnati	*All Purpose Circus*
OH	Cincinnati	*Genesis*
OH	Cincinnati	*Ideoplastos*
OH	Cincinnati	*Voice*
OH	Cleveland	*Fist*
OH	Cleveland	*Heights Free Press*
OH	Cleveland	*Student Voice*
OH	Cleveland	*Truth (The)*
OH	Cleveland	*West Tech Truth*
OH	Columbus	*Doubloon*
OH	Columbus	*Juventas*
OH	Columbus	*Omega*
OH	Columbus	*Rumble (The)*
OH	Columbus	*Shamble (The)*
OH	Columbus	*Subversive Scholastic*
OH	Columbus	*Times Change*
OH	Columbus	*W.T.W. Gazette*
OH	Cuyahoga County	*Hunter (The)*
OH	Dayton	*Alternative (The)*
OH	Dayton	*Free Press (The)*
OH	Dayton	*Sedition (The)*
OH	Enon	*Bight Times*
OH	Euclid	*Trucking*
OH	Garrettsville	*Soliearist (The)*
OH	Geneva	*Sub*
OH	Hamilton	*In-Between*
OH	Hudson	*Student's Voice*
OH	Jewett	*Loose Stuffing*
OH	Jewett	*Strobe*
OH	Kent	*Open Forum*
OH	La Grange	*Rolling Rock*
OH	Marietta	*Poiuyt*
OH	Middlebranch	*Bite*
OH	Middleburg Heights	*Revelations*
OH	Middletown	*Students Together Under Democracy*
OH	Montpelier	*Heavenly Blue Flash Press*
OH	Munroe Falls	*Dark Horse*
OH	North Industry	*Liberator II*

State	City	Name of Publication
OH	Shaker Heights	Alice's Restaurant
OH	Shaker Heights	Fresh Wind
OH	Toledo	Don't Read This Paper
OH	Toledo	Panther's Claws
OH	Upper Arlington	Gilded Bare (The)
OH	Warsaw	Threshold
OH	West Union	Milestone
OH	Xenia	Alternative
OH	Youngstown	Free
OH	Youngstown	Gloryosky
OK	Norman	Termite
OK	Oklahoma City	Get Down
OK	Oklahoma City	Get Smart
OK	Oklahoma City	Leaves of Grass
OR	Corvallis	Class Struggle
OR	Corvallis	Common Sense
OR	Corvallis	Jail Break
OR	Corvallis	Open Mind
OR	Eugene	Alternative
OR	Eugene	Sweat
OR	Grants Pass	Altogether
OR	Hermiston	Vox Libera
OR	Newberg	Hedoist (The)
OR	Portland	Behiston Rock
OR	Portland	Daily Planet
OR	Portland	DayBreak
OR	Portland	Equinox
OR	Portland	Flowers
OR	Portland	Free Press
OR	Portland	Nonkrempft
OR	Portland	Purple
OR	Portland	Shutters
OR	Portland	Smelt
OR	Portland	South West Sun
OR	Salem	Phoenix (The)
PA	Allentown	1st Amendment
PA	Allentown	Open Valley
PA	Bechtelsville	Minors Lamp
PA	Bethlehem	Feet
PA	Camp Hill	Ob-Scene (The)
PA	Camp Hill	Rap-Up
PA	Chambersburg	Hole in the Wall
PA	Chester	New Voice
PA	Conemaugh	untitled

State	City	Name of Publication
PA	Dallastown	*Underground Unlimited*
PA	Easton	*Pooh Gazzette*
PA	Easton	*Public Ledger*
PA	Edwardsville	*Cry Out*
PA	Flourtown	*Saturday Evening Roach*
PA	Gettysburg	*Gadfly (The)*
PA	Gettysburg	*Little Peoples' Blues Gazette*
PA	Harrisburg	*I Am*
PA	Harrisburg	*Rebellion*
PA	Hellertown	*Hellertown Free Press*
PA	Kingston	*Apple Red*
PA	Kingstown	*We're Back*
PA	Kintnersville	*Voice (The)*
PA	Lehigh Valley	*Teen Times*
PA	Lehigh Valley	*Yia Street Sheet*
PA	McConnellsburg	*Whippersnapper*
PA	Media	*Stand Together*
PA	Media	*Student Free Press*
PA	Media	*Student Independent Press*
PA	Media	*Phantom Press (The)*
PA	Media	*Phoenix (The)*
PA	Narberth	*Vast Majority (The)*
PA	Northampton	*Students for Intellectual Freedom*
PA	North Hills	*Org*
PA	North Hills	*Peace Pipe*
PA	Palmerton	*Open 1*
PA	Perkasie	*Message*
PA	Philadelphia	*Blus Bus*
PA	Philadelphia	*Fusion*
PA	Philadelphia	*Heavy, Heavy Streak Brothers*
PA	Philadelphia	*Individual*
PA	Philadelphia	*Observer*
PA	Philadelphia	*Paper (The)*
PA	Philadelphia	*Philadelphia Freedom Writer*
PA	Philadelphia	*Red Army*
PA	Philadelphia	*Screwdriver*
PA	Philadelphia	*Student Free Press*
PA	Philadelphia	*Vast Majority (The)*
PA	Philadelphia	*Youth in Action*
PA	Pittsburgh	*Conch*
PA	Pittsburgh	*I'm All Right*
PA	Pittsburgh	*Voice (The)*
PA	Pottsville	*Minor's Lamp*
PA	Quakertown	*Pantleg Gazette*

State	City	Name of Publication
PA	Quakertown	*Splinter*
PA	Stroudsburg	*Last Word*
PA	Upper Darby	*Student Action*
PA	Warren	*Probe (The)*
PA	Wayne	*Edge (The)*
PA	Whitehall	*Bathroom Bomber*
RI	Middletown	*Whipped Establishment & Other Delights*
RI	Newport	*Red Devil*
RI	Providence	*Amendment One*
RI	Providence	*Skool Break*
SC	Columbia	*Sparkleberry Free Press*
SC	Rock Hill	*Open End (The)*
SD	Aberdeen	*Dakota Whippersnapper*
SD	Aberdeen	*Do it*
SD	Aberdeen	*Furor Scri-Ben-I*
SD	Aberdeen	*South Dakota Seditionist Monthly*
SD	Aberdeen	*Up the System*
SD	Rapid City	*Finial*
SD	Sioux Falls	*Ergo*
SD	Sioux Falls	*Options*
SD	Sioux Falls	*Up From Slavery*
TN	Nashville	*Iceberg*
TN	Nashville	*Insight*
TX	Austin	*Bitter End*
TX	Austin	*Grapevine*
TX	Austin	*Roach*
TX	Bryan	*Issue*
TX	Dallas	*Chicken Scratch*
TX	El Paso	*Ball and Chain*
TX	El Paso	*Truck (The)*
TX	El Paso	*Word (The)*
TX	Galveston	*One Per Cent*
TX	Houston	*ARMAS*
TX	Houston	*Dork City! News & Plain Brown Police Gazette*
TX	Houston	*Houston Student Dispatch (The)*
TX	Houston	*Janus*
TX	Houston	*Latent Tendency*
TX	Houston	*Little Red Schoolhouse*
TX	Houston	*Phlashlyte*
TX	Houston	*Plain Brown Watermelon*
TX	Houston	*Reality*
TX	Killeen	*Revolution in the Halls*
TX	Lubbock	*Thorn (The)*

State	City	Name of Publication
TX	Odessa	*Mandala*
TX	Pecos	*Renaissance II*
TX	San Antonio	*Awakening McArthur Free Press (The)*
TX	San Antonio	*MacArthur Free Press*
TX	San Antonio	*Revolution in the Hallways*
TX	San Antonio	*San Antonio High School Notes*
UT	Bountiful	*LEFT*
UT	Salt Lake City	*Synchro*
VA	Alexandria	*Philos*
VA	Arlington	*Black Bird Shantif*
VA	Arlington	*Green Orange*
VA	Blacksburg	*Quack*
VA	Burke	*My Weekly Reefer*
VA	Charlottesville	*Blast*
VA	Dun Loring	*We're Not Gonna Take It*
VA	Springfield	*Annandale Free Press*
VA	Springfield	*Eye Witness*
VT	Barre	*Greenfeel*
VT	Johnson	*Outhouse by Upward Bound*
VT	Ludlow	*Iris*
VT	Plainfield	*New Zoo Review*
VT	Rutland	*Other Thing (The)*
WA	Longview	*Student Underground Chronicle*
WA	Longview	*Submerged Log*
WA	Port Orchard	*Mind-Body*
WA	Port Orchard	*Your First Amendment*
WA	Seattle	*Antidote*
WA	Seattle	*Boss*
WA	Seattle	*Dare*
WA	Seattle	*Plebiscite*
WA	Seattle	*To the Point*
WA	Seattle	*Voice (The)*
WA	Seattle	*Zig-Zag*
WA	Snohomish	*Free Observer*
WA	Spanaway	*Dafka*
WA	Spokane	*Mushroom*
WA	Spokane	*Student Free Press*
WI	Appleton	*Appleton Post-Mortem*
WI	Ashland	*Bell (The)*
WI	Ashland	*North Country Student Free Press*
WI	Brookfield	*Free Rein*
WI	Eau Claire	*Traditions*
WI	Fond du lac	*Other Side*
WI	Fond du lac	*Street Sheet*

State	City	Name of Publication
WI	Green Bay	*Gadfly*
WI	Green Bay	*Irregular Channel (The)*
WI	Green Bay	*Tower of Babble*
WI	Green Bay	*Trial Balloon*
WI	Hartford	*Cranial Awakener*
WI	Hartford	*New Awakening*
WI	Hudson	*Hudson Free Press*
WI	Kenosha	*Parafinn Clouds Express Press*
WI	Madison	*Bad Moon Rising*
WI	Madison	*Behind the Shield*
WI	Madison	*Connections*
WI	Madison	*Free Thinker*
WI	Madison	*Hickory Nuts*
WI	Madison	*LINKS*
WI	Madison	*Madison Area High School Free Press*
WI	Madison	*Running Dog (The)*
WI	Madison	*Student Voice*
WI	Madison	*Wisconsin Youth World Development Newsletter*
WI	Madison	*W.S.L.J. Newsletter*
WI	Milwaukee	*Apocalypse*
WI	Milwaukee	*Custer Harlequin*
WI	Milwaukee	*Down and Out*
WI	Milwaukee	*Iskra*
WI	Milwaukee	*Milwaukee Student Union Paper*
WI	Milwaukee	*Nude King*
WI	Milwaukee	*Open Door*
WI	Milwaukee	*Pentagram*
WI	Milwaukee	*Red Pencil*
WI	Milwaukee	*Stomp*
WI	Milwaukee	*Underground Rag*
WI	Milwaukee	*Zap!*
WI	Monona	*Waves*
WI	Oshkosh	*Spectrum*
WI	Port Washington	*Why Not?*
WI	Rothschild	*Trash*
WI	Shorewood	*Free Pest*
WI	Shorewood	*Union Voice*
WI	Spring Greens	*Ins and Outs*
WI	Sussex	*Hamilton Gazette*
WI	Verona	*Great Society, aka Verona Free Press*
WI	Waukesha	*Candor*
WI	Wausau	*Peach*
WI	Whitewater	*Give a Damn*

State	City	Name of Publication
WI	Wisconsin Rapids	*Inside Looking Out*
WI	Wisconsin Rapids	*Rapids Flying Saucers Investigators*
WV	Beckley	*Time Machine (The)*
WV	Charleston	*Freedom Rider*
WV	Hinton	unidentified
WV	St. Albans	*Electric Dragon*
WV	St. Albans	*Liberator (The)*
WY	Cheyenne	*Candor*
WY	Laramie	*Paper (The)*
WY	Wyoming Valley	*Daily Bulletin*
WY	Wyoming Valley	*Force*

Notes

Abbreviations

Dilworth Papers	Richardson Dilworth Papers, 1881–2002, Historical Society of Pennsylvania, Philadelphia
FBI-FOIA	FBI Files and Records obtained through the Freedom of Information Act
Hoover Archives	Hoover Institution Archives, Stanford University, Stanford, CA
MSL SC	Michael Schwartz Library Special Collections, Cleveland State University, Cleveland, OH
OHA-CU	Oral History Archives, Rare Book and Manuscript Library, Columbia University in the City of New York
PAHA	Palo Alto Historical Association
Spears MSS	Spears Manuscripts, Lilly Library, Indiana University, Bloomington
TLWA LA	Tamiment Library and Robert F. Wagner Labor Archives, New York University, New York
YLPR	Youth Liberation Press Records, SCRC 175, Special Collections Research Center, Temple University Libraries, Philadelphia, PA

Prologue

1. Wasserman, interview; Srebrnik, *Dreams of Nationhood*, 2.
2. Wasserman, interview.
3. Wasserman, interview.
4. Wasserman, interview.
5. W. J. Rorabaugh examines all these subsequent events and others in *Berkeley at War*. For more information on the student strike at San Francisco State College, see Biondi, *Black Revolution on Campus*, 43–73.
6. Wasserman, interview; Herring, *America's Longest War*, 43–45.
7. "School Walkout Hinted," *Berkeley Daily Gazette*, October 13, 1967; Fountain Jr., "War in the School," 25–26.
8. "100 Walk Out at BHS; Applauded on Campus," *Berkeley Daily Gazette*, October 17, 1967; "22 BHS Students Arrested," *Berkeley Daily Gazette*, October 19, 1967; "100 BH Students Walk-Out Per. 5," *Daily Jacket*, October 18, 1967, Berkeley High School Library, Berkeley, CA; Wasserman, interview.
9. Wasserman, interview.

10. Wasserman, interview; Rorabaugh, *Berkeley at War*, 156–62; "Group Vows to Stay in School until Guard Quits," *Berkeley Daily Gazette*, May 26, 1969; "40 Students Continue Sleep-In," *Berkeley Daily Gazette*, May 28, 1969.

11. Wasserman, interview; Schwendinger, interview; "Pack Rat . . . Radical Paper on HS Level," *Berkeley Daily Gazette*, October 31, 1969; "BHS Students, Parents, Administrators Compromise," *Berkeley Daily Gazette*, November 6, 1969.

12. Steve Wasserman, clipping, courtesy of David Smith, in possession of author.

13. Merritt Clifton, "The Reign of Steve Wasserman," *Olla Podrida*, 1970 (Berkeley High School), Berkeley Public Library, Berkeley, CA.

14. FBI Director to Chicago SAC, June 22, 1970, Berkeley High School Student Union (100–459248), Federal Bureau of Investigation, Freedom of Information Act request (hereafter cited FBI–FOIA).

15. "National H.S. Conference, Chicago June 22–27," *New York Herald Tribune*, June 1970, box 279, Boxed Newspaper Collection, TLWA LA.

16. "National High School Convention," *Indianapolis High School Free Press* 1, no. 1, box 1, Ronald W. Haldeman Collection of Local Publications, Indianapolis Public Library, Indianapolis, Indiana.

17. Chicago SAC to FBI Director, July 9, 1970; San Francisco SAC to FBI Director, September 30, 1970, Berkeley High School Student Union, FBI–FOIA.

18. Wasserman, interview; Libarle and Seligson, *High School Revolutionaries*, 229–37; Ernest Dunbar, "Trouble: The High School Radicals," *Look*, March 24, 1970, 70–80.

19. Wasserman, interview.

Introduction

1. This data comes from the National Center for Education Statistics, https://nces.ed.gov/programs/digest/d21/tables/dt21_214.10.asp, accessed May 24, 2024.

2. Diane Divoky, "Revolt in the High Schools: The Ways It's Going to be," *Saturday Review*, February 15, 1969, 83–84.

3. *Freed Speak* (Lawrence, KS), [n.d.], box 7; "Where We Came From," *Root* (Vancouver, BC) 1, no. 1, September 1975, box 21, YLPR.

4. Oritz, "La Voz de la Gente," 229–244; V. Franklin, "Black High School Student," 3–8; Zimmerman, *Whose America?*; New, "Fire in the Sky"; Wright, "Black Pride Day, 1968," 151–62; Danns, *Something Better*; Barrera, "1968 Edcouch-Elsa," 93–122. Graham, *Young Activists*; Countryman, *Up South*, chapter 6; Schweinitz, *If We Could Change*; B. Franklin, "Community, Race, and Curriculum"; Theoharis, "'W-A-L-K-O-U-T!,'" 107–29; Titus, *Brown's Battleground*; García and Castro, *Blowout!*; Hale, "'Fight Was Instilled,'" 4–28; Rury and Hill, "End of Innocence," 486–508; Bynum, *NAACP Youth*; J. Williams, *From the Bullet to the Ballot*, 66–74; S. Franklin, *After the Rebellion*; Echeverria, *Aztlán Arizona*, chapter 3; Vaden, "High School Students," 65–79; Petrzela, *Classroom Wars*; Bundy, "'Revolutions Happen,'" 273–93; Loomis, "'As Far as I'm Concerned'"; Hale, *Freedom Schools*; Kinchen, *Black Power*; Berghel, "'What My Generation Makes,'" 422–40; Barrera, "1960s Chicano Movement," 82–97; Schumaker, *Troublemakers*; Buffett, "Crossing the Line," 1212–36; D. Walker,

"Black Power, Education"; Davis and Wiener, *Set the Night on Fire*, chapters 21–23; V. Franklin, *Young Crusaders*; Sinta and Rivas-Rodriguez, "1970 Uvalde School Walkout," 151–76; Remnick, "Disruptive Children"; Hale, *New Kind of Youth*; Suttell, *Campus to Counter*; Frost, *"Let us Vote!"*; Hyres, "'Whole Mess Is American History,'" 14–28; D. Walker, "Learning to Struggle," 1–18; Remnick, "Police State," 1–17; Robinson, *Washington State Rising*, chapter 2; Ballantyne, *Radical Volunteers*; Hyres, "Barbara Johns and Beyond," 449–66.

5. Howlett, "Anti-Vietnam War Movement," 56–75; Gilbert, "Lock and Load High," 174–93; Howlett, "When the Bell Rings," 194–215; Cohen, *Gay Liberation*; Graham, "Flaunting the Freak Flag," 522–43; Buffett, "Black, White and Green"; Sink, "Fueling the Southern Underground," 129–43; Ides, "'Dare to Free Yourself,'" 295–319; Fountain, "Right to Sit"; Fountain, "War in the School"; Lovell, "Girls Are Equal Too," 71–95; Fountain, "Building a Student Movement," 202–37; Ajunwa "It's Our School Too"; Stern, "Hidden Politics," 237–75; Stern "School Violence," 483–534; Stern, "'We Got to Fight,'" 1–31; Wall, "'Don't Touch Race,'" 427. For works about high school student activism in other countries, see Adamson, *Secondary Student Revolt*; Krob and Davis, "El Día de los Mártires"; Zolov, "Cuba si, Yanquis no"; and Meyering, "Margaret Bailey Case."

6. Chainey, *The High School Revolt*; Gudridge, *High School Student Unrest*; Reeves, *Notes of a Processed Brother*; *Room 222*; *Seventeen*, May 1969; Wall, "Indiana High School Newspaper."

7. "Recalling the Walkouts of 1968," *San Antonio Express-News*, August 16, 2015, https://www.expressnews.com/150years/education-health/article/In-1968-students-here-defied-prejudice-and-6446428.php; "East L.A., 1968: 'Walkout!" *Los Angeles Times*, March 1, 2018, https://www.latimes.com/nation/la-na-1968-east-la-walkouts-20180301-htmlstory.html; "Chicano Progress Today Owes Much To the Denver West High Blowouts Of 50 Years Ago," *Colorado Public Radio*, March 18, 1969, https://www.cpr.org/2019/03/18/chicano-progress-today-owes-much-to-the-denver-west-high-blowouts-of-50-years-ago/; "Asheville High Walkout, Riot, in 1969 Revisited by Students 50 Years," *Ashville Citizen Times*, September 26, 2019, https://www.citizen-times.com/story/news/local/2019/09/26/asheville-high-walkout-riot-1969-revisited-students-50-years/2353198001/; "1967 Black Student Walkout Historical Market Unveiling," *The Bullhorn News*, April 7, 2022, https://www.thebullhornnews.com/article/2022/04/1967-black-student-walkout-historical-marker-unveiling.

8. "Historical Markers are Everywhere in America. Some get History Wrong," *NPR*, April 21, 2024, https://www.npr.org/2024/04/21/1244899635/civil-war-confederate-statue-markers-sign-history; The Historical Marker Database, hmdb.org, accessed January 2, 2025.

9. Emily Balboa, email message to author, December 19, 2014.

10. Cleveland Restoration Society, Cleveland Civil Rights Trail, clevelandcivilrightstrail.org.

11. O'Neill, *Coming Apart*; Sale, *SDS*; Unger, *Movement*; Matusow, *Unraveling of America*; J. Miller, *"Democracy Is in the Streets"*; Gitlin, *Sixties*; Isserman and Kazin, *America Divided*.

12. Hale, *New Kind of Youth*, 4.

13. Church and Sedlak, *Education in the United States*; Butts, *Public Education*; Tyack and Cuban, *Tinkering toward Utopia*; Ravitch, *Left Back*; Comer, *Leave No Child Behind*; Hartman, *Education and the Cold War*; Leiding, *Reform Can Make a Difference*; Petrzela, "Revisiting the Rightward Turn," 143–71; Laats, *Other School Reformers*; Sanders, *Chance for Change*; Gordon, *This is Our School!*; Moak, *From the New Deal*.

14. Johnson, *Struggle for Student Rights*.

15. Thernstrom, "Where Did All the Order Go?" 299–327; Hymowitz, "Who Killed School Discipline?"; Arum, *Judging School Discipline*; Dupre, *Speaking Up*.

16. Stirling, interview.

17. Glasser, interview.

18. "A Concerned Student," *J.H.S. Student Union Voice* 3, June 5, 1969, used with permission from Joel Schwartz. In possession of the author.

19. Aimee Sands, letter to the editors, *New York Times*, April 19, 1969.

20. Birmingham, *Our Time Is Now*, 4–5.

21. "Jansen Opposes Police in Schools: Calls Proposal 'Unthinkable'—Leibowitz Backs Idea," *New York Times*, November 27, 1957.

22. Thompson, "Why Mass Incarceration Matters," 703–34, here 710; Kautz, "From Segregation to Suspension"; Hinton, *America on Fire*, 145–49; Remnick, "Police State."

23. Stern, "'We Got to Fight'"; Stern, "Hidden Politics," 237–75; Stern "School Violence," 483–534.

24. Remnick, "Police State," 3.

25. Social scientist and education scholars have largely documented this history, but most works are contemporary. See Kafka, *The History of "Zero Tolerance" in American Public Schooling*; Kim, Losen, and Hewitt, *The School-to-Prison Pipeline*; Monahan and Torres, *Schools under Surveillance*; Nolan, *Police in the Hallways*; Shedd, *Unequal City*; Erickson, *Making the Unequal Metropolis*; Heitzeg, *The School-to-Prison Pipeline*; Morris, *Pushout*; Kupchik, *The Real School Safety Problem*; Vitale, *The End of Policing*; Okilwa, Khalifa, and Briscoe, *The School to Prison Pipeline*; Rios, *Human Targets*; Stern, *Race and Education in New Orleans*; Erickson and Morrell, *Educating Harlem*; Love, *We Want to Do More Than Survive*; Bell, *Suspended*; Hale, "'If You Want Police, We Will Have Them,'" 1–14; Kautz, "From Segregation to Suspension," 1049–70.

26. Garrow, *FBI and Martin Luther King*; Churchill and Wall, *Agents of Repression*; Echols, *Daring to Be Bad*; Pyle, *Military Surveillance*; Jensen, *Army Surveillance in America*; Stephan, *"Communazis"*; Jerome, *The Einstein File*; Cunningham, *There's Something Happening Here*; Montejano, *Quixote's Soliders*; Rosenfeld, *Subversives*; Leonard and Gallagher, *Heavy Radicals*; Perrusquia, *A Spy in Canaan*; Felker-Kantor, *Policing Los Angeles*; Martin, "Bureau Clergyman," 1–51; Janda, *Prairie Power*; Fernández, *Young Lords*; Balto, *Occupied Territory*; Michel, *Spying on Students*.

27. McKnight, *Australia's Spies and Their Secrets*; Sethna, "High-School Confidential," 121–30. There's little to no secondary scholarship on other countries. To learn more, see "Spooks Spied on High School Revolutionaries," *Stuff*, June 28,

2009, https://www.stuff.co.nz/national/politics/2524921/Spooks-spied-on-high-school-revolutionaries; "Edward Heath Ordered MI5 to Watch School Revolutionaries," *Times*, April 13, 2009, https://www.thetimes.com/article/edward-heath-ordered-mi5-to-watch-school-revolutionaries-wzq7cvbzrtt.

28. There are two works that briefly mention examples of high school students and government surveillance: see Donner, *Protectors of Privilege*, 136; and Davis, *Assault on the Left*, 96, 112, and 185.

29. Eklund, email.

30. Marc Arsell Robinson documented the collaborative work of high school and college students in Black Student Unions in Seattle, Washington. See *Washington State Rising*, chapter 2.

31. Kitty Cone, "Political Organizer for Disability Rights, 1970s–1990s, and Strategist for Section 504 Demonstrations, 1977," an oral history conducted in 1996–1998 by David Landes, Regional Oral History Office, The Bancroft Library, University of California, Berkeley, 2000.

32. Historians and education scholars have long dealt with the scarcity of records created by children and teenagers themselves. For more information on this problem, see Hyres and Steele, "Reimagining the High School Experience."

33. Hefner, interview.

34. Reminiscences of Estelle Schneider (June 20, 2009), OHA–CU.

35. Teishan A. Latner referred to the FBI as "unauthorized archivists." See "'Agrarians or Anarchists?'" 119–40. Other scholars like Seth Kershner called New York State Police Red Squad files "accidental archivists." See "Investigating 'Subversives,'" 7–9.

36. According to Sarah Eppler Janda, Governor Dewey Barlett of Oklahoma established the Office of Inter-Agency Coordination in June 1968 as a covert organization to collect intelligence on suspected radicals within the state. His successor instructed his staff to destroy the documents to prevent public humiliation. See "'Even Mild Protest is not Generally Considered to be very Patriotic,'" 393–414; Michel, *Spying on Students*, chapter 2.

37. SA to Omaha SAC, March 19, 1969, The Form (100–62–3017), FBI–FOIA.

38. "W.G.U. responds to criticism," *Warren Owl*, December 10, 1971, Warren Central High School Archives, Indianapolis, IN.

39. Carol Pittman, email message to author, November 5, 2018.

40. M. Hoyman, email.

41. Hefner, email.

Chapter 1

1. Cohen, *When the Old Left Was Young*; Hale, *New Kind of Youth*.

2. Johnson, *Struggle for Student Rights*; "War Protests Bring Penalty," *Record* (Hackensack, NJ), March 28, 1966; "Antiwar Forces Infiltrate High Schools," *Plain Dealer* (Cleveland), December 10, 1965; "School Suspends 13-Year-Old Leader of Garfield Protest," *Berkeley Daily Gazette*, January 14, 1966; "Schoolboy's Peace Button Pits Principal, ACLU," *Chicago Sun-Times*, May 21, 1966.

3. "'Junior FSM' Pops Up Here," *San Francisco News-Call Bulletin*, April 28, 1965.

4. The Reminiscences of Peter Shapiro, April 11, 1984, box 1, Student Movements of the 1960s, OHA–CU.

5. Tepper, interview.

6. Tepper, interview. For more information on Burbridge, see P. Miller, *Postwar Struggle for Civil Rights*.

7. Jim Brumell, "Biography of Archie Brown (unfinished M.S.)," box 1, folder 1, Archie Brown Collection, 1933–1978, Labor Archives and Research Center, San Francisco State University, San Francisco, CA.

8. "Biography of Archie Brown."

9. Heale, "Red Scare Politics," 5–32; Foster, "Red Alert!" 2.

10. "Alleged 'Red' List Given Congress," *San Francisco Examiner*, October 16, 1947; Fulton Lewis Jr., "Candidate Role of Archie Brown," *San Francisco Examiner*, October 10, 1961; "Archie Brown, 79, Union Leader in Landmark Case on Communists," *New York Times*, November 25, 1990; "East Bay Red Army 'Routed,'" *San Francisco Examiner*, December 28, 1929; "Trial Dates Set for Oakland Demonstrators," *Oakland Tribune*, February 27, 1930; Molly Martin, "Betsy Brown Traveled Around," *tradeswomn musings* (blog), December 5, 2018, https://mollymartin.blog/2018/12/05/betsy-brown-traveled-around/.

11. Brown, interview.

12. Bennett, interview.

13. Shapiro reminisces, CU–OHA; Shapiro, interview.

14. Pittman, interview. Pittman's father is profiled in Thomas Fleming, "The Black Press," https://www.foundsf.org/index.php?title=The_Black_Press, accessed June 18, 2024.

15. Citret, interview.

16. Semel, interview.

17. Northcott, interview.

18. Garb, interview. For more information, see Pipes, *Russian Revolution*, and Budnitskii, *Russian Jews*.

19. Garb, interview.

20. Garb, interview.

21. Citret, interview; Garb, interview.

22. "The Activist Opinion: What Is It," *Activist Opinion* 1, no. 1, [February 1965?], Betsy Brown copy, in possession of author; "We Need News," *Activist Opinion* 1, no. 2 (March 21–April 9) , 1965, SOEAL (100–54888), FBI–FOIA.

23. Tepper, interview; Pittman, interview; Garb, interview; Citret, interview.

24. Citret, interview.

25. "Editorial: The Selma Outrage," *Activist Opinion* 1, no. 2 (March 21–April 9), 1965, SOEAL, FBI–FOIA.

26. "Continued Madness in Vietnam," *Activist Opinion* 1, no. 4 (May 10–May 28), 1965, SOEAL, FBI–FOIA.

27. Letter to SAC, San Francisco, March 25, 1965, SOEAL, FBI–FOIA; Curtis O. Lynum, SAC to anonymous, March 29, 1965, SOEAL, FBI–FOIA.

28. SE Cecil J. C. M. Le Blanc to San Francisco SAC, April 6, 1965, SOEAL, FBI–FOIA.

29. Anonymous to Cecil Pharris, San Francisco Police Department Intelligence Unit, April 19, 1965 [incorrect date], SOEAL, FBI-FOIA.

30. "Betsy Brown Traveled Around"; Brown, interview.

31. Tepper, interview. For an analysis on Northern racism, see Purnell, Theoharis, and Woodard, *Strange Careers of the Jim Crow North*. On colorblind ideology, see Sokol, *All Eyes Are Upon Us*, 72.

32. "Expose of S.F. School Segregation," *Activist Opinion* 1, no. 2, March 21–April 9, 1965, SOEAL, FBI-FOIA.

33. "Expose of S.F. School Segregation," *Activist Opinion* 1, no. 2, March 21–April 9, 1965, SOEAL, FBI-FOIA. "New Figures on S.F. School Segregation," *Activist Opinion* 1, no. 5, June 7–June 28, 1965, Jesse Tepper copy, in possession of the author; "Schools Facing Bias Suit," *San Francisco Examiner*, May 29, 1961.

34. Quinn, *Class Action*, 16–17; "S.F. School Study Urged," *San Francisco Examiner*, July 12, 1959.

35. "Schools Facing Bias Suit," *San Francisco Examiner*, May 29, 1961.

36. Quinn, *Class Action*, 20–21.

37. "Spears Bans 'Activist' Newsletter," *San Francisco Chronicle*, April 7, 1965; "School Pamphlet Ban Upheld," *San Francisco Examiner*, April 25, 1965.

38. "All Students Beware," *Activist Opinion* 1, no. 3, April 19–May 8, 1965, SOEAL, FBI-FOIA.

39. "A.O. Banned—The Way It Happened," *Activist Opinion* 1, no. 3, April 19–May 8, 1965, SOEAL, FBI-FOIA.

40. "All Students Beware: This Newspaper Is Banned," *Activist Opinion* 1, no. 3, April 19–May 8, 1965, SOEAL, FBI-FOIA.

41. "John Burton Strikes Again," *Activist Opinion* 1, no. 2, March 21–April 9, 1965, SOEAL, FBI-FOIA.

42. "Lowell Administrators vs. Democracy," *Activist Opinion* 1, no. 2, March 21–April 9, 1965, SOEAL, FBI-FOIA.

43. "Academic Freedom and the Lowell Image," *Activist Opinion* 1, no. 3, April 19–May 8, 1965, SOEAL, FBI-FOIA.

44. "Lincoln Principal States Policy on Leaflets," *Activist Opinion* 1, no. 3, April 19–May 8, 1965, SOEAL, FBI-FOIA.

45. "Free Speech at Berkeley High," *Activist Opinion* 1, no. 3, April 19–May 8, 1965, SOEAL, FBI-FOIA; "Tamalpais Free Speech Controversy," *Activist Opinion* 1, no. 3, April 19–May 8, 1965, SOEAL, FBI-FOIA.

46. "Editorial: Censorship of School Papers," *Activist Opinion* 1, no. 3, April 19–May 8, 1965, SOEAL, FBI-FOIA.

47. San Francisco Board of Education meeting transcript, April 27, 1965, 20–23, box 5, Spears MSS.

48. San Francisco Board of Education meeting transcript, April 27, 1965, 24–29, box 5, Spears MSS; Tepper interview.

49. San Francisco Board of Education meeting transcript, April 27, 1965, 24–29, box 5, Spears MSS.

50. San Francisco Board of Education meeting transcript, April 27, 1965, 29–32, box 5, Spears MSS.

51. San Francisco Board of Education meeting transcript, April 27, 1965, 33–35, box 5, Spears MSS.

52. San Francisco Board of Education meeting transcript, April 27, 1965, 37–42, box 5, Spears MSS.

53. San Francisco Board of Education meeting transcript, April 27, 1965, 38–54, box 5, Spears MSS.

54. Ravitch, *Left Back*.

55. Bruner, *Toward a Theory of Instruction*; Zacharias, "Zacharias on Professional Education," 30–32; Darling-Hammond, *Flat World of Education*.

56. "On the Fringe of a Golden Era," *Time*, January 29, 1965, https://time.com/3680943/on-the-fringe-of-a-golden-era.

57. "School Board Refuses to Lift Ban on AO," *Activist Opinion* 1, no. 4, May 10–28, 1965, SOEAL, FBI–FOIA.

58. Ronald Merenbach, letter to the editor, *Activist Opinion* 1, no. 4, May 10–28, 1965, SOEAL, FBI–FOIA.

59. School Board Says 'No' to Student Plea," *San Francisco Chronicle*, May 12, 1965, MSS Spears.

60. San Francisco Board of Education meeting transcript, May 11, 1965, 85–97, 101–3, box 5; "'The Activist' Inactivated in S.F. Schools," *News Call Bulletin*, May 12, 1965, Spears MSS.

61. "High School Pickets," *San Francisco Chronicle*, May 27, 1965; "Teen-Agers Protest Ban on Paper," *San Francisco Examiner*, May 27, 1965, Spears MSS.

62. "'Scholastic Rebel' Editor Barred from Lowell High," *San Francisco Chronicle*, February 2, 1916; "A 1916 Incident Student Expelled," *San Francisco Chronicle*, June 1, 1965, Spears MSS.

63. "A Maverick Newspaper Loses Again," *San Francisco Chronicle*, June 16, 1965, Spears MSS.

64. "New Administrative Policies Revealed," *Lowell* (Lowell High School, San Francisco), October 5, 1965; "Mr. Perino OK's Circulation of Controversial Petition," *Lowell*, October 22, 1965, Lowell High School archives, San Francisco, CA.

65. Paula Garb, "SOEAL's Representative of the World Peace Conference," *Activist Opinion* 2, no. 1, September 20–October 7, 1965, SOEAL, FBI–FOIA; Klimke, *Other Alliance*, 1–3.

66. Garb, interview.

67. "Teen Gangs 'Peace March,'" *San Francisco Examiner*, May 23, 1966.

68. Semel, interview; Northcott, interview; Citret interview.

Chapter 2

1. Maurice Isserman, "My First Antiwar Protest," *New York Times*, April 14, 1967, https://www.nytimes.com/2017/04/14/opinion/my-first-antiwar-protest.html.

2. Isserman, "My First Antiwar Protest."

3. Mike Klare, "An Approach to High School Organizing," *Peace & Freedom News*, no. 30, July 26, 1966, United Food & Commercial Workers International

Union District 427 Records, 1937–1973, Western Reserve Historical Society, Case Western Reserve University, Cleveland, OH.

4. Jorma Williams to Margie, September 15, 1969, West Virginia, 1967–1969, reel 12, folder 124, *America in Protest: Records of Anti-Vietnam War Organization, Part 3: Student Mobilization Committee to End the War in Vietnam, 1966–1973* (hereafter SMC papers).

5. "The 'Fall Offensive' continues," microfilm reel 4, part 2, Social Protest Collection, Bancroft Library, University of California, Berkeley.

6. Harer, interview.

7. Harer, interview. Hitchhiking was a common practice in the United States at the time. See Reid, *Roadside Americans*.

8. Harer, interview.

9. Harer, interview.

10. Kathie Harer, "High Schoolers Organized," *Activist* 1, no. 1, September 1966, High School Students Against the War (100–57544), FBI-FOIA; "High School Students Form Group," *San Francisco State College Vietnam Day Committee Newsletter* [1966?], FBI-FOIA.

11. "High School Students Form Group"; "3,000 Protest Viet War in Market St. March," *San Francisco Examiner*, August 7, 1966; DeBenedetti and Chatfield, *American Ordeal*, 157; Harer, interview.

12. Cohen, *When the Old Left Was Young*; "The Student and the War," pamphlet, [n.d.], box 8, Student Peace Union Records, Swarthmore College Peace College, Swarthmore College, Swarthmore, PA (hereafter SCPC); "Local SSFP," *Student Peace Union Bulletin*, November 1961, box 30, folder 2, Office of Student Activities Records, University of Chicago Library Department of Special Collections, Chicago, IL (hereafter UCL).

13. Howlett, "Anti-Vietnam War Movement," 56–57; Ehrhart "Aftermath," 229–38; *The Lowell*, April 29, 1966.

14. "High Schoolers Demonstrate for Vietnam Negotiations," *Baltimore Sun*, April 4, 1965.

15. Larry Sigmond, "High School Students for Peace in Vietnam," in *National Coordinating Committee to End the War in Vietnam, 1964–1967*, reel 13, folder 146, Pennsylvania, 1965–1966, Pittsburgh–York.

16. "Until Ninth Grade, she was 'Apathetic,'" *Providence Journal*, May 17, 1968, Rhode Island High School Students for Peace (100–38507), FBI-FOIA.

17. "High School Committee," *Activist Opinion* 1, no. 2, October 1966, FBI-FOIA; "High School Viet Protests Increase," *Sunday Ramparts*, November 6–13, 1966, FBI-FOIA.

18. "The United Committee against the War," *Bring the Troops Home Newsletter* 1, no. 15, October 17, 1966, FBI-FOIA.

19. Halstead, *Out Now!*, 270–81; "Introducing Ourselves," *Student Mobilizer* 1, no. 1, January 17, 1967, GI Press Collection, 1964–1977, Wisconsin Historical Society, https://content.wisconsinhistory.org/digital/collection/p15932coll8, accessed July 3, 2021 (hereafter GI Press Collection).

20. "Los Angeles High School Student Activity Report," February 16, 1967, *Southern California Student Mobilizer*, no. 1, March 8, 1867, reel 13, folder 137, SMC papers.

21. "Report on High School Mobilization," [1967?], reel 13, folder 136, SMC papers.

22. Minutes of the steering committee meeting, February 13, 1967; minutes of the steering committee meeting, February 20, 1967, SMC papers.

23. Kipp [Dawson] to Kathy Harer [1967?], reel 7, folder 64, SMC papers.

24. Dawson, interview.

25. Dawson, interview.

26. Dawson, interview. Her work at Berkeley High is outlined in Ramey and Evans, "'We Came Together,'" 181–92.

27. Dawson, interview.

28. Halstead, *Out Now!*, 336–37; "Youth Dominates March," *San Francisco Examiner*, April 16, 1967.

29. "Hippies, Clergymen Parade on W. Coast," *Boston Globe*, April 16, 1967; Kipp Dawson recalled her memories in "April 15, 1967: Massive Anti-Vietnam War Demonstration," *Zinn Education Project*, https://www.zinnedproject.org/news/tdih/massive-anti-war-demonstrations/#kipp, accessed April 21, 2024.

30. "High School Students: Why March against the War?" [April 1967?], leaflet, FBI–FOIA; Harer, interview.

31. Harer, interview.

32. Halstead, *Out Now!*, 347–50; "Student Mobilization Committee Chicago Conference Proposed Agenda," [1967?], box 30, folder 2, UCL.

33. "The Student Mobilization Committee," pamphlet, box 30, folder 2, Office of Student Activities Records, University of Chicago Library Department of Special Collections, Chicago, IL (hereafter cited UCL).

34. Halstead, *Out Now!*, 350; Anonymous to Terri Dawson and Suzi Montauk, letter received, May 1, 1967, reel 7, folder 64, SMC papers.

35. "The Chicago Conference: May 1967," High School Organizing, reel 12, folder 130, SMC papers.

36. Maxine Orris, "Attention: Student Mobilization Committee," May 1967, SMC papers.

37. "The Chicago Conference: May, 1967," reel 12, folder 130, SMC papers.

38. "Here is a list of contacts made at the Chicago conference," [May 1967?], reel 13, folder 138, SMC papers.

39. Fox, interview.

40. Fox, interview.

41. "Cass Tech Ousts 4 Pupils for 'Mourning' Viet Dead," *Detroit Free Press*, December 17, 1965. As of now, there is no comprehensive history of this group. Records of the Detroit Committee to End the War in Vietnam are held in the Archives of Labor and Urban Affairs at Wayne State University in Detroit, Michigan.

42. "City's Clergy Help to Form School for Draft Dodgers," *Detroit Free Press*, December 29, 1966; Gordon Fox, letter to the editor, "Distorted News," *Detroit Free Press*, January 10, 1967.

43. Fox, interview.

44. "H.S. Students Form Nat'l Group," *Student Mobilizer* 1, no. 3, July 1967, GI Press Collection.

45. Student Mobilization Committee, "October 21 Confrontation, Progress Report #4," August 11, 1967, GI Press Collection; Halstead, *Out Now!*, 366.

46. "The Editors Speak Their Piece!" *High School Mobilizer*, June 1967, GI Press Collection.

47. G. Berman, letters to the editors; "Canadians Demonstrate Against War at Expo," *High School Mobilizer*, June 1967, GI Press Collection.

48. "Boston Conf." *High School Mobilizer* 1, no. 3, October [1967?], GI Press Collection.

49. "H.S. Students Form Nat'l Group," *Student Mobilizer* 1, no. 3, July 1967, GI Press Collection.

50. "Detroit High School Student Mobilization Committee to End the War in Vietnam," August 30, 1967, Detroit High School Student Mobilization Committee (100-34265), FBI-FOIA.

51. "Detroit Conference," *High School Mobilizer* 1, no. 3, October [1967?], GI Press Collection.

52. Dave Watson, "High School Anti-War Conference Report," [September 1967?], Detroit High School Student Mobilization Committee, FBI-FOIA.

53. Watson, "High School Anti-War Conference Report."

54. Wells, *War Within*, 174–75.

55. Mark B. Rue to SMC, October 8, 1967, reel 7, folder 64, SMC papers.

56. Student Mobilization Committee, "October 21 Confrontation, Progress Report #8," September 15, 1967, GI Press Collection.

57. James Maynard Williamson III to Student Mobilization Committee, August 3, 1967; Kipp Dawson to James Maynard Williamson III, August 8, 1967, reel 8, folder 73, SMC papers.

58. Lytle, *America's Uncivil Wars*, 191, 217, 242–43; Tim Rowton, "High School Students and the War," May 13, 1967, reel 13, folder 138, SMC papers.

59. Wells, *War Within*, 195–203; Halstead, *Out Now!*, 393.

60. "Young Radicals Run Show in Washington Peace Rally," *Detroit Free Press*, October 22, 1967; Gordon Fox, letter to the editors, *Detroit Free Press*, October 28, 1967; Smalls, *Covering Dissent*.

61. Bill Scheer, "National High School Conference Held," *Minnesota Mobilizer* 3, no. 12, December 16, 1967, GI Press Collection; Fox, interview.

62. "High School Movement against the War," (November 27, 1967), WBAI Broadcast, Pacifica Radio Archives.

63. "High School Movement."

64. "High School Movement."

Chapter 3

1. Fred Ferretti, "High School Students of the City, Unite!" *New York Magazine*, April 28, 1969, 43–44; Orris, interview; Stewart, *On the Ground*, 33; "High School

Student Union," *New York High School Free Press*, no. 9, December 1969, Underground Newspaper Collection-Roll 38 (hereafter UNC-Roll); New York High School Student Mobilization Committee, July 19, 1968, reel 12, folder 130, SMC papers.

2. Ferretti, "High School Students," 43–44.

3. Marta Gutman, "Editorial Statement," *Union Times*, no. 2, September 1969, Resist Collection, box 10, folder 1, High School Kit, Watkinson Library, Trinity College, Hartford, CT (hereafter Watkinson Library); "'We Do Not Seek Formal Victories; We Seek Reform': An Interview with Don Vagstad, Chairman, Minnesota Student Union," *Minnesota Journal of Education*, September 1969, 18–19.

4. "What Student Activists Are Doing," *Nation's Schools* 83, no. 3, March 1969, 62; Ferretti, "High School Students," 42.

5. Trigg, interview.

6. Trigg, interview.

7. Macleod, *Building Character*, xi; Trigg, interview.

8. Trigg, interview.

9. Josh Kiok, "All I Really Need to Know About Politics I Learned in High School," unpublished paper, courtesy of Josh Kiok, in author's possession.

10. Trigg, interview; "Peace-Sticker Booby Trap Hurts Boy," *New York Daily News*, April 14, 1967.

11. Kiok, "All I Really Need"; Trigg, interview.

12. Small, *Covering Dissent*, 87; "High Schoolers Join Chorus," *Daily News*, April 27, 1968; Kiok, "All I Really Need."

13. Trigg, interview.

14. Trigg, interview; Stewart, *On the Ground*, 33.

15. Buffet, "Crossing the Line," 1213–14.

16. Schwartz, interview.

17. Reminiscences of Elk Gene (June 20, 2009), OHA-CU.

18. Reminiscences of Estelle Schneider (June 20, 2009), OHA-CU.

19. Buffet, "Crossing the Line," 1214–15; Newton, interview.

20. Swerdloff, interview; Howard Swerdloff, "Life in these United States," *New York High School Free Press*, no. 3, Nov. 20–Dec. 11, 1968, Boxed Newspaper Collection, box 281, TLWA LA.

21. Bloom and Martin, *Black Against Empire*, 206–8.

22. Bloom and Martin, *Black Against Empire*, 208–9.

23. Trigg, interview; Howard Swerdloff, "Czechago," *New York High School Free Press*, October 9–22, 1968, no. 1, October 9–22, 1968, Boxed Newspaper Collection, box 281, TLWA LA; Buffett, "Crossing the Line," 1216.

24. Podair, *Strike That Changed New York*, 1–8.

25. "Now we have a Union! Up Against the Wall BD of ED," *New York High School Free Press*, no. 1, October 9–22, 1968, Boxed Newspaper Collection, box 281, TLWA LA; Buffet, "Crossing the Line," 1216; Trigg, interview.

26. "Position Paper for the Structure of the Union," document, courtesy of Howard Swerdloff.

27. Buffett, "Crossing the Line," 1216.

28. New York High School Student Union pamphlet, undated (October 1968?), courtesy of Howard Swerdloff.

29. New York High School Student Union pamphlet.

30. Graham, *Young Activists*, 114.

31. McMillian, *Smoking Typewriters*, 4-7.

32. McMillian, *Smoking Typewriters*, 73 and 82; *High School Independent Press Service*, UNC-Roll 8; Glessing, *Underground Press in America*, 76.

33. Divoky, *How Old Will You*, n.p.

34. "High School Independent Press Service," *Fifth Estate*, no. 66, November 14-27, 1968, https://www.fifthestate.org/archive/66-november-14-27-1968/high-school-independent-press-service/, accessed December 30, 2024.

35. Libarle and Seligson, *High School Revolutionaries*, 238-42.

36. *High School Independent Press Service*, UNC-Roll 8; Glessing, *Underground Press in America*, 76.

37. Nicholas Pileggi, "Revolutionaries Who Have to be Home by 7:30," *New York Times*, March 16, 1969; Stewart, *On the Ground*, 33.

38. Pileggi, "Revolutionaries."

39. Divoky, "Revolt in the High School," 88.

40. *New York High School Free Press*, no. 1, October 9-22, 1968, TLWA LA; Ferretti, "High School Students," 43; Reminiscences of Jamie Friar (June 20, 2009), OHA-CU; Ingus, *Tonight at Noon*, 97.

41. Swerdloff, interview; Reminiscences of Jamie Friar (June 20, 2009), OHA-CU.

42. Stepenoff, "Gender at the Barricades," 10.

43. "Male Chauvinism," *Serve the People* 1, no. 3 (March 25, 1969): p. 7, box 18, folder 1. High School Movement, 1965-1970, New Left Collection, Hoover Archives.

44. Ides, "'Dare to Free Yourself,'" 305-9.

45. "What do Girls Learn in High School?" [n.d.], High School Student Union of Baltimore (100-26046), FBI-FOIA.

46. Schneider, reminiscences; Reminiscences of Katherine Mulvihill, (June 20, 2009), OHA-CU.

47. Sbarge, *Ira, You'll Get into Trouble*. The student who made this comment is unidentified.

48. "Stop Racist Shaker Now!" flyer, October 31, 1969, courtesy of Howard Swerdloff; Trigg, interview.

49. Newton, interview.

50. Buffet, "Crossing the Line," 1223-25.

51. "Fuck Your 45 Minutes," *New York High School Free Press*, no. 4, December 19-January 8, 1969, 3 and 12, UNC-Roll 38; "35% of Students Boycott Schools," *New York Times*, November 30, 1968; Buffet, "Crossing the Line," 1225.

52. "Protest the New Time Schedule," flyer by the Martin Van Buren HSSU local and the G.O. Executive Committee, courtesy of Josh Kiok, in author's possession.

53. Buffet, "Crossing the Line," 1226.

54. Trigg, interview.

55. Maurice Bleifeld to Helen Kiok, November 27, 1968, courtesy of Josh Kiok.

56. Trigg, interview.

57. "Union May Agree to Alter School Make-Up Schedule," *New York Times*, December 9, 1968; "Schools to be Closed for all of Easter Week," *New York Times*, January 30, 1969.

58. Sbarge, *Ira, You'll Get into Trouble*.

59. Buffet, "Crossing the Line," 1227.

60. "High School Student Union Defines Itself!" *New York High School Free Press*, no. 4, December-January 8, 1969, UNC-Roll 38.

61. Swerdloff, interview.

62. Committee on Student Unrest of the High School Principal Association of the City of New York, "The Nature and Limits of Student Dissent and Participation," January 16, 1969, reprinted in US House, Committee on Education and Labor, *Campus Unrest*, 91st Cong., 1st sess., February 3; March 19, 20, 21, 25, and 26; April 18; May 7, 8, 9, 15, 20, and 22, 1969 (Washington, DC: Government Printing Office, 1969), 626-30.

63. Divoky, "Revolt in the High Schools," 101; Pileggi, "Revolutionaries."

64. Sbarge, *Ira, You'll Get into Trouble*.

65. Swerdloff, interview.

66. Pileggi, "Revolutionaries."

67. Ferretti, "High School Students," 42.

68. Ferretti, "High School Students," 42.

69. Sbarge, *Ira, You'll Get into Trouble*.

70. "New York High School Student Union," August 21, 1969, FOIA-obtained document, courtesy of Howard Swerdloff. FBI documents on the NYHSSU were destroyed on three separate occasions. Estelle Schneider filed a FOIA in the late 1970s and received the NYHSSU's file, which is not in my possession.

71. *Schwartz v. Schuker*, 298 F. Supp. 238; 1969 US Dist. (1969).

72. "Spring Offensive," *New York High School Free Press*, no. 7, March-April 1969, UNC-Roll 38; "Hunter Demands & HSSU & More," *New York Herald Tribune*, May 1969, UNC-37; Newton, interview.

73. Buffett, "Crossing the Line," 1228-29.

74. "Brooklyn High School Closed After Student Riot," *New York Times*, April 19, 1969; "Negro Students Present Demands," *New York Times*, April 20, 1969; "2 High Schools Shut Down in Disorders," *New York Post*, April 23, 1969; "Washington HS Closed by Fires," *New York Post*, May 7, 1969.

75. Newton, interview; Swerdloff interview; Buffett, "Crossing the Line," 1229.

76. Newton, interview; Reminiscences of Katherine Mulvihill, OHA-CU.

77. Trigg, interview; Diane Fowler, "School is Revolting," *Good Times* 2, no. 31, August 14, 1969, UNC-Roll 36.

Chapter 4

1. Joanna Misnik to Romona Ripston, April 22, 1969, reel 12, folder 130, SMC papers.

2. Libarle and Seligson, *High School Revolutionaries*, 213-14.

3. Mirelowitz, interview.

4. "Bare Student Recruiting by Trotskyites," *Chicago Tribune*, November 8, 1968; Intelligence Division, Interview Report, November 11, 1968; Interview Report, "HSSATW Rally," April 9, 1969, box 230, folder 1136, CPD Intelligence Section, Chicago Police Department, Red Squad, and Selected Records, Chicago History Museum Research Center, Chicago.

5. Cone interview, Bancroft Library; Mirelowitz, email message to author, July 19, 2024.

6. Mirelowitz, email.

7. "Chicago High School Activists Organize!" *High School Strikeback!* 1, no. 1, n.d., box 229, folder 1, William T. Poole Collection, Hoover Archives; Cone, interview.

8. "Chicago High School Activists Organize!" *High School Strikeback!* 1, no. 1, n.d., box 229, folder 1, William T. Poole Collection, Hoover Archives.

9. "Report on High School Students Against the War," June 9, 1969, High School Students Against the War (100-44706), FBI-FOIA; Mike Maggi to Geoff Mirelowitz, January 10, 1969, reel 8, folder 79, SMC papers.

10. Libarle and Seligson, *High School Revolutionaries*, 215–17.

11. Libarle and Seligson, *High School Revolutionaries*, 218–21.

12. "School Board of Catholics Faces Pickets," *Chicago Tribune*, March 6, 1969; "Chicago Student Fights Expulsion," *The Militant*, March 14, 1969, news clipping provided by David Smith, in possession of author; Libarle and Seligson, *High School Revolutionaries*, 220.

13. "An Attack on Free Speech at Academy of Our Lady," [February 1969?], High School Students Against the War, FBI-FOIA.

14. "Chicago Student Fights Expulsion"; "School Board of Catholic Faces Pickets," *Chicago Tribune*, March 6, 1969; "Protest Expulsion."

15. Schaffner, interview.

16. "Shaw Pupil Loses Suit Over Antiwar Button," *Plain Dealer*, April 3, 1969; "Guzick Case Goes to Top Court," *Plain Dealer*, December 16, 1970; Saunders, "The Expansion of Constitutional Rights to Public School Pupils through the Due Process Clause of the Fourteenth Amendment," 106–8.

17. Sauders, "Expansion of Constitutional Rights"; Schumaker, *Troublemakers*, 50. Schumaker covers the entire trial in chapter 1.

18. "High School Students Use & Defend Rights," *Student Mobilizer Wallposter*, no. 4, May 5, 1969, UNC-Roll 41; "700 Walk Out a 2 Schools, 40 Suspended at Another," *Paterson News*, March 28, 1969, 40.

19. "Binghamton Central High School," [May 1969?], reel 12, folder 130, SMC papers.

20. "How Will the War End?" Flyer, 1969; Newsletter, November 1969, reel 7, folder 66, SMC papers.

21. Julie Simon and Nancy Morawetz to SMC, [1969?], reel 12, folder 130, SMC papers.

22. "High School Student Rights Conference," 1969, reel 10, folder 103, SMC papers.

23. "Re: The New York City High School Bill of Rights," February 18, 1970, reel 12, folder 130, SMC papers.

24. Halstead, *Out Now!*, 612; "Thousands Attend Session at Adelbert Gym," *Case Western Reserve Observer*, February 17, 1970; "Preliminary Workshop Discusses Mass Action," *Case Western Reserve Observer*, February 17, 1970.

25. "3,000 Conferenced in Cleveland," *Great Speckled Bird* 3, no. 8, February 23, 1970, UNC–Roll 44.

26. "High School Mobe," *Great Speckled Bird* 3, no. 2, January 5, 1970, UNC–Roll 44.

27. "H.S. Unity: End the War!" *Great Speckled Bird* 3, no. 5, February 2, 1970, UNC–Roll 44; "Frank Smith Gets School Board Post," *Atlanta Journal*, February 10, 1970.

28. "3,000 Conferenced in Cleveland," *Great Speckled Bird* 3, no. 8, February 23, 1970, UNC Roll 44; "SMC Workshops Formulate Proposals," *Case Western Reserve Observer*, February 17, 1970.

29. A Document of Struggle," *Student Mobilizer* 3, no. 1, January 21, 1970, box 52, folder 7, New Left Collection, Hoover Archives; "High School Bill of Rights, *Student Mobilizer* 3, no. 2, February 8, 1970, GI Press Collection; "High School Bill of Rights," *Student Mobilizer* 3, no. 3, March 10, 1970, box 52, folder 7, New Left Collection, Hoover Archives.

30. "High School Bill of Rights," *Student Mobilizer* 3, no. 3, March 10, 1970, box 52, folder 7, New Left Collection, Hoover Archives; "High School Bill of Rights," *Student Mobilizer* 3, no. 2, February 8, 1970, GI Press Collection.

31. "Support the Struggle for Student Rights," February 22, 1970, reel 12, folder 130, SMC papers; "High School Bill of Rights," *Student Mobilizer* 3, no. 2, February 8, 1970, 8, GI Press Collection.

32. "High School Rights," *Great Speckled Bird* 3, no. 12, March 23, 1970, 11; Illona Stanton to National SMC, March 24, 1970, reel 12, folder 130, SMC papers.

33. "Student-Teacher Council to Probe School 'Rights,'" *Atlanta Journal*, March 31, 1970.

34. "H.S. Bill of Rights: McNary," *Phoenix* 4, no. 1, [1970?], box 16, YLPR; Bill Vilonza to SMC, May 5, 1971, reel 12, folder 122, SMC papers; Portland HSSMC Wins Rights Fight," *Student Mobilizer* 5, no. 2, February 1972, 10, GI Press Collection; "Rights Talk Plans Laid by Students," *Austin American*, March 10, 1971.

35. "In N. Bethesda Fighting Breaks Out Over Student Picketing," *Montgomery County Sentinel*, March 26, 1970.

36. "Six Winter Park High Protesters Suspended," *Orlando Sentinel*, September 26, 1970; "30 Student Meet, Mum on Officers," *Orlando Sentinel*, September 27, 1970.

37. "Letters," *Student Mobilizer* 3, no. 8, September 16, 1970, GI Press Collection.

38. "Arlington Students Ask for Reforms," *Washington Post*, March 5, 1970, reel 12, folder 132, SMC papers.

39. All of these files have been retrieved through FOIA requests.

40. Cleveland SAC to FBI Director, March 31, 1970; Cleveland SAC to FBI Director, July 24, 1970; FBI Director to SAC Cleveland, July 31, 1970; Cleveland SAC to FBI Di-

rector, August 20, 1970, FBI Vault–New Left, https://vault.fbi.gov/cointel-pro/new-left/cointel-pro-new-left-cleveland-part-01-of-01/view, accessed May 29, 2024.

41. "Open Letter from the Parents' Committee to Citizens of Cleveland Heights-University Heights School District," April 17, 1970, reel 12, folder 130, SMC papers. Data on Cleveland Heights comes from "Cleveland Heights," *Encyclopedia of Cleveland History*, https://case.edu/ech/articles/c/cleveland-heights, accessed May 29, 2024.

42. "Parents' Bill of Rights and Responsibilities," April 17, 1970, reel 12, folder 130, SMC papers.

43. "What Does the SMC Demand of our Schools?" April 17, 1970, reel 12, folder 130, SMC papers.

44. Tittle, *Welcome to Heights High*, 152–53; "Board Backs Gerhardt Ban of SMC in Heights Schools," *Sun Press* (Cleveland Heights, OH), April 10, 1970, box 13, folder 8, Cleveland Heights-University Heights Public Library.

45. "Guidelines Adopted for School Groups," *Plain Dealer*, May 12, 1971.

46. "SMC on High School Movement," *Great Swamp Erie da da Boom* 1, no. 10, May 28–June 13, 1971, MSL SC.

47. "Court Blocks Peary Speakers," *Daily News*, May 14, 1971, news clipping, reel 12, folder 130, SMC papers.

48. "State of the War Cont." *Student Mobilizer* 5, no. 1, February 1972, GI Press Collection.

49. Sandy Modell, Randy Price, and John Linder, "Proposal for a National High School Speak-Out Against the War," *Student Mobilizer* 5, no. 2, February 1972, 11, GI Press Collection; Halstead, *Out Now!*, 770.

Chapter 5

1. *The S.W. Sun*, [1969?], box 16, YLPR.
2. High School Collective to CHIPS, box, 16, folder *S.W. Sun*, YLPR.
3. Jenny Lavelle to CHIPS, [n.d.], box 4, folder 18, YLPR.
4. *Open Valley*, no. 4, High School Issue, Open Valley (100–51751), FBI-FOIA.
5. "Application for 69–70 *Paper* Staff Positions," [n.d.], box 1, folder 1, Barbara Kuck Alternative Press Collection, Special Collections, Chicago Public Library, Chicago, IL (hereafter Kuck Collections).
6. Cooper, interview.
7. Cooper, interview.
8. Cooper, interview; "New Orleans High School Students Organizing as chapter of Students for a Democratic Society," *Finger* 1, no. 1, October 1968, 7, UNC-Roll 29.
9. A–2 to New Orleans Police Department Intelligence Division, August 29, 1968; "In the Name of Student Rights We Demand," leaflet, [September 1968?], Fortier High School SDS (100–17884), FBI-FOIA.
10. Cooper, interview; "New Orleans High School Students Organizing as chapter of Students for a Democratic Society," *Finger* 1, no. 1, October 1968, 7, UNC-Roll 29.

11. New Orleans SAC to FBI Director, May 29, 1968; New Orleans SAC to FBI Director, October 30, 1968; New Orleans SAC to FBI Director, December 31, 1968, COINTELPRO, New Left, File: 100-44968, reel 3.

12. "New Orleans High School Students Organizing as chapter of Students for a Democratic Society."

13. Michel, *Struggle for a Better South*, 1–10.

14. Cooper, interview; Grant Cooper, "The High School Scene," *Southern Movement Press* 1, no. 6, March 1969, UNC-Roll 41; Michel, *Struggle for a Better South*, 138.

15. "An Introduction," *Iceberg*, no. 1, January 1969, box 9, folder S.S.O.C. Newsletters-High School "Iceberg!" Southern Student Organizing Committee records, 1948–1994, University Archives, University of Virginia Library, Charlottesville, VA (here after SSOC records).

16. Cooper, interview.

17. "School Unrest Said Settled," *Richmond Times-Dispatch*, October 4, 1968, B1.

18. "What's Happening . . ." *Iceberg*, no. 1, January 1969, box 9, folder S.S.O.C. Newsletters-High School "Iceberg!" SSOC records.

19. "High School," *NC-SSOC Worklist*, no. 2, December 16 [1968?], box 9, folder SSOC Newsletter-North Carolina, SSOC records.

20. Cooper, interview.

21. "Iceberg!" *GA SSOC Newsletter*, February 1969, box 9, folder SSOC Newsletter-Georgia, SSOC records.

22. "Introduction."

23. "What's Happening"; Cooper, interview.

24. "Malcom X . . . The Autobiography of Malcolm X: Impressions of a Revolutionary"; Student Power: New York Style," *Iceberg*, no. 1, January 1969, box 9, folder S.S.O.C. Newsletters-High School "Iceberg!" SSOC records.

25. "Hell Out There . . ." *Iceberg*, no. 2, February 1969, box 9, folder SSOC Newsletter-Georgia, SSOC records.

26. San Antonio SAC to FBI Director, April 17, 1969, FBI Vault-New Left, https://vault.fbi.gov/cointel-pro/new-left/cointel-pro-new-left-san-antonio-part-01-of-01/view, accessed July 29, 2021.

27. "Jonesboro Students Protest Smoking Ban," *Atlanta Journal*, February 8, 1969, 3A; "It Can Happen Here . . ." *Iceberg*, no. 2, February 1969, box 9, folder SSOC Newsletter-Georgia, SSOC records.

28. Cooper, "High School Scene."

29. "High School Conference!!!" *Iceberg*, no. 2, February 1969, box 9, folder SSOC Newsletter-Georgia, SSOC records.

30. "High School Conference Easter Weekend!" *Iceberg*, [March 1969?], box 9, folder SSOC Newsletter-Georgia, SSOC records.

31. Boye Jacobs, "High School Conference," *Great Speckled Bird* 2, no. 5, April 14, 1969, https://digitalcollections.library.gsu.edu/digital/collection/GSB, accessed May 8, 2024; "SSOC it to me," *The Finger* 1, no. 7, [April 1969?], UNC-Roll 35; Cooper, interview.

32. Shepard Samuels, "Political Prisoner," *The Finger* 1, no. 7, [May 1969?], UNC–Roll 35; FBI Director to New Orleans SAC, March 21, 1969, COINTELPRO, New Left, File: 100–44968, reel 3.

33. Cooper, interview.

34. Allyson, interview.

35. Allyson, interview.

36. John Schaller, "A Short History of CHIPS and FPS," *FPS*, no. 6, February 4, 1971, box 9, folder FPS, YLPR.

37. Schaller, "Short History of CHIPS."

38. "High School Undergrounds," *Indianapolis Free Press*, June 11–25, 1970, UNC–Roll 58.

39. Schaller, "Short History of CHIPS."

40. *How to Start a High School Underground Newspaper*, [1970?], CHIPS (100–40133), FBI–FOIA.

41. "A Short History of CHIPS and FPS."

42. Graham, *Young Activists*, 99–102; Hefner, interview.

43. "Students Want to Show Concern," *Plain Dealer* (Cleveland, OH), December 17, 1972.

44. *How to Start*.

45. Allyson, interview.

46. John Drugger to CHIPS, [n.d.]; "Information about High School Independent Papers for a CHIPS directory," box 6, folder New Amerikan Mercury, YLPR.

47. Eric M. Berg to John Schaller, January 18 1970, box 1, folder Local Rocks, YLPR.

48. Allyson interview; "Judge Refuses to Order Bellaire Students Admitted," *Houston Chronicle*, October 22, 1969.

49. Schaller, "Short History of CHIPS."

50. Schaller, "Short History of CHIPS."

51. Allyson, interview.

52. "An Introduction to FPS—What We Are, Where We Came from, and What We Hope to Do," *FPS*, no. 1, September 11, 1970, box 9, folder FPS, YLPR.

53. "Screw Your School"; "National High School Conference"; "School is like Military Prison"; "Talking Public Skools"; "Don't Miss the Next Action-Packed Issue of FPS," *FPS*, no. 1, September 11, 1970, box 9, folder FPS, YLPR.

54. Schaller, "Short History of CHIPS."; Allyson, interview; *FPS*, no. 2 and no. 3, box 8, folder FPS, YLPR

55. Schaller, "Short History of CHIPS."; Allyson, interview; A. J. Moffett Jr., "Youth Gets a Voice in New Student Center," *Nation's Schools* 85, no. 5 (May 1970): 57–59.

56. "Nixon Welcomes Groups to D.C.," *FPS*, no. 4, December 16, 1970, CHIPS, box 9, folder FPS, YLPR.

57. "FPS to DC with SIC," *FPS*, no. 4, December 16, 1970, box 9, folder FPS, YLPR.

58. "Culture (?) . . . Freak!!-Part II," *FPS*, no. 11, May 14, 1971, box 9, folder, FPS, YLPR.

59. "Sample of Underground High School Papers," *Great Swamp Erie da da Boom* 1, no. 5, March 9–22 [1971?], MSL SC.

60. Allyson, interview.

61. Hefner, interview.

62. Hefner, interview.

63. Hefner, interview.

64. "Pupils' Suspensions Rapped by Parents," *Ann Arbor News*, September 26, 1968, Disruption Ann Arbor High School (100–3536), FBI-FOIA.

65. Pupils' Suspensions Rapped by Parents"; "Walkout," [September 1968?], Disruption Ann Arbor High School, FBI-FOIA.

66. Hefner, interview; Oriard, *Brand NFL*, 214.

67. Hefner, interview.

68. Hefner, interview; Keith Hefner, "The Evolution of Youth Empowerment at a Youth Newspaper," *Social Policy*, Summer 1988; "Student Sues to Run for School Board," *Detroit Free Press*, May 23, 1972.

69. Hefner, interview.

70. Hefner, interview.

71. "A Word from the Staff," *FPS*, October 7, 1971, FPS (100–40133), FBI-FOIA.

72. Phobe Pollitt to FPS, [n.d], November 6, 1971, box 15, folder Virgin, YLPR.

73. Mark De Pecal to CHIPS, [n.d.]; Leonard C. Yannielli to CHIPS, August 10, 1972, box 3, folder Reynolds Bridge, YLPR.

74. Inter–High to CHIPS, [n.d.], box 21, folder Inter–High, YLPR.

75. Richard Katz to CHIPS, January 5, 1971, box 1, folder 38, YLPR.

76. Glessing, *Underground Press in America*, 129.

77. "CHIPS membership Questionnaire," box 7, folder Chronicle of Current Events, YLPR.

78. The Chronicle Staff to Youth Liberation, May 19, 1974, box 7, folder Chronicle of Current Events, YLPR.

79. Bill Male to FPS, June 17, 1973, box 2, folder Asian Face, CHIPS, archives.

80. For more information, see Fountain, "Building a Student Movement."

81. To learn more about conservative student activism, see Shepherd, *Resistance from the Right*.

82. "Fights Flare at School; Some Parents Say Their Children Will Not Return," *Daily Oklahoman* (Oklahoma City, OK), September 9, 1969; "Second Newsletter Answers First One," *Daily Oklahoman*, September 16, 1969, 13; "Paper Pops Up at Classen," *Daily Oklahoman*, October 1, 1969, 12.

83. "Kids' Paper Prints Both Sides," *Kansas City Star*, June 22, 1970, 4; Sheperd, *Resistance from the Right*, 6.

84. "Students Unite!" *Dare to Struggle* 1, no. 1, April 27, 1971, box 1, folder 9, Steve Louie Asian American Movement Collection, Charles E. Young Research Library, Department of Special Collection, University of California, Los Angeles (hereafter Young Research Library).

85. "Robbed," *Street Sheet*, [1970?], Street Sheet (157–19926), FBI-FOIA.

86. Hefner, interview; *FPS*, no. 55; *FPS*, no. 62, box 9, folder FPS, YLPR.

Chapter 6

1. "Attendance Slumps at Hughes," *Cincinnati Post*, October 12, 1967; "Police to Stay at Schools, Miller Says," *Cincinnati Post*, April 24, 1968; "1400 Students Stage Sit-Ins at 6 Schools," *Cincinnati Post*, April 30, 1968; Rod Pennington, letter to the editor, "A School Editor's Story," *Cincinnati Post*, May 9, 1968; "Evolution of Disorder," *Cincinnati Enquirer*, May 19, 1968.

2. "Joseph Smithmeyer on Cincy High Schools," *Independent Eye*, May 17, 1968, Cincinnati and Hamilton County Public Library, https://digital.cincinnatilibrary.org/digital/collection/p16998coll17/id/64344/.

3. "Sit-ins Staged at 4 Schools," *Cincinnati Post*, April 30, 1968; Evolution of Disorder."

4. "1,306 Students are Suspended," May 1, 1968, *Cincinnati Enquirer*.

5. "Court Readies Crackdown on School Demonstrators," *Cincinnati Post*, May 1, 1968.

6. Pennington, "School Editor's Story."

7. "Black Students Win in Cincy!" *Independent Eye*, May 17, 1968; "Evolution of Disorder."

8. Bundy, "'Revolutions Happen!'"; Rury and Hill, "End of Innocence"; B. Franklin, "Community, Race, and Curriculum"; Hale, *New Kind of Youth*; García and Castro, *Blowout!*

9. Divoky, *How Old Will You*; Birmingham, *Our Time is Now*.

10. These articles are far too numerous to list. For an example of a newspaper article, see "Until Ninth Grade, She was 'Apathetic.'"

11. "High School Unrest Rises, Alarming U.S. Educators," *New York Times*, May 9, 1969; Schumaker, *Troublemakers*, 107; Shepherd, *Resistance from the Right*, 17.

12. "Unrest Cited in High Schools," *Atlanta Journal*, June 1, 1969.

13. Rest in Peace and Power Francisco Flores Landa: a Community Rebel at Heart," *El Tecolote*, March 10, 2022, https://eltecolote.org/content/en/rest-in-peace-and-power-francisco-flores-landa-a-community-rebel-at-heart/.

14. Ferreira, "All Power to the People," 156, 180–84; Heins, *Strictly Ghetto Property*, 25–27; Contreras, *Latinos and the Liberal City*, 5–8, and 133. For another study on the Mission District, see Summers, *Latinos at the Golden Gate*.

15. "Mission High Closes Door," *San Francisco Chronicle*, September 29, 1966; "6 Hurt in Mission High Fights," *San Francisco Examiner*, April 17, 1968; "Anti-Riot Move at Mission," *San Francisco Examiner*, April 18, 1968.

16. Francisco FloresLanda, "Mission High School Student Organizing 1969," FoundSF, http://foundsf.org/index.php?title=Mission_High_School_Student_Organizing_1969, accessed June 23, 2022.

17. FloresLanda, "Mission High School Student."

18. Heins, *Strictly Ghetto Property*, 25–27; FloresLanda, "Mission High School Riot," FoundSF, http://foundsf.org/index.php?title=Mission_High_School_Riot_1969, accessed June 23, 2022.

19. FloresLanda, "Mission High School Student."

20. FloresLanda, "Mission High School Student."

21. Schumaker, *Troublemakers*, chapter 2; Robinson, *Washington State Rising*, chapter 2.

22. Biondi, *Black Revolution on Campus*, 56–73.

23. "Violence Rips S.F. Schools," *San Francisco Examiner*, October 22, 1968.

24. "Problems Erupt at SF Schools," *San Francisco Examiner*, October 24, 1968; Several former Polytechnic graduates recalled the walk in a 1996 article. See Venise Wagner, "Poly High Alums Seek Spirit of '68," *SFGate*, October 4, 1996, http://www.sfgate.com/news/article/Poly-High-alums-seek-spirit-of-68-3121056.php.

25. "Poly Students Win Demands," *San Francisco Examiner*, October 25, 1968; "Polytechnic Teachers' Letter," *San Francisco Examiner*, October 25, 1968; "Poly Black Students Boo Off School Chief," *San Francisco Examiner*, October 25, 1968; "500 Poly Parents Look at Problems," *San Francisco Examiner*, October 31, 1968.

26. Herbert R. Simon to Robert E. Jenkins, October 29, 1968, San Francisco Unified School District Department of Art Education, box 54, folder 4, San Francisco History Center, San Francisco, CA (hereafter cited as SFHC).

27. Herbert R. Simon to Robert Jenkins, November 4, 1968, SFUSD Department of Art Education, SFHC.

28. Vitale, *End of Policing*, 55.

29. Hinton, *America on Fire*, 10–11.

30. Hinton, *America on Fire*, 147–49.

31. Stern, "Hidden Politics," 239; Suddler, *Presumed Criminal*, 150.

32. "Newark Schools get Guard Cops," *New York Times*, March 9, 1969.

33. Remnick, "Police State," 13.

34. "490 Armed Guards Patrol Public Schools in Chicago," *Chicago Tribune*, March 26, 1982.

35. Petition letter to Thomas Cahill, chief of police, October 22, 1968, box 15, folder 26, Alioto Papers, SFHC.

36. Statement by Mayor Alioto on problems in San Francisco schools, October 24, 1968, box 15, folder 26, Alioto Papers, SFHC; "Problems Erupt at SF Schools."

37. "Hard-Nosed Policy for S.F. Schools—Jenkins," *San Francisco Examiner*, October 28, 1968.

38. "S.F. Police Probe Balboa High Bomb," *San Francisco Examiner*, November 2, 1968; "Arsonists Hit 2 High Schools," *San Francisco Examiner*, November 15, 1968.

39. Scribner, *A Is for Arson*, 1.

40. "Schools to Hire Guards," *San Francisco Examiner*, November 13, 1968; "School Board Hears Foes, OKs Guards," *San Francisco Examiner*, December 4, 1968.

41. Robert Jenkins to all principals and assistant principals, December 9, 1968, Office of the Superintendent, "Positive Provisions for a Sound and Safe Educational Environment," box 15, folder 26, Alioto Papers, SFHC.

42. "Sympathy Rally at Lincoln High," *San Francisco Examiner*, December 6, 1968, 18; "Sympathy Walkouts Fizzle," *San Francisco Examiner*, December 10, 1968.

43. "Violence in S.F. Schools Our Most Serious Problem," *San Francisco Examiner*, December 10, 1968.

44. Concerned Black Parents to Dr. Robert E. Jenkins, March 20, 1969, box 15, folder 26, Alioto Papers, SFHC.

45. "Blacks Seek School Power," *San Francisco Examiner*, October 19, 1968.

46. Wang, "Chinese-American Student," 53–57.

47. "Yellow Power," *Lowell*, February 25, 1969.

48. "Chinese at Washington Turn Militant," *San Francisco Examiner*, February 18, 1969; "Chinatown Meet on Schools: Changes Asked in Education," *San Francisco Examiner*, February 26, 1969.

49. FloresLanda, "Mission High School Students"; FloresLanda, "Mission High School Riot."

50. FloresLanda, "Mission High School Students"; FloresLanda, "Mission High School Riot."

51. "Violence at Mission High Again," *San Francisco Examiner*, January 25, 1969.

52. Ferreira, "All Power to the People," 249–50

53. "2 Lincoln High Students Stabbed," *San Francisco Examiner*, February 21, 1969; "Rumors Stir Anger at Lincoln High," *San Francisco Examiner*, February 27, 1969.

54. "Set Probe of Tac Role in School Riots," *San Francisco Examiner*, March 19, 1969; Cohen, "Prophetic Minority," 1–39.

55. "At Mission High: Parents Want Police," *San Francisco Examiner*, January 26, 1969.

56. "More Violence at Mission High," *San Francisco Examiner*, January 27, 1969; "Police Halt Violence at Mission High," *San Francisco Chronicle*, January 28, 1969.

57. Quoted in Heins, *Strictly Ghetto Property*, 137.

58. "New Mission High Student Demands," *San Francisco Chronicle*, January 29, 1969; Joe Johnson to Mike McCone, February 6, 1969, Office of the Mayor, "Mission High School," box 15, folder 26, Alioto Papers, SFHC.

59. FloresLanda, "Mission High School Student."

60. "17 Demands at Mission HS," *San Francisco Examiner*, February 5, 1969; "Mission High School Organizing, 1969."

61. Biondi, *Black Revolution on Campus*, 43–53.

62. Biondi, *Black Revolution on Campus*, 56–73.

63. "33 Mission Arrests–Tac Squad Called," *San Francisco Chronicle*, February 5, 1969; FloresLanda, "Mission High School Student."

64. "'Unrest Coming to High School,'" *San Francisco Examiner*, February 6, 1969.

65. "Blueprint for Takeover," *San Francisco Examiner*, February 7, 1969.

66. "Seeking the Way at Mission High," *San Francisco Examiner*, February 8, 1969.

67. "Conference on Latin-American Problems Set," *San Francisco Examiner*, February 9, 1969; "Latino Youth Hits Teachers' 'Image,'" *San Francisco Examiner*, February 16, 1969; "'Pressure' Protest by S.F. Teachers," *San Francisco Examiner*, February 23, 1969; "Mission Coalition Warning," *San Francisco Examiner*, April 2, 1969.

68. "Mission High Demands Set for Tonight," *San Francisco Examiner*, March 18, 1969.

69. "5 City Principals Shifted," *San Francisco Examiner*, June 24, 1969; "School Board Jeered," *San Francisco Examiner*, June 26, 1969; "Mission Students Coalition Seeks School Board Probe," *San Francisco Examiner*, June 27, 1969; FloresLanda, "Mission High School Student."

70. California Newsreel, *High School Rising*.

71. California Newsreel, *High School Rising*.

72. California Newsreel, *High School Rising*.

73. Fowler, "School is Revolting."

74. FloresLanda, "Mission High School Student."

75. "Walkout Gets Slim Backing in School," *San Francisco Chronicle*, September 17, 1969; Fountain, "War in the Schools," 34-35.

76. Schumaker, *Troublemakers*, 178.

Chapter 7

1. "Students Granted Rights—They Want to Use Them," *Philadelphia Inquirer*, January 23, 1972.

2. "Student Grievances," [March 1968?], Lincoln High School (157-2163), FBI-FOIA.

3. One of the earliest efforts occurred in Washington, DC, at Anacostia High School. See "Students Write 'Rights," *Washington Daily News*, April 28, 1967.

4. Buffet, "Crossing the Line," 1229-30; "Area School Resists Student Demands That They Help Write the Regulations," *Courier-Journal*, February 21, 1970.

5. "Backers of Sargent Health Reorganization Will Try to Save It With a Compromise," *Boston Globe*, July 21, 1974.

6. Susan Bailey, email; "George Bailey, Former Committeeman," *Philadelphia Tribune*, October 30, 1992; "Martha Bailey, 63, Educator, Leader," *Philadelphia Tribune*, February 20, 1987.

7. "Martha Bailey."

8. Perkiss, "Mount Airy (West)." To learn more about housing integration in Mount Airy, see Perkiss, *Making Good Neighbors*.

9. Bailey, email; "What is Resistance? Strategy, Tactics, Purpose," [n.d.], Box 1, folder 10/93, Philadelphia Resistance, SCPC.

10. Bailey, email; Punnett, interview.

11. Countryman, *Up South*, 237-38.

12. "Schools are Targets for Unrest," *Philadelphia Inquirer*, November 18, 1967, 7.

13. Countryman, *Up South*, 228-36.

14. Countryman, *Up South*, 236-37; "200 Gratz Students Stage Black Power Demonstration," *Philadelphia Inquirer*, October 27, 1967.

15. Countryman, *Up South*, 228-36.

16. Bailey, email.

17. Bredell, "Black Panther High," 75-79.

18. Countryman, *Up South*, 238–39; "Students Ask Right to Legal Counsel in Disputes with Schools," *Philadelphia Tribune*, May 30, 1970. School Board President Richard Dilworth kept a news clipping of the bill of rights campaign in New York City; see box 10, folder 4, Dilworth Papers.

19. Mark F. Lloyd, "The Need for a Student Bill of Rights in the High Schools of Philadelphia," [1970?], box 152, folder 2, Dilworth Papers.

20. "Students Charge School System Suppresses Desire for Learning," *Philadelphia Inquirer*, July 19, 1970.

21. "Pupil Bill of Rights Calls for Caution," *Philadelphia Inquirer*, June 21, 1970; The Fellowship Commission to Board of Education, July 27, 1970; Philadelphia Federation of Teachers to School Board, July 27, 1970, box 153, folder 2, Dilworth papers.

22. "Views Differ on Students Rights," *Philadelphia Inquirer*, July 28, 1970; "On Student Rights: Dad, Son, Big Brother," *Philadelphia Daily News*, July 28, 1970; Al Haas, "School Hearings: Talk, Talk, Talk," *Philadelphia Inquirer*, July 29, 1970.

23. Robert Lee Williams, "Student Bill of Rights," [July 1970?], box 153, folder 2, Dilworth Papers.

24. "Bill of Rights for Students Debated Again," *Philadelphia Daily News*, November 10, 1970; "School Board Vows Action on Pupils' Rights," *Philadelphia Inquirer*, November 22, 1970.

25. "Antiwar Group Begins Drive," *Philadelphia Inquirer*, November 22, 1970; "Bar to Sponsor Student Forum," *Philadelphia Inquirer*, December 6, 1970; "Student Strike Feared if Vote on Bill of Rights is Delayed," *Philadelphia Inquirer*, December 21, 1970; "Student Rights Pass Board but Shedd Feels Heat," *Philadelphia Daily News*, December 22, 1970.

26. School District of Philadelphia, "Bill of Rights and Responsibilities for High School Students," December 21, 1970, box 153, folder 2, Dillworth papers.

27. "Student Rights Pass Board."

28. David A. Horowtiz, "Principals' Concerns Regarding the Student Bill of Rights and Responsibilities," January 18, 1971, box 153, folder 2, Dillworth papers.

29. "High School 'Bill of Rights'—Bullshit!" *Red Army*, January 11, 1971, Red Army (100–52653), FBI–FOIA.

30. "High School 'Bill of Rights'—Bullshit!"; "Shedd Hints at Probe of Student's Transfer," *Philadelphia Daily News*, December 8, 1970; "Curb These Student Uprisings," *Philadelphia Inquirer*, January 4, 1971.

31. "Student Protest at Board of Ed. Set for Thursday," *Philadelphia Tribune*, January 12, 1971; "Do High School Students Need a Bill of Rights?" *Philadelphia Tribune*, January 16, 1971; "Bill of Rights not Implemented Yet, Student Demonstrators Claim," *Philadelphia Tribune*, January 19, 1971.

32. Bailey, email.

33. "Mount Airy Teacher Shot, Killed; Union Calls for Protest," *Philadelphia Inquirer*, February 2, 1971.

34. "5,000 Attend Rites for Slain Teacher," *Philadelphia Inquirer*, February 4, 1971.

35. "PFT, Angered by Slaying, asks Repeal of Student Bill of Rights," *Philadelphia Daily News*, February 4, 1971.

36. Bailey, email.

37. "Teachers' Union Asks for Ouster of Shedd," *Philadelphia Inquirer*, February 6, 1971; "Student Bill of Rights Should go, Union's Ryan Says," *Philadelphia Daily News*, February 18, 1971; "Teachers Want Shedd to Quit Poll Reveals," *Philadelphia Inquirer*, February 27, 1971.

38. "Killing of Teacher by Student," *Philadelphia Inquirer*, February 8, 1971.

39. "Shedd's Resignation is Accepted by Board at Cost of at least $58,500," *Philadelphia Inquirer*, December 10, 1971.

40. "An Environment of Violence," *Philadelphia Inquirer*, February 8, 1971; "Battle of '67: Finally a Decision," *Philadelphia Daily News*, December 7, 1971.

41. "Trust Yourself, Book Tells Students," *Philadelphia Inquirer*, December 2, 1971; "Ross Threatens Pupil Rights Bill," *Philadelphia Daily News*, January 11, 1972.

42. Bailey, email; "Students Granted Rights."

43. "Susan Lobbies for School Change," *Philadelphia Daily News*, February 11, 1972.

44. Bailey, email.

45. "City Schools Are Accused of Failing Students," *Philadelphia Daily News*, March 8, 1972.

46. "Pupil Rights Bill Backed by Costanzo," *Philadelphia Inquirer*, June 11, 1972; "Student Rights Bill Under Fire as Vote Nears," *Philadelphia Daily News*, July 6, 1972; "Student Rights Bill Retained by Board—With Adjustments," *Philadelphia Inquirer*, July 18, 1972.

47. "Ombudsmen-Pupils Note Apathy," *Philadelphia Daily News*, October 15, 1975.

48. "Students Union: 'We're Not Radical Anymore,'" *Philadelphia Daily News*, December 13, 1976.

49. "Students' Rights Platform of Philadelphia," *Teiresias* 1, no. 8, [1969?]; North Central High School Statement of Students' Rights and Responsibilities," January 1972, box 1, folder 13, Bugher Collection, North Central High School Library, Indianapolis, IN; "Where do our Students Stand," *Indianapolis News*, March 8, 1969.

50. Kate Cunningham to Priscilla Robertson, December 21, 1971, box 1, folder Academic Freedom 1971, Kentucky Civil Liberties Union, University Archives and Historical Research Center, University of Louisville, Louisville, KY (hereafter UAHRC). Reproduction of Philadelphia Student Bill of Rights is in the same box, but in folder "Academic Freedom Conference 1971."

51. "Proposed Student Bill of Rights and Responsibilities," [1975?], box 7, folder Students' Rights Jeff. Co. Schools 1975–1976, Progress in Education Records, UAHRC.

52. Ruhl, "'Forward You Must Go,'" 55–56.

Chapter 8

1. "Briggs to Keep Collinwood Closed if Danger Lingers," *Plain Dealer*, April 7, 1970; "News on Collinwood Spurred Stokes to Act," *Plain Dealer*, April 9, 1970; "Bigoted Whites Storm Collinwood," *Call and Post*, April 11, 1970.

2. "News on Collinwood Spurred."

3. "News on Collinwood Spurred"; Police to Remain at Collinwood," *Plain Dealer*, April 9, 1970.

4. Stern, "School Violence," 492; Levy, *Great Uprising*, 290–91.

5. "Black Students at Collinwood Launch Activities Boycott," *Call and Post*, April 25, 1970.

6. Stern, "Hidden Politics," 238–42; "Outbursts of Racial Violence Plague Nation's High School," *Philadelphia Inquirer*, January 6, 1970.

7. "'Probe Teens Racial 'Rumble,'" *Call and Post*, March 20, 1965.

8. Roy, "Collinwood."

9. "Collinwood Tension Building up 15 Years," *Plain Dealer*, March 19, 1965.

10. Fraser, *Hillbilly Highway*, 112–13.

11. V. Franklin, *Young Crusaders*, 144; Moore, "School Desegregation Crisis," 135–36.

12. Moore, "School Desegregation Crisis," 137.

13. Moore, *Carl B. Stokes*, 30; "Collinwood is Focus of Tense, Changing Area," *Plain Dealer*, April 8, 1970.

14. V. Franklin, *Young Crusaders*, 145–46.

15. V. Franklin, *Young Crusaders*, 146–51.

16. "Behind the Collinwood Caper," *Call and Post*, March 22, 1969; "Collinwood is Focus of Tense, Changing Area," *Plain Dealer*, April 8, 1970.

17. Linda Murray, interview by HistoryMakers®, August 30, 2004.

18. Murray, interview.

19. Murray, interview; Nick Castele, "Listen to Testimony from the 1966 U.S. Civil Rights Commission Hearing in Cleveland," *Ideastream Public Media*, July 12, 2016, https://www.ideastream.org/arts-culture/2016-07-12/listen-to-testimony-from-the-1966-u-s-civil-rights-commission-hearing-in-cleveland; "Peace Pledged at Collinwood," *Plain Dealer*, March 19, 1965.

20. "Anti-Negro Slogans Painted on School," *Cleveland Press*, September 10, 1964, MSL SC.

21. Murray, interview.

22. Murray, interview; "Listen to Testimony."

23. "Listen to Testimony"; "Collinwood Fighting Breaks Out," *Cleveland Press*, March 18, 1965, Possible Race Riot at Collinwood High (157–354), FBI-FOIA.

24. "Peace Pledged at Collinwood"; "Say Cops Stand Idle as Mob Stones Negroes," *Call and Post*, June 22, 1963.

25. "Peace Pledged at Collinwood."

26. "Collinwood Fighting Breaks Out."

27. "Peace Pledged at Collinwood"; "Collinwood Tension Building up 15 Years," *Plain Dealer*, March 19, 1965, 10; Cleveland SAC to FBI Director, March 18, 1965, Possible Race Riot Involving Collinwood High School Students, FBI-FOIA.

28. Murray, interview.

29. "Peace Pledged at Collinwood"; "Beaten in Rescue of Collinwood Negro Resident," *Call and Post*, March 27, 1965.

30. "Collinwood is Quiet After Arrests of 24," *Plain Dealer*, March 20, 1965.

31. Barber, *Latino City*, 122–23.
32. Stern, "'We Got to Fight,'" 5 and 13; Stern, "Hidden Politics," 237–75.
33. Graham, *Young Activists*, 65; Stern, "'We Got to Fight,'" 5 and 13.
34. "Behind the Collinwood Disorder," *Call and Post*, March 27, 1965.
35. "Cleveland on the Spot," *Call and Post*, April 9, 1966; "Listen to Testimony."
36. "Police Guard School in Collinwood," *Cleveland Press*, March 13, 1969; "Adults Join Student Group in Uproar Collinwood High," *Cleveland Press*, March 14, 1969; "Tense Collinwood Tells on Principal," *Cleveland Press*, March 15, 1969, MSL SC; Picketing Collinwood High School (157-2018), FBI-FOIA; "Bigotry Sparked Collinwood Revolt," *Call and Post*, March 22, 1969.
37. "Tense Collinwood Tells." To learn more about the Ludlow Community Association, see Meckler, *Dream Town*.
38. "Tense Collinwood Tells"; "Behind the Collinwood Caper," *Call and Post*, March 22, 1969, 4B.
39. "Tense Collinwood Tells"; "Behind the Collinwood Caper."
40. "Behind the Collinwood Caper"; "Officials, Parents Attend Collinwood Peace Meeting," *Cleveland Press*, March 17, 1969, Picketing Collinwood High School, FBI-FOIA.
41. "Tense City Watches School Outbreaks," *Call and Post*, June 14, 1969.
42. "Bigoted Whites Storm Collinwood"; "Student Walkout, Bomb Threat Follow Racial Bias Charges," *Call and Post*, November 22, 1969.
43. "Bigoted Whites Storm Collinwood.".
44. Mohamed, "Of Monsters and Men," 1157–216.
45. "Guard on Alert as Classes Resume at Collinwood High," *Call and Post*, April 11, 1970; "Parents Mobilize to Stifle Violence"; "'Rumor Clinics' Considered for Collinwood Community."
46. Naomi Donerson to Honorable Carl B. Stokes, December 15, 1969, reprinted in *Proceedings of the Board of Education* 91, January–December 1970, January 5, 1970, 5, Cleveland Metropolitan School District Woodland Warehouse archives, Cleveland, OH.
47. Paul Stein, "A Day at Collinwood: 'Just a Skirmish,'" *Cleveland Press*, April 21, 1970, MSL SC.
48. "Student Walkout, Bomb Threat."
49. "Glassboro Imposes Curfew," *Central New Jersey Home News* (New Brunswick, NJ), September 30, 1971.
50. "Black Students at Collinwood Launch Activities Boycott," *Call and Post*, April 25, 1970.
51. "Parents Mobilize to Stifle Violence," *Call and Post*, April 18, 1970; "'Rumor Clinics' Considered for Collinwood Community,'? *Call and Post*, May 9, 1970.
52. "Two Wounded in Collinwood White-Black Clash," *Call and Post*, September 26, 1970; "Police Break up Collinwood Fight," *Call and Post*, May 1, 1971.
53. "Collinwood Blacks, Whites Sit-in for Student Rights," *Call and Post*, March 6, 1971.
54. "Police Break up Collinwood Fight"; "Black Unity Kept it Cool in Collinwood," *Call and Post*, October 13, 1973.

55. "School Fights Disturb Parents," *Call and Post*, September 23, 1972.

56. "Racial Melee Erupts at Collinwood High," *Call and Post*, September 28, 1974.

57. "High School Pupil Slain at Playground in Collinwood Area," *Plain Dealer*, October 7, 1974; "Collinwood Youth is Slain Group Plans Peace Session," *Call and Post*, October 12, 1974; "Collinwood Killing Suspects to Face Trial as Adults," *Plain Dealer*, October 18, 1974.

58. "The Collinwood Tinderbox," *Cleveland Press*, October 8, 1974, MSL SC.

59. "Police Sirens Wail, 500 Bolt Collinwood," *Plain Dealer*, October 15, 1974, MSL SC.

60. "Conciliation Seems Keynote at Collinwood Talk," *Plain Dealer*, October 18, 1974.

61. "Collinwood Guard Charged in Rape," *Plain Dealer*, October 28, 1974.

62. "Collinwood Principal Quits—'I Can't Take Any More,'" *Cleveland Press*, June 26, 1975; "Retiring Principal Blames Collinwood Adults for Ills," *Plain Dealer*, June 27, 1975; "DiZinno Gives Up," *Cleveland Press*, June 27, 1975; "6 Collinwood Pupils Suspended in Knifing," *Cleveland Press*, December 17, 1974; "Collinwood—a Day of Confusion and Agony," *Cleveland Press*, February 21, 1975; "Collinwood High Shut after Clash of Blacks, Whites," *Plain Dealer*, February 21, 1975; "$5,000 Fire Hit Stage at Collinwood," *Plain Dealer*, February 26, 1975; "Three Pupils Injured in Collinwood Fight," *Plain Dealer*, April 30, 1975, MSL SC.

63. "Collinwood Principal Davis Works to Solve Race Problem," *Call and Post*, December 6, 1975.

Chapter 9

1. FBI, Director to Milwaukee SAC, December 3, 1968; "Join Us," leaflet, [1968?]; Beatrice M. Gudridge, "Is Student Protest Spreading to the High School?" [1968?], Milwaukee Student Alliance (100–15877), FBI–FOIA.

2. SA Dennis P. Joyce to Milwaukee SAC, December 31, 1968, Milwaukee Student Alliance, FBI–FOIA.

3. Joyce to SAC; Milwaukee SAC to FBI Director, "Counterintelligence Program Internal Security Disruption of the New Left," February 14, 1969, FBI Vault–New Left, http://vault.fbi.gov/cointel-pro/new-left/cointel-pro-new-left-milwaukee-part-01-of-01/view, accessed January 24, 2015.

4. Milwaukee SAC, "Counterintelligence Program Internal Security."

5. Hale, *New Kind of Youth*, 189–90.

6. Auten, interview; "New Sandia High to Accommodate 2000 Students," *Albuquerque Journal*, August 10, 1958.

7. Wood, *Postwar Transformation of Albuquerque*, 232.

8. Hillman, *Dressing for the Culture Wars*, xv–xvi.

9. Hillman, *Dressing for the Culture Wars*, 18.

10. Graham, "Flaunting the Freak Flag," 522–23, and 525.

11. "Students Ask for Explanations," *Albuquerque Journal*, March 18, 1969; "Slack-Wearing School Girls Debate Rage," *Albuquerque Journal*, November 27, 1969; "West

Mesa Suspends Girl for Wearing Bell-Bottoms," *Albuquerque Journal*, December 3, 1969.

12. Auten, interview.

13. "Coffeehouses are Open for Albuquerque Teenagers," *Albuquerque Journal*, October 13, 1969.

14. Auten, interview.

15. "A.S.D. Active Students for Democracy," *Joint Effort*, no. 2, [1969?], Joint Effort (100–3441), FBI–FOIA.

16. Active Students for Democracy, "Awareness," leaflet, [1969?], Youth for Radical Progress (100–3419), FBI–FOIA.

17. Auten, interview.

18. All of these flyers appear in the FBI files after a memo titled, "Youth for Radical Progress, also known as Active Students for Democracy (ASD)," December 24, 1969, Youth for Radical Progress, FBI–FOIA. Although the date is marked 1969, the memo summarizes the incidents that occurred in November 1968.

19. "Campus Unrest: City Schools No Longer Ignore Student Gripes," *Albuquerque Journal*, March 16, 1969; Wood, *The Postwar Transformation of Albuquerque*, 234.

20. "Campus Unrest."

21. "Campus Unrest"; Auten, interview.

22. SA Joseph F. Condon to Albuquerque SAC, April 17, 1969, Joint Effort, FBI–FOIA; "Harrell Led Security at APS for 23 Years," *Albuquerque Journal*, July 31, 2001.

23. "Campus Unrest"; SA Joseph F. Condon to Albuquerque SAC, March 17, 1969, Youth for Radical Progress, FBI–FOIA. Although the informant's name is redacted, Harrell likely is the informant given that he was the administrator that student Ken Sanchez contacted for a special session with the school board via an article that appeared in the *Albuquerque Journal*.

24. Youth for Radical Progress, "Youth Identity," leaflet, [October 1969?], Youth for Radical Progress, FBI–FOIA.

25. Dr. Tom Wiley, letter received, "Potential Militant Student Activity," September 26, 1969; SA Joseph F. Condon to Albuquerque SAC, October 1, 1969, Youth for Radical Progress, FBI–FOIA.

26. "'M-Day' Bus One for Hundreds Here," *Albuquerque Journal*, October 16, 1969.

27. Counterintelligence Operation Branch, 901st MI Detachment, Sandia Base, "Summary of Information," October 20, 1969, Youth for Radical Progress, FBI–FOIA.

28. SA Joseph F. Condon to Albuquerque SAC November 7, 1969, Youth for Radical Progress, FBI–FOIA.

29. FBI Director to Albuquerque SAC, "Youth for Radical Progress," November 25, 1969, Youth for Radical Progress, FBI–FOIA.

30. SAC Albuquerque to FBI Director, "Youth for Radical Progress," December 24, 1969. Given matching details with another FBI investigation regarding Joint Effort, AQ T-2 matches identically with Darryl Harrell's actions.

31. Graham, *Young Activists*, 138–41; "Rebel SDS Moving into Area High Schools," *Plain Dealer*, October 30, 1968; "High School SDS Fades," *Honolulu Advertiser*, March 24, 1969. To learn more about the Columbia University protest, see Bradley, *Harlem vs. Columbia University*.

32. Mark Kleiman, *High School Reform: Towards A Student Movement*, box 9, folder 12, Civil Rights Movement in the United States, Young Research Library.

33. US House, Committee on Internal Security, *SDS Plans for America's High Schools*, 91st Cong., 1st sess., 1969 (Washington, DC: Government Printing Office, 1969).

34. "State School Board's Anti-SDS Resolution," *San Francisco Chronicle*, September 12, 1969; "Council Moves for S.D.S. Charter; Greenham Hesitant to Approve it," *The Shakerite*, February 6, 1969, Local History Archives, Shaker Heights Public Library, Shaker Heights, OH.

35. J. Edgar Hoover, "The SDS and the High Schools: A Study in Student Extremism," *PTA Magazine*, January–February 1970, 2–5.

36. Davis and Wiener, *Set the Night on Fire*.

37. Hoover, "SDS and the High Schools."

38. Cunningham, *There's Something Happening Here*, 102.

39. Gregg, *Spying on Students*, 41–43.

40. WFO SAC to FBI Director, September 11, 1968; FBI Director to WFO SAC, October 1, 1968, FBI Vault–New Left, https://vault.fbi.gov/cointel-pro/new-left/cointel-pro-new-left-washington-part-01-of-01/view, accessed July 29, 2021.

41. Los Angeles SAC to FBI Director, January 20, 1969; FBI Director to Los Angeles SAC, February 2, 1969, FBI Vault–New Left, https://vault.fbi.gov/cointel-pro/new-left/cointel-pro-new-left-los-angeles-part-01-of-02/view, accessed July 29, 2021.

42. SAC Sacramento to FBI Director, April 7, 1970; Sacramento SAC to FBI Director, October 28, 1970, reel 1, section 3, Disruption of the New Left.

43. Davis, *Assault on the Left*, 96; St. Louis SAC to FBI Director, October 10, 1968, FBI Vault–New Left, https://vault.fbi.gov/cointel-pro/new-left/cointel-pro-new-left-st.-louis-part-01-of-01/view, accessed July 29, 2021.

44. "Central Students Plan SDS Chapter," *Times-Democrat* (Davenport-Bettendorf, IA), November 6, 1970.

45. Omaha SAC to FBI Director, December 31, 1970, reel 1, section 3, Disruption of the New Left; "Faculty Votes Against SDS," *Times-Democrat*, November 6, 1970.

46. For a study on theoretical concepts of Blackness and surveillance, see Browne, *Dark Matters*.

47. FBI Director to Baltimore SAC, February 25, 1969; Baltimore SAC to FBI Director, March 17, 1969; Baltimore SAC to FBI Director, March 28, 1969, FBI Vault–Black Extremists, https://vault.fbi.gov/cointel-pro/cointel-pro-black-extremists/cointelpro-black-extremists-part-09-of/view, accessed August 4, 2021; "School Talk by Black Panthers Banned," *Baltimore Sun*, March 28, 1969.

48. Columbia SAC to FBI Director, April 5, 1968, https://vault.fbi.gov/cointel-pro/cointel-pro-black-extremists/cointelpro-black-extremists-part-02-of/view; Columbia

SAC to FBI Director, May 31, 1968, https://vault.fbi.gov/cointel-pro/cointel-pro-black-extremists/cointelpro-black-extremists-part-04-of/view, accessed August 4, 2021.

49. Sacramento SAC to FBI Director, October 11, 1968, https://vault.fbi.gov/cointel-pro/cointel-pro-black-extremists/cointelpro-black-extremists-part-06-of/view; Sacramento SAC to FBI Director, October 31, 1968, https://vault.fbi.gov/cointel-pro/cointel-pro-black-extremists/cointelpro-black-extremists-part-07-of/view, accessed August 4, 2021.

50. G. C. Moor to W. C. Sullivan, April 4, 1969, https://vault.fbi.go FBI Director to Seattle SAC, April 7, 1969, https://vault.fbi.gov/cointel-pro/cointel-pro-black-extremists/cointelpro-black-extremists-part-11-of/viewv/cointel-pro/cointel-pro-black-extremists/cointelpro-black-extremists-part-11-of/view, accessed August 4, 2021.

51. "High School SDS Action Said Planned," *Austin American* (Austin, TX), June 27, 1968.

52. "High School SDS?" *Bristol Herald Courier*, April 10, 1969.

53. "High School Students Cool to the SDS Pitch," *Oakland Tribune*, March 6, 1969.

54. US House, Committee on Internal Security, *Investigation of Students for a Democratic Society Part 6-A (Columbus, Ohio, High Schools)*, 91st Cong., 1st sess., October 20–22, 1969 (Washington, DC: Government Printing Office, 1969).

55. "SDS Plans in Schools Revealed," *Times Recorder* (Zanesville, OH), November 5, 1969.

56. "'Radical Left' Recruits in America's High Schools," *Jefferson City Post-Tribune* (Jefferson City, MO), December 19, 1969.

57. "High School Students Cool"; "S.D.S. Loses Word Battles at Schools," *Seattle Times*, October 2, 1969.

58. "Effort Planned?" *Albuquerque Journal*, March 31, 1969.

59. "Misinterpreted?" *Albuquerque Journal*, April 9, 1969.

60. Memo, "Youth for Radical Progress," December 24, 1969, Youth for Radical Progress, FBI–FOIA.

61. SA Joseph F. Condon to Albuquerque SAC, December 17, 1969, Youth for Radical Progress, FBI–FOIA.

62. Joseph F. Condon, SA to SAC, Albuquerque, "Youth for Radical Progress," January 29, 1970, Youth for Radical Progress, FBI–FOIA.

63. W. D. Iverson to A. T. Swallows, April 7, 1970, Youth for Radical Progress, FBI–FOIA.

64. Jewell Brown to Dr. Tom Wiley, May 6, 1970; "An Explanation to our Fellow Students," leaflet, [May 1970?], Youth for Radical Progress, FBI–FOIA; Miretsky, interview. A similar incident occurred at Highland High where the principal expelled one student, who was already on disciplinary probation, for trying to lower the flag. See "HHS Student Expelled; Manzano Suspends 7," *Albuquerque Tribune*, May 7, 1970.

65. W. J. Atkins to Cary Carlton, June 14, 1970, Youth for Radical Progress, FBI–FOIA.

66. FBI Director to Albuquerque SAC, March 3, 1970; Albuquerque SAC to FBI Director, April 1, 1970; and Albuquerque SAC to FBI Director, June 30, 1970, FBI Vault–New Left, https://vault.fbi.gov/cointel-pro/new-left/cointel-pro-new-left-albuquerque-part-01-of-01/view, accessed July 29, 2021.

67. Robert Smith, *New Mexico Lobo*, February 11, 1971, Youth for Radical Progress, FBI–FOIA.

68. "A 'Piece of Paper' Rocks Albq Like a Bomb Explosion," *Albuquerque Tribune*, November 17, 1971.

69. "School Rights, Responsibilities Text Presented," *Albuquerque Journal*, May 11, 1972; "Statement Adopted on Student Rights," *Albuquerque Journal*, May 12, 1972.

70. Auten, interview; Miretsky, interview.

71. SA Jerry D. Winchester to Minneapolis SAC, April 23, 1969, Minneapolis High School Student Mobilization Committee (100–13837), FBI–FOIA.

72. Morris Fineberg to FBI Philadelphia, February 24, 1971, Red Army, FBI–FOIA.

73. Detroit SAC to FBI Director, May 26, 1970; "High School Liberation Front," September 18, 1970, High School Liberation Front (100–457605), FBI–FOIA.

74. Milton B. Kuhl to SAC, January 31, 1972, *South Dakota Whippersnapper* (100–16051), FBI–FOIA.

75. SA to El Paso SAC, September 27, 1971, Organization for Student Rights (100–62–1996), FBI–FOIA.

76. Richmond SAC to FBI Director, May 15, 1970, Student Action Movement (100–11158), FBI–FOIA; "Possible Walk Out at Holy Ghost Roman Catholic High School," April 14, 1969, Holy Ghost Roman Catholic High School, FBI–FOIA; "Negro Student Disturbance R. H. Watkins High School," February 18, 1972, R. H. Watkins High School (157–15404), FBI–FOIA.

77. Donner, *Protectors of Privilege*, 1.

78. John N. Baader, Principal Union Springs Central School, April 25, 1969, box 48, folder b, New York State Division of State Police Non-Criminal Investigation Case Files, New York State Archives, Albany, NY.

79. SA William M. Chapin to Cleveland SAC, March 25, 1969, Student Coalition for Constructive Social Reform (100–29719), FBI–FOIA; "Against High School ROTC," *Akron Beacon Journal*, June 11, 1969.

80. Cincinnati SAC to FBI Director, November 5, 1971; and Cincinnati SAC to FBI Director, November 15, 1971, Demonstration by Aiken High School Students (100–20258), FBI–FOIA.

81. "'We Do Not Seek Formal Victories; We Seek Reform," 18–19; "Students Seeking High-School Reform Organize," *Minneapolis Tribune*, March 23, 1969; "Mutual Respect Sought in Schools," *Minneapolis Star*, October 17, 1969.

82. Kim Heikkila, interview with Leah Rutchick, October 3, 2018, Oral History Interviews of the Vietnam Era Oral History Project, Minnesota Historical Society, St. Paul, MN.

83. SA H. Clifford Miller to Minneapolis SAC, April 18, 1969, Minnesota Student Union (100–14544), FBI–FOIA.

84. "2 Suspended Marshall Girls are Reinstated," *Minneapolis Tribune*, November 19, 1968.

85. "Twin Cities Students Press Blake School Haircut Protest," *Minneapolis Tribune*, January 10, 1969; "100 Robbinsdale High School Suspended for Clothing Protest," *Minneapolis Star,* February 13, 1969; Celeste Fulju, Alison Grab, Debbie Pulju, Linda Moretter, "Democracy at Robbinsdale High," letter to the editor, *Minneapolis Tribune*, February 20, 1969; "William J. Petroski, "Appealed by Student Action," letter to the editor, *Minneapolis Tribune*, February 21, 1969.

86. SA Charles R. Wiley to Seattle SAC, February 11, 1970, Nathan Hale High School SDS (100-27151), FBI-FOIA; "S.D.S. Loses Word Battles at Schools," *Seattle Times*, October 2, 1969, Lincoln High School SDS (100-29855), FBI-FOIA.

87. SA Donald L. Hoppert to Seattle SAC, February 13, 1970, SDS Queen Anne High School (100-27151), FBI-FOIA.

88. "Army Spied on Nilehi," *Skokie Life*, March 18, 1971, reel 4, US Army Surveillance of Dissidents, 1955-1972: Records of the US Army's ACSI Task Force. To learn more about military surveillance, see Lyman, "In the Eye of the Sphinx."

89. SA Jesse R. Bowie to Milwaukee SAC, May 15, 1972; SA Russell J. Horner to Milwaukee SAC, July 25, 1972, Iskra (100-15247), FBI-FOIA.

90. "Student Protests Minority Image," *Black and Gold* (Cleveland Heights High School), March 21, 1969, Cleveland Heights-University Heights Public Library.

91. SA Joseph R. Shea to Chicago SAC, September 24, 1968, Suburban Liberation Front (100-46488), FBI-FOIA.

92. Portland FBI, letter received, September 23, 1970, High School Collective (100-11912), FBI-FOIA.

93. "Long Hair Called 'Symbol of Sickness,'" *Minneapolis Tribune*, April 5, 1969; Gordon Raup, "Students Seek to Run Schools," letter to the editor, *Minneapolis Tribune*, April 10, 1969.

94. William P. Effertz, SA to SAC, Minneapolis, April 30, 1969; SA John Joseph Mulhern to Minneapolis SAC, May 21, 1969, Minnesota Student Union, FBI-FOIA.

95. SA, "Flyer Regarding Demo," Minneapolis, July 30, 1970; SA Ralph S. Russell, "Closed Meeting of SWP Held," April 20, 1973, Minnesota Student Union, FBI-FOIA.

Chapter 10

1. Clerk William J. Herr to Baltimore SAC, March 22, 1969; SA Arthur S. Hamilton to Baltimore SAC, March 24, 1969, High School Student Union of Baltimore, FBI-FOIA.

2. Warren J. Bauer to Art Hamilton, March 24, 1969, High School Student Union of Baltimore, FBI-FOIA.

3. Gage, *G-Man*, 173-77.

4. To learn more about society's general concern about children in different social contexts, see Clapp, *Mothers of All Children*; Odem, *Delinquent Daughters*;

Rivers, *Radical Relations*; Grieve, *Little Cold Warriors*; Agyepong, *Criminalization of Black Children*.

5. Harris, *Palo Alto*.

6. Steve Staiger, "History of Palo Alto," City of Palo Alto Planning & Development, https://www.cityofpaloalto.org/Departments/Planning-Development-Services/Historic-Preservation/History-of-Palo-Alto, accessed January 4, 2024.

7. "History of Palto Alto."

8. "Singer Baez Defends Pacifism," *Campanile* (Palo Alto High School), February 26, 1965, Palo Alto High School Library, Palo Alto, CA; Hatfield, *Over Time*.

9. "Viet Marches Decried; Yet, Bullets Kill Ideas," *Campanile*, October 28, 1965.

10. "The Axiom," *Catamount* (Cubberley High School, Palo Alto, CA), April 7, 1967, http://www.cubberleycatamount.com, accessed August 12, 2018.

11. *The USM Newsletter*, no. 1 [December 1966?], "United Student Movement," (100–58113), FBI-FOIA.

12. "First U.S.M. Reports—17 High Schools, 10 Advisors, 250 Students," *U.S.M. Newsletter* 1 [1967?], PAHA; Williams, *Hassling*, 13–14.

13. *U.S.M. Newsletter* 1, [1967?], folder United Student Movement, PAHA.

14. SA R. E. Thau to San Francisco SAC, December 30, 1966, United Student Movement, FBI-FOIA.

15. Jacobs, interview.

16. Williams, *Hassling*, 18; DeBenedetti and Chatfield, *American Ordeal*, 153.

17. "Ashamed?" [March 1967?], leaflet, United Student Movement, FBI-FOIA; Williams, *Hassling*, 17–18.

18. "United Student Movement," May 22, 1967, United Student Movement, FBI-FOIA.

19. "Copy of Membership List of United Student Movement," April 26, 1967, United Student Movement, FBI-FOIA.

20. "Antiwar Forces Infiltrate High Schools," *Plain Dealer*, December 10, 1965; Memo, "High School Activist League," January 20, 1966; Cleveland SAC to FBI Director, April 4, 1966, High School Activist League (100–27710), FBI-FOIA.

21. SA Thomas J. Lardner to Boston SAC, July 12, 1968, Rhode Island High School Students for Peace, FBI-FOIA.

22. F. J. von Mering to J. Edgar Hoover, October 5, 1969, Right On (100–462679), FBI-FOIA.

23. SA Leo E. Brunnick to SAC Sup. B. McCabe, September 19, 1969, High School SDS (100–40070–1A), FBI-FOIA.

24. WFO SAC to Baltimore SAC, March 17, 1969, Montgomery County Student Alliance (100–49008), FBI-FOIA.

25. Sagirard M. Annino to Chicago SAC, September 24, 1968, Suburban Liberation Front, FBI-FOIA.

26. SA David R. Hirtz to Cleveland FBI, January 11, 1974, Youth Liberation (100–42144), FBI-FOIA.

27. SAC, New Orleans to FBI, Director, October 30, 1968, microfilm, reel 3, COINTELPRO: Counterintelligence Program of the FBI New Left.

28. WFO SAC to FBI Director, November 13, 1968; FBI Director to New York SAC, December 27, 1968, FBI Vault–New Left, https://vault.fbi.gov/cointel-pro/new-left/cointel-pro-new-left-new-york-part-01-of-02/view, accessed July 29, 2021.

29. "The Monicle," *Catamount*, October 26, 1967, http://www.cubberleycatamount.com/Content/67-68/Catamount%20Pages/V12No3/671026.pdf, accessed October 12, 2018.

30. Scott D. Thomson to Cubberley Parents, December 15, 1967, PAHA; Palo Alto Unified School District meeting minutes, December 19, 1967, Palo Alto, CA; Andrew M. Spears to Bernard M. Oliver, December 22, 1967, PAHA.

31. John E. Austin to Bernard M. Oliver, December 20, 1967, PAHA.

32. Martin J. Dreyfuss to Scott D. Thomson, December 16, 1967, PAHA; Scott D. Thomson to Martin Dreyfuss, December 21, 1967, PAHA.

33. Kenneth W. Kolence to Agnes Robinson, December 15, 1967, PAHA.

34. "Susan Lynn Keller," July 18, 1969, PAHA; San Francisco SAC to FBI Director, September 19, 1967, United Student Movement, FBI–FOIA.

35. "United Student Movement," memo, February 23, 1968, United Student Movement, FBI–FOIA.

36. "Witch Hunt: USM Red-Baited," *Serve the People* 1, no. 4, April 17, 1969, 3, New Left Collection, Hoover Archives.

37. "United Student Movement," memo, June 12, 1969, PAHA.

38. Palo Alto High School to SA Brent T. Palmer, March 10, 1969, United Student Movement, FBI–FOIA.

39. Jacobs, interview.

40. San Francisco SAC to FBI Director, February 12, 1970, Radical Student Union (100–457307), FBI–FOIA.

41. San Francisco SAC to FBI Director, December 1, 1970, FBI–FOIA.

42. "Laura Mackay Irwin 'Diddy,'" *Charlotte Observer*, January 5, 2005; "Basil L. Irwin," *Charlotte Observer*, November 16, 2008.

43. Charlotte Student Union, "Statement of Purpose," Charlotte Student Union (100–10690), FBI–FOIA.

44. "Spark of Teen Revolt Burns Here," *Charlotte Observer*, April 25, 1969, Charlotte Student Union, FBI–FOIA.

45. Laura Mackay Irwin to J. Edgar Hoover, March 21, 1968, Charlotte Student Union, FBI–FOIA.

46. Irwin to Hoover.

47. J. Edgar Hoover to Basil L. Irwin, March 27, 1969; FBI Director to Charlotte SAC, April 4, 1969, Charlotte Student Union, FBI–FOIA.

48. SA Thomas J. Moore, Jr. to Buffalo SAC, October 11, 1968, Nickel Bag (100–19820), FBI–FOIA.

49. Mrs. John E. Gill to FBI San Antonio, September 10, 1970, San Antonio High School Student Union (100–12020), FBI–FOIA.

50. Jean Mills to FBI New York, March 1, 1972, Renegade (100–175134), FBI–FOIA.

51. Cohen, "Prophetic Minority," 16. For a broader study on student activism in the South, see Turner, *Sitting In and Speaking Out*.

52. Sink, "Fueling the Southern Underground," 132.

53. Michel, *Struggle for a Better South*, 142.

54. Charles H. Crutchfield to J. C. Goodman, April 14, 1970, Inquisition (100–10874), FBI-FOIA.

55. Hoyman, email. For an oral history on Scott Hoyman, see William Finger, interview with Scott Hoyman, July 15, 1974, Southern Oral History Program Collection, University of North Carolina, https://docsouth.unc.edu/sohp/E-0010/E-0010.html, accessed October 1, 2023.

56. "Spark of Teen Revolt."

57. SA George Koons to Charlotte SAC, April 7, 1969; "Are Myers Park Students Ready to Unite?" leaflet, [1969?], Charlotte Student Union, FBI-FOIA.

58. George C. Koons, SA to SAC, Charlotte, April 7, 1969; "Charlotte Student Union," Memo, April 15, 1969, FBI-FOIA.

59. SA Leonard H. McCoy to Charlotte SAC, April 9, 1969, Charlotte Student Union, FBI-FOIA.

60. Charlotte SAC to FBI Director, April 15, 1969, Charlotte Student Union, FBI-FOIA.

Epilogue

1. Tepper, interview.

2. Pittman, interview; Brown, interview; Northcott, interview; Shapiro, interview; Shapiro, *Song of the Stubborn*.

3. Semel, interview; Garb, interview.

4. Citret, interview.

5. Harer, interview; Fox, interview.

6. Dawson, interview; Mirelowitz, interview.

7. Trigg, interview; Schneider, interview; Gene, interview; W. Friar, interview; J. Friar, interview, OHA-CU; Schwartz, interview.

8. Josh Kiok, email; Newton, interview; Orris, interview; Swerdloff interview.

9. Hefner, interview; Allyson, interview; Cooper, interview.

10. Cooper, interview; Gregg Michel, email message to author, July 12, 2024.

11. "Rest in Peace and Power Francisco Flores Landa."

12. Bailey, email; Punnett, interview; Murray, interview.

13. Auten, interview.

14. George A. Chauncey Jr., "Up Against the Blackboard," *Equinox* 1, no. 2. Dec.20–Jan.15 [1971?], New Left, box 18, folder 2, Hoover Archives; *Union Times*, no. 2, September 1969, box 10, folder 1, High School Kit, Resist Collection, Watkinson Archives.

15. Scales, *In a Time of Panthers*.

16. Schwendinger, interview.

17. Finger, interview.

18. Hefner, email.

19. Adam Gabbatt, "Vietnam to Parkland: How America's Protesters are Getting Younger," *Guardian*, April 15, 2018, https://www.theguardian.com/world/2018

/apr/15/us-protests-vietnam-war-parkland-shooting-young-people; "Florida School Shooting Survivors are Not 'Crisis Actors,'" *Associated Press*, February 21, 2018, https://www.rollingstone.com/culture/culture-news/read-obamas-heartfelt-letter-to-parkland-shooting-students-204535/?sub_action=logged_in; "7 Times in History When Students Turned to Activism," *New York Times*, March 5, 2018, https://www.nytimes.com/2018/03/05/us/student-protest-movements.html; "Read Obamas' Heartfelt Letter to Parkland Shooting Students," *Rolling Stone*, March 21, 2018, https://www.rollingstone.com/culture/culture-news/read-obamas-heartfelt-letter-to-parkland-shooting-students-204535/?sub_action=logged_in."

20. "'Nicholas Senn High School: Division of Daily's Pig State," *Paper* 3, no. 8, January 8, 1969, box 1, folder 17, Kuck Collection.

21. "Hundreds Walk out of Allentown schools, Then Lose Interest," *Morning Call* (Allentown, PA), September 28, 2015, https://www.mcall.com/2015/09/28/hundreds-walk-out-of-allentown-schools-then-lose-interest/.

22. Aaron G. Fountain Jr., "Allentown Students' Activism Harkens to Protests of 1960s, 1970s," October 27, 2015, *Lehigh Valley Live*, https://www.lehighvalleylive.com/opinion/2015/10/allentown_students_activism_ha.html.

23. The South Dakota State Archives holds original copies and oral history interviews with the publishers of the *South Dakota Seditionist Monthly*.

24. Aaron Fountain, letter to the editor, *Indianapolis Star*, December 21, 2017, https://www.indystar.com/story/opinion/readers/2017/12/21/letters-hollingsworth-should-show-evidence-threat/973163001/.

25. For Palo Alto High School's archives, see https://palyjournalismarchive.pausd.org/, accessed July 2, 2024. I only came across the archives at North Central High inadvertently. I originally asked to see the school newspaper, but the librarian informed me that the school had an archive.

Bibliography

Archival and Manuscript Collections

Albany, NY
    New York State Archives
        New York State Division of State Police Non-Criminal Investigation Case Files

Berkeley, CA
    Bancroft Library, University of California, Berkeley
        Social Protest Collection
    Berkeley High School Library
        Daily Jacket Collection
    Berkeley Public Library Central History Room
        Daily Jacket Collection
        Olla Podrida

Bloomington, IN
    Lily Library, Indiana University
        Spears MSS

Charlottesville, VA
    University Archives, University of Virginia Library
        Southern Student Organizing Committee Records

Chicago, IL
    Chicago History Museum Research Center
        CPD Intelligence Section
            Chicago Police Department, Red Squad, and Selected Records
    Department of Special Collections, University of Chicago Library
        Office of Student Activities Records
    Special Collections, Chicago Public Library
        Barbara Kuck Alternative Press Collection

Cleveland, OH
    Cleveland Heights-University Heights Public Library Local History Room
        Sun Press
    Cleveland Metropolitan School District Woodland Warehouse
        Proceedings of the Board of Education
    Michael Schwartz Library Special Collection, Cleveland State University
        Great Swamp Erie da da Boom
        Newspaper Clippings
    Western Reserve Historical Society, Case Western Reserve University

United Food & Commercial Workers International Union District 427
 Records, 1937–1973
Hartford, CT
 Watkinson Library and College Archives, Trinity College
  Resist Collection
Indianapolis, IN
 Indianapolis Public Library
  Ronald W. Haldeman Collection of Local Publications
 North Central High School Library
  Bugher Collection
 Warren Central High School Archives
  Warren Owl
Los Angeles, CA
 Charles E. Young Research Library, University of California,
   Los Angeles
  Steve Louie Asian American Movement Collection
  Civil Rights Movement in the United States
Louisville, KY
 University Archives and Historical Research Center, University of Louisville
  Kentucky Civil Liberties Union
  Progress in Education Records
New York, NY
 Columbia Center for Oral History, Columbia University
  Student Movements of the 1960s
 Tamiment Library and Robert F. Wagner Labor Archives, New York University
  Boxed Newspaper Collection
Palo Alto, CA
 Palo Alto High School Library
  The Campanile Collection
 Palo Alto Historical Association
  Robert French papers
 Palo Alto Unified School District
  Board of Education Meeting Minutes
Philadelphia, PA
 Historical Society of Pennsylvania
  Richardson Dilworth Papers, 1881–2002
 Special Collections Research Center, Temple University
  Youth Liberation Press Records
 Swarthmore College Peace Collection
  Philadelphia Resistance
  Student Peace Union Records
St. Paul, MN
 Minnesota Historical Society
  Oral History Interviews of the Vietnam Era Oral History Project
San Francisco, CA

History Center, San Francisco Public Library
    Joseph Alioto papers
    Lowell High School
        Lowell
    San Francisco Unified School District
    Labor Archives and Research Center, San Francisco State University
        Archie Brown Collection, 1933–1978
Shaker Heights, OH
    Local History Archives, Shaker Heights Public Library
        Shakerite
Stanford, CA
    Hoover Institution, Stanford University
        New Left Collection
        William T. Poole

Audio and Video Recordings

California Newsreel. *High School Rising*. Internet Archive. University of California, Berkeley Art Museum and Pacific Film Archive, 1 Reel of 1: Film: 16mm. Accessed June 23, 2022. https://archive.org/details/cbpf_000093.

Castele, Nick. "Listen to Testimony from the 1966 U.S. Civil Rights Commission Hearing in Cleveland." *Ideastream Public Media*, July 12, 2016.

"High School Students against the War." WBAI Broadcast, Pacifica Radio Archives, January 27, 1967.

Room 222. Created by James L. Brooks. 1969–1974. Los Angeles, CA: Twentieth Century Fox Film Corporation, 2009, DVD.

Sbrage, Stephen. *Ira, You'll Get into Trouble*. Newsreel, 1970, 16mm b&w, 85 min. 1968–1970. http://www.stevesbarge.com/stevesbargemovie.html.

Digital Archives

Berkeley Library Digital Collections
    Kitty Cone interview
Cincinnati and Hamilton County Public Library Digital Collection
    Independent Eye
Cleveland Heights-University Heights Public Library Digital Archive
    Black and Gold (Cleveland Heights High School)
FBI Vault
    Black Extremists
    New Left
Fifth Estate
    Fifth Estate Archives
FoundSF
    The Black Press
    Mission High School Riot, 1969

Mission High School Students Organizing, 1969
HistoryMakers® African American Video Oral History Collection
Dr. Linda Rae Murray interview
Irvington Oral History Project
Thomas Stirling interview, April 9, 1979
Southern Oral History Program Collection, University of North Carolina
Scott Hoyman interview, July 15, 1974
Wisconsin Historical Society
GI Press Collection, 1964–1977
Zinn Education Project
Massive Anti-Vietnam War Demonstration

Government Documents

Federal Bureau of Investigation, National Records Administration, College Park, MD.
Schwartz v. Schuker, 298 F. Supp. 238; 1969 US Dist. (1969).
US House Committee on Education and Labor. *Campus Unrest*. 91st Cong., 1st sess., February 3; March 19, 20, 21, 25, and 26; April 18; May 7, 8, 9, 15, 20, and 22, 1969. Washington, D.C.: Government Printing Office, 1969.
US House Committee on Internal Security. *Investigation of Students for a Democratic Society Part 6-A (Columbus, Ohio, High Schools)*. 91st Cong., 1st sess., October 20–22, 1969. Washington, D.C.: Government Printing Office, 1969.
US House Committee on Internal Security. *SDS Plans for America's High Schools*. 91st Cong., 1st sess., 1969. Washington, D.C.: Government Printing Office, 1969.

Interviews

Allyson, Sasha. Telephone interview with author. October 14, 2023.
Auten, Barbara (Voldahl). Video interview with author. July 20, 2023.
Bailey, Susan. Email message to author. March 20, 2024.
Bennett, Johnathan. Interview with author. September 17, 2016, Manhattan, NY.
Brown, Betsy. Video interview with author. September 13, 2023.
Citret, Mark. Interview with author. August 6, 2015, Daly City, CA.
Cooper, Grant. Video interview with author. June 29, 2023, and November 4, 2023.
Dawson, Kipp. Interview with author. December 8, 2018, Pittsburgh, PA.
Eklund, John. Email message to author. November 29, 2023.
Finger, Anne. Interview with author. July 18, 2023.
Fox, Gordon. Telephone interview with author. September 1, 2017.
Friar, Jamie. Reminiscences with Columbia University. June 20, 2009.
Friar, Wendy. Reminiscences with Columbia University. June 20, 2009.
Garb, Paula. Telephone interview with author. August 8, 2015.
Gene, Elk. Reminiscences with Columbia University. June 20, 2009.
Glasser, Ira. Telephone interview with author. July 9, 2013.
Harer, Katharine. Interview with author. August 8, 2016, Berkeley, CA.
Hefner, Keith. Email message to author. June 19, 2023.

Hefner, Keith. Video interview with author. September 14, 2023.
Hoyman, Michele. Email message to author. June 15, 2023.
Hoyman, Neal. Email message to author. August 31, 2015.
Jacobs, David. Interview with author. August 7, 2015, Stanford, CA.
Kiok, Josh. Email message to author. July 30, 2024.
Michel, Gregg. Email message to author. July 12, 2024.
Mirelowitz, Geoff. Telephone interview with author. July 28, 2017.
Mirelowitz, Geoff. Email message to author. July 19, 2024.
Miretsky, Bonnie (Bank). Video interview with author. November 20, 2023.
Mulvihill, Katherine. Reminiscences with Columbia University. June 20, 2009.
Newton, Robert. Telephone interview with author. March 4, 2015.
Northcott, Kate. Interview with author. August 11, 2015, San Francisco, CA.
Orris, Maxine. Telephone interview with author. March 19, 2015.
Pittman, Carol. Telephone interview with author. January 11, 2019.
Punnett, Laura. Video interview with author. July 20, 2023.
Rutchick, Leah. Interview with Kim Heikkila. October 3, 2018.
Schaffner, Jay. Video interview with author. March 20, 2024.
Schneider, Estelle. Reminiscences with Columbia University. June 20, 2009.
Schwartz, Jeffrey. Telephone interview with author. March 8, 2015.
Schwendinger, Leni. Telephone interview with author. July 9, 2013.
Semel, Elisabeth. Interview with author. August 11, 2015, San Francisco, CA.
Shapiro, Peter. Interview with Ronald J. Grele. April 11, 1984.
Shapiro, Peter. Interview with author. September 28, 2023.
Swerdloff, Howard. Telephone interview with author. March 16, 2015.
Tepper, Jesse. Interview with author. August 7, 2015, San Francisco, CA.
Trigg, Bruce. Reminiscences with Columbia University. June 20, 2009.
Wasserman, Steve. Interview with author. May 23, June 18, 2013, and August 16, 2016, Berkeley, CA.

Microfilm Collections

America in Protest: Records of Anti-Vietnam War Organization, Part 3: Student Mobilization Committee to End the War in Vietnam, 1966–1973; High School Organizing, 1967–1972.
COINTELPRO, New Left.
National Coordinating Committee to End the War in Vietnam, 1964–1967, Pennsylvania, 1965–1966, Pittsburgh-York.
US Army Surveillance of Dissidents, 1955–1972: Records of the US Army's ACSI Task Force.

Miscellaneous Documents

David Smith private collections
Harrell Graham private collections
Howard Swerdloff private collections

Joel Schwartz private collections
Josh Kiok private collections

Newspapers

Akron Beacon Journal (Akron, OH)
Albuquerque Journal
Albuquerque Tribune
Atlanta Journal
Austin American (Austin, TX)
Baltimore Sun
Berkeley Daily Gazette (Berkeley, CA)
Boston Globe
Bristol Herald Courier (Bristol, TN)
Call and Post (Cleveland, OH)
Case Western Reserve Observer (Cleveland, OH)
Catamount (Cubberley High School, Palo Alto)
Central New Jersey Home News (New Brunswick, NJ)
Charlotte Observer
Chicago Sun-Times
Chicago Tribune
Cincinnati Enquirer
Cincinnati Post
Cleveland Press
Courier-Journal (Louisville, KY)
Daily Jacket (Berkeley High School, Berkeley, CA)
Daily Oklahoman (Oklahoma City, OK)
Detroit Free Press
Finger (New Orleans, LA)
Good Times (San Francisco, CA)
Great Speckled Bird (Atlanta, GA)
High School Independent Press Service (New York, NY)
Honolulu Advertiser
Houston Chronicle
Indianapolis News
Jefferson City Post-Tribune (Jefferson City, MO)
Kansas City Star (Kansas City, MO)
Los Angeles Times
Lowell (Lowell High School, San Francisco, CA)
Minneapolis Star
Minneapolis Tribune
Montgomery County Sentinel (Rockville, MD)
Morning Call (Allentown, PA)
New York Daily News
New York Herald Tribune
New York High School Free Press
New York Post
New York Times
Oakland Tribune
Orlando Sentinel
Paterson News (Paterson, NJ)
Philadelphia Daily News
Philadelphia Inquirer
Philadelphia Tribune
Plain Dealer (Cleveland, OH)
Record (Hackensack, NJ)
Richmond Times-Dispatch (Richmond, VA)
San Francisco Chronicle
San Francisco Examiner
San Francisco News-Call Bulletin
Seattle Times
Southern Movement Press
Student Mobilizer
Student Mobilizer Wallposter
Sun-Reporter (San Francisco, CA)
Times (San Mateo, CA)
Times-Democrat (Davenport-Bettendorf, IA)
Times Recorder (Zanesville, OH)
Underground Newspaper Collection
Washington Daily News (Washington, DC)
Washington Post

Other Oral Histories

The HistoryMakers® Video Oral History Interview with Dr. Linda Rae Murray, August 30, 2004. TheHistoryMakers® African American Video Oral History Collection, 1900 S. Michigan Avenue, Chicago, Illinois.

Periodicals

Look
Minnesota Journal of Education
Nation's Schools
New York Magazine
PTA Magazine
Saturday Review
Seventeen Magazine
Social Policy
Time

Published Primary Literature

Birmingham, John. *Our Time is Now: Notes from the High School Underground*. New York: Bantam Books, 1970.
Bruner, Jerome. *Toward a Theory of Instruction*. Cambridge, MA: Harvard University Press, 1966.
Butts, R. Freeman. *Public Education in the United States: From Revolution to Reform*. New York: Holt, Rinehart and Winston, 1978.
Chainey, Steve. *The High School Revolt*. New York: Pathfinder Press, 1972.
Divoky, Diane. *How Old Will You Be In 1984? Expressions of Student Outrage from the High School Free Press*. New York: Avon, 1969.
Glessing, Robert J. *The Underground Press in America*. Bloomington: Indiana University Press, 1970.
Gudridge, Beatrice M. *High School Student Unrest*. Washington, DC: National School Public Relations Association, 1969.
Heins, Marjorie. *Strictly Ghetto Property: The Story of Los Siete de la Raza*. Berkeley, CA: Ramparts Press, 1972.
Hoover, J. Edgar. "The SDS and the High Schools: A Study in Student Extremism." *PTA Magazine*, January–February 1970, 2–5.
Libarle, Marc, and Tom Seligson. *The High School Revolutionaries*. New York: Random House, 1970.
Reeves, Donald. *Notes of a Processed Brother*. New York: Pantheon, 1972.
Sauders, Hubert E. "The Expansion of Constitutional Rights to Public School Pupils through the Due Process Clause of the Fourteenth Amendment." PhD diss., University of Massachusetts Amherst, 1972.

Wall, Kathryn MacKinnon. "An Indiana High School Newspaper and its Underground Newspaper: An Attitude Study." Master's thesis, Indiana University Bloomington, 1971.

Wang, L. Ling Chi. "The Chinese-American Student in San Francisco." Reprinted in *Chinese-Americans: School and Community Problems*. Chicago: Integrated Education Associates, 1972, 53–57.

Williams, Sylvia Berry. *Hassling*. Boston: Little, Brown and Company, 1970.

Zacharias, William J. "Zacharias on Professional Education." *Change in Higher Education* 1, no. 1 (1969): 30–32.

Secondary Sources

Adamson, Greg. *25 Years of Secondary Student Revolt*. Sydney: Resistance: 1993.

Agyepong, Tera Eva. *The Criminalization of Black Children: Race, Gender, and Delinquency in Chicago's Juvenile Justice System, 1899–1945*. Chapel Hill: University of North Carolina Press, 2018.

Ajunwa, Kelechi. "It's Our School Too: Youth Activism as Educational Reform, 1951–1979." PhD diss., Temple University, 2011.

Arum, Richard. *Judging School Discipline: The Crisis of Moral Authority*. Cambridge, MA: Harvard University Press, 2003.

Ballantyne, Katherine J. *Radical Volunteers: Dissent, Desegregation, and Student Power in Tennessee*. Athens: University of Georgia Press, 2024.

Balto, Simon. *Occupied Territory: Policing Black Chicago from Red Summer to Black Power*. Chapel Hill: University of North Carolina Press, 2020.

Barber, Llana. *Latino City: Immigration and Urban Crisis in Lawrence, Massachusetts*. Chapel Hill: University of North Carolina Press, 2017.

Barrera, James. "The 1960s Chicano Movement for Educational Reform and the Rise of Student Protest Activism in San Antonio's West Side." *US Latina & Latino Oral History Journal* 1 (2017): 82–97.

———. "The 1968 Edcouch-Elsa High School Walkout: Chicano Student Activism in a South Texas Community." *Aztlán* 29, no. 2 (2004): 93–122.

Bell, Charles. *Suspended: Punishment, Violence, and the Failure of School Safety*. Baltimore, MD: Johns Hopkins University Press, 2021.

Berghel, Susan Eckelmann. "'What My Generation Makes of America': American Youth Citizenship, Civil Rights Allies, and 1960s Black Freedom Struggle." *Journal of the History of Childhood and Youth* 10, no. 3 (Fall 2017): 422–40.

Biondi, Martha. *The Black Revolution on Campus*. Berkeley: University of California Press, 2012.

Bloom, Joshua, and Waldo E. Martin Jr. *Black Against Empire: The History and Politics of the Black Panther Party*. Berkeley: University of California Press, 2013.

Bradley, Stefan M. *Harlem vs. Columbia University: Black Student Power in the Late 1960s*. Urbana: University of Illinois Press, 2009.

Bredell, Kyle Hampton. "Black Panther High: Racial Violence, Student Activism, and the Policing of Philadelphia Public Schools." Master's thesis, Temple University, 2013.

Browne, Simone. *Dark Matters on the Surveillance of Blackness*. Durham, NC: Duke University Press, 2015.

Budnitskii, Oleg. *Russian Jews between the Reds and the Whites, 1917–1920*. Philadelphia: University of Pennsylvania, 2011.

Buffett, Neil Philip. "Black, White and Green: High School Student Civil Rights and Environmental Activism in New York City and on Long Island, 1968–1975." PhD diss., Stony Brook University, 2011.

———. "Crossing the Line: High School Student Activism, the New York High School Student Union, and the 1968 Ocean Hill-Brownsville Teachers' Strike." *Journal of Urban History* 45, no. 6 (2019): 1212–36.

Bundy, Tess. "'Revolutions Happen through Young People!' The Black Student Movement in the Boston Public Schools, 1968–1971." *Journal of Urban History* 42, no. 2 (March 2017): 273–93.

Butts, R. Freeman. *Public Education in the United States: From Revolution to Reform*. New York: Holt, Rinehart and Winston, 1978.

Bynum, Thomas L. *NAACP Youth and the Fight for Black Freedom, 1936–1965*. Knoxville: University of Tennessee Press, 2013.

Church, Robert, and Michael W. Sedlak. *Education in the United States: An Interpretive History*. New York: Free Press, 1976.

Churchill, Ward, and Jim Vander Wall. *Agents of Repression: The FBI's Secret War Against the Black Panther Party and the American Indiana Movement*. Cambridge, MA: South End Press, 1988.

Clapp, Elizabeth J. *Mothers of All Children: Women Reformers and the Rise of Juvenile Courts in Progressive Era America*. University Park: Pennsylvania State University Press, 1998.

Cohen, Robert. "Prophetic Minority versus Recalcitrant Majority." In *Rebellion in Black and White: Southern Student Activism in the 1960s*, edited by Robert Cohen and David J. Snyder, 1–39. Baltimore, MD: Johns Hopkins University Press, 2013.

———. *When the Old Left Was Young: Student Radicals and America's First Mass Student Movement, 1929–1941*. New York: Oxford University Press, 1993.

Cohen, Stephan L. *The Gay Liberation Youth Movement in New York: "An Army of Lovers Cannot Fail."* New York: Taylor & Francis Group, 2008.

Comer, James P. *Leave No Child Behind: Preparing Today's Youth for Tomorrow's World*. New Haven, CT: Yale University Press, 2004.

Contreras, Eduardo. *Latinos and the Liberal City: Politics and Protest in San Francisco*. Philadelphia: University of Pennsylvania Press, 2019.

Countryman, Matthew J. *Up South: Civil Rights and Black Power in Philadelphia*. Philadelphia: University of Pennsylvania Press, 2006.

Cunningham, David. *There's Something Happening Here: The New Left, the Klan, and FBI Counterintelligence*. Berkeley: University of California Press, 2004.

Danns, Dianne. *Something Better for Our Children: Black Organization in the Chicago Public Schools, 1963–1971*. New York: Routledge, 2002.

Darling-Hammond, Linda. *The Flat World of Education: How America's Commitment to Equity Will Determine Our Future*. New York: Teacher's College Press, 2010.

Davis, James Kirkpatrick. *Assault on the Left: The FBI and the Sixties Antiwar Movement.* Westport, CT: Praeger, 1997.

Davis, Mike, and Jon Wiener. *Set the Night on Fire: L.A. in the Sixties.* New York: Verso, 2021.

DeBenedetti, Charles, and Charles Chatfield. *An American Ordeal: The Antiwar Movement of the Vietnam Era.* Syracuse, NY: Syracuse University Press, 1990.

Donner, Frank J. *Protectors of Privilege: Red Squads and Police Repression in Urban America.* Berkeley: University of California Press, 1990.

Dupre, Anne Proffitt. *Speaking Up: The Unintended Costs of Free Speech in Public Schools.* Cambridge, MA: Harvard University Press, 2009.

Echeverria, Darius V. *Aztlán Arizona: Mexican American Educational Empowerment, 1968–1978.* Tucson: University of Arizona Press, 2014.

Echols, Alice. *Daring to be Bad: Radical Feminism in America, 1967–1975.* Minneapolis: University of Minnesota Press, 2003.

Ehrhart, W. D. "Aftermath: Pennridge High School and the Vietnam War." In *The Vietnam War on Campus: Other Voices, More Distant Drums*, edited by Marc Jason Gilbert. Westport, CT: Praeger Publishers, 2001.

Erickson, Ansley T. *Making the Unequal Metropolis: School Desegregation and Its Limits.* Chicago: University of Chicago Press, 2016.

Erickson, Ansley T., and Ernest Morell, eds. *Educating Harlem: A Century of Schooling and Resistance in a Black Community.* New York: Columbia University Press, 2019.

Felker-Kantor, Max. *Policing Los Angeles: Race, Resistance, and the Rise of the LAPD.* Chapel Hill: University of North Carolina Press, 2018.

Fernández, Johanna. *The Young Lords: A Radical History.* Chapel Hill: University of North Carolina Press, 2018.

Ferreira, Jason Michael. "All Power to the People: A Comparative History of Third World Radicalism in San Francisco, 1968–1974." PhD diss., University of California Berkeley, 2003.

Foster, Stuart J. "Red Alert!: The National Education Association Confronts the 'Red Scare' in American Public Schools, 1947–1954." *Education and Culture* 14, no. 2 (1997): 1–16.

Fountain, Aaron G., Jr. "Building a Student Movement in Naptown: The *Corn Cob Curtain* Controversy, Free Speech, and 1960s and 1970s High School Activism in Indianapolis." *Indiana Magazine of History* 114, no. 3 (September 2018): 202–37.

———. "The Right to Sit: Symbolic Expression and the Pledge of Allegiance in New York Public Schools, 1969–1973." *New York History* 96, no. 1 (Winter 2015): 84–100.

———. "The War in the Schools: San Francisco Bay Area High Schools and the Anti-Vietnam War, 1965–1973." *California History* 92, no. 2 (Summer 2015): 22–41.

Franklin, Barry M. "Community, Race and Curriculum in Detroit: The Northern High School Walkout." *History of Education* 33, no. 2 (March 2004): 137–56.

Franklin, Sekou M. *After the Rebellion: Black Youth, Social Movement Activism, and the Post-Civil Rights Generation.* New York: New York University Press, 2014.

Franklin, V. P. "Black High School Student Activism in the 1960s: An Urban Phenomenon?" *Journal of Research in Education* 10, no. 1 (2000): 3–8.

———. *The Young Crusaders: The Untold Story of the Children and Teenagers Who Galvanized the Civil Rights Movement.* Boston: Beacon Press, 2021.

Fraser, Max. *Hillbilly Highway: The Transappalachian Migration and the Making of a White Working Class.* Princeton, NJ: Princeton University Press, 2023.

Frost, Jennifer. *"Let Us Vote!": Youth Voting Rights and the 26th Amendment.* New York: New York University Press, 2021.

Gage, Beverly. *G-Man: J. Edgar Hoover and the Making of the American Century.* New York: Viking, 2022.

García, Mario T., and Sal Castro. *Blowout!: Sal Castro and the Chicano Struggle for Educational Justice.* Chapel Hill: University of North Carolina Press, 2011.

Garrow, David J. *FBI and Martin Luther King, Jr.: "Solo" to Memphis.* New York: W. W. Norton & Company, 1981.

Gilbert, Marc Jason. "Lock and Load High: The Vietnam War Comes to a Los Angeles Secondary School." In *The Vietnam War on Campus: Other Voices, More Distant Drums*, edited by Marc Jason Gilbert. Westport CT: Praeger Publishers, 2001.

Gitlin, Todd. *The Sixties: Years of Hope, Days of Rage.* New York: Bantam, 1993.

Gordon, Hava Rachel. *This is Our School!: Race and Community Resistance to School Reform.* New York: New York University Press, 2021.

Graham, Gael. "Flaunting the Freak Flag: Karr v. Schmidt and the Great Hair Debate in American High Schools, 1965–1975." *Journal of American History* 91, no. 2 (September 2004): 522–43.

———. *Young Activists: American High School Students in the Age of Protest.* DeKalb: Northern Illinois University Press, 2006.

Grieve, Victoria M. *Little Cold Warriors: American Childhood in the 1950s.* New York: Oxford University Press, 2018.

Hale, Jon H. "'The Fight Was Instilled in Us': High School Student Activism and the Civil Rights Movement in Charleston." *South Carolina Historical Magazine* 114, no. 1 (January 2013): 4–28.

———. *The Freedom Schools: Student Activists in the Mississippi Civil Rights Movement.* New York: Columbia University Press, 2016.

———. "'If You Want Police, We Will Have Them': Anti-Black Student Discipline in Southern Schools and the Rise of a New Carceral Logic, 1961–1975." *Journal of Urban History* 49, no. 5 (2022): 1–14.

———. *A New Kind of Youth: Historically Black High Schools and Southern Student Activism, 1920–1975.* Chapel Hill: University of North Carolina Press, 2022.

Halstead, Fred. *Out Now!: A Participant's Account of the American Movement against the Vietnam War.* New York: Pathfinders, 1978.

Harris, Malcolm. *Palo Alto: A History of California, Capitalism, and the World.* Boston: Little, Brown and Company, 2023.

Hartman, Andrew. *Education and the Cold War: The Battle for the American School*. New York: Palgrave Macmillan, 2008.
Hatfield, Ben. *Over Time: Palo Alto, 1947–1980*. Charleston, SC: Arcadia, 2008.
Heale, M. J. "Red Scare Politics: California's Campaign against Un-American Activities, 1940–1970." *Journal of American Studies* 20, no. 1 (April 1986): 5–32.
Heitzeg, Nancy A. *The School-to-Prison Pipeline: Education, Discipline, and Racialized Double Standards*. Santa Barbara, CA: Praeger, 2016.
Herring, George C. *America's Longest War: The United States and Vietnam, 1950–1975*. 3rd ed. New York: John Wiley & Sons, 1996.
Hillman, Betty Luther. *Dressing for the Culture Wars: Style and the Politics of Self-Presentation in the 1960s and 1970s*. Lincoln: University of Nebraska Press, 2015.
Hinton, Elizabeth. *America on Fire: The Untold History of Police Violence and Black Rebellion since the 1960s*. New York: Liveright Publishing, 2021.
Howlett, Charles F. "The Anti-Vietnam War Movement on Long Island Part Two: The High Schools, the October 1969 Moratorium, and Kent State (1970)." *Long Island Historical Journal* 8, no. 1 (September 1995): 56–75.
———. "When the Bell Rings: Public High Schools, the Courts, and Anti-Vietnam War Dissent." In *The Vietnam War on Campus: Other Voices, More Distant Drums*, edited by Marc Jason Gilbert. Westport, CT: Praeger Publishers, 2001.
Hymowitz, Kay. "Who Killed School Discipline?" *City Journal* (Spring 2000). https://www.city-journal.org/html/who-killed-school-discipline-11749.html.
Hyres, Alexander. "Barbara Johns and Beyond: Black Male Youth Activists, School Desegregation, and the Black Freedom Struggle in Virginia, 1951–1970." *Journal of the History of Childhood and Youth* 17, no. 3 (Fall 2024): 449–66.
———. "'The Whole Mess Is American History': Protest, Pedagogy, and Black Studies at a Desegregated High School in the South, 1967–1974." *History of Education Review* 52, no. 1 (2023): 14–28.
Hyres, Alexander, and Kyle P. Steele. "Reimagining the High School Experience: The Uses and Limitations of Student-Generated Documents for Understanding the Past and Present." *Teacher College Record*, April 12, 2022.
Ides, Matthew. "'Dare to Free Yourself': The Red Tide, Feminism, and High School Activism in the Early 1970s." *Journal of the History of Childhood and Youth* 7, no. 2 (2014): 295–319.
Ingus, Sue Graham. *Tonight at Noon: A Love Story*. Cambridge, MA: Da Capo Press, 2003.
Isserman, Maurice, and Michael Kazin. *America Divided: The Civil War of the 1960s*. New York: Oxford University Press, 2000.
Janda, Sarah Eppler. "'Even Mild Protest is Not Generally Considered to be Very Patriotic': Surveillance Culture and the Rise of the 'Sooner CIA.'" *Western Historical Quarterly* 48, (Winter 2017): 393–414.
———. *Prairie Power: Student Activism, Counterculture, and Backlash in Oklahoma, 1962–1972*. Norman: University of Oklahoma Press, 2018.
Jensen, Joan M. *Army Surveillance in America, 1775–1980*. New Haven, CT: Yale University Press, 1991.

Jerome, Fred. *The Einstein File: J. Edgar Hoover's Secret War Against the World's Most Famous Scientist*. New York: St. Martin's Griffin, 2002.

Johnson, John W. *The Struggle for Student Rights: Tinker v. Des Moines and the 1960s*. Lawrence: University of Kansas Press, 1997.

Kafka, Judith. *The History of "Zero Tolerance" in American Public Schooling*. New York: Palgrave Macmillan, 2011.

Kautz, Matthew B. "From Segregation to Suspension: The Solidification of the Contemporary School-Prison Nexus in Boston, 1963–1985." *Journal of Urban History* 49, no. 5 (2023): 1049–70.

Kendi, Ibram X. *The Black Campus Movement: Black Students and the Racial Reconstitution of Higher Education, 1965–1972*. New York: Palgrave Macmillan, 2012.

Kershner, Seth. "Investigating 'Subversives.'" *New York Archives* 22, no. 3 (Winter 2022): 7–9.

Kim, Catherine Y., Daniel J. Losen, and Damon T. Hewitt. *The School-to-Prison Pipeline: Structuring Legal Reform*. New York: New York University Press, 2010.

Kinchen, Shirletta J. *Black Power in the Bluff City: African American Youth and Student Activism in Memphis, 1965–1975*. Knoxville: University of Tennessee Press, 2016.

Klimke, Martin. *The Other Alliance: Student Protest in West Germany and the United States in the Global Sixties*. Princeton, NJ: Princeton University Press, 2010.

Krob, Melanie G., and Stephanie Enseñat Davis. "El Día de los Mártires: High-School Student Revolution and the Emergence of Panamanian National Identity." *Latin Americanist* 58, no. 1 (March 2014): 55–66.

Kupchik, Aaron. *The Real School Safety Problem: The Long-Term Consequences of Harsh School Punishment*. Berkeley: University of California Press, 2016.

Laats, Adam. *The Other School Reformers: Conservative Activism in American Education*. Cambridge, MA: Harvard University Press, 2015.

Latner. Teishan A. "'Agrarians or Anarchists?': The Venceremos Brigades to Cuba, State Surveillance, and the FBI as Biographer and Archivist." *Journal of Transnational American Studies* 9, no. 1 (2018): 119–40.

Leiding, Darlene. *Reform Can Make a Difference: A Guide to School Reform*. Lanham, MD: Rowman & Littlefield, 2009.

Leonard, Aaron J., and Conor A. Gallagher. *Heavy Radicals: The FBI's Secret War on America's Maoists*. Alresford, UK: Zero Books, 2014.

Levy, Peter B. *The Great Uprising: Race Riots in Urban America during the 1960s*. New York: Cambridge University Press, 2018.

Loomis, Caroline. "'As Far as I'm Concerned, They're on Strike because They're against Me:' Children's Voices in the Ocean Hill-Brownsville Community Control Struggle, 1968–69." *Theory, Research, and Action in Urban Education* 3, no. 1 (Fall 2014). https://traue.commons.gc.cuny.edu/far-im-concerned-theyre-strike-theyre-childrens-voices-ocean-hill-brownsville-community-control-struggle-1968-69.

Love, Bettina. *We Want to Do More Than Survive: Abolitionist Teaching and the Pursuit of Educational Freedom*. New York: Beacon Press, 2019.

Lovell, Kera. "*Girls Are Equal Too*: Education, Body Politics, and the Making of Teenage Feminism." *Gender Issues* 33 (2016): 71–95.

Lyman, Benjamin J. "In the Eye of the Sphinx: US Army Intelligence Collection and Surveillance, 1965–1970." *Journal of Intelligence History* 22, no. 3 (2023): 376–97.

Lytle, Mark Hamilton. *America's Uncivil Wars: The Sixties Era from Elvis to the Fall of Richard Nixon*. New York: Oxford University Press, 2006.

Macleod, David D. *Building Character in the American Boy: The Boy Scouts, YMCA, and their Forerunners, 1870–1920*. Madison: University of Wisconsin Press, 2004.

Martin, Lerone. "Bureau Clergyman: How the FBI Colluded with an African American Televangelist to Destroy Dr. Martin Luther King, Jr." *Religion and American Culture: A Journal of Interpretation* 28, no. 1 (Winter 2018): 1–51.

Matusow, Allen J. *The Unraveling of America: A History of Liberalism in the 1960s*. New York: Harper & Row, 1984.

McKnight, David. *Australia's Spies and their Secrets*. Sydney: Allen & Unwin, 1994.

McMillian, John. *Smoking Typewriters: The Sixties Underground Press and the Rise of Alternative Media in America*. New York: Oxford University Press, 2011.

Meckler, Laura. *Dream Town: Shaker Heights and the Quest for Racial Equity*. New York: Henry Holt and Company, 2023.

Meyering, Isobelle Barrett. "The Margaret Bailey Case: High School Activism, the Right to Education and Modern Citizenship in Late 1960s Australia." *History of Education Review* 48, no. 2 (2019): 183–97.

Michel, Gregg. *Spying on Students: The FBI, Red Squads, and Student Activists in the 1960s South*. Baton Rouge: Louisiana State University Press, 2024.

———. *Struggle for a Better South: The Southern Student Organizing Committee, 1964–1969*. New York: Palgrave Macmillan, 2004.

Miller, James. *Democracy Is in the Streets: From Port Huron to the Siege of Chicago*. New York: Simon & Schuster, 1987.

Miller, Paul T. *The Postwar Struggle for Civil Rights: African Americans in San Francisco*. New York: Routledge, 2010.

Moak, Daniel S. *From the New Deal to the War on Schools: Race, Inequality, and the Rise of the Punitive Education State*. Chapel Hill: University of North Carolina Press, 2022.

Mohamed, Saira. "Of Monsters and Men: Perpetrator Trauma and Mass Atrocity." *Columbia Law Review* 115, no. 5 (2015): 1157–216.

Monahan, Torin, and Rodolfo D. Torres. *Schools under Surveillance: Cultures of Control in Public Education*. New Brunswick, NJ: Rutgers University Press, 2011.

Montejano, David. *Quixote's Soldiers: A Local History of the Chicano Movement, 1966–1981*. Austin: University of Texas Press, 2010.

Moore, Leonard Nathaniel. *Carl B. Stokes and the Rise of Black Political Power*. Urbana: University of Illinois Press, 2002.

———. "The School Desegregation Crisis of Cleveland, Ohio, 1963–1964: The Catalyst for Black Political Power in a Northern City." *Journal of Urban History* 28, no. 2 (January 2002): 135–57.

Morris, Monique W. *Pushout: The Criminalization of Black Girls in Schools.* New York: New Press, 2016.
New, Beryl Ann. "A Fire in the Sky: Student Activism in Topeka, Kansas and Lawrence, Kansas High Schools in 1969 and 1970." Master's thesis, Washburn University, 2002.
Nolan, Kathleen. *Police in the Hallways: Discipline in an Urban High School.* Minneapolis: University of Minnesota Press, 2011.
Odem, Mary E. *Delinquent Daughters: Protecting and Policing Adolescent Female Sexuality in the United States, 1885–1920.* Chapel Hill: University of North Carolina Press, 2000.
Okilwa, Nathern, Muhammad Khalifa, and Felecia Briscoe. *The School to Prison Pipeline: The Role of Culture and Discipline in School.* Leeds, UK: Emerald Publishing Limited, 2017.
O'Neill, William. *Coming Apart: An Informal History of America in the 1960s.* Chicago: Quadrangle Books, 1971.
Oriard, Michael. *Brand NFL: Making and Selling America's Favorite Sport.* Chapel Hill: University of North Carolina Press, 2007.
Oritz, Leonard David. "La Voz de la Gente: Chicano Activist Publications in the Kansas City Area, 1968–1989." *Kansas City* 22, no. 2 (Autumn 1999): 229–44.
Perkiss, Abigail. *Making Good Neighbors: Civil Rights, Liberalism, and Integration in Postwar Philadelphia.* Ithaca, NY: Cornell University Press, 2014.
———. "Mount Airy (West)." *Encyclopedia of Philadelphia.* https://philadelphiaencyclopedia.org/essays/mount-airy-west/.
Perrusquia, Marc. *A Spy in Canaan: How the FBI Used a Famous Photographer to Infiltrate the Civil Rights Movement.* New York: Melville House Publishing, 2017.
Petrzela, Natalia Mehlman. *Classroom Wars: Language, Sex, and the Making of Modern Political Culture.* New York: Oxford University Press, 2015.
———. "Revisiting the Rightward Turn: Max Rafferty, Education, and Modern American Politics." *Sixties: A Journal of History, Politics, and Culture* 6, no. 2 (2013): 143–71.
Pipes, Richard. *The Russian Revolution.* New York: Vintage Books, 1990.
Podair, Jerald E. *The Strike that Changed New York: Blacks, Whites, and the Ocean Hill-Brownsville Crisis.* New Haven, CT: Yale University Press, 2002.
Purnell, Brian, Jeanne Theoharis, and Komozi Woodard, eds. *The Strange Careers of the Jim Crow North: Segregation and Struggle Outside of the South.* New York: New York University Press, 2019
Pyle, Christopher. *Military Surveillance of Civilian Politics, 1967–1970.* New York: Garland Publishing, 1986.
Quinn, Rand. *Class Action: Desegregation and Diversity in San Francisco Schools.* Minneapolis: University of Minnesota Press, 2020.
Ramey, Jessie B., and Catherine A. Evans. "'We Came Together and We Fought': Kipp Dawson and Resistance to State Violence in US Social Movements since the 1950s." *Radical History Review*, no. 148 (2024): 181–92.
Ravitch, Diane. *Left Back: A Century of Failed School Reforms.* New York: Simon & Schuster, 2000.

Reid, Jack. *Roadside Americans: The Rise and Fall of Hitchhiking in a Changing Nation*. Chapel Hill: University of North Carolina Press, 2020.

Remnick, Noah. "Disruptive Children: Desegregation, Student Resistance, and the Carceral Turn in New York City Schools." PhD diss., University of Oxford, 2021.

———. "The Police State in Franklin K. Lane: Desegregation, Student Resistance, and the Carceral Turn at a New York City High School." *Journal of Urban History* 49, no. 5 (January 2023): 1–17.

Rios, Victor M. *Human Targets: Schools, Police, and the Criminalization of Latino Youth*. Chicago: University of Chicago Press, 2017.

Rivers, Daniel Winunwe. *Radical Relations: Lesbian Mothers, Gay Fathers, and their Children in the United States since World War II*. Chapel Hill: University of North Carolina Press, 2013.

Robinson, Marc Arsell. *Washington State Rising: Black Power on Campus in the Pacific Northwest*. New York: New York University Press, 2023.

Rorabaugh, W. J. *Berkeley at War: The 1960s*. New York: Oxford University Press, 1989.

Rosenfeld, Seth. *Subversives: The FBI's War on Student Radicals, and Reagan's Rise to Power*. New York: Farrar, Straus and Giroux, 2012.

Roy, Christopher. "Collinwood." Encyclopedia of Cleveland History. https://case.edu/ech/articles/c/collinwood.

Ruhl, Melissa. "'Forward You Must Go': Chemawa Indian Boarding School and Student Activism in the 1960s and 1970s." Master's thesis, University of Oregon, 2011.

Rury, John L., and Shirley Hill. "An End of Innocence: African-American High School Protest in the 1960s and 1970s." *History of Education* 42, no. 4 (2013): 486–508.

Sale, Kirkpatrick. *SDS*. New York: Random House, 1973.

Sanders, Crystal R. *A Chance for Change: Head Start and Mississippi's Black Freedom Struggle*. Chapel Hill: University of North Carolina Press, 2016.

Scales, Jeffrey Henson. *In a Time of Panthers: Early Photographs*. New York: Powerhouse Books, 2022.

Schumaker, Kathryn. *Troublemakers: Students' Rights and Racial Justice in the Long 1960s*. New York: New York University Press, 2019.

Schweinitz, Rebecca De. *If We Could Change the World: Young People and American's Long Struggle for Racial Equality*. Chapel Hill: University of North Carolina Press, 2009.

Scribner, Campbell F. *A is for Arson: A History of Vandalism in American Education*. Ithaca, NY: Cornell University Press, 2023.

Sethna, Christabelle. "High-School Confidential: RCMP Surveillance of Secondary School Student Activists." In *Whose National Security?: Canadian State Surveillance and the Creation of Enemies*, edited by Gary Kinsman, Dieter K. Buse, and Mercedes Steedman. Toronto: Between the Lines, 2000.

Shapiro, Peter. *Song of the Stubborn One Thousand: The Watsonville Canning Strike, 1985–1987*. Chicago: Haymarket Books, 2016.

Shedd, Carla. *Unequal City: Race, Schools, and Perceptions of Injustice.* New York: Russell Sage Foundation, 2015.

Shepherd, Lauren Lassabe. *Resistance from the Right: Conservatives and the Campus Wars in Modern America.* Chapel Hill: University of North Carolina Press, 2023.

Sink, Suzanne Parenti. "Fueling the Southern Underground Movement: *Inquisition v. The City of Charlotte.*" *Studies in American Culture* 31, no. 1 (October 2011): 129–43.

Sinta, Vinicio, and Maggie Rivas-Rodriguez. "The 1970 Uvalde School Walkout." In *Civil Rights in Black and Brown: Histories of Resistance and Struggle in Texas*, edited by Max Krochmal and Todd Moye. Austin: University of Texas Press, 2021.

Small, Melvin. *Covering Dissent: The Media and the Anti-Vietnam War Movement.* New Brunswick, NJ: Rutgers University Press, 1994.

Sokol, Jason. *All Eyes Are Upon Us: Race and Politics from Boston to Brooklyn.* New York: Basic Books, 2014.

Srebrnik, Henry Felix. *Dreams of Nationhood: American Jewish Communist and the Soviet Birodbizhan Project, 1925–1951.* Brighton, MA: Academic Studies Press, 2010.

Stepenoff, Bonnie. "Gender at the Barricades: Women and the Columbia University Uprising of 1968." *New York History* 95, no. 1 (Winter 2014): 8–25.

Stephan, Alexander. *"Communazis": FBI Surveillance of German Emigré Writers.* New Haven, CT: Yale University Press, 2000.

Stern, Walter. "The Hidden Politics of High School Violence." In *New Perspectives on the History of the Twentieth-Century American High School*, edited by Kyle P. Steele. New York: Palgrave Macmillan, 2021.

———. *Race and Education in New Orleans: Creating the Segregated City, 1764–1960.* Baton Rouge: Louisiana State University Press, 2018.

———. "School Violence and the Carceral State in the 1970s: Desegregation and the New Educational Inequality in Louisiana." *Journal of Southern History* 89, no. 3 (August 2023): 483–534.

———. "'We Got to Fight for What We Want': Black School Rebellions in Louisiana, 1965–1974." *Teachers College Record* 125, no. 3 (2023): 1–31.

Stewart, Sean. *On the Ground: An Illustrated Anecdotal History of the Sixties Underground Press in America.* Oakland, CA: PM Press, 2011.

Suddler, Carl. *Presumed Criminal: Black Youth and the Justice System in Postwar New York.* New York: New York University Press, 2019.

Summers, Tomás F. Sandoval, Jr. *Latinos at the Golden Gate: Creating Community and Identity in San Francisco.* Chapel Hill: University of North Carolina Press, 2013.

Suttell, Brian. *Campus to Counter: Civil Rights Activism in Raleigh and Durham, North Carolina, 1960–1963.* Macon, GA: Mercer University Press, 2023.

Theoharis, Jeanne. "'W-A-L-K-O-U-T!': High School Students and the Development of Black Power in L.A." In *Neighborhood Rebels: Black Power at the Local Level*, edited by Peniel E. Joseph. New York: Palgrave Macmillan, 2010.

Thernstrom, Abigail. "Where Did All the Order Go? School Discipline and the Law." In *Brookings Papers of Education Policy*, edited by Diane Ravitch. Washington, DC: Brookings Institution Press, 1999.

Thompson, Heather Ann. "Why Mass Incarceration Matters: Rethinking Crisis, Decline, and Transformation in Postwar American History." *Journal of American History* 97, no. 3 (December 2010): 703-34.

Tittle, Diana. *Welcome to Heights High: The Crippling Politics of Restructuring America's Public Schools.* Columbus: Ohio State University Press, 1995.

Titus, Jill Ogline. *Brown's Battleground: Students, Segregationists, and the Struggle for Justice in Prince Edward County, Virginia.* Chapel Hill: University of North Carolina Press, 2011.

Turner, Jeffrey A. *Sitting In and Speaking Out: Student Movements in the American South 1960-1970.* Athens: University of Georgia Press, 2010.

Tyack, David, and Larry Cuban. *Tinkering Toward Utopia: A Century of Public School Reform.* Cambridge, MA: Harvard University Press, 1995.

Unger, Irwin. *The Movement: A History of the American New Left, 1959-1972.* New York: Dodd Mead, 1974.

Vaden, Luci. "High School Students, the Catholic Church, and the Struggle for Black Inclusion and Citizenship in Rock Hill, South Carolina." In *Contesting Post-Racialism: Conflicted Churches in the United States and South Africa*, edited by R. Drew Smith, William Ackah, Anthony G. Reddie, and Rothney S. Tshaka. Jackson: University Press of Mississippi, 2015.

Vitale, Alex S. *The End of Policing.* New York: Verso, 2017.

Walker, Dara. "Black Power, Education, and Youth Politics, 1966-1973." PhD diss., Rutgers University, 2018.

———. "Learning to Struggle, Learning to Govern: How Black Youth Marshaled Education to Navigate Urban Transformations in the Motor City, 1967-1972." *Journal of Urban History* 51, no. 2 (2023): 1-18.

Wall, Maeve K. "'Don't Touch Race': Nice White Leadership and Calls for Equity in Salt Lake City Schools, 1969-Present." *Education Sciences* 14, no. 4 (2024): 427.

Wells, Tom. *The War Within: America's Battle over Vietnam.* New York: Henry Holt, 1994.

Williams, Jakobi. *From the Bullet to the Ballot: The Illinois Chapter of the Black Panther Party and Racial Coalition Politics in Chicago.* Chapel Hill: University of North Carolina Press, 2013.

Wood, Robert Turner. *The Postwar Transformation of Albuquerque, New Mexico, 1945-1972.* Santa Fe, NM: Sunstone Press, 2014.

Wright, Dwayne C. "Black Pride Day, 1968: High School Student Activism in York, Pennsylvania." *Journal of African American History* 88, no. 2 (Spring 2003): 151-62.

Zimmerman, Jonathan. *Whose America? Culture Wars in the Public Schools.* Cambridge, MA: Harvard University Press, 2002.

Zolov, Eric. "Cuba si, Yanquis no: The Sacking of the Instituto Cultural Mexico-Norteamericano in Morelia, Michoacan, 1961." In *In from the Cold: Latin America's New Encounter with the Cold War*, edited by Gilbert M. Joseph and Daniela Spenser. Durham, NC: Duke University Press, 2008), 214-52.

Index

Page numbers in italics refer to illustrations.

Aberdeen, SD, 235
Abraham Lincoln Brigade, 29, 77
Academic Freedom in the Secondary Schools (ACLU), 127, 222
Active Students for Democracy (ASD), 219–20; FBI surveillance of, 220
Activist Opinion (newsletter), 33–37, *35*; bans on, 37–46
Adler, Margrit, 30
adult leadership of student organizations, 92; SMC, 96–97, *97*
African American Student Association, 89, 91
Akron, OH, 235
Albuquerque, NM, 184, 217–23, 230–34; Sandia High School, 217–20, 221–22, 232–33
Albuquerque Christian Youth Council, 219
Albuquerque Journal (newspaper), 220, 221
Alexander, Reginald Y., 155
Alioto, Joseph L., 150, 155
Allentown, PA, 268
American Civil Liberties Union (ACLU), 2, 69, 174; *Academic Freedom in the Secondary School*, 127
American Coalition of Patriotic Societies, 29
American Federation of Labor, 28
American-Russian Institute, 37
American Student Union, 52
anarchists, 94, 247
The Anarchists (Joll), 247
Anderson, Roger Y., 230–31

Andreas, Joel, 265
Andreotti, Dante, 154–55
Andrews, Mattie Lou, 167
Ann Arbor, MI, 131–33
Anti-Anti Club, 56
antisemitism, 27, 31
antiwar movement, 47–70, 96–113; in Albuquerque, 222–23; Chicago High School Students Against the War (HSSAW), 97–102; Chicago SMC conference (1967), 58–60; Detroit mobilization committee, 61–68; early years of, 31–32; in East Cleveland, OH, 102–5; high school activists' roles in, 47–49; in San Francisco, 50–58; SMC (Student Mobilization Committee), 105–13; and student rights, 68–70; Trotskyites vs. Independents, 71; youth support for war pre-1967, 47, 53. *See also* Student Mobilization Committee (SMC)
archival material: and author's methodology, 17–21; destruction of, 18; FBI files, 17–18; gaps in, 16–17; preservation of, 268–69
Arlington, VA, 184
Armed Forces of National Liberation (Venezuela), 251
Army surveillance of high schools, 238–39
Arnoni, M. S., 3
Art and News (newspaper), 260
Ashbrook, John, 229
Asian American students, 136; in San Francisco, 152–53

Atkins, W. Jack, 232–33
Atlanta, GA: Emory University conference (1970), 106; High School Mobe, 105–6, 107–8

Baez, Joan, 245
Bailey, George, Jr., 167
Bailey, George, Sr., 167
Bailey, Susan, 164, 166–69, 171, 172–73, 177, 180–82, 264–65
Baker, Gary, 182
Ballew, Albert, 201
Baltimore High School Students for Peace, 53
Bank, Bonnie, 231, 234
Banko, John, 196
Banning, Jack, 84
Barber, Lana, 198–99
Bauer, Warren, 242
Bay Area: Bay Area High School Liberation Conference, 94, 162; Bay Area High School Student Union, 94–95. *See also* Berkeley, CA; San Francisco Bay Area, CA
Beibel, Richard, 6
Belafonte, Harry, 185
Bennett, Jonathan, 29–30, 38, 259
Bennett, Reubin, 44
Berchenko, Jeff, 105–6, 107
Berg, Eric M., 128
Berkeley, CA: Berkeley High School, 4; Board of Control (BOC), 6; Free Speech Movement, 3; High School Student Union (HSSU), 5, 6–7; National High School Conference (1970), 7; *Pack Rat* (newspaper), 5, 6; Vietnam Day Committee (VDC), 3
Berkeley Daily Gazette (newspaper), 5
Bermann, Georgina, 63
Berschinski, Robert, 118
Besser, Howard, 266
Better America Federation, 28
Bill of Rights (high school), 105–8
Birdsong, Howard, 199–200

Black history, 4–5
Black Nationalism, 170, 202, 228
Black Panther Party, 3, 94, 102, 129, 132, 226, 228; *Off the Pigs* (film), 229; Bobby Seale, 6
Black People's Unity Movement (BPUM), 170
Black students: Black Southern youth, 25; enrollment rates of in higher education, 157–58; FBI surveillance of, 228–29; hairstyles of, 165; and Latino students, 153–54
Black Student Unions (BSUs), 4–5, 72, 141; George Washington High School (San Francisco), 148
Black studies programs, 151
Black Unity Recreation Center, 206
Blackwell, Michael J., 197
Blackwell v. Issaquena Board of Education, 103
Blakey, Michael, 265
Blatch, Melvin, 34
Bleifeld, Maurice, 90
Boa, Leonard, 68–69
Board of the Union of Student Government (USG), 180–81
Bock, Al, 30
Bock, Mini, 30
Bolsheviks, 31
Boy Scouts, 73, 74
Braun, Ginny, 136
Braver Angels, 265
Breyer, Irving, 37, 38
Briggs, Paul, 185–86, 191, 197, 199–200, 201–2, 209
Bright Hope Baptist Church (Philadelphia), 167, 168
Bring the Troops Home Now Newsletter, 58
Britton, David, 208–9
Bronx Science Committee for Political Action, 77
Bronxville, NY, 255
Brown (Manzano High School principal), 231–32

Brown, Archie, 27–29, 36
Brown, Charlotte, 71–72, 77, 92
Brown, Dale, 112
Brown, Elizabeth "Betsy," 27, 29, 36, 260
Brown, Esther, 29
Brown Berets, 94, 156
Brown v. Board of Education, 36
Bruner, Jerome, 42
Bryant, Mrs. Henry, 257
Burbridge, Nathaniel, 27
Burnside, Canzetta, 25
Burton, John, 38
buttons and insignia, 102–5

Cahill, Thomas, 149, 154–55
California: higher education system, 157; State Board of Education, 45; *see also* San Francisco Bay Area, CA
Call and Post (newspaper), 199, 201, 202, 203, 204, 206
Canada, 64
Canty, Mark, 176
Carlson, James, 196
censorship, 115, 220; *Activist Opinion* ban, 37–46. *See also* First Amendment rights; *Tinker v. Des Moines*
Center for Citizen Peacebuilding, 261
Charlotte, NC, 253–58; Charlotte Student Union, 21, 253–55, 256
Charlottesville, VA, 235
Chauncey, George, 265
Chenoweth, Cary, 256–57
Chesterland, OH, 250
Chicago, IL: Arlington Heights, 250; Chicago Area Draft Resisters, 125, 127; Chicago Area High School Independent Press Syndicate, 127; High School Students Against the War (HSSAW), 51–52, 53, 54, 57–58, 97–102; Police Department Red Squad, 98–99; police security in schools, 149; SMC antiwar conference (1967), 58–60, 59
Chicago Seven, 6

childhood, 42–43
Childress, Ruth, 192
Chisholm, Robert L., 220
Christian Science Monitor (newspaper), 230
Christopher Street Liberation Day, 262
Cincinnati, OH, 235
Cincinnati History Library and Archives, 268
Citret, Mark, 30, 32, 33–34, 46, 261
City Magazine of San Francisco, 8
Citywide Student Strike Committee (New York City), 88–89, 90–91
civil rights, student rights as, 164–84; Susan Bailey's work in, 166–69; New York City demonstration, 166; Philadelphia Student Demonstration (1967), 169–71; Student Bill of Rights (Philadelphia), 171–77
civil rights movement, 25, 193; and high school activists, 26–27; in Selma, AL, 34; white leadership positions in, 29–30
Claus, Sue, 64
Cleaver, Eldridge, 229
Cleveland, OH: FBI counterintelligence operation in, 109–10; *Great Swamp Erie da da Boom* (newspaper), 130–31; High School Activist League, 248; National Student Antiwar Conference, 105; school desegregation and busing plans in, 188–92. *See also* Collinwood High School (Cleveland)
Cleveland Civil Rights Trail, 12, 211
Cleveland Press (newspaper), 200–201, 205, 209
Cleveland State Law Review (journal), 103
Clifton, Merritt, 6
COINTELPRO (FBI counterintelligence program), 215, 223–30, 250
Collins, Judy, 57
Collinwood Area Police Citizen Committee, 201

Collinwood Committee of Black Concerns, 206–7
Collinwood community (Cleveland), 188–89
Collinwood High School (Cleveland), 185–212; and lack of resources recording racial history, 211–12; opposition of to school integration, 191–92; riots, 192–200, *195*; school reform efforts in, 200–203; violence in, 203–12; white attacks on Black students in, 193–94, 203–4
Collinwood Improvement Association, 190, 201
Columbia, SC, 228–29
Columbia Center for Oral History Research, 17
Columbia University antiwar protest (1968), 224
Committee for America, 44
Committee for Non-Violent Action, 29
Committee on Un-American Activities (California), 28
Committee to Defend the Rights of High School Students, 102
The Communist Manifesto (Karl Marx), 193
Communist Party, 26, 248; and high school activists, 27; and SOEAL, 30–31; and trade unions, 28
Conant, James B., 42
Concerned Black Parents (San Francisco), 152
Concerned Chinese for Action and Change, 153
Concerned Mission Parents, 162
Concerned Students Against the War Within the Catholic High School, 100–101
Condon, Joseph F., 223
Cone, Kitty, 99
Congress of Racial Equality (CORE), 193
constructivism, 42
Cooper, Arthur, 116

Cooper, Grant, 116–24, *117*, 264
Cooperative High School Independent Press Syndicate (CHIPS), 114–16, 124–31, 133–37
Coppola, Francis Ford, 8
Costanzo, Matthew, 182
Cox, Special Agent, 257
Craggett, Daisy, 189–90
critical thinking skills, 40, 172–73
Crutchfield, Charles H., 256
Cuba: Cuban Revolution, 50; and Steve Wasserman, 7
Curtice, Emery, 4

Daily News (Philadelphia), 179, 181, 183
Daley, Richard, 79
Davenport, IA, 227–28
Davies, Paul, 130
Davis, Benjamin O., Jr., 186
Davis, Rennie, 67
Dawson, Kipp, 55–57, 58, 262
Deaton, David, 208–9
Del Corso, Sylvester T., 186
Democratic Party: Democratic National Convention (1968), 6, 77, 78–79, 100; on war, 78
demonstrations: in Cincinnati, OH, 141–43, *142*; Collinwood High School (Cleveland) riots, 192–200; at Mission High School (San Francisco), 144–47, 153–63; non-white vs. white activists and, 143–44; in Philadelphia, 170–71; rioting at Collinwood High School (Cleveland), 194–200, *195*; in San Francisco, 147–53; against school busing plans, 190–91
Detroit, MI: Detroit Committee to End the War in Vietnam (DCEWV), 61, 62, 65; Detroit High School Students for Peace, 67; Student Mobilization Committee, 61–68
Detroit Free Press (newspaper), 61, 67
Dickerson, Walt, 219
DiGiacomo, Dennis, 200

Dilworth, Richardson, 170–71, 173
Dittrick, Alva R., 197
Divoky, Diane, 83, 92
Dixon, Lauren, 215–16
Dixon, Ralph, 221
DiZinno, Joseph A., 205–6, 207–8, 209–10
domino theory, 53
Donerson, Naomi, 204
Donovan, Bernard E., 92
D'Ortona, Paul, 171
Dragoon, Ann, 1
Drebus, Donald L., 102–3
dress codes, 75, 84; hair length policies, 132, 218; violations, 237
Driskell, Dana, 76
DuBridge, Lee, 43

Earnest, Wayne, 135
East Cleveland, OH, 102–5
East Los Angeles uprising (1968), 147
Ebony (magazine), 131–32
education. *See* schools
Educational Opportunity Program, 157
Ehrhart, W. D., 53
Eklund, John, 16
elementary schools: Boulevard Elementary School (Shaker Heights, OH), 192–93; William H. Brett Elementary School (Cleveland), 191
Ellis, Willard, 235
El Paso, TX, 235
El Tecolote (newspaper), 264
Estok, Edward, 111
Estrella, Marta, 146, 154
Ethnic Studies program, 156; at San Francisco State, 158
expulsion of students, 44, 89–90, 91, 94, 101, 119–20, 216

Fabian Society, 247
Fadley, David, 219–20
Fairfield (CT) Students Against the War, 65

Fall, Wendy Wilson, 265
Farber, Jerry, 82
FBI (Federal Bureau of Investigation): in Albuquerque, 217–23, 230–34; Berkeley HSSU investigation by, 7; COINTELPRO, 215, 223–30, 250; counterintelligence in high schools by, 16; files and archival material, 17–18; and Minnesota Student Union (MSU), 236–38, 240–41; student informants for, 234–36, 238–40; and student surveillance in Charlotte, NC, 253–58; surveillance of high school activists by, 19–20, 108–13, 215–17; surveillance of SOEAL by, 34–36; surveillance of student publications by, 242–43; undermining of student movements by, 258
Feagler, Dick, 201
Feldman, Samuel, 134
Fencil, George, 171
Fenton, David, 76–77
Ferrell, Robert B., 234, 237
Ferretti, Fred, 71
Fifth Avenue Peace Parade Committee, 76, 78, 90
Finch, Robert, 207
Fineberg, Morris, 234
Finger, Anne, 53–54, 266
First Amendment rights, 14, 39–40, 101, 165, 173–74
Fisher, Wendy, 69
flag, American, 231–32
Flores, Francisco, 144–47, 153–54, 156–57, 158, 160, 162, 264
football players, 132
Ford, Mrs. D. W., 257
Fox, Gordon, 61–62, 63, 67, 261–62
Franklin, Benjamin, 43
FRED (alternative press syndicate), 124, 125
Freedman, Samson L., 177–79
Freedom of Information Act (FOIA) requests, 17–18

Freedom Schools, 77
Free Speech Movement, 3; SOEAL, 26–32
free speech rights. *See* censorship; First Amendment rights; symbolic expression; *Tinker v. Des Moines*
French, John, 265
French, Robert, 17
Friar, Jamie, 86, 262–63
Friar, Wendy, 262
Friedman, Saul, 67

Galamison, Milton A., 91
Garb, Paula, 31–32, 33, 44, 45, 260–61
Garcia, Cathy, 160
gendered roles, 86–87
Gene, Elk, 77, 262
Geneva Accords (1954), 4
George, Martha Ann, 167–68
Gerhardt, Frank, 111
German American (newspaper), 30
Glasser, Ira, 13, 69
Glessing, Robert J., 134
G-Men (film), 244
Gold, Steve, 181
Golden, Miriam, 266
Goodlett, Carlton B., 36–37
Graham, Harrell, 128
Gray, William H. "Dallas," Jr., 167–68
Gray, William H., Sr., 167
Greater Rochester High School Student Union (New York), 72
Greenberg, Alvin J., 44–45
Greene, Graham, 31
Greenham, William, 225
Greer, Gene, 248
Greninger, Carl, 238
Griffin, Virginia, 141
Grimsby, Roger, 90–91
Gruening, Ernest, 3
Grundy, Dale, 183
Guevara, Che, 75
Gutman, Marta, 265
Guzick, Thomas, Jr., 102–3

Haight-Ashbury district (San Francisco), 51
hair length policies, 218, 240. *See also* dress codes
Hale, James, 248
Hale, Jon, 12
Hale, Sally, 248
Halstead, Fred, 65, 67, 105
Hamilton, Arthur S., 242–43
Hamilton, Robbie, 199
Hampton, Fred, 6
Harer, Katharine, 50–52, 55, 57, 261
Harrell, Daryl, 221, 222, 223
Harris, Odette, 164
Harvey, Louella, 203
Hatcher, Evelyn, 235
Hayakawa, S. I., 158
Hayden, Tom, 6, 98
Hazeldell Parents Association (HPA), 190
Heart of America Conservative Club, 136
Hefner, Keith, 17, 21, 131–33, 136, 263, 265, 266
Heming, Laura, 69–70
Herr, William J., 242
Herreshoff, David, 64
Heyday Press, 8
High School Activist League (Cleveland, OH), 248
High School Bill of Rights, 105–8
High School Free Press (newspaper), 88, 93
High School Independent Press Service (HIPS), 10, 83–84
High School Legal Defense Committee, 91
High School Liberation Front, 234
High School Mobilizer (newsletter). *See Mobilizer* (newsletter)
High School Principals Association (HSPA), 91–92
High School Reform (pamphlet), 224–25

The High School Revolutionaries (Libarle and Seligson), 7

High School Rising (documentary), 160–62

high schools: Academy of Our Lady, Chicago, 100–101; Balboa High School (San Francisco), 41–42, 50, 147, 150, 151; Beverly Hills High School (California), 127–28; Bok Vocational High School (Philadelphia), 169, 170; Bronx High School of Science, 69, 77; Central High School (Davenport, Iowa), 227–28; Cleveland Heights High School, 109–10, 239; Cubberley High School (Palo Alto, California), 245, 251; Custer High School (Milwaukee), 215, 239; Fortier High School (New Orleans), 117–18; Galileo High School (San Francisco), 151, 152; George Washington High School (San Francisco), 34, 136, 148, 150, 152; Germantown High School (Philadelphia), 160, 181; Glenville High School (Cleveland), 193, 196, 206–7; Homestead High School (Cupertino, California), 246, 248; Homestead High School (Mequon, Wisconsin), 215–16; James Monroe High School (Queens), 17, 77; John Bowne High School (Queens), 68–69, 77, 91; Lick-Wilmerding High School (San Francisco), 27, 29, 33; Lincoln High School (San Francisco), 38, 39, 44, 150, 151, 155; Lowell High School (San Francisco), 32, 33, 38, 44–45, 152–53; Manzano High School (Albuquerque), 222, 231, 232; Marjory Stoneman Douglas High School (Florida), 266–67; Martin Van Buren High School (New York City), 74, *89*; Mission High School (San Francisco), 144–47, 153–63; Palo Alto High School (California), 17, 245–46, 251–53; Philadelphia High School for Girls, 164, 169, 177; Polytechnic High School (San Francisco), 46, 51, 147–48, 150; Sandia High School (Albuquerque), 217–20, 221–22, 232–33; security and police presence, 15, 148–49; Shaw High School (East Cleveland), 102–5; South Philadelphia High School, 169, 181, 182; Woodrow Wilson High School (San Francisco), 33, 151, 155. *See also* Collinwood High School (Cleveland)

high school students: conservative activists, 135; need for resources and help, 16; as oppressed group, 14, 81–82; and sense of empowerment, 164–65

High School Students Against the War (HSSAW), Chicago, 51–52, 53, 54, 57–58, 97–102

"High School Students Unite!" slogan, 9–10, *11*, 83

Historical Marker Database, 11

Hitchens, Christopher, 8

Hoover, J. Edgar, 7, 118, 124, 213; Milwaukee Student Alliance, surveillance of, 215; SDS, distrust of, 223–24, 225–26. *See also* FBI (Federal Bureau of Investigation)

House Committee on Internal Security, 224

House Un-American Activities Committee (HUAC), 29, 39

Hoyman, Neal, 21, 256

Hoyman, Scott, 256

Humphrey, Hubert, 78, 79

Hunter's Point Naval Reservation, 36; riots, 145, 154

Huntsman, A. Blaine, 252

Hutt, George, 179

Iceberg (newspaper), 119–20, 121–23

Ichord, Richard, 230

I. F. Stone's Weekly (newspaper), 2

Indianapolis, IN, 183

Indianapolis High School Press Service, 126

Indianapolis News (newspaper), 183
Indian Student Bill of Rights, 184
informants, parents as, 244, 248–50
Intermountain Indian School (UT), 184
International Longshoremen and Warehousemen's Union, 50, 55
International Student Strike Day, 75–76
Ira, You'll Get into Trouble (film), 92
Irwin, Basil, 253–55
Irwin, Basil, Jr., 253–55
Irwin, Laura Mackay, 253–55
Isserman, Maurice, 47

Jackson, Dan, 40–41
Jackson, MS, 235
Jacobs, Bonye, 122, 123
Jacobs, David, 20–21, 246–47, 252
Jansen, William, 15
Jeffersonville, IN, 165
Jenkins, Robert, 150, 151, 155, 159
Jewish culture and social justice, 1–2
Jobs with Justice, 260
John Birch Society, 250
John Bowne Students for Peace, 77
John Hay High School (Cleveland), 12
Johnson, Lyndon, 34; and draft, 66; war on crime, 148–49
Joll, James, 247
Jones, Jimmie L., Jr., 209
journalism. *See* news media; underground newspapers
junior high schools: Aptos Junior High School, 34–35; Denman Junior High School (San Francisco), 147; Leeds Junior High School (Philadelphia), 177; Patrick Henry Junior High School (Cleveland), 197; Presidio Junior High School (San Francisco), 159–60; Roxboro Junior High School (Cleveland), 109–10; Spellacy Junior High School (Cleveland), 203, 207

Kalamazoo, MI, 234
Kelley, C. Franklin, 40
Kellman, Barry, 265–66

Kemmitt, Edward, 40, 42, 44
Kennedy, Robert, 78, 79
Kent State University shootings (1970), 231
Kentucky Civil Liberties Union, 184
King, Coretta Scott, 57
King, Martin Luther, Jr., 4, 57; assassination of, 76
Kiok, Josh, 74–75, 89–90, 263
Kleiman, Mark, 224–25
Klein, Ruth, 177
Klonsky, Mike, 123
Klunder, Bruce, 191
Koons, George, 257
KPFA radio station, 94
Krassner, Paul, 3
Krytzer, Harry, 154, 157, 159–60

Lancaster, Oliver, 174
Lanen, Teuvo, 249
La Raza, 94
Latino immigrants, 144–46
Laubach, Martin, 265
Laura, Annette, 265
Laurel, MS, 235
Lavelle, Jenny, 114–15
Lawrence, Howard, 194–95, 198
League of Revolutionary Struggle, 260
Lee, John, 194, 197
Leland Stanford Junior University, 245
Lenin, Vladimir, 193
Lesko, Joseph, 198
Levenson, William, 190
Levy, David, 121
Liberation News Service (LNS), 7, 83, 129
Lilienthal, Ernest, 41
Lincoln Memorial, antiwar demonstration (1967), 66–67
Lindsay, Tom, 83–84
Lloyd, Mark, 172
Loney, Richard, 234
Lorain, Ohio, 66
Los Angeles Institute for the Humanities, 8

Los Angeles's Special Weapons and Tactical Team, 154
Los Angeles Times Festival of Books, 8
Los Siete de la Raza, 162
Lucas, Reginald, 76, 86
A Lump of Sugar (newspaper), 121
Lundstrom, John, 239
Lundstrom, Richard, 239
Lynch, Lawrence, 253
Lynd, Staughton, 98
Lynum, Curtis, 34
Lytle, James T., 180, 181

Madison, Clyde, 206–7
Mailer, Norman, 3
Malveaux, Brenda, 56
Maplewood, NJ, 104
March for Our Lives rally, 267
March on the Pentagon (1967), 65, 67, 75, 78, 84
March on Washington (1963), 77
Marcuse, Herbert, 5
Marion, Bob, 227–28
Market, Leon, 41
martial law, 5
Martinez, Ben, 159
Mathias, Joseph M., 112
Mathis, David, 199
Matson, Harold B., 44–45
Maye, Roy, 210
McAdams, Doug, 266
McArthur, Brenda, 155
McCallister, Ralph, 190, 191
McCarthy, Eugene, 79, 125
McCarty, Frankie, 220–21, 230
McCoy, Rhody, 88
McMurray, Frank, 33, 38, 39–40, 42, 44, 260
McNamara, Robert, 34
McWilliams, Carey, 145
Meade, David, 240–41
Medford, MA, 249
Meglich, Gary, 206
Mendez, Marcla, 206

Michalak, R. F., 215
Michel, Gregg, 264
military recruitment, 75, 107
Mill, Jean, 255
Millar, George, 253
Miller, H. Clifford, 237
Miller, Laura, 102
Miller, Paul, 141–43
Mills, C. Wright, 5
Milwaukee, WI, 215–16, 239
Milwaukee Student Alliance, 215
Minnesota Education Association, 240
Minnesota Student Union (MSU), 72, 236–38, 240–41
Minority of One (magazine), 2–3
Mirelowitz, Geoff, 68, 98, 99–100, 262
Mirsch, James H., 209
Misnik, Joanna, 96
Mission Coalition Organization, 159–60
Mission District (San Francisco), 144–45
Mission High Parents Group, 155
Mission High School (San Francisco), 144–47; district's attempts to address issues, 159; strike (1969), 153–63
Mobilizer (newsletter), 54, 62–63, 136
Montauk, Susi, 55
Montgomery County Student Alliance (MD), 72
Moore, Joseph A., Jr., 41
Morales, Edgar "Edy," 146, 153–54
Moratorium to End the War in Vietnam, 162
Morgen Freiheit (newspaper), 1
Morris, Phillip, 211
Morse, Linda, 94
Morse High School Student Government, 135
Mulvihill, Katherin, 87, 94
Murray, Linda Rae, 192–200, 265
Murray, Mrs. Ken, 174–75
Murray, Randall, 196
Murray, Raymond, 192
Music and Art Students Against the War in Vietnam, 77

Index   373

Nashville, TN, 119–20
National Archives, 18
National Association for the Advancement of Colored People (NAACP), 27
National Committee for a Sane Nuclear Policy, 61
National Coordinating Committee, 48
National High School Conference, 7, 67, 129
National High School Speak-Out Against the War, 112
National High School Student Mobilization Committee, 62
National Student Antiwar Conference, 105
National Student Strike Against the War (1968), 75
Newark, NJ, 149
New Mexico Lobo (newspaper), 233
New Republic Books, 8
news media: HSSU attention and criticism from, 92–93; inaccurate journalism, 61, 67
newspapers, underground. *See* underground newspapers
Newsreel (film production company), 92, 94, 123, 160
Newton, Huey, 148
Newton, Robert, 77, 90, 94, 263
New York City: teacher strike, 80, 87–92. *See also* New York High School Student Union (HSSU)
New York Civil Liberties Union, 13, 69, 96
New York Free Press (newspaper), 84
New York High School Free Press (newspaper), 72, 84–87, *85*
New York High School Student Union (HSSU), 71, 72–73, 162; formation of, 73–79; media attention and criticism for, 92–93; newspaper syndicates, 82–87; Spring Offensive (1969), 93–95; structure and organization of, 80–82; and teacher strike, 87–92

New York Magazine, 71, 92
New York Review of Sex (newspaper), 84
New York Society of Ethical Culture, 80
Nickel Bag (newspaper), 255
1984 (Orwell), 41
Nixon, Richard, 130
Norden, Eric, 3
North American Alliance for White People, 190
North Bethesda, MD, 108
North Carolina, 120
Northcott, Kate, 31, 32, 46, 260
Northeast Health and Welfare Council, 174
North from Mexico (McWilliams), 145
nuclear weapons, 53

Oak Ridge, TN, 121
Oberholtzer, Dolores, 180
Oberlin College, 66
O'Brien, John, 238–39
obscenity charges, 104
October Revolution (1917), 31
Off the Pigs (film), 229
Oglesby, Carl, 123
O'Glover, Frederic, 246
Oliver, Bernard M., 251
"ombudsman" role, 172, 177
Omnibus Crime Control and Safe Streets Act (1968), 149
Orlando, FL, 108
Orris, Maxine, 55, 60, 77, 263
Orwell, George, 41
Our Time is Now (Vonnegut), 9
"outside agitator" myth, 16, 92–93, 146, 150, 155, 164, 188, 229, 258, 267

Palo Alto, CA, 244–45. *See also* San Francisco Bay Area, CA
Palo Alto High School, 17, 245–46; FBI surveillance of, 251–53
parents, 242–58; FBI reliance on, 242–44; FBI surveillance of in Silicon Valley, 244–48; as informants, 244, 248–50; public complaints of,

250–53; rights and responsibilities of, 110
Parents' Against Relay Classes, 189–90
Parkland, FL, 266–67
patriotism, 78; and Boy Scouts, 73
Paul, John, 219–20, 223, 231, 232–33, 234
Pennington, Ron, 141–43
Pentagon, March on (1967), 65, 67
People's Park (San Francisco), 3
Perino, J. A., 45
"perpetrator trauma," 203
Pharris, Cecil M., 34–35
Philadelphia, MS, 25
Philadelphia, PA: Board of Education, 164; Philadelphia Student Demonstration (1967), 169–71; Student Bill of Rights, 164, 165–66, 171–77; West Mount Airy neighborhood, 168
Philadelphia Federation of Teachers (PFT), 173, 178–79
Philadelphia Fellowship Commission, 173
Philadelphia Inquirer (newspaper), 179
Philadelphia Principals Association, 174, 175
Philadelphia Resistance, 168
Philadelphia Student Bill of Rights, 169–70
Philadelphia Tribune (newspaper), 176
Pierce, Rufus, 198
Pileggi, Nicholas, 85, 92
Pittman, Carol, 30, 33, 259–60
Pittman, John, 30
Pittsburgh High School Students for Peace in Vietnam, 53
Plain Dealer (newspaper), 239; High School Activist League, 248
Pledge of Allegiance, 14, 117
police: brutality and violence, 5, 156; militarization of, 149, 153 protection of students from racial violence by, 187; Red Squads, 235, 239; and school administrators, 235; in schools, 148–49, 206; in schools, demands to remove, 210–11
Pollitt, Phoebe, 265
Poor People's Campaign, 75
Portland, OR, 239–40
Portland High School Rights Coalition, 72
The Power Elite (Mills), 5
Prairie Village, KS, 136
protests. *See* demonstrations
Providence, RI, 53–54, 249
PTA Magazine, 225
Punnett, Laura, 169, 181, 265

Quaker education, 50
The Quiet American (Greene), 31

racial issues, 131–32; Black and Latino students' collaboration, 156–57; Black and white student clashes, 155; Black militancy, white fears of, 202; Collinwood High School (Cleveland), 200–203; mixed race families, 30, 56; in New York teacher strikes, 87–88; non-white vs. white activists, 143–44; racial violence and high school activism, 186–87; racial violence in East Cleveland, 103; riots at Collinwood High School (Cleveland), 185; school busing plans, 189–91; school desegregation, 121, 169–70, 188–92; and students' rights, 164–65; and white middle-class activists, 26
Radical Student Union (RSU), 252–53
Radical Student Union (Palo Alto, CA), 21
Rafferty, Bernard, 180
Rasmussen, David, 257–58
Raup, Gordon, 240
Reagan, Ronald, 3, 157–58, 229
Red Balloon Collective, 263
"red diaper babies," 30, 76, 116
Red Scare, 28
Red Squads, 235, 239
rent strikes, 193

Repressive Tolerance (Marcuse), 5
Rhode Island High School Students for Peace, 53–54, 249
Rhodes, James A., 186
Rice, Emily, 181
Richard, Larry, 196
Richmond, VA, 120
Rikers Island Penitentiary, 149
Risher, John, 112
Rizzo, Frank, 170–71, 179–80
Robinson, Agnes, 251
Rochester, NY, 255
Room 222 (television series), 10
Rose, Mark, 85–86
Ross, William, 164, 175, 180, 182
ROTC and military recruitment, 107
Rowton, Tim, 66
Rubin, Jerry, 6, 65
Rudd, Mark, 229
Rude, De Floren, 240
Rumley, Jim, 119
Rusk, Dean, 78
Russell, Bertrand, 3
Russian Revolution (1917), 31
Rutchick, Leah, 236–37
Ryan, John, 179

Salop, Claire, 158
San Antonio, TX, 255; FBI field office in, 122
Sanchez, Ken, 221
Sanders, Margaret, 257
Sandow, Laurie, 71, 77
Sandperl, Ira, 245
Sands, Aimee, 14
San Francisco Bay Area, CA: antiwar movement in, 50–58; Asian American activism in, 152–53; Balboa High School, 41–42, 50, 147, 150, 151; counterculture of 1960s in, 3; Free Speech Movement in high schools, 25–46; Haight-Ashbury district, 51; high school demonstrations in, 147–53; High School Students Against the War (HSSAW), 51–52, 53, 54, 57–58; Kezar Stadium gathering, 57; martial law in, 5; Mission District, 144–45; Mission High School, 144–47, 153–63; People's Park, 3; police security in schools in, 149–51; racial violence in, 36; school system and racial imbalance in, 36–37; Silicon Valley, 244–48; Tactical Squad of San Francisco Police Dept., 154–55. *See also* Berkeley, CA
San Francisco Chronicle (newspaper), 31, 44, 156, 158
San Francisco Classroom Teachers Association, 159
San Francisco Conference on Religion, Race, and Social Concerns, 31
San Francisco Examiner (newspaper), 158–59
San Francisco Federation of Teachers, 40
San Francisco General Strike (1934), 30
San Francisco Jewish Community Relations Council, 31
San Francisco Police Department: Community Relations Unit (CRU), 154; Tactical Squad, 154–56
San Francisco Spokesman (newsletter), 30
San Francisco State College, 3; strike (1968), 3, 147, 151, 156, 157–58
Savio, Mario, 3, 25
Sbarge, Stephen, 92, 93
Scales, Jeffrey Henson, 266
Schaffner, Jay, 102
Schaller, John, 124–31, 263–64; Ann Arbor Youth Liberation, 131–33
Scheer, Bill, 64, 67
Schenkman, Robert A., 172
Schneider, Estelle, 17, 77, 87, 262
Scholastic Rebel (newspaper), 44–45
Scholten, Paul, 151–52
schools: activists' impact on, 13; and evolving concepts of education, 42–43; expulsion of students from, 44, 89–90, 91, 94, 101, 119–20, 216;

function of in society, 80; gifted student programs in, 193; school resource officers, 148–49; security in, 15; teacher strikes, 87–92. *See also* elementary schools; high schools; junior high schools
Schuker, Louis, 93
Schwartz, Benjamin, 142
Schwartz, Jeffrey, 77, 93, 263
Schwendinger, Leni, 5, 266
Scribner, Campbell F., 151
"The SDS and the High Schools" (Hoover), 225, 227
Seale, Bobby, 6
Seattle, WA, 238
Selma, AL, 34
Semel, Elisabeth, 30–31, 32, 46, 260
Seneca Student Rights Committee (Louisville, KY), 72
sexism, 86–87
Shamalie, Phillip, 239
Shapiro, Peter, 26, 30, 42, 44, 260
Share, Steven, 68
Sharkey County, MS, 25
Shedd, Mark, 170, 171–72, 173, 175, 179, 182; resignation of, 179–80
Shneyer, Paul, 77
Shreve, Mary Jean, 237, 240
Silicon Valley, CA, 244–48
Simmons, Al, 228
Simmons, Kevin, 178
Simpkins, Bill, 235
Sims, Tracy, 56
sit-ins. *See* demonstrations
Skokie, IL, 238
SLATE (UC Berkeley), 30
Smith, David, 265
Smith, L. Barrett, 200–202
Smith, Paula, 97–102
Smith, Robert, 157–58, 233
Smith, Stephen, 18
Smoker, Dave, 221
Socialist Workers Party, 51, 262
Sonstein, Shelli, 176–77
Sorrell, Clyde, 249

Southern Christian Leadership Conference (SCLC), 75
Southern conservatism, 255–56
Southern Students Organizing Committee (SSOC), 116–24, 256–57, 264
Sowinski Park (Cleveland), 196
Spanish Civil War, 77
Spears, Harold, 26, 37–38, 42, 43–45
Spitzer, E. E., 246
Spock, Benjamin, 66
Spring Mobilization to End the War in Vietnam (1967), 47, 55
Spring Offensive (1969), 93–95
Stack, Mary, 38
Stahl, Matt, 245
Stanford, Jane, 245
Stanford, Leland, 245
Stanford University, 245
Stein, Paul, 205
Stevenson, Ronald, 4
Stewart, Robert "Bobby," 176, 177
St. Louis, MO, 227
St. Louis Globe-Democrat (newspaper), 227
Stokes, Carl, 185–86
Stone, George, 185
Stone, I. F., 3
Stone, Jenny, 5
Stop the Draft Week, 4, 251
Stratten, James E., 40–41
Struggle for a Better South (Michel), 264
"The Student as Nigger" (Farber), 82
Student Bill of Rights (Philadelphia), 171–77; PFT's efforts to amend, 178–79; preservation of, 179–84
Student Coalition for Constructive Social Reform, 235
Student Congress of Racial Equality (SCORE), 29–30
Student Information Center (SIC), 130
Student Mobilization Committee (SMC), 48, 54–55; Chicago antiwar conference (1967), 58–60, 59;

Student Mobilization Committee (SMC) (cont.)
  FBI surveillance of, 108–13; High School Bill of Rights, 105–8; National High School wing, 60; National Student Antiwar Conference, 105; purpose of, 96; student rights focus, 104–5
Student Mobilizer (newsletter), 48, 62, 100, 112
Student Mobilizer Wallposter (newspaper), 103
Student Nonviolent Coordinating Committee (SNCC), 25, 77, 118–19
student organizations, independent, 71–72, 95; and adult leadership, 92. *See also* New York High School Student Union (HSSU)
Student Peace Union, 53
student rights, 25; and high school antiwar movement, 68–70. *See also* civil rights, student rights as
Students Against the War in Vietnam, Oakland, 54
Students Against the War in Vietnam, Toronto, 64
Students for a Democratic Society (SDS), 71; FBI's surveillance of, 223–24; school chapters, 118
Students for Equality, 56
Students for Mission High, 160
Students Open Forum (Albuquerque), 220–21
Students' Organized Education and Action League (SOEAL), 26–32; *Activist Opinion*, 33–37, 35; *Activist Opinion* ban, 37–46; on civil rights issues and desegregation, 36; FBI surveillance of, 34–36
Students' Rights Coalition (Philadelphia), 176–77
Study Our Schools committee (San Francisco), 36–37
Suburban Liberation Front, 239, 250
Sullivan, Frank, 178–79
Sullivan, William, 226
Sun-Reporter (newspaper), 154
Supporters of American Ideals, 6
surveillance, of high school students, 108–13; parents as informants, 244, 248–50. *See also* FBI (Federal Bureau of Investigation)
Swan Quarter, NC, 121
Swerdloff, Howard, 77, 78, 79, 84, 85, 91, 94, 263
symbolic expression: buttons and insignia, 103; Lowell High School art displays, 38–39

Tactical Squads, 152, 154, 158
Tanner, Kathie Ilene, 229
Tate, James, 171
Taulbee, Charles, Jr., 238
teacher strikes, 87–92
Temple University, 17
Tepper, Jesse, 26–27, 32, 33, 35, 40, 44, 259
Textile Workers Union of America, 256
Third World Liberation Front, 151, 156–57, 158
Thomas, Emma, 208
Thomas, Larry, 206
Thomaston, CT, 134
Thomson (Cubberley High School principal), 251–52
Tinker v. Des Moines, 13, 96, 104, 233, 268; legacy of, 112–13
Trade Union Education League, 28
Trigg, Bernice, 73–74
Trigg, Bruce, 73–79, 87, 89–90, 94, 95, 162, 262
Trigg, Maurie, 73–74
Trudelle, Ernest, 249

underground newspapers: *Activist Opinion* (SOEAL), 33–46, 35; *Corn Cob Curtain*, 135, 269; *Demobilizer*, 136; *Finger*, 117–18, 124; *FPS*, 128–30, 136–37; *Great Speckled Bird*, 105–6, 107, 123; *Great Swamp Erie da da*

Boom (Cleveland), 130–31; *Inquisition*, 120, 121, 256; *Kaleidoscope*, 215–16; *Mobilizer* (SMC newsletter), 54, 62–63, 136; *Open Door*, 215; *Pack Rat* (HSSU newspaper), 5, 6; *Red Army*, 176, 234; *Right On*, 213, 249; *South West Sun*, 114; *Space City News*, 128–29; *Spark*, 242–43; *Student Mobilizer* (SMC newsletter), 48, 62, 100, 112
underground press, 82; conservative newspapers, 135–36; Cooperative High School Independent Press Syndicate (CHIPS), 114–16, 124–31, 133–37; instruction booklet for, 126–27; loose networks, 83–84; *New York High School Free Press*, 84–87, 85; overview of, 114–16; Southern Student Organizing Committee (SSOC), 116–24; syndicates, 82–87
Underground Press Syndicate (UPS), 83
Union of Student Government (USG), 180–82
United Citizens' Council of America, 200
United Committee, Bay Area, 51
United Farm Workers Union, 146, 162
United Federation of Teachers (UFT), 87, 88, 90
United Freedom Movement (UFM), 190–91
United Student Movement (USM), 86, 245–48; parents' public complaints about, 250–53
Unity (newspaper), 260
University of California (UC), Berkeley: Free Speech Movement, 3; SLATE, 30; Vietnam teach-in, 3. *See also* Berkeley, CA
University of Minnesota, 237
Urban American Inc., 199

Vagstad, Don, 236
Van Buren Students Against Militarism (VBSAM), 74–75, 76
Vancouver, British Columbia, 134
Vaughan, Leah, 177

Venezuela, 251
Vietnam Analysis Committee (VAC), 3–4
Vietnam Day Committee (VDC), Berkeley, 3, 52
Vietnam Moratorium Day, 6
Viet Nam Peace Action (Wellesley High School), 249
Vietnam Summer Committee, 168–69
Vietnam War: antiwar armbands, 13, 25; antiwar demonstrations, 3–4; Department of Defense stance on, 34. *See also* antiwar movement
Vietnam Week (1966), 54, 55
violence: rioting at Collinwood High School (Cleveland), 194–200, *195*; riots, 198–99
Vocations for Social Change (newspaper), 130
Voldahl, Barbara, 217–21, 234, 265
Voldahl, Lowell, 217
von Merling, F. J., 213
Vonnegut, Kurt, Jr., 9
Voters' Peace Pledge March, 61

Wagner, Richard, 235
Wang, Ling-Chi, 152
Wasserman, Abraham "Al," 1–2
Wasserman, Rebecca, 1
Wasserman, Rena, 1
Wasserman, Sherry, 1
Wasserman, Solomon, 1
Wasserman, Steve, 1–8, *2*, 259
Watson, Dave, 139
Watson, Paul G., 120
WBAI radio, 68
Weaver, Michael, 209
W. E. B. Du Bois Club, 33
Weinglass, Leonard, 6
Wells, Lynn, 119
West Coast High School Students Against the War, 55
Western Reserve Women's Republican Club, 109, 111
West of Twin Peaks Council, 41
Wildin, M. W., 230–31

Wiley, Tom, 222, 231–32
Williams, Duncan, 111
Williams, Jorma (pseudonym), 48
Williams, Robert Lee, 173–74
Williams, Sylvia, 247
Wilson, Julian, 196
Wilson, Kit, 41–42
Women for Peace, 61
Women's Strike for Equality, 262
Wood, Jim, 156
World Congress for Peace, National Independence, and General Disarmament (1965), 45
Wormuth, John F., 44

X, Malcolm, 56, 121, 164

Young, Amy, 234
Young Americans for Freedom, 160, 229
Young Communist League, 28, 77
Young Lords, 102
Young Socialist Alliance (YSA), 51, 99–100, 262
youth: autonomy of, 46; childhood vs. adulthood roles, 41–42; empowerment of, 33; evolving conceptions of, 43
Youth Against the War and Fascism, 239
Youth Communication, 263
Youth for Radical Progress (YRP), 222–23, 231, 232–33
Youth Liberation, 114, 263; Ann Arbor, MI, 131–33; Student Organizing Kit, 134

Zacharias, Jerrold, 42
Zeleski, Jim, 64

www.ingramcontent.com/pod-product-compliance
Lightning Source LLC
Chambersburg PA
CBHW030516230426
43665CB00010B/645